攻殻機動隊

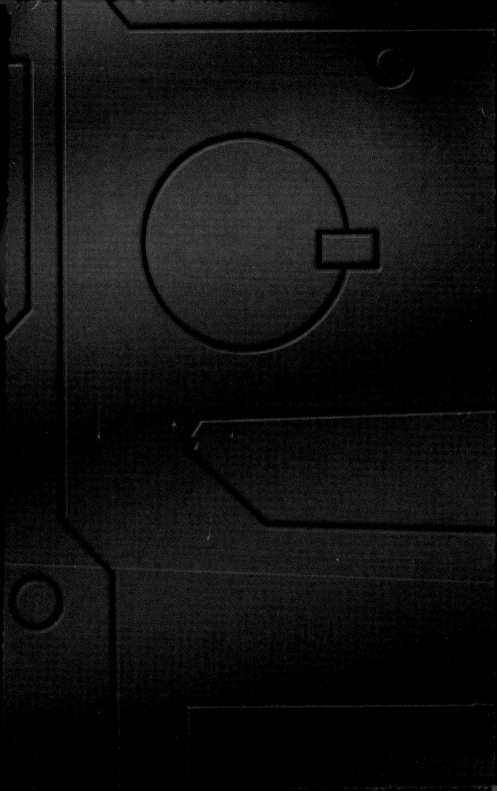

GHOST IN THE SHELL
HUMAN-ERROR PROCESSOR

攻殻機動隊

STORY AND ART BY
SHIROW MASAMUNE

TRANSLATION BY >> FREDERIK L. SCHODT LETTERING BY >> TOM ORZECHOWSKI

DARK
HORSE
MANGA

PUBLISHER ›› MIKE RICHARDSON   EDITOR ›› CHRIS WARNER
COLLECTION DESIGNER ›› DAVID NESTELLE   ART DIRECTOR ›› LIA RIBACCHI

GHOST IN THE SHELL 1.5
HUMAN-ERROR PROCESSOR

This volume collects issues one through eight of the Dark Horse comic-book series *Ghost in the Shell 1.5: Human-Error Processor*.

Published by Dark Horse Manga, a division of Dark Horse Comics, Inc. 10956 SE Main Street, Milwaukie OR 97222 ›› darkhorse.com ›› To find a comics shop in your area, call the Comic Shop Locator Service toll-free at 1-888-266-4226.

1st edition: October 2007 ›› ISBN-10: 1-59307-815-3
ISBN-13: 978-1-59307-815-7 ›› 10 9 8 7 6 5 4 3 2 1

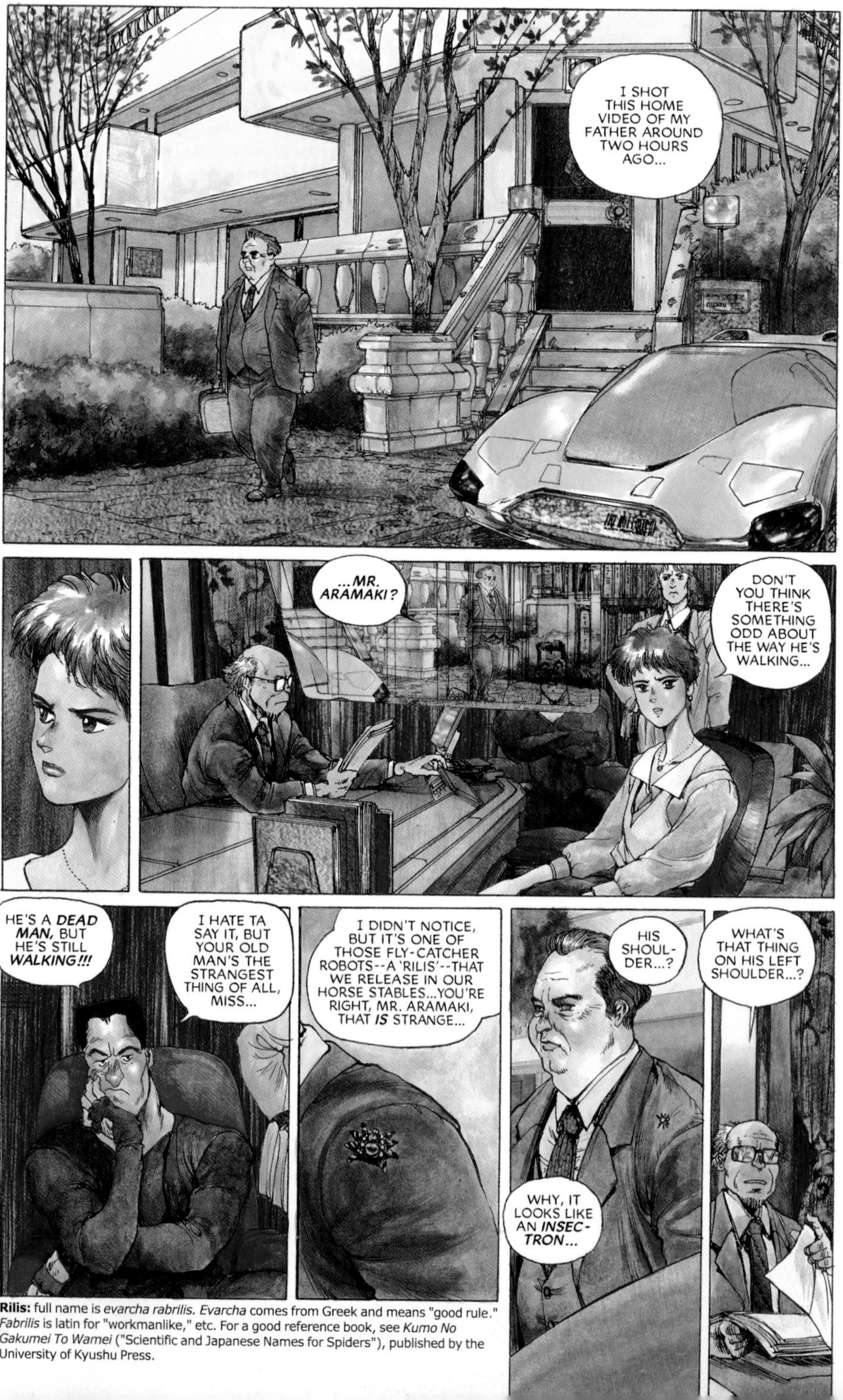
I SHOT THIS HOME VIDEO OF MY FATHER AROUND TWO HOURS AGO...
DON'T YOU THINK THERE'S SOMETHING ODD ABOUT THE WAY HE'S WALKING...
...MR. ARAMAKI?
WHAT'S THAT THING ON HIS LEFT SHOULDER...?
HIS SHOUL-DER...?
WHY, IT LOOKS LIKE AN *INSEC-TRON*...
I DIDN'T NOTICE, BUT IT'S ONE OF THOSE FLY-CATCHER ROBOTS--A 'RILIS'--THAT WE RELEASE IN OUR HORSE STABLES...YOU'RE RIGHT, MR. ARAMAKI, THAT *IS* STRANGE...
I HATE TA SAY IT, BUT YOUR OLD MAN'S THE STRANGEST THING OF ALL, MISS...
HE'S A *DEAD MAN,* BUT HE'S STILL *WALKING!!!*

Rilis: full name is *evarcha rabrilis. Evarcha* comes from Greek and means "good rule." *Fabrilis* is latin for "workmanlike," etc. For a good reference book, see *Kumo No Gakumei To Wamei* ("Scientific and Japanese Names for Spiders"), published by the University of Kyushu Press.

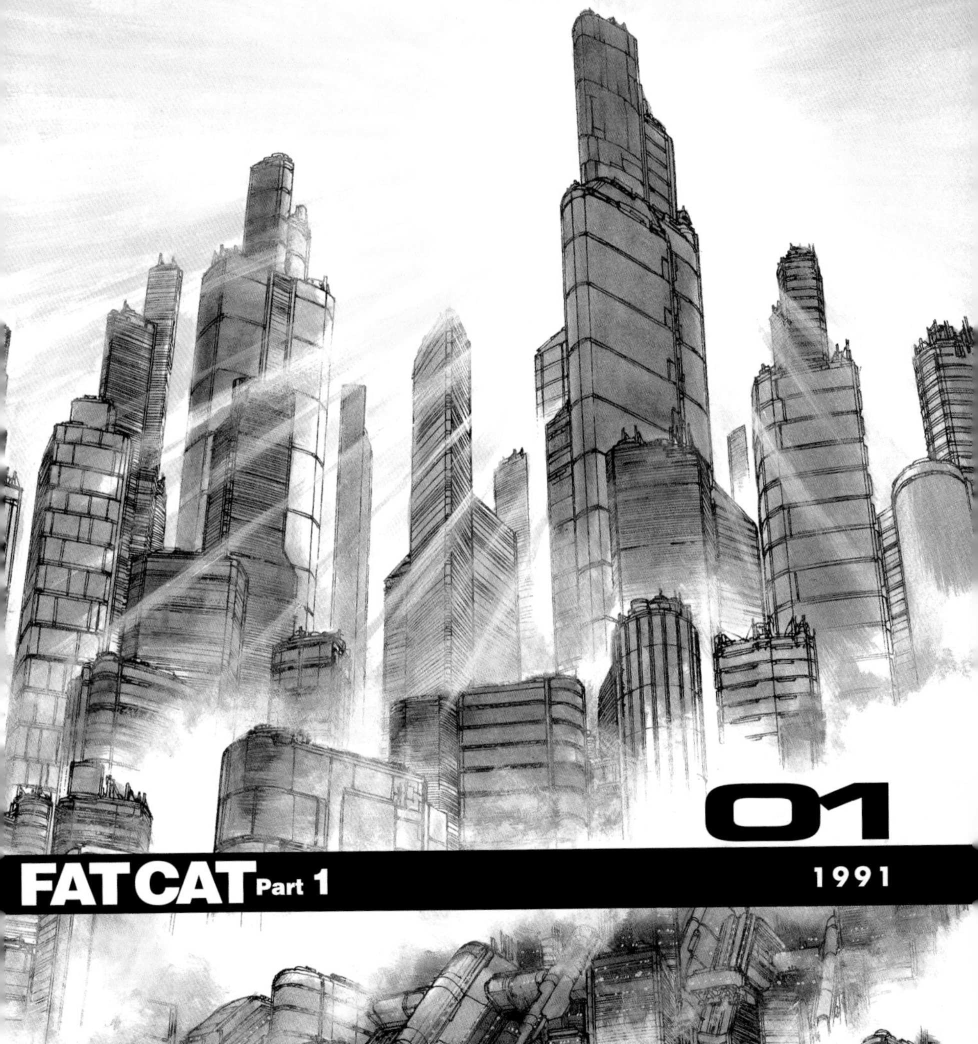

01

FAT CAT Part 1

1991

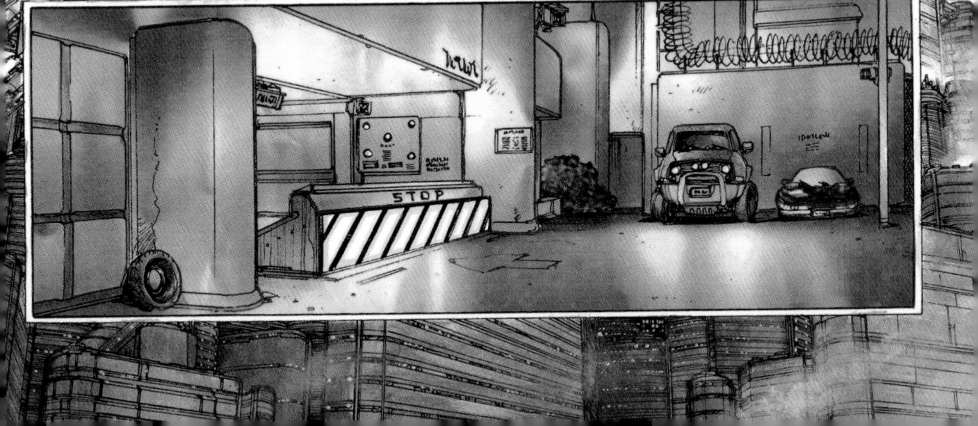
STOP

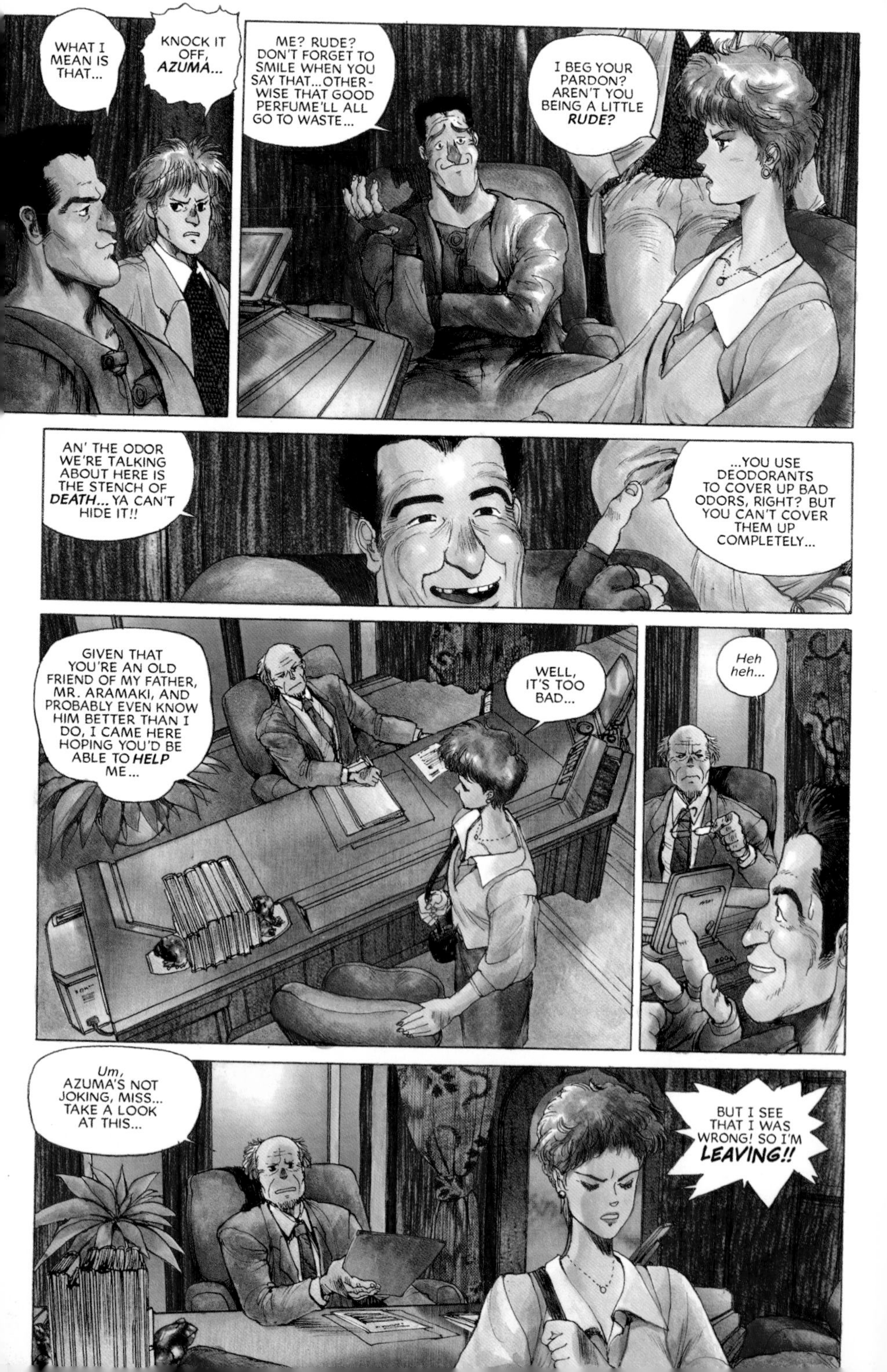
I BEG YOUR PARDON? AREN'T YOU BEING A LITTLE *RUDE?*
ME? RUDE? DON'T FORGET TO SMILE WHEN YOU SAY THAT...OTHER-WISE THAT GOOD PERFUME'LL ALL GO TO WASTE...
KNOCK IT OFF, *AZUMA...*
WHAT I MEAN IS THAT...
...YOU USE DEODORANTS TO COVER UP BAD ODORS, RIGHT? BUT YOU CAN'T COVER THEM UP COMPLETELY...
AN' THE ODOR WE'RE TALKING ABOUT HERE IS THE STENCH OF *DEATH...* YA CAN'T HIDE IT!!
Heh heh...
WELL, IT'S TOO BAD...
GIVEN THAT YOU'RE AN OLD FRIEND OF MY FATHER, MR. ARAMAKI, AND PROBABLY EVEN KNOW HIM BETTER THAN I DO, I CAME HERE HOPING YOU'D BE ABLE TO *HELP* ME...
BUT I SEE THAT I WAS WRONG! SO I'M *LEAVING!!*
Um, AZUMA'S NOT JOKING, MISS... TAKE A LOOK AT THIS...

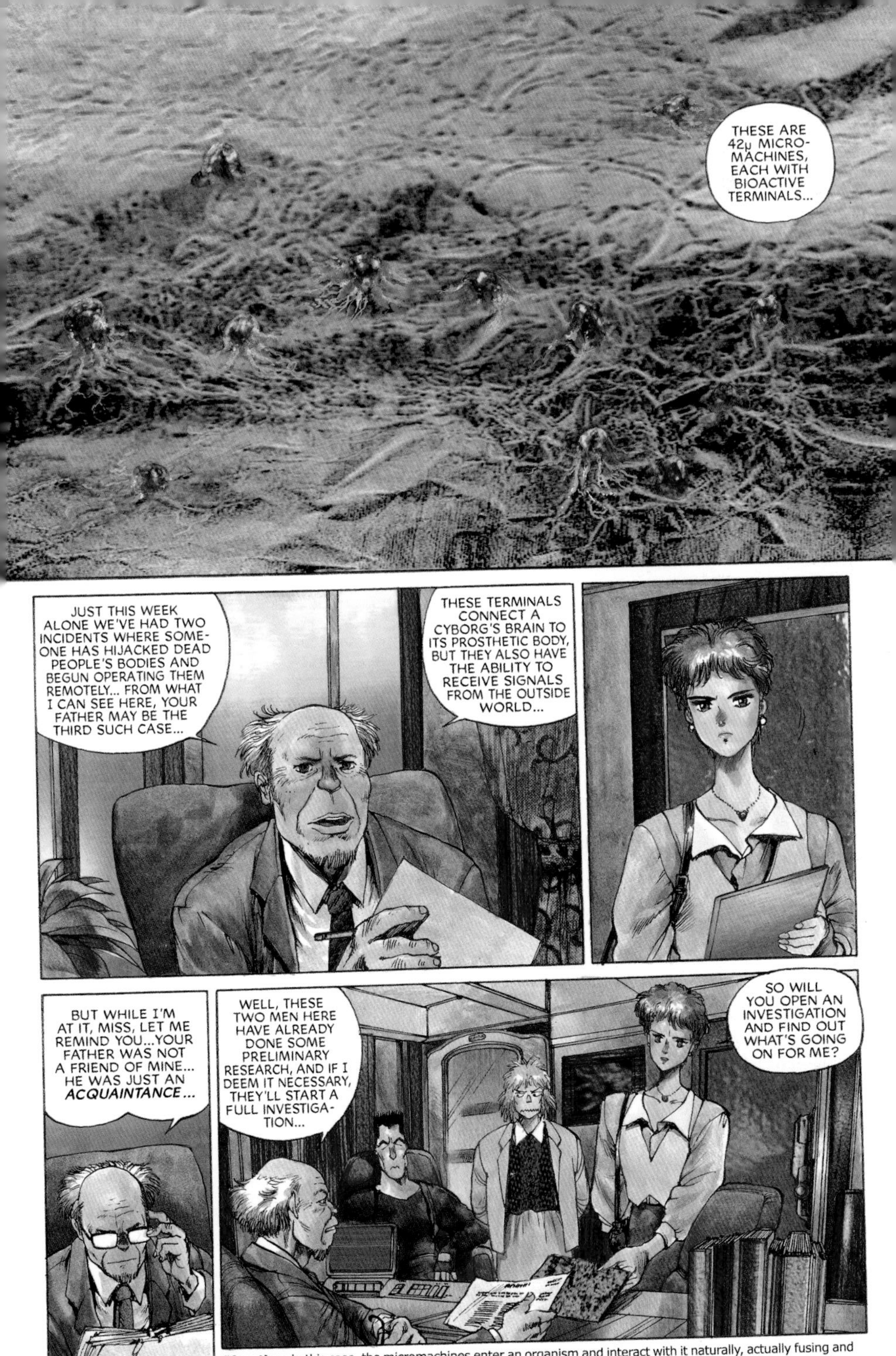
THESE ARE 42μ MICRO-MACHINES, EACH WITH BIOACTIVE TERMINALS...
THESE TERMINALS CONNECT A CYBORG'S BRAIN TO ITS PROSTHETIC BODY, BUT THEY ALSO HAVE THE ABILITY TO RECEIVE SIGNALS FROM THE OUTSIDE WORLD...
JUST THIS WEEK ALONE WE'VE HAD TWO INCIDENTS WHERE SOMEONE HAS HIJACKED DEAD PEOPLE'S BODIES AND BEGUN OPERATING THEM REMOTELY... FROM WHAT I CAN SEE HERE, YOUR FATHER MAY BE THE THIRD SUCH CASE...
SO WILL YOU OPEN AN INVESTIGATION AND FIND OUT WHAT'S GOING ON FOR ME?
WELL, THESE TWO MEN HERE HAVE ALREADY DONE SOME PRELIMINARY RESEARCH, AND IF I DEEM IT NECESSARY, THEY'LL START A FULL INVESTIGATION...
BUT WHILE I'M AT IT, MISS, LET ME REMIND YOU...YOUR FATHER WAS NOT A FRIEND OF MINE... HE WAS JUST AN *ACQUAINTANCE...*

Bioactive: in this case, the micromachines enter an organism and interact with it naturally, actually fusing and functioning with it. Inactive materials, such as titanium or ceramics, do not fuse with biological material and are essentially treated by the body as foreign matter.

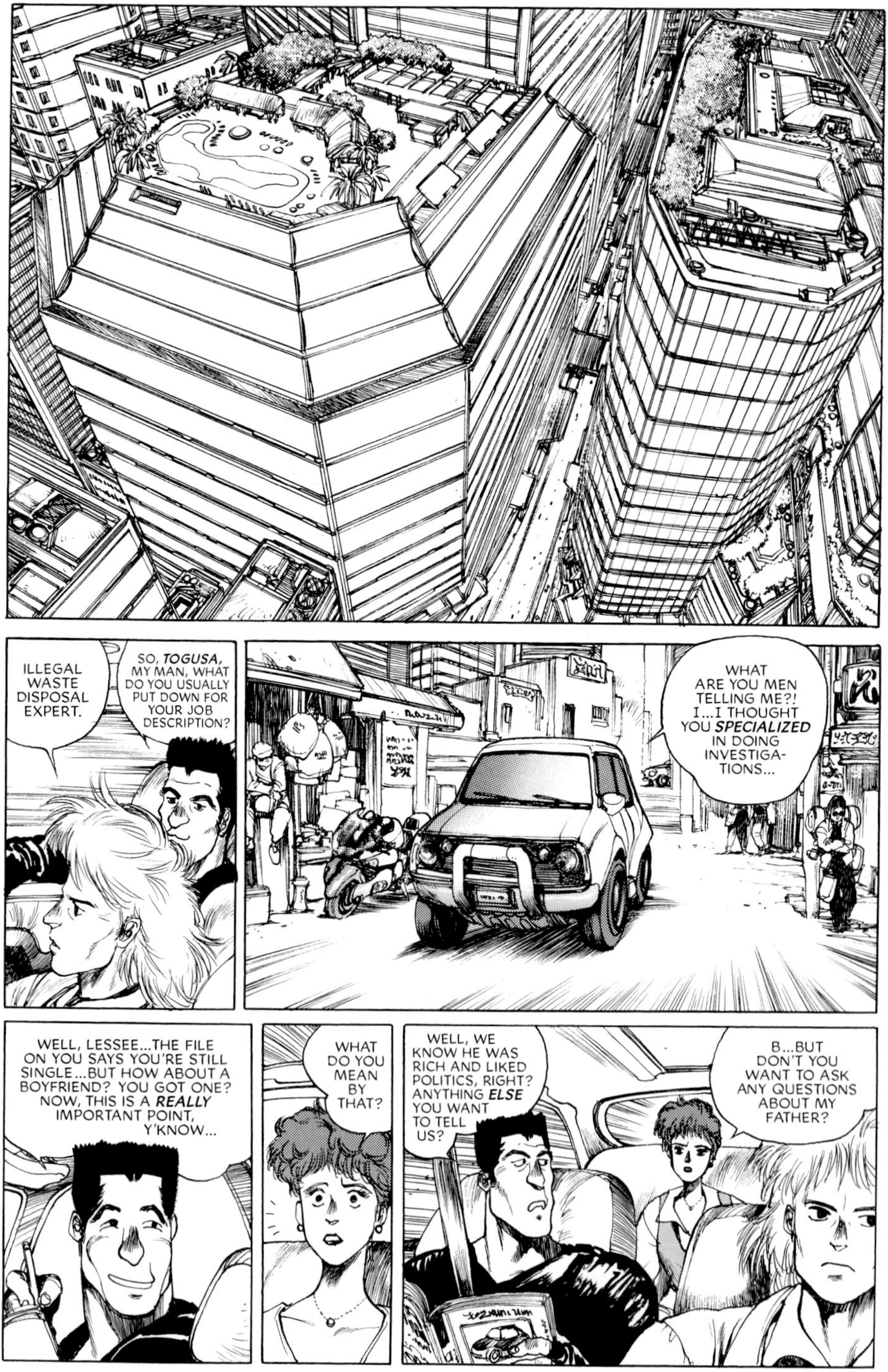
SO, *TOGUSA,* MY MAN, WHAT DO YOU USUALLY PUT DOWN FOR YOUR JOB DESCRIPTION?
ILLEGAL WASTE DISPOSAL EXPERT.
WHAT ARE YOU MEN TELLING ME?! I...I THOUGHT YOU ***SPECIALIZED*** IN DOING INVESTIGA-TIONS...
WELL, LESSEE...THE FILE ON YOU SAYS YOU'RE STILL SINGLE...BUT HOW ABOUT A BOYFRIEND? YOU GOT ONE? NOW, THIS IS A ***REALLY*** IMPORTANT POINT, Y'KNOW...
WHAT DO YOU MEAN BY THAT?
WELL, WE KNOW HE WAS RICH AND LIKED POLITICS, RIGHT? ANYTHING ***ELSE*** YOU WANT TO TELL US?
B...BUT DON'T YOU WANT TO ASK ANY QUESTIONS ABOUT MY FATHER?

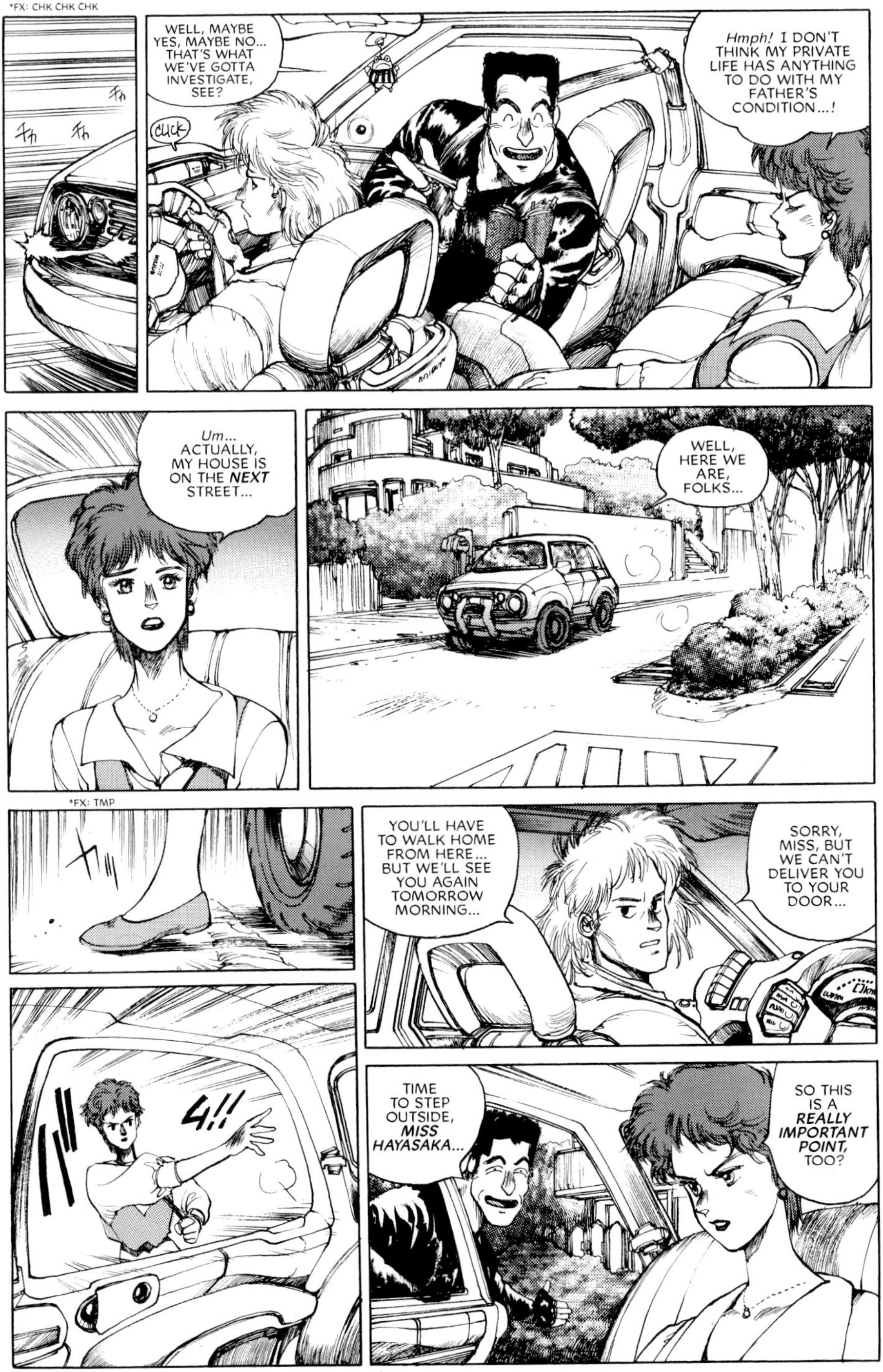
Hmph! I DON'T THINK MY PRIVATE LIFE HAS ANYTHING TO DO WITH MY FATHER'S CONDITION...!
WELL, MAYBE YES, MAYBE NO... THAT'S WHAT WE'VE GOTTA INVESTIGATE, SEE?
CLICK
WELL, HERE WE ARE, FOLKS...
Um... ACTUALLY, MY HOUSE IS ON THE NEXT STREET...
SORRY, MISS, BUT WE CAN'T DELIVER YOU TO YOUR DOOR...
YOU'LL HAVE TO WALK HOME FROM HERE... BUT WE'LL SEE YOU AGAIN TOMORROW MORNING...
SO THIS IS A REALLY IMPORTANT POINT, TOO?
TIME TO STEP OUTSIDE, MISS HAYASAKA...
*FX: CHK CHK CHK
*FX: TMP
*FX: SLAM

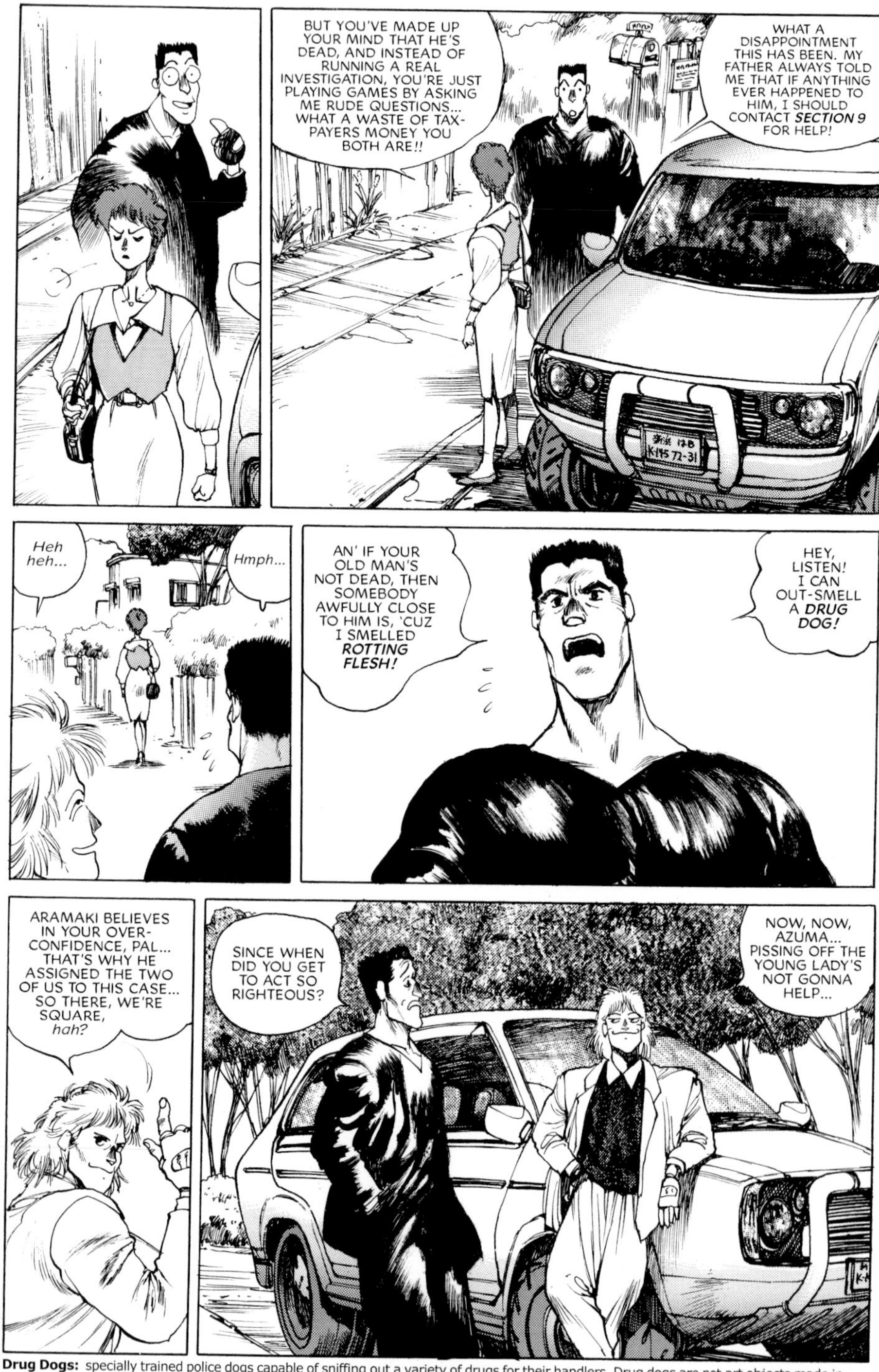
WHAT A DISAPPOINTMENT THIS HAS BEEN. MY FATHER ALWAYS TOLD ME THAT IF ANYTHING EVER HAPPENED TO HIM, I SHOULD CONTACT ***SECTION 9*** FOR HELP!
BUT YOU'VE MADE UP YOUR MIND THAT HE'S DEAD, AND INSTEAD OF RUNNING A REAL INVESTIGATION, YOU'RE JUST PLAYING GAMES BY ASKING ME RUDE QUESTIONS... WHAT A WASTE OF TAX-PAYERS MONEY YOU BOTH ARE!!
HEY, LISTEN! I CAN OUT-SMELL A ***DRUG DOG!***
AN' IF YOUR OLD MAN'S NOT DEAD, THEN SOMEBODY AWFULLY CLOSE TO HIM IS, 'CUZ I SMELLED ***ROTTING FLESH!***
Hmph...
Heh heh...
NOW, NOW, AZUMA... PISSING OFF THE YOUNG LADY'S NOT GONNA HELP...
SINCE WHEN DID YOU GET TO ACT SO RIGHTEOUS?
ARAMAKI BELIEVES IN YOUR OVER-CONFIDENCE, PAL... THAT'S WHY HE ASSIGNED THE TWO OF US TO THIS CASE... SO THERE, WE'RE SQUARE, *hah?*

Drug Dogs: specially trained police dogs capable of sniffing out a variety of drugs for their handlers. Drug dogs are not art objects made in the shape of dogs, then stuffed with drugs and used for smuggling. Nor are they dogs that are stoned silly from doing too many drugs...

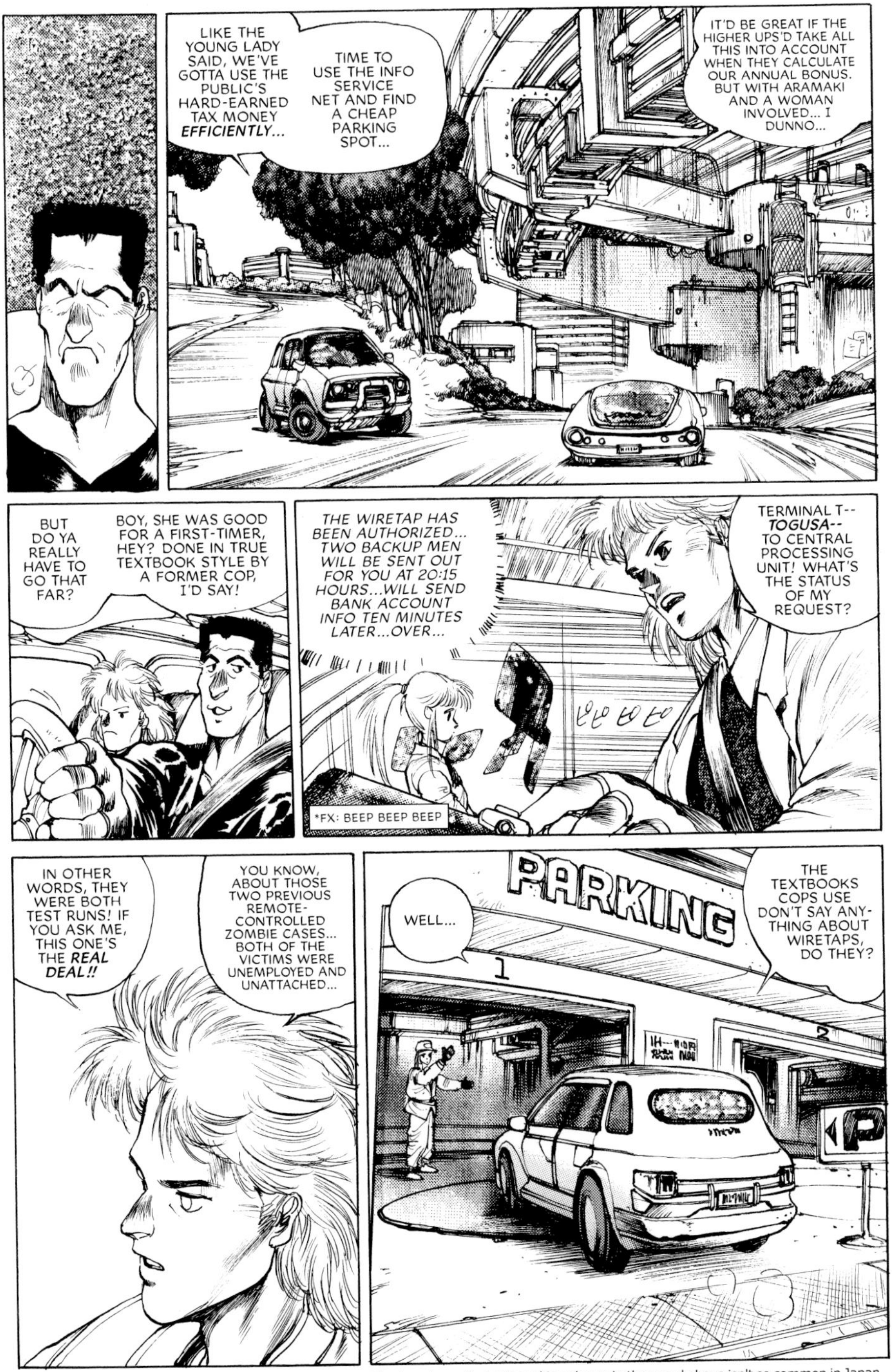
IT'D BE GREAT IF THE HIGHER UPS'D TAKE ALL THIS INTO ACCOUNT WHEN THEY CALCULATE OUR ANNUAL BONUS. BUT WITH ARAMAKI AND A WOMAN INVOLVED... I DUNNO...
TIME TO USE THE INFO SERVICE NET AND FIND A CHEAP PARKING SPOT...
LIKE THE YOUNG LADY SAID, WE'VE GOTTA USE THE PUBLIC'S HARD-EARNED TAX MONEY *EFFICIENTLY*...
TERMINAL T-- *TOGUSA*-- TO CENTRAL PROCESSING UNIT! WHAT'S THE STATUS OF MY REQUEST?
ピピピピ
THE WIRETAP HAS BEEN AUTHORIZED... TWO BACKUP MEN WILL BE SENT OUT FOR YOU AT 20:15 HOURS...WILL SEND BANK ACCOUNT INFO TEN MINUTES LATER...OVER...
*FX: BEEP BEEP BEEP
BOY, SHE WAS GOOD FOR A FIRST-TIMER, HEY? DONE IN TRUE TEXTBOOK STYLE BY A FORMER COP, I'D SAY!
BUT DO YA REALLY HAVE TO GO THAT FAR?
PARKING
THE TEXTBOOKS COPS USE DON'T SAY ANY-THING ABOUT WIRETAPS, DO THEY?
WELL...
YOU KNOW, ABOUT THOSE TWO PREVIOUS REMOTE-CONTROLLED ZOMBIE CASES... BOTH OF THE VICTIMS WERE UNEMPLOYED AND UNATTACHED...
IN OTHER WORDS, THEY WERE BOTH TEST RUNS! IF YOU ASK ME, THIS ONE'S THE *REAL DEAL!!*

The tray-type of robotic parking shown in the panel above isn't so common in Japan anymore. Instead, auto-parking systems tend to rotate the cargo horizontally. This saves time and trouble, since it's no longer necessary to back out of the facility.

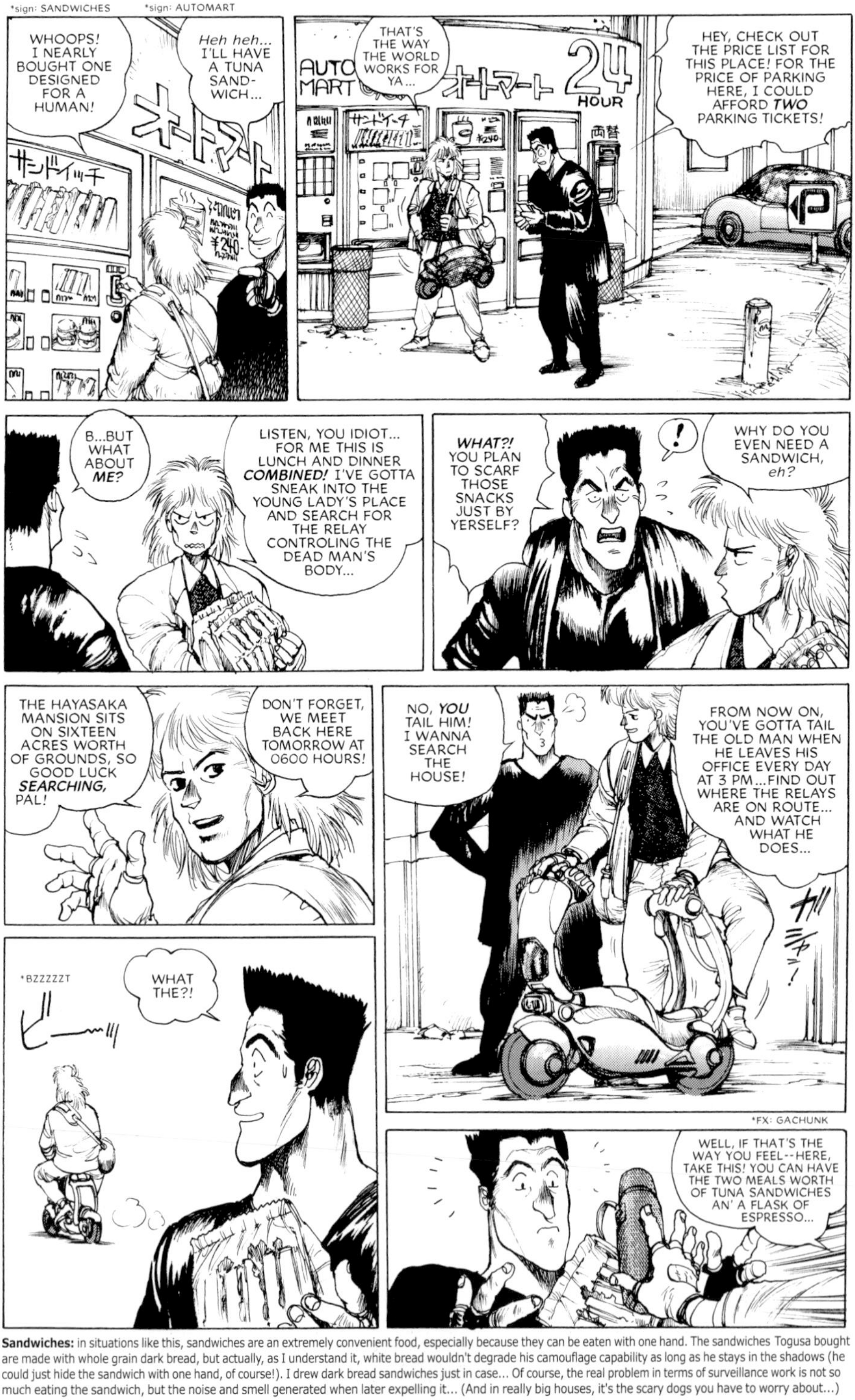
*sign: SANDWICHES
*sign: AUTOMART
HEY, CHECK OUT THE PRICE LIST FOR THIS PLACE! FOR THE PRICE OF PARKING HERE, I COULD AFFORD *TWO* PARKING TICKETS!
THAT'S THE WAY THE WORLD WORKS FOR YA...
AUTO MART
24 HOUR
Heh heh... I'LL HAVE A TUNA SANDWICH...
WHOOPS! I NEARLY BOUGHT ONE DESIGNED FOR A HUMAN!
WHY DO YOU EVEN NEED A SANDWICH, *eh?*
!
WHAT?! YOU PLAN TO SCARF THOSE SNACKS JUST BY YERSELF?
LISTEN, YOU IDIOT... FOR ME THIS IS LUNCH AND DINNER ***COMBINED!*** I'VE GOTTA SNEAK INTO THE YOUNG LADY'S PLACE AND SEARCH FOR THE RELAY CONTROLING THE DEAD MAN'S BODY...
B...BUT WHAT ABOUT ***ME?***
FROM NOW ON, YOU'VE GOTTA TAIL THE OLD MAN WHEN HE LEAVES HIS OFFICE EVERY DAY AT 3 PM...FIND OUT WHERE THE RELAYS ARE ON ROUTE... AND WATCH WHAT HE DOES...
NO, ***YOU*** TAIL HIM! I WANNA SEARCH THE HOUSE!
*FX: GACHUNK
DON'T FORGET, WE MEET BACK HERE TOMORROW AT 0600 HOURS!
THE HAYASAKA MANSION SITS ON SIXTEEN ACRES WORTH OF GROUNDS, SO GOOD LUCK ***SEARCHING,*** PAL!
WELL, IF THAT'S THE WAY YOU FEEL--HERE, TAKE THIS! YOU CAN HAVE THE TWO MEALS WORTH OF TUNA SANDWICHES AN' A FLASK OF ESPRESSO...
*BZZZZZT
WHAT THE?!

Sandwiches: in situations like this, sandwiches are an extremely convenient food, especially because they can be eaten with one hand. The sandwiches Togusa bought are made with whole grain dark bread, but actually, as I understand it, white bread wouldn't degrade his camouflage capability as long as he stays in the shadows (he could just hide the sandwich with one hand, of course!). I drew dark bread sandwiches just in case... Of course, the real problem in terms of surveillance work is not so much eating the sandwich, but the noise and smell generated when later expelling it... (And in really big houses, it's the scary dogs you have to worry about...)

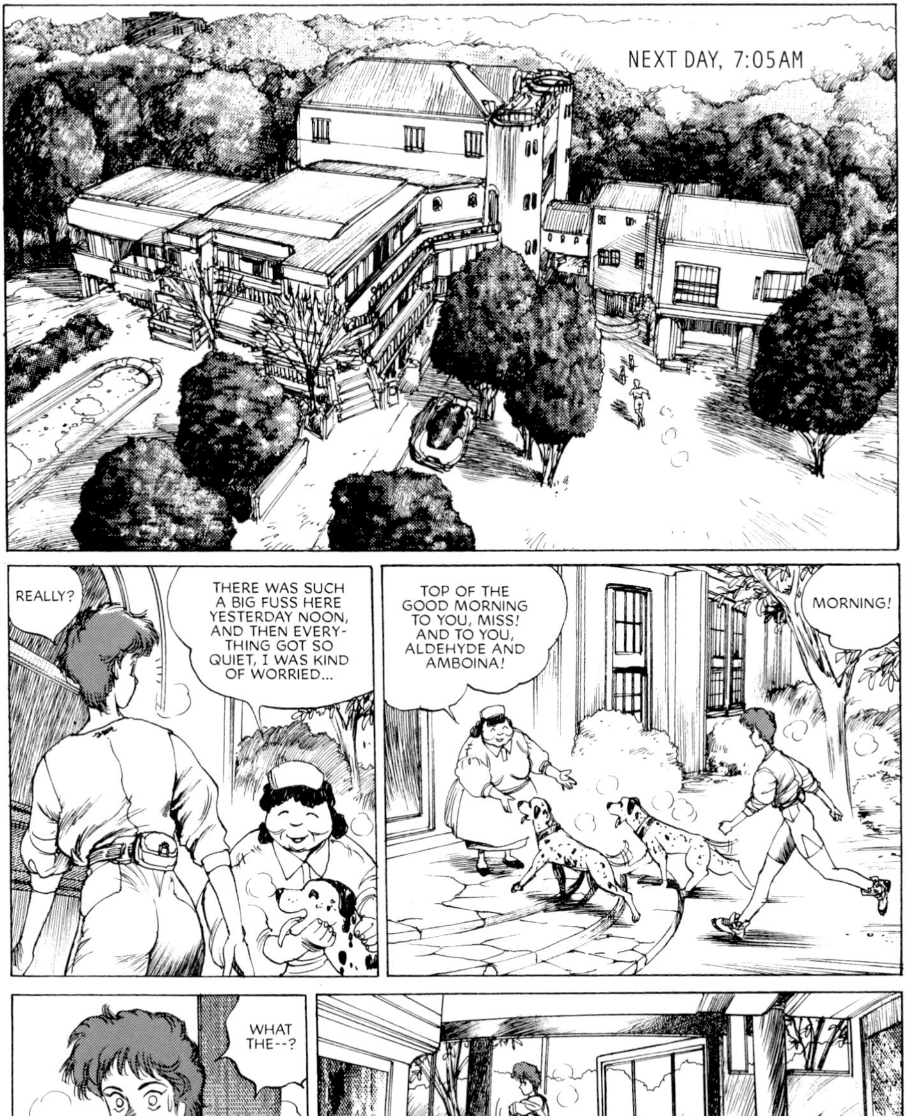
NEXT DAY, 7:05AM
MORNING!
TOP OF THE GOOD MORNING TO YOU, MISS! AND TO YOU, ALDEHYDE AND AMBOINA!
THERE WAS SUCH A BIG FUSS HERE YESTERDAY NOON, AND THEN EVERY-THING GOT SO QUIET, I WAS KIND OF WORRIED...
REALLY?
Ehem
WHAT THE--?

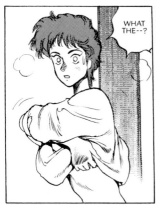

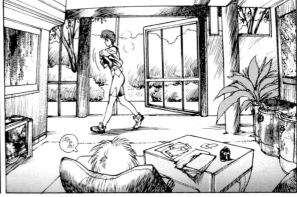

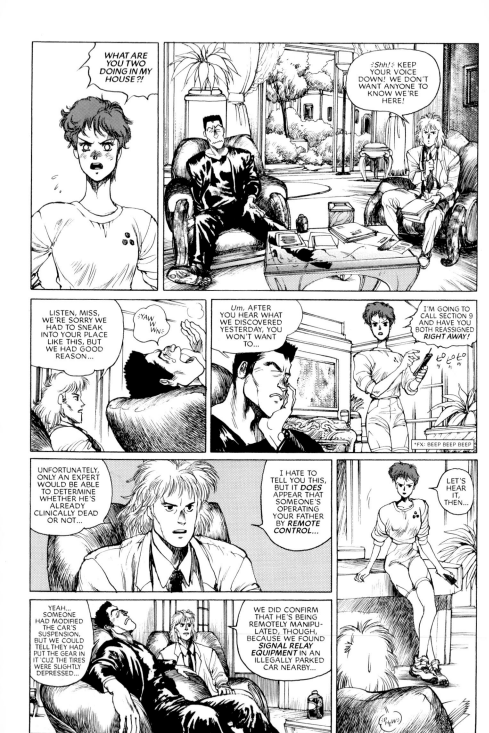

15

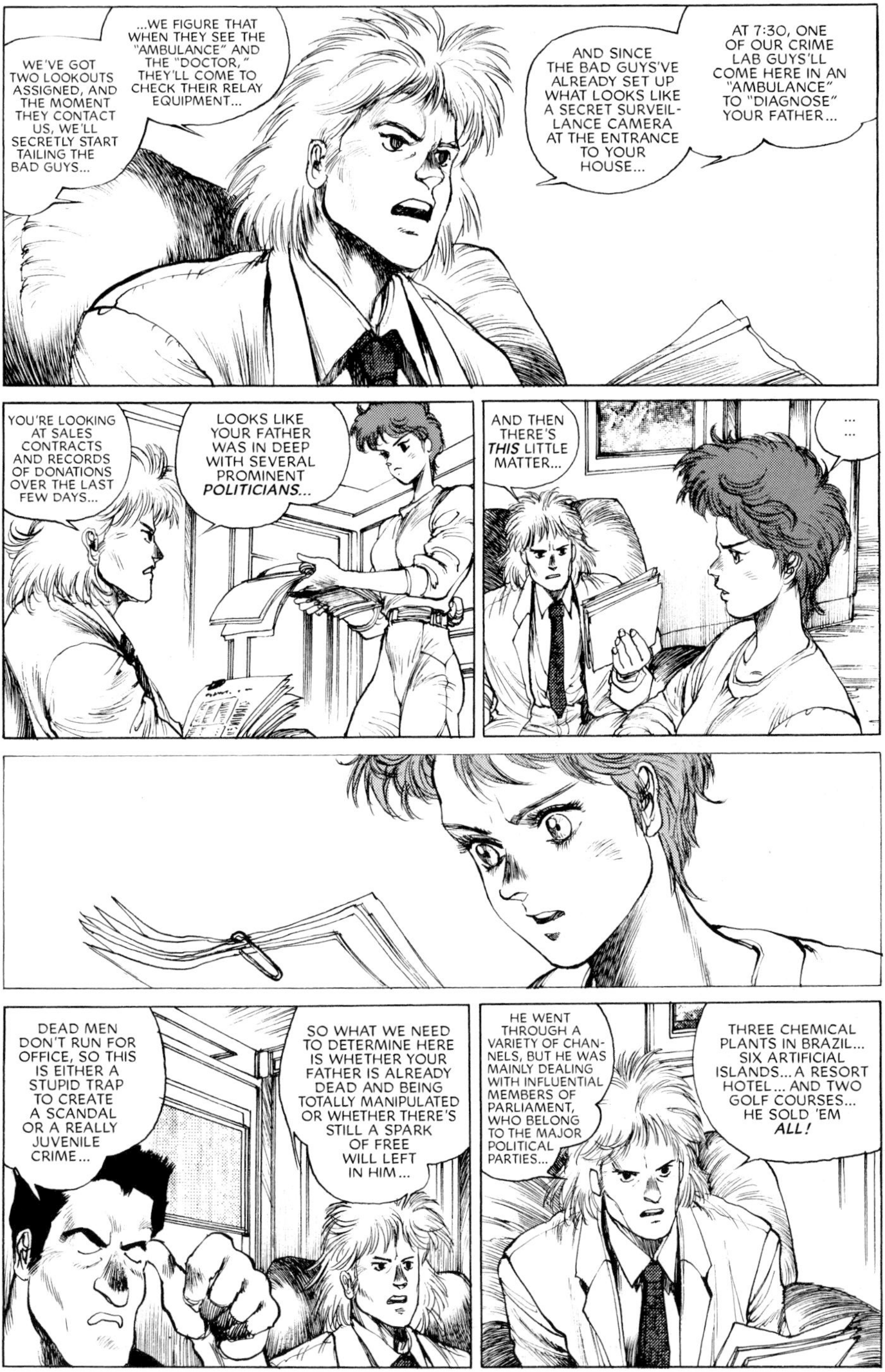
AT 7:30, ONE OF OUR CRIME LAB GUYS'LL COME HERE IN AN "AMBULANCE" TO "DIAGNOSE" YOUR FATHER...
AND SINCE THE BAD GUYS'VE ALREADY SET UP WHAT LOOKS LIKE A SECRET SURVEIL-LANCE CAMERA AT THE ENTRANCE TO YOUR HOUSE...
...WE FIGURE THAT WHEN THEY SEE THE "AMBULANCE" AND THE "DOCTOR," THEY'LL COME TO CHECK THEIR RELAY EQUIPMENT...
WE'VE GOT TWO LOOKOUTS ASSIGNED, AND THE MOMENT THEY CONTACT US, WE'LL SECRETLY START TAILING THE BAD GUYS...
... ...
AND THEN THERE'S *THIS* LITTLE MATTER...
LOOKS LIKE YOUR FATHER WAS IN DEEP WITH SEVERAL PROMINENT *POLITICIANS...*
YOU'RE LOOKING AT SALES CONTRACTS AND RECORDS OF DONATIONS OVER THE LAST FEW DAYS...
THREE CHEMICAL PLANTS IN BRAZIL... SIX ARTIFICIAL ISLANDS... A RESORT HOTEL... AND TWO GOLF COURSES... HE SOLD 'EM *ALL!*
HE WENT THROUGH A VARIETY OF CHAN-NELS, BUT HE WAS MAINLY DEALING WITH INFLUENTIAL MEMBERS OF PARLIAMENT, WHO BELONG TO THE MAJOR POLITICAL PARTIES...
SO WHAT WE NEED TO DETERMINE HERE IS WHETHER YOUR FATHER IS ALREADY DEAD AND BEING TOTALLY MANIPULATED OR WHETHER THERE'S STILL A SPARK OF FREE WILL LEFT IN HIM...
DEAD MEN DON'T RUN FOR OFFICE, SO THIS IS EITHER A STUPID TRAP TO CREATE A SCANDAL OR A REALLY JUVENILE CRIME...

*FX: BEEP BEEP BEEEP BEEP

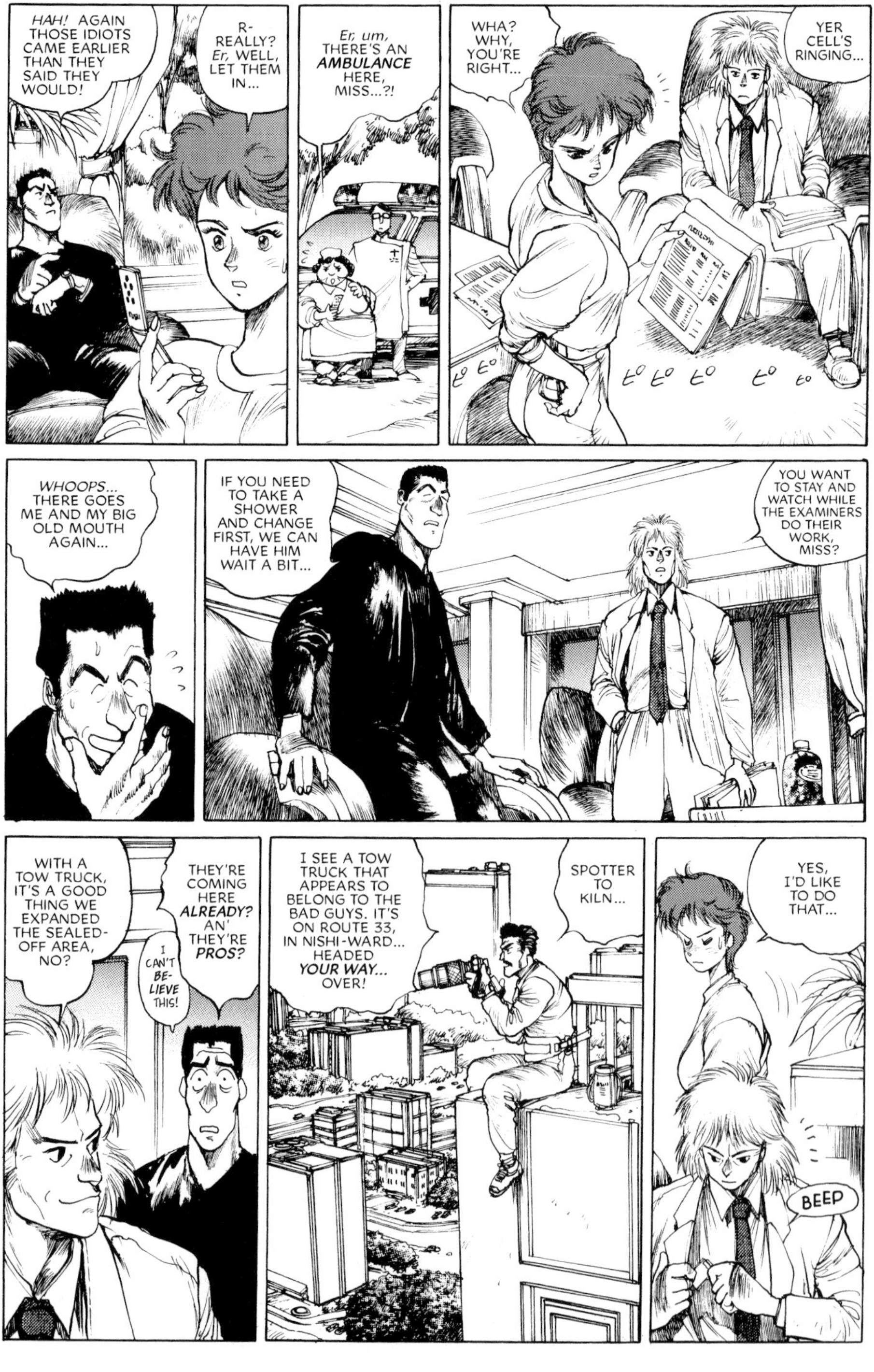
YER CELL'S RINGING...
WHA? WHY, YOU'RE RIGHT...
Er, um, THERE'S AN AMBULANCE HERE, MISS...?!
R- REALLY? Er, WELL, LET THEM IN...
HAH! AGAIN THOSE IDIOTS CAME EARLIER THAN THEY SAID THEY WOULD!
YOU WANT TO STAY AND WATCH WHILE THE EXAMINERS DO THEIR WORK, MISS?
IF YOU NEED TO TAKE A SHOWER AND CHANGE FIRST, WE CAN HAVE HIM WAIT A BIT...
WHOOPS... THERE GOES ME AND MY BIG OLD MOUTH AGAIN...
YES, I'D LIKE TO DO THAT...
BEEP
SPOTTER TO KILN...
I SEE A TOW TRUCK THAT APPEARS TO BELONG TO THE BAD GUYS. IT'S ON ROUTE 33, IN NISHI-WARD... HEADED YOUR WAY... OVER!
THEY'RE COMING HERE ALREADY? AN' THEY'RE PROS?
I CAN'T BE- LIEVE THIS!
WITH A TOW TRUCK, IT'S A GOOD THING WE EXPANDED THE SEALED- OFF AREA, NO?

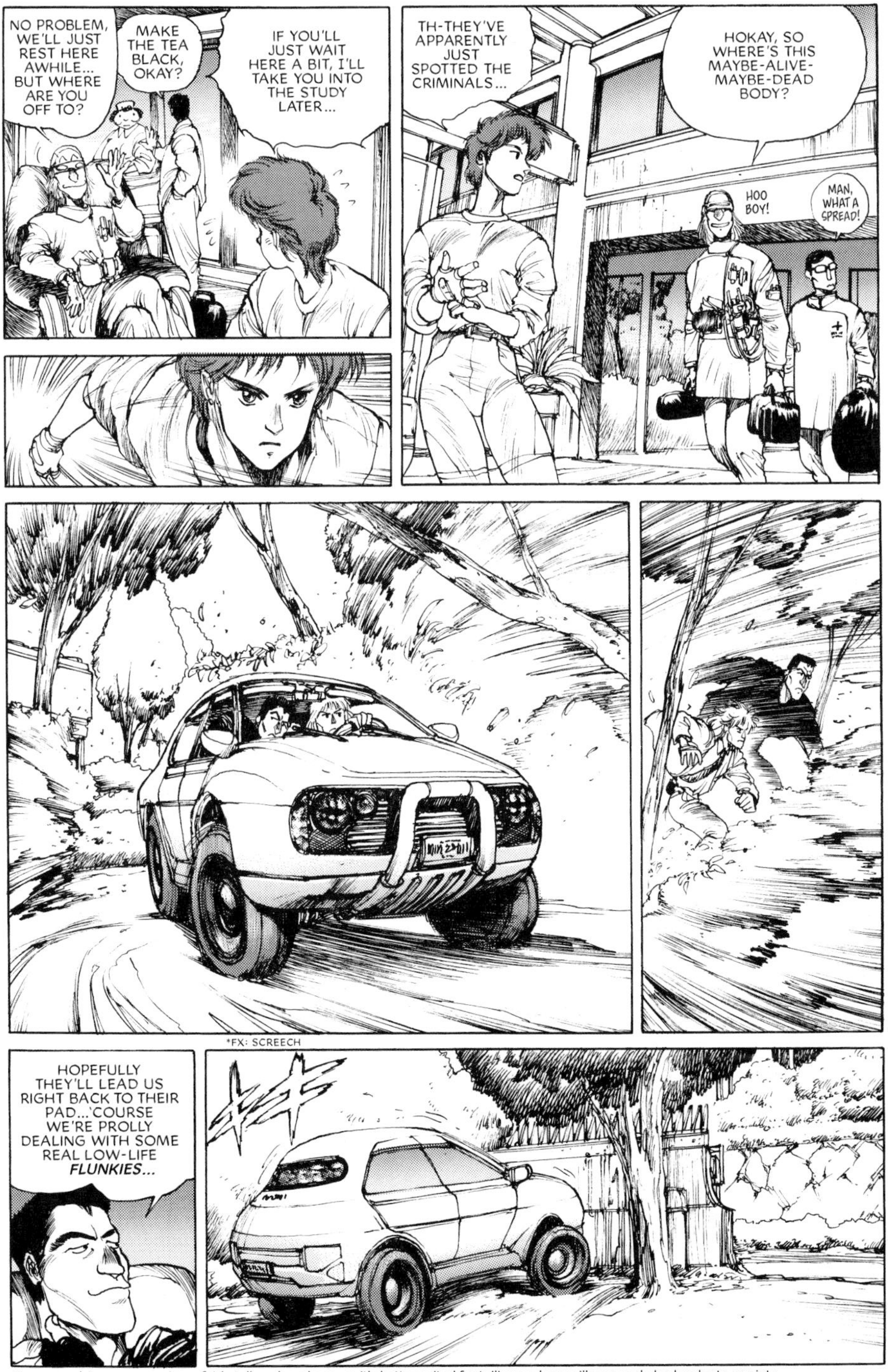
MAN, WHAT A SPREAD!
HOO BOY!
HOKAY, SO WHERE'S THIS MAYBE-ALIVE-MAYBE-DEAD BODY?
TH-THEY'VE APPARENTLY JUST SPOTTED THE CRIMINALS...
IF YOU'LL JUST WAIT HERE A BIT, I'LL TAKE YOU INTO THE STUDY LATER...
MAKE THE TEA BLACK, OKAY?
NO PROBLEM, WE'LL JUST REST HERE AWHILE... BUT WHERE ARE YOU OFF TO?
*FX: SCREECH
HOPEFULLY THEY'LL LEAD US RIGHT BACK TO THEIR PAD...'COURSE WE'RE PROLLY DEALING WITH SOME REAL LOW-LIFE *FLUNKIES*...

Togusa and Azuma are using a fairly tall car here because it's better suited for tailing and surveillance and also harder to see into. Choice of vehicle does not necessarily reflect the personal preference of the characters or the artist...

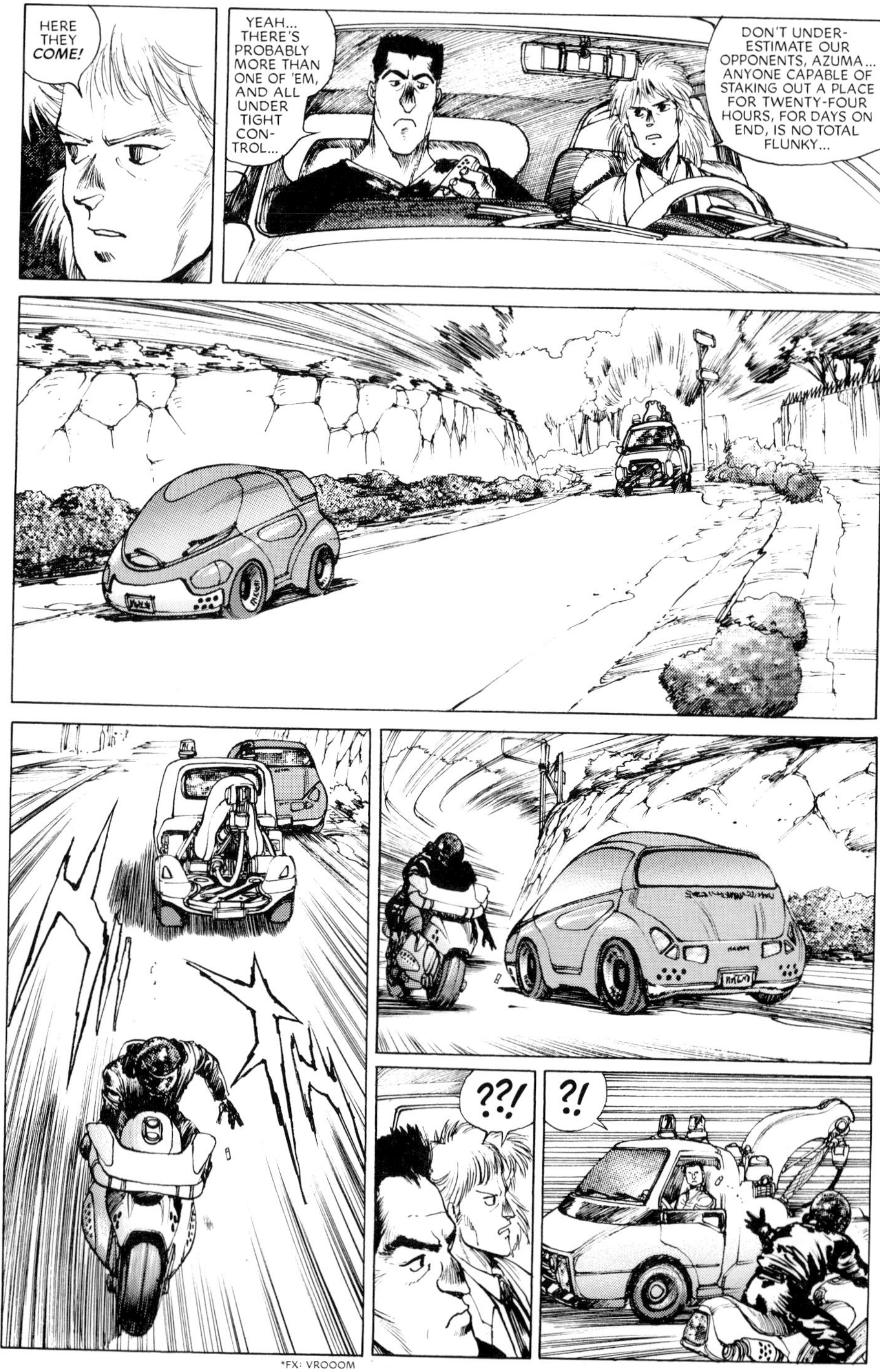
HERE THEY *COME!*
YEAH... THERE'S PROBABLY MORE THAN ONE OF 'EM, AND ALL UNDER TIGHT CON-TROL...
DON'T UNDER-ESTIMATE OUR OPPONENTS, AZUMA... ANYONE CAPABLE OF STAKING OUT A PLACE FOR TWENTY-FOUR HOURS, FOR DAYS ON END, IS NO TOTAL FLUNKY...
??!
?!

*FX: VROOOM

*FX: KABOOOM

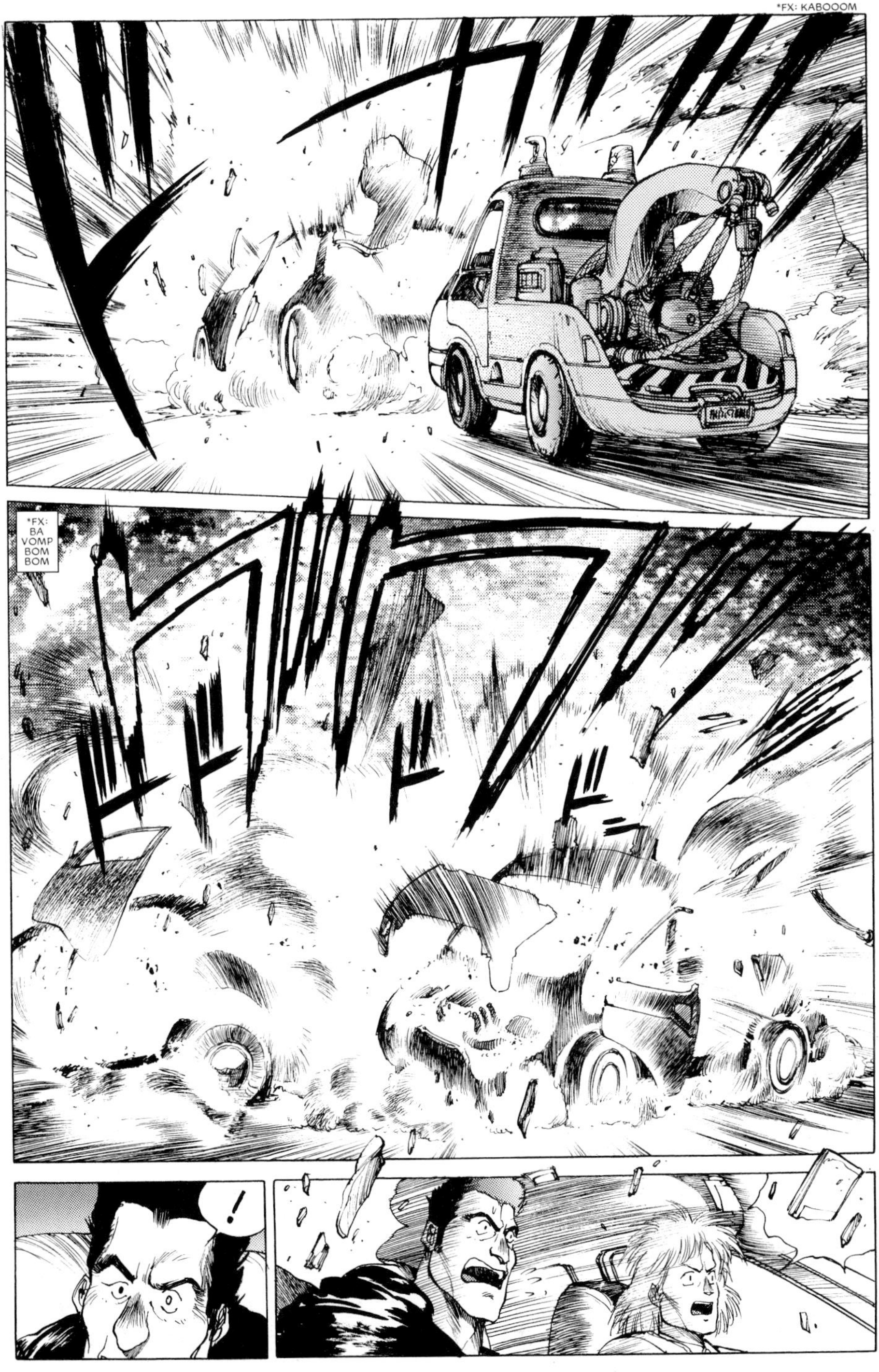
*FX: BA VOMP BOM BOM
!

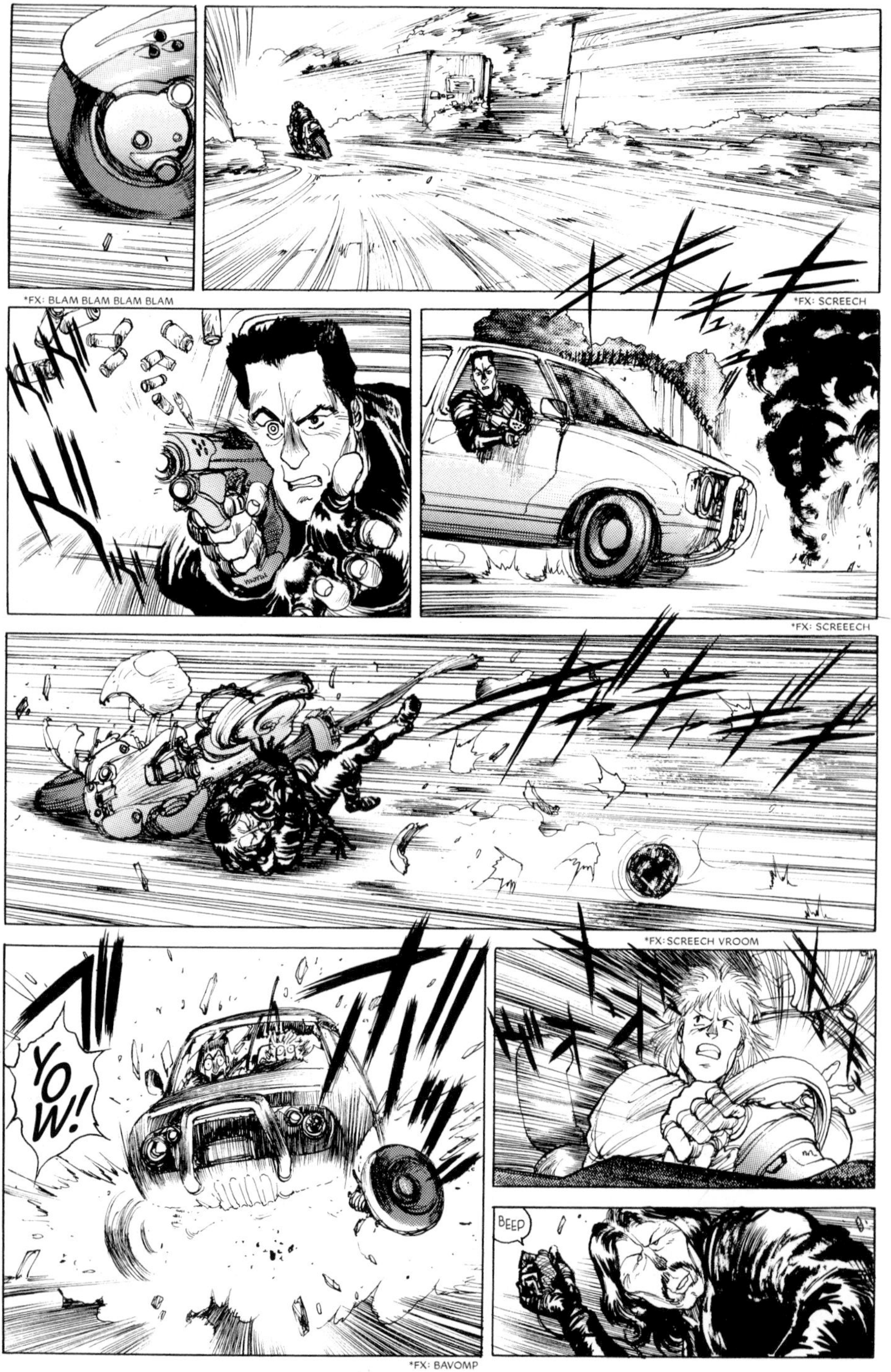
*FX: SCREECH
*FX: BLAM BLAM BLAM BLAM
*FX: SCREEECH
*FX: SCREECH VROOM
BEEP
YOW!
*FX: BAVOMP

*FX: FLICK *FX: TROMP TROMP TROMP

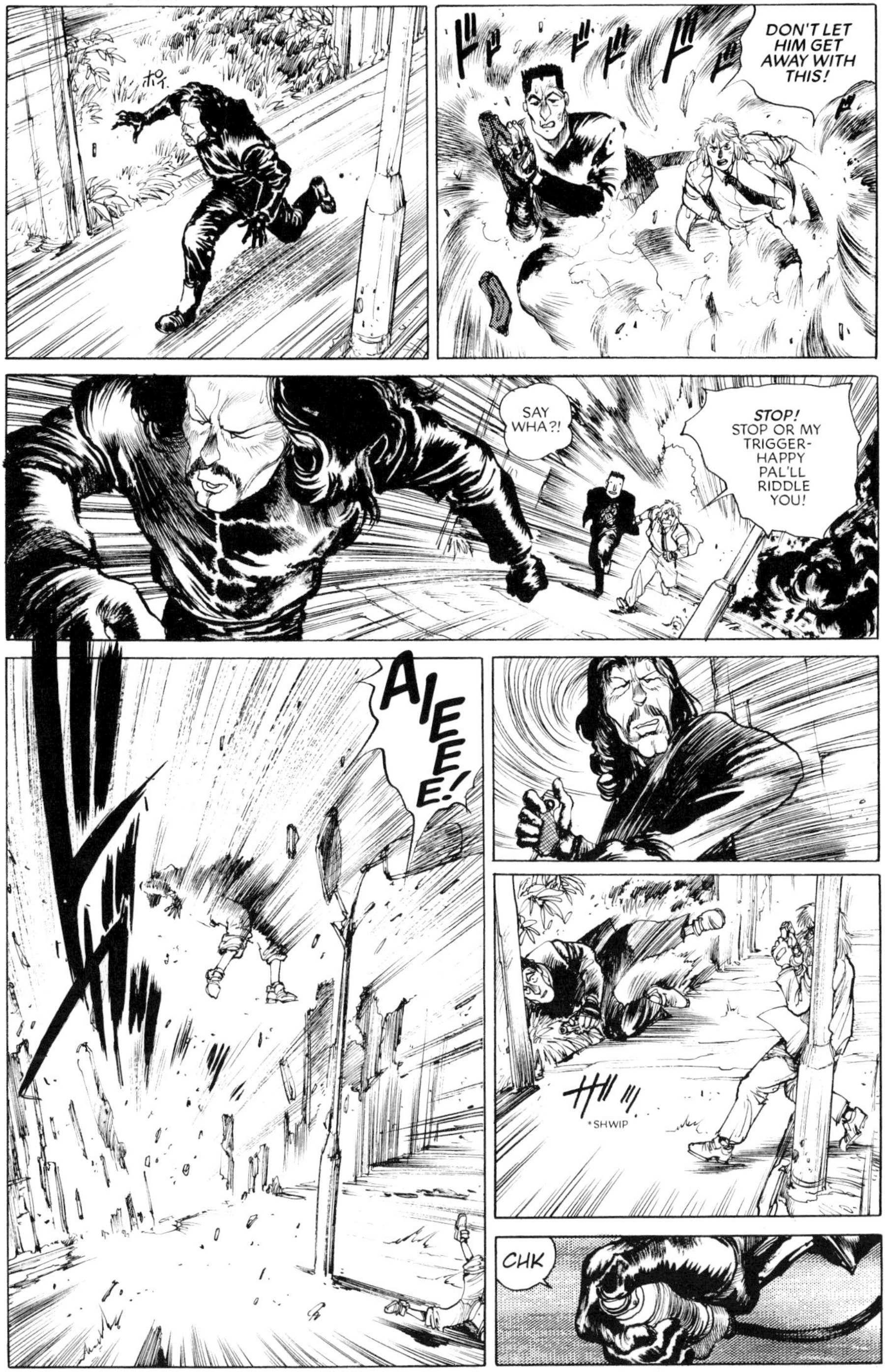
DON'T LET HIM GET AWAY WITH THIS!
STOP! STOP OR MY TRIGGER-HAPPY PAL'LL RIDDLE YOU!
SAY WHA?!
*SHWIP
CHK
AIEEEE!

*FX: KVAM!

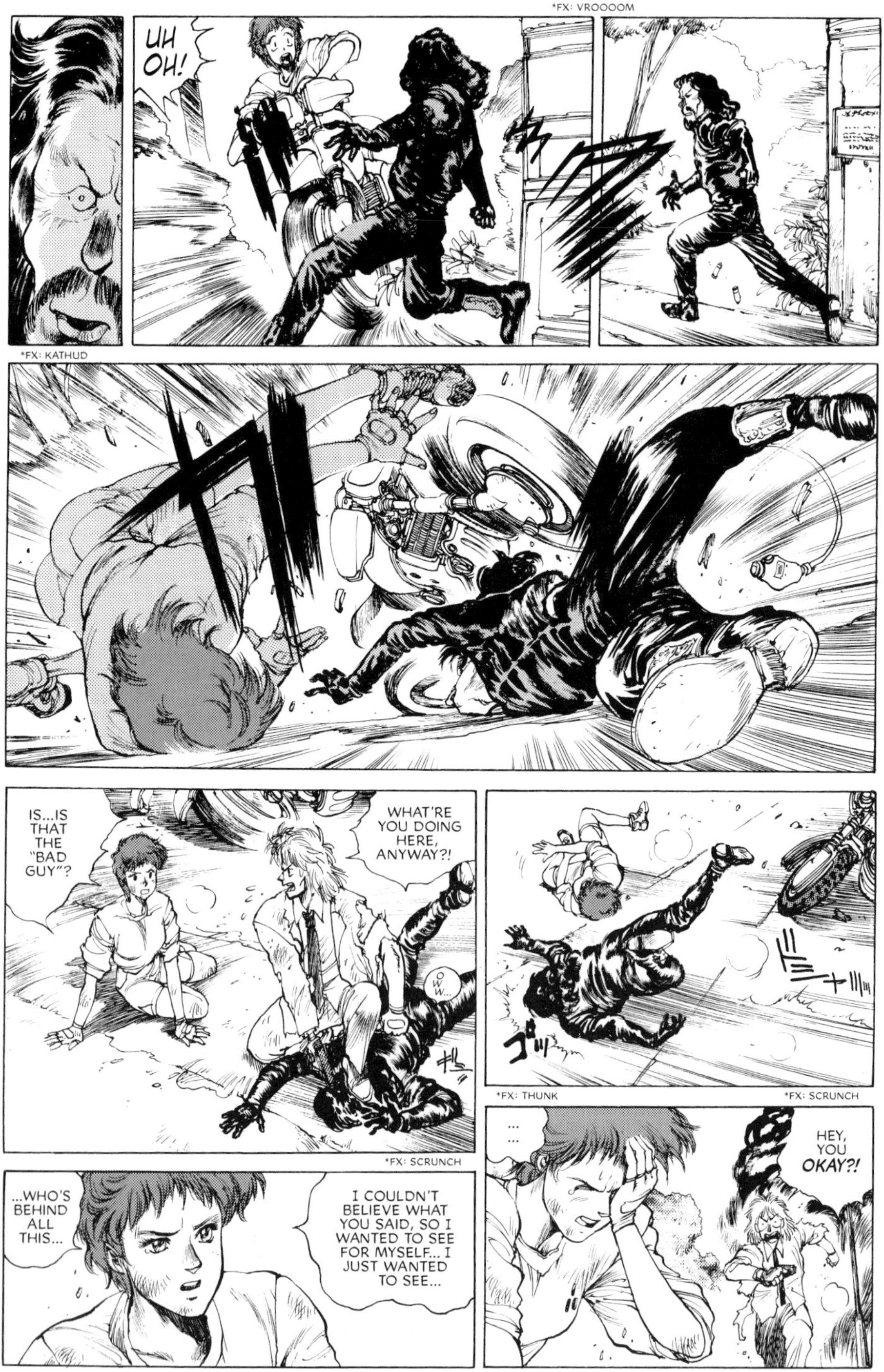
*FX: VROOOOM
UH OH!
*FX: KATHUD
*FX: THUNK
*FX: SCRUNCH
WHAT'RE YOU DOING HERE, ANYWAY?!
IS...IS THAT THE "BAD GUY"?
OWW...
*FX: SCRUNCH
HEY, YOU OKAY?!
... ...
I COULDN'T BELIEVE WHAT YOU SAID, SO I WANTED TO SEE FOR MYSELF... I JUST WANTED TO SEE...
...WHO'S BEHIND ALL THIS...

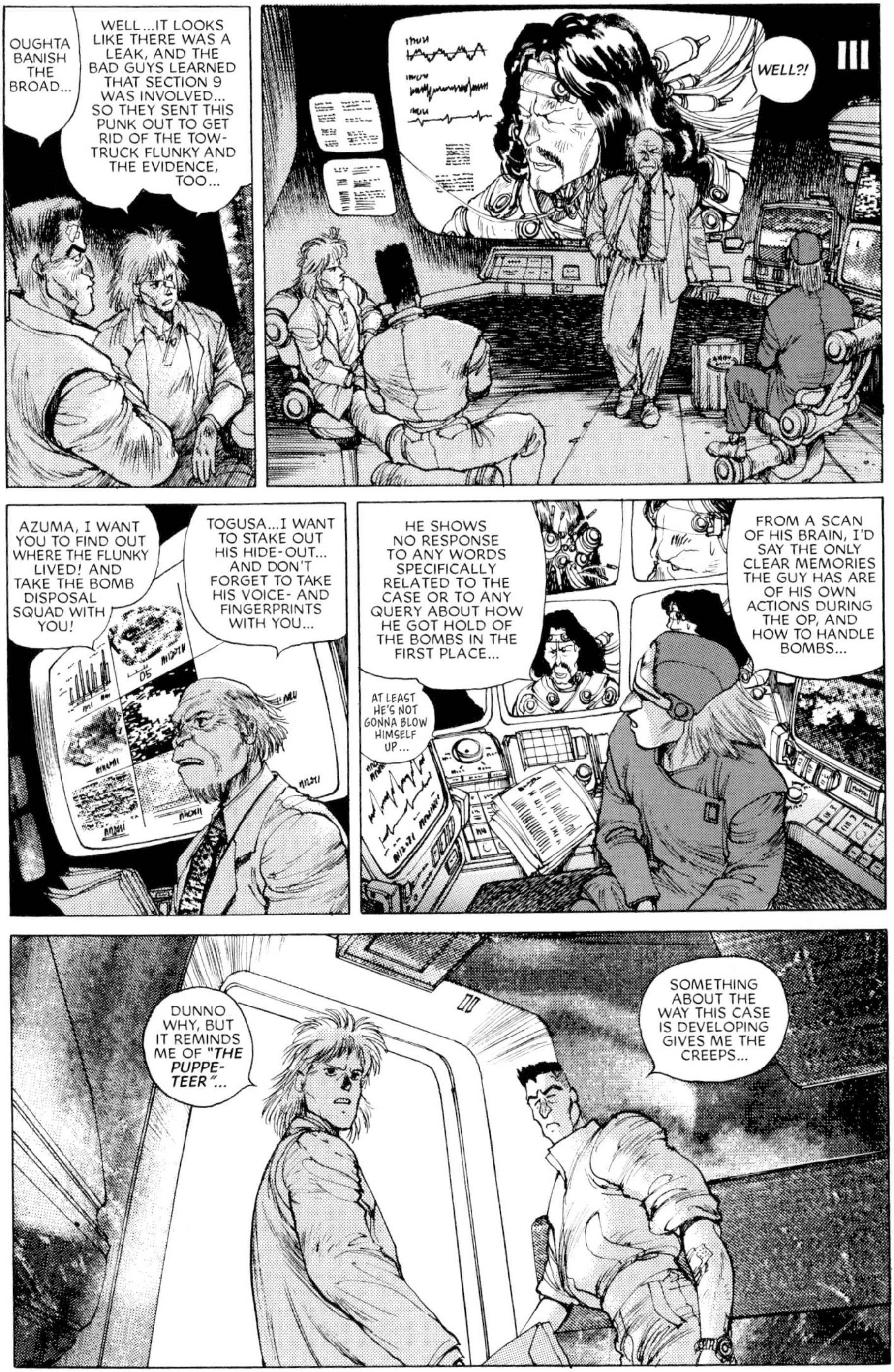

WELL...IT LOOKS LIKE THERE WAS A LEAK, AND THE BAD GUYS LEARNED THAT SECTION 9 WAS INVOLVED... SO THEY SENT THIS PUNK OUT TO GET RID OF THE TOW-TRUCK FLUNKY AND THE EVIDENCE, TOO...
OUGHTA BANISH THE BROAD...
WELL?!
AZUMA, I WANT YOU TO FIND OUT WHERE THE FLUNKY LIVED! AND TAKE THE BOMB DISPOSAL SQUAD WITH YOU!
TOGUSA...I WANT TO STAKE OUT HIS HIDE-OUT... AND DON'T FORGET TO TAKE HIS VOICE- AND FINGERPRINTS WITH YOU...
HE SHOWS NO RESPONSE TO ANY WORDS SPECIFICALLY RELATED TO THE CASE OR TO ANY QUERY ABOUT HOW HE GOT HOLD OF THE BOMBS IN THE FIRST PLACE...
FROM A SCAN OF HIS BRAIN, I'D SAY THE ONLY CLEAR MEMORIES THE GUY HAS ARE OF HIS OWN ACTIONS DURING THE OP, AND HOW TO HANDLE BOMBS...
AT LEAST HE'S NOT GONNA BLOW HIMSELF UP...
SOMETHING ABOUT THE WAY THIS CASE IS DEVELOPING GIVES ME THE CREEPS...
DUNNO WHY, BUT IT REMINDS ME OF "THE PUPPETEER"...

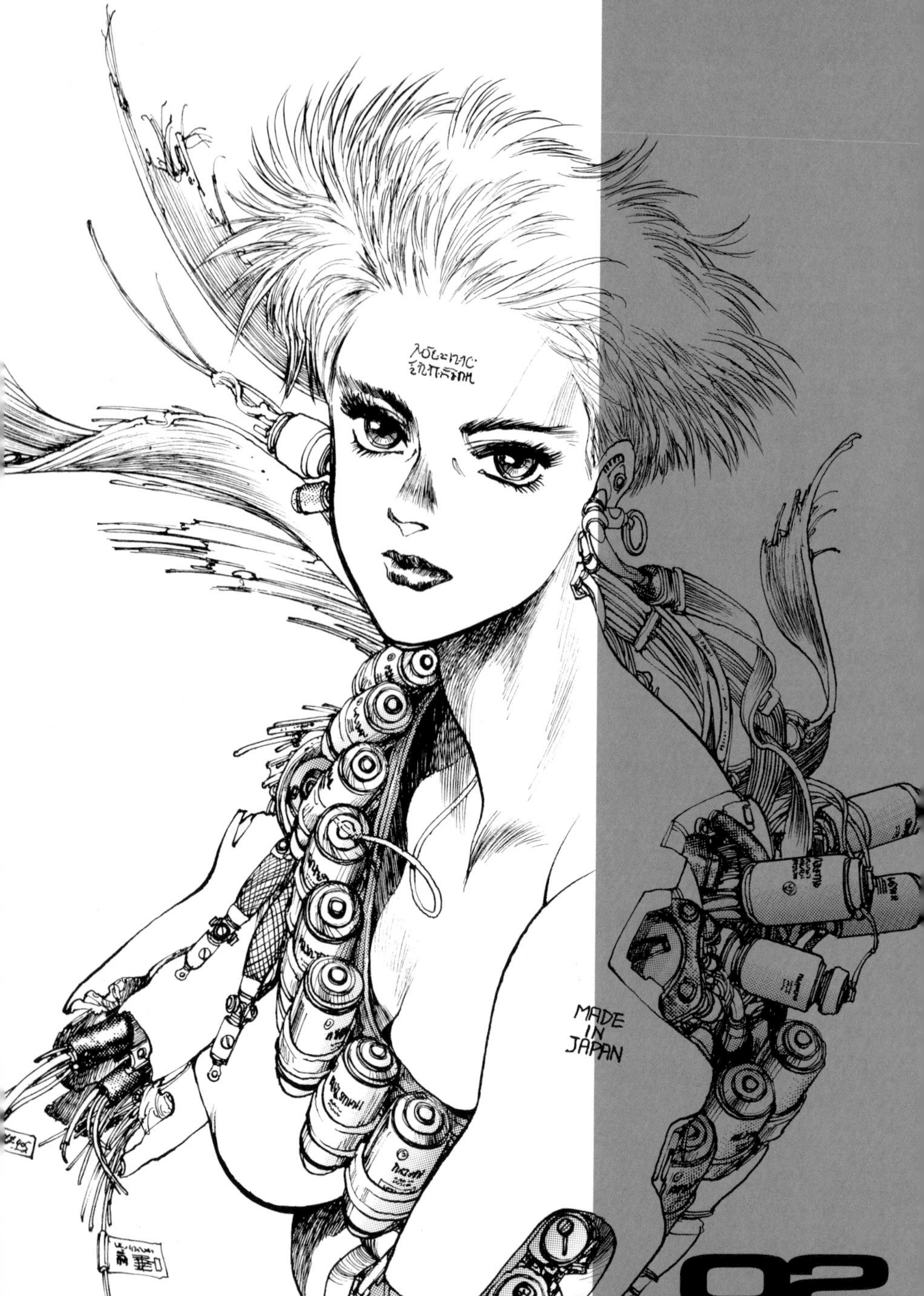
MADE IN JAPAN

02

FAT CAT Part 2

1991

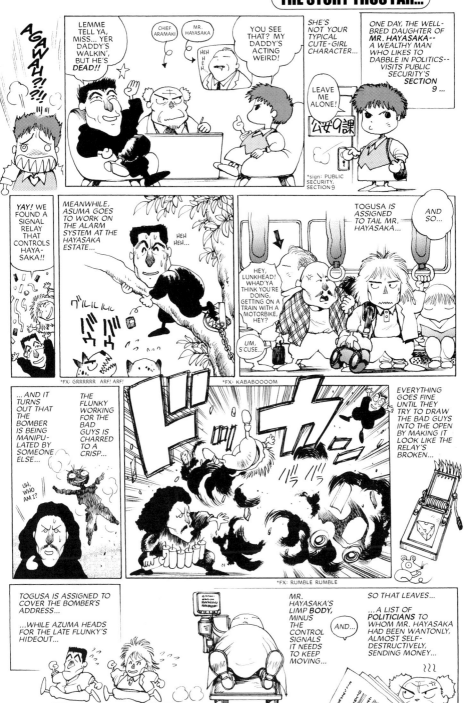

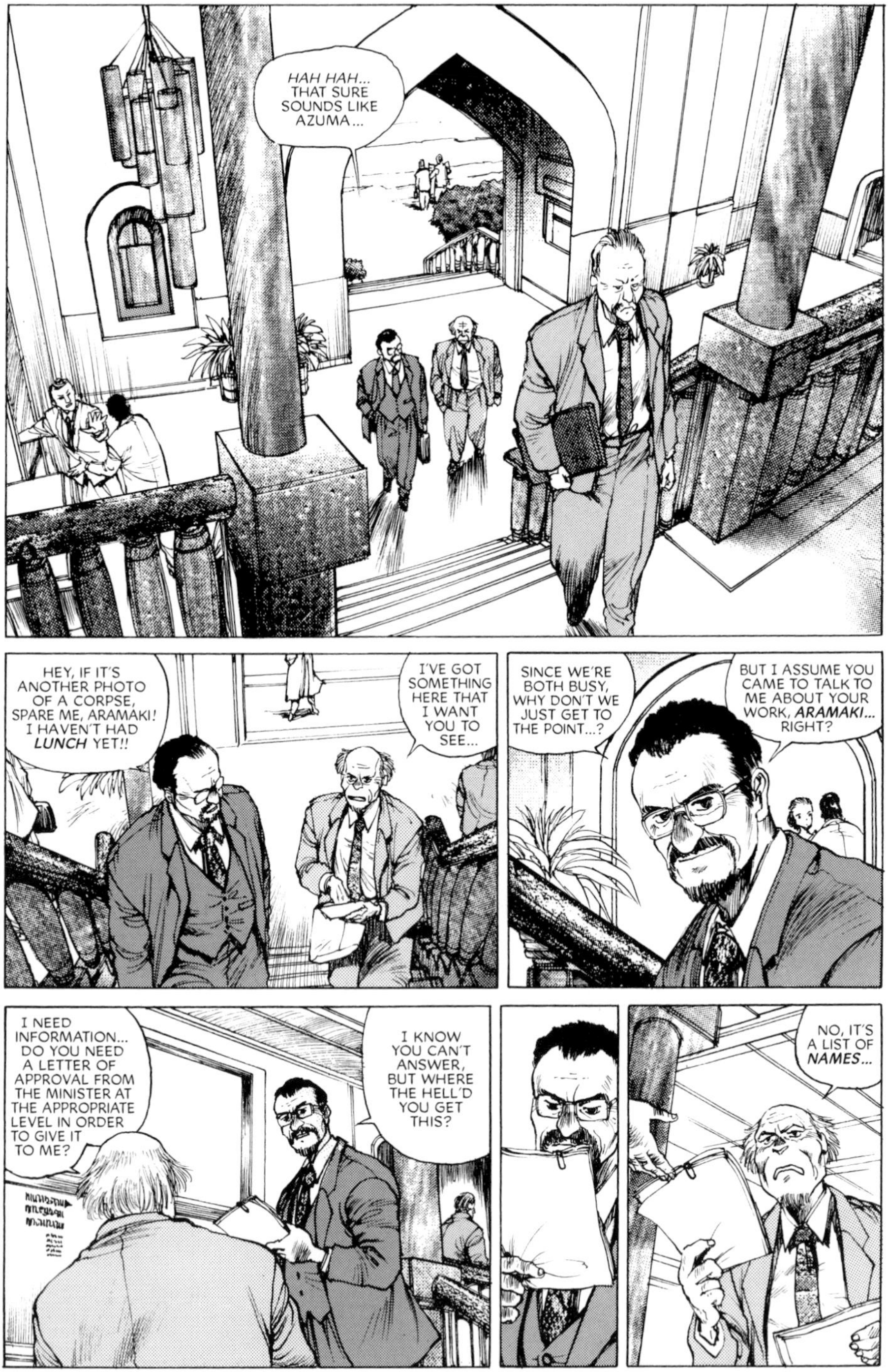
HAH HAH... THAT SURE SOUNDS LIKE AZUMA...
HEY, IF IT'S ANOTHER PHOTO OF A CORPSE, SPARE ME, ARAMAKI! I HAVEN'T HAD *LUNCH* YET!!
I'VE GOT SOMETHING HERE THAT I WANT YOU TO SEE...
SINCE WE'RE BOTH BUSY, WHY DON'T WE JUST GET TO THE POINT...?
BUT I ASSUME YOU CAME TO TALK TO ME ABOUT YOUR WORK, *ARAMAKI...* RIGHT?
I NEED INFORMATION... DO YOU NEED A LETTER OF APPROVAL FROM THE MINISTER AT THE APPROPRIATE LEVEL IN ORDER TO GIVE IT TO ME?
I KNOW YOU CAN'T ANSWER, BUT WHERE THE HELL'D YOU GET THIS?
NO, IT'S A LIST OF *NAMES...*

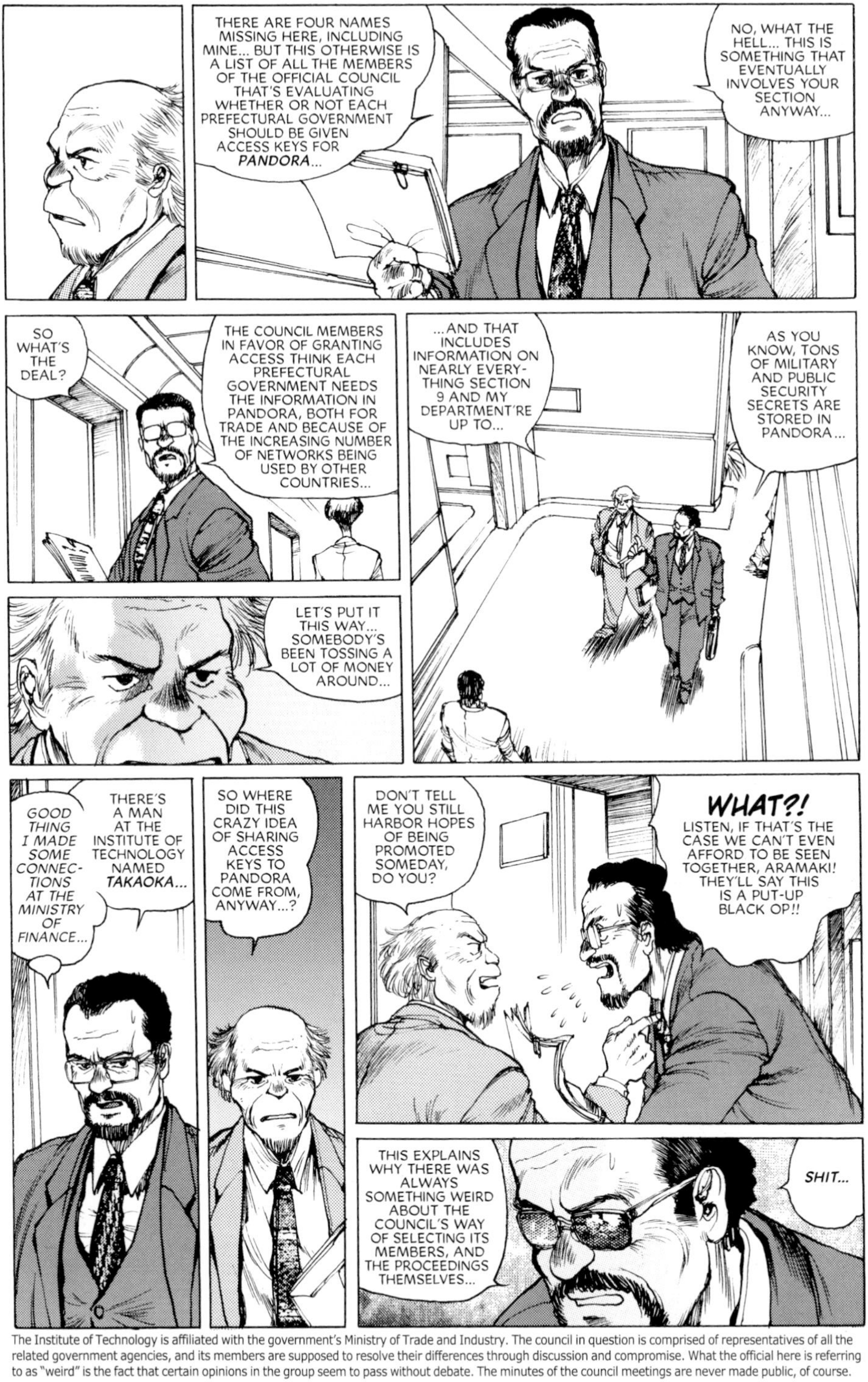
NO, WHAT THE HELL... THIS IS SOMETHING THAT EVENTUALLY INVOLVES YOUR SECTION ANYWAY...
THERE ARE FOUR NAMES MISSING HERE, INCLUDING MINE... BUT THIS OTHERWISE IS A LIST OF ALL THE MEMBERS OF THE OFFICIAL COUNCIL THAT'S EVALUATING WHETHER OR NOT EACH PREFECTURAL GOVERNMENT SHOULD BE GIVEN ACCESS KEYS FOR PANDORA...
AS YOU KNOW, TONS OF MILITARY AND PUBLIC SECURITY SECRETS ARE STORED IN PANDORA...
...AND THAT INCLUDES INFORMATION ON NEARLY EVERY-THING SECTION 9 AND MY DEPARTMENT'RE UP TO...
THE COUNCIL MEMBERS IN FAVOR OF GRANTING ACCESS THINK EACH PREFECTURAL GOVERNMENT NEEDS THE INFORMATION IN PANDORA, BOTH FOR TRADE AND BECAUSE OF THE INCREASING NUMBER OF NETWORKS BEING USED BY OTHER COUNTRIES...
SO WHAT'S THE DEAL?
LET'S PUT IT THIS WAY... SOMEBODY'S BEEN TOSSING A LOT OF MONEY AROUND...
WHAT?! LISTEN, IF THAT'S THE CASE WE CAN'T EVEN AFFORD TO BE SEEN TOGETHER, ARAMAKI! THEY'LL SAY THIS IS A PUT-UP BLACK OP!!
DON'T TELL ME YOU STILL HARBOR HOPES OF BEING PROMOTED SOMEDAY, DO YOU?
SHIT...
THIS EXPLAINS WHY THERE WAS ALWAYS SOMETHING WEIRD ABOUT THE COUNCIL'S WAY OF SELECTING ITS MEMBERS, AND THE PROCEEDINGS THEMSELVES...
SO WHERE DID THIS CRAZY IDEA OF SHARING ACCESS KEYS TO PANDORA COME FROM, ANYWAY...?
THERE'S A MAN AT THE INSTITUTE OF TECHNOLOGY NAMED TAKAOKA...
GOOD THING I MADE SOME CONNEC-TIONS AT THE MINISTRY OF FINANCE...

The Institute of Technology is affiliated with the government's Ministry of Trade and Industry. The council in question is comprised of representatives of all the related government agencies, and its members are supposed to resolve their differences through discussion and compromise. What the official here is referring to as "weird" is the fact that certain opinions in the group seem to pass without debate. The minutes of the council meetings are never made public, of course.

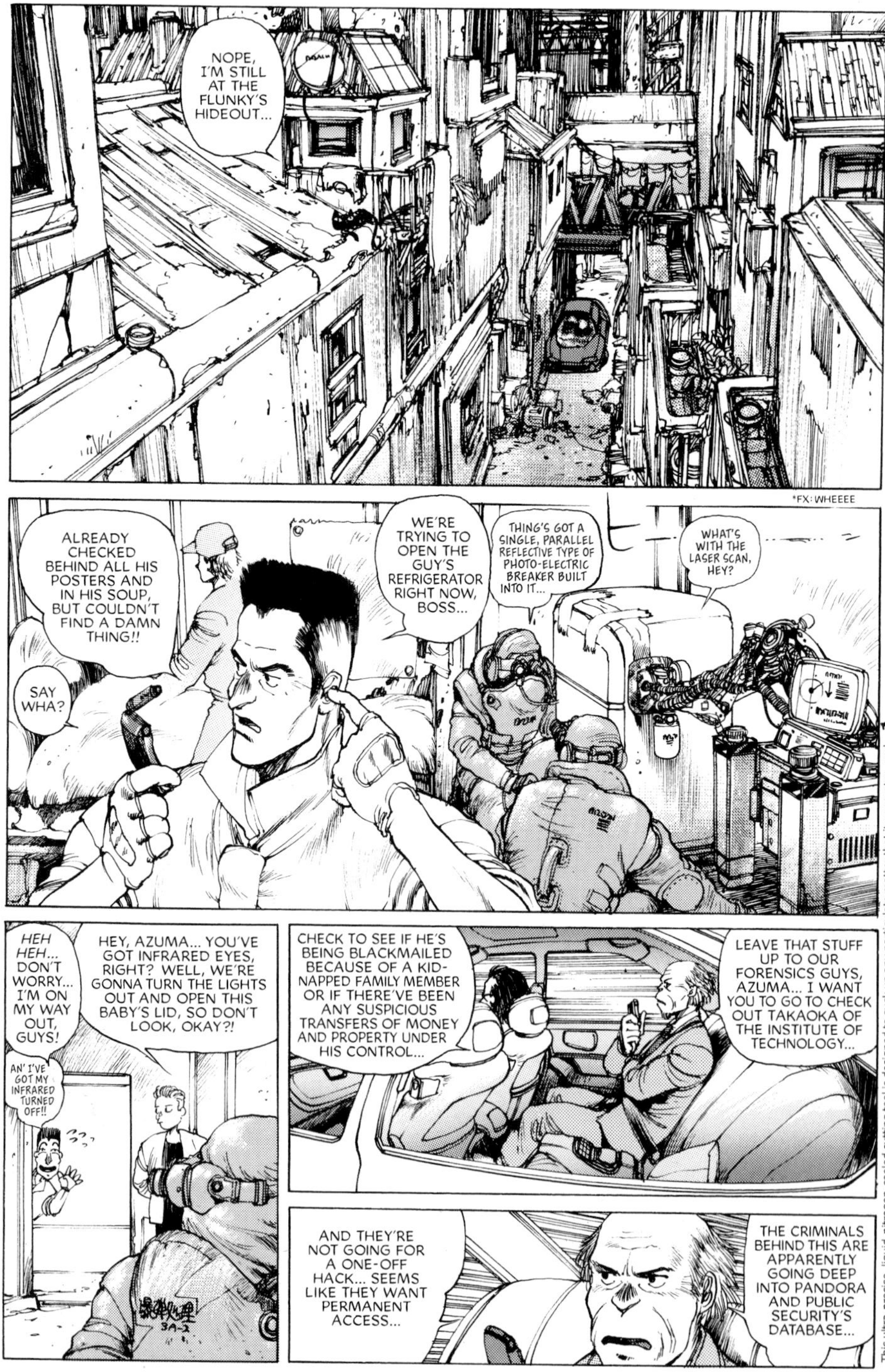
NOPE, I'M STILL AT THE FLUNKY'S HIDEOUT...
ALREADY CHECKED BEHIND ALL HIS POSTERS AND IN HIS SOUP, BUT COULDN'T FIND A DAMN THING!!
SAY WHA?
WE'RE TRYING TO OPEN THE GUY'S REFRIGERATOR RIGHT NOW, BOSS...
WHAT'S WITH THE LASER SCAN, HEY?
THING'S GOT A SINGLE, PARALLEL REFLECTIVE TYPE OF PHOTO-ELECTRIC BREAKER BUILT INTO IT...
HEH HEH... DON'T WORRY... I'M ON MY WAY OUT, GUYS!
AN' I'VE GOT MY INFRARED TURNED OFF!!
HEY, AZUMA... YOU'VE GOT INFRARED EYES, RIGHT? WELL, WE'RE GONNA TURN THE LIGHTS OUT AND OPEN THIS BABY'S LID, SO DON'T LOOK, OKAY?!
CHECK TO SEE IF HE'S BEING BLACKMAILED BECAUSE OF A KID-NAPPED FAMILY MEMBER OR IF THERE'VE BEEN ANY SUSPICIOUS TRANSFERS OF MONEY AND PROPERTY UNDER HIS CONTROL...
LEAVE THAT STUFF UP TO OUR FORENSICS GUYS, AZUMA... I WANT YOU TO GO TO CHECK OUT TAKAOKA OF THE INSTITUTE OF TECHNOLOGY...
THE CRIMINALS BEHIND THIS ARE APPARENTLY GOING DEEP INTO PANDORA AND PUBLIC SECURITY'S DATABASE...
AND THEY'RE NOT GOING FOR A ONE-OFF HACK... SEEMS LIKE THEY WANT PERMANENT ACCESS...

*FX: WHEEEE

This ultra-precise, liquid-nitrogen-cooled cutting tool is designed to suck up any particulate matter that it generates, and also to be vibration-free. In other words, it is designed to not activate any vibration or motion sensors built into the bomb

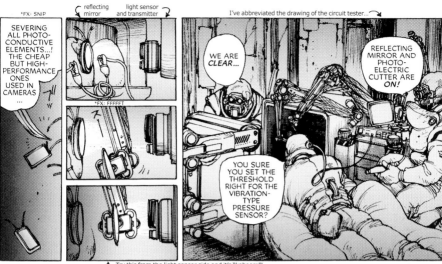

reflecting mirror | light sensor and transmitter

I've abbreviated the drawing of the circuit tester...

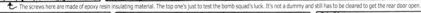
↳ Try this from the light sensor side and it's "kaboom"!

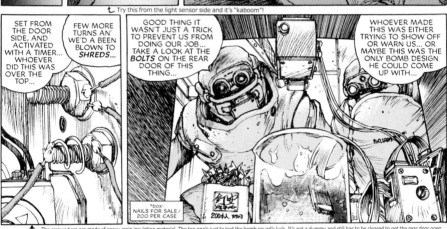

↳ The screws here are made of epoxy resin insulating material. The top one's just to test the bomb squad's luck. It's not a dummy and still has to be cleared to get the rear door open...

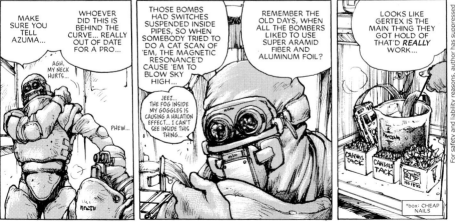

For safety and liability reasons, author has suppressed use of some terminology here... —the editors

Re: the warning referred to in panel 6. If the goal had been to kill the flunky, all it would take is for something far more primitive to be connected to the door of the apartment or to one of the many consumer appliances in the room. If the goal were to blow up the police along with the whole room, all it would take is a lookout nearby to spot them entering. The lookout could then hightail it to safety a klik or two away by car, and send a password or simple execution string back to the room by radio, or set the system to blow when the phone rings (then place a call and wait for someone to answer, etc). In other words, there would have been lots of easier ways to get the job done...

*FX: BEEP BEEP BEEP

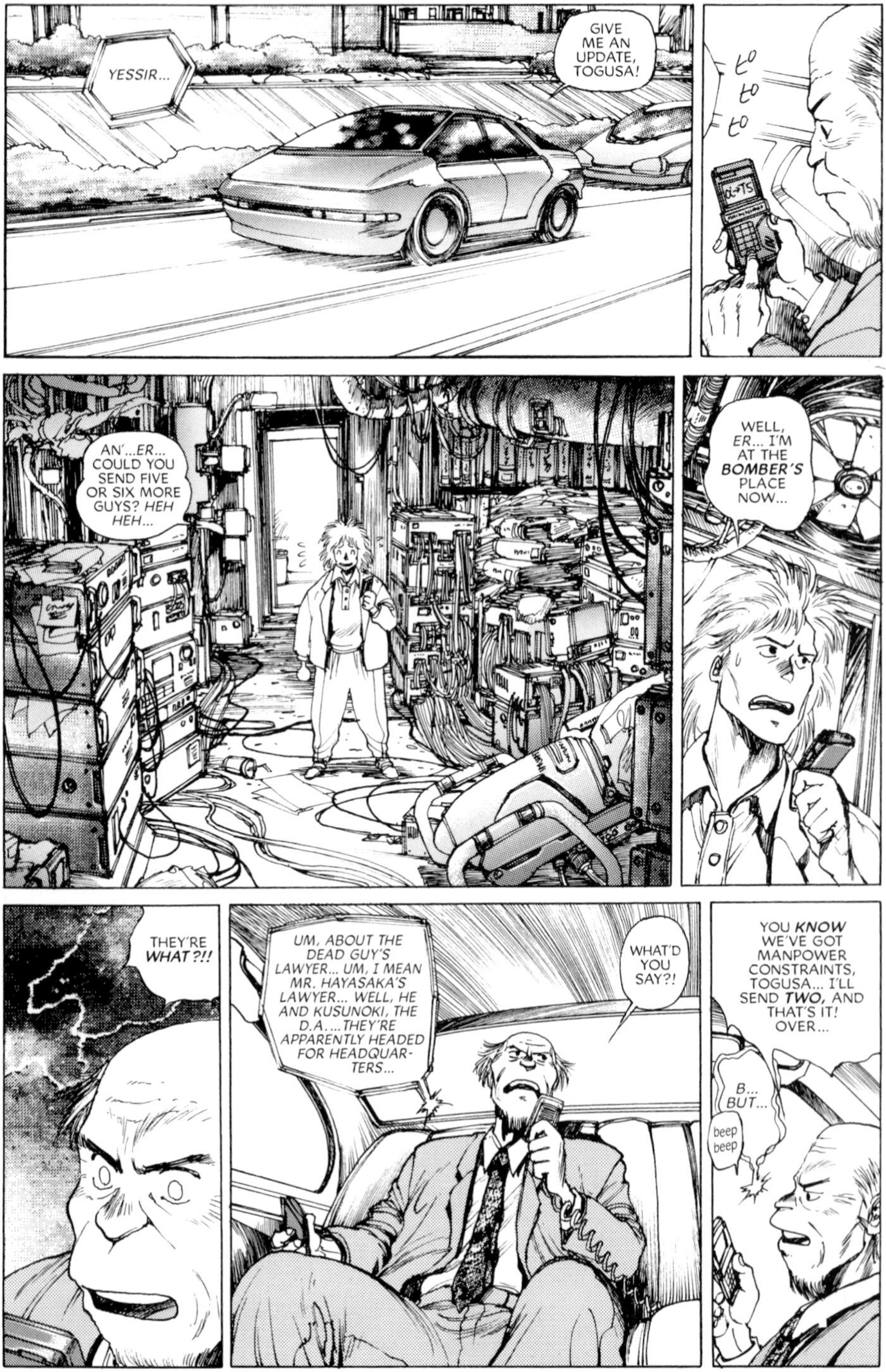
ピ
ピ
ピ
ピ
GIVE ME AN UPDATE, TOGUSA!
YESSIR...
WELL, ER... I'M AT THE BOMBER'S PLACE NOW...
AN'...ER... COULD YOU SEND FIVE OR SIX MORE GUYS? HEH HEH...
YOU KNOW WE'VE GOT MANPOWER CONSTRAINTS, TOGUSA... I'LL SEND TWO, AND THAT'S IT! OVER...
B... BUT...
beep beep
WHAT'D YOU SAY?!
UM, ABOUT THE DEAD GUY'S LAWYER... UM, I MEAN MR. HAYASAKA'S LAWYER... WELL, HE AND KUSUNOKI, THE D.A.... THEY'RE APPARENTLY HEADED FOR HEADQUARTERS...
THEY'RE WHAT?!!

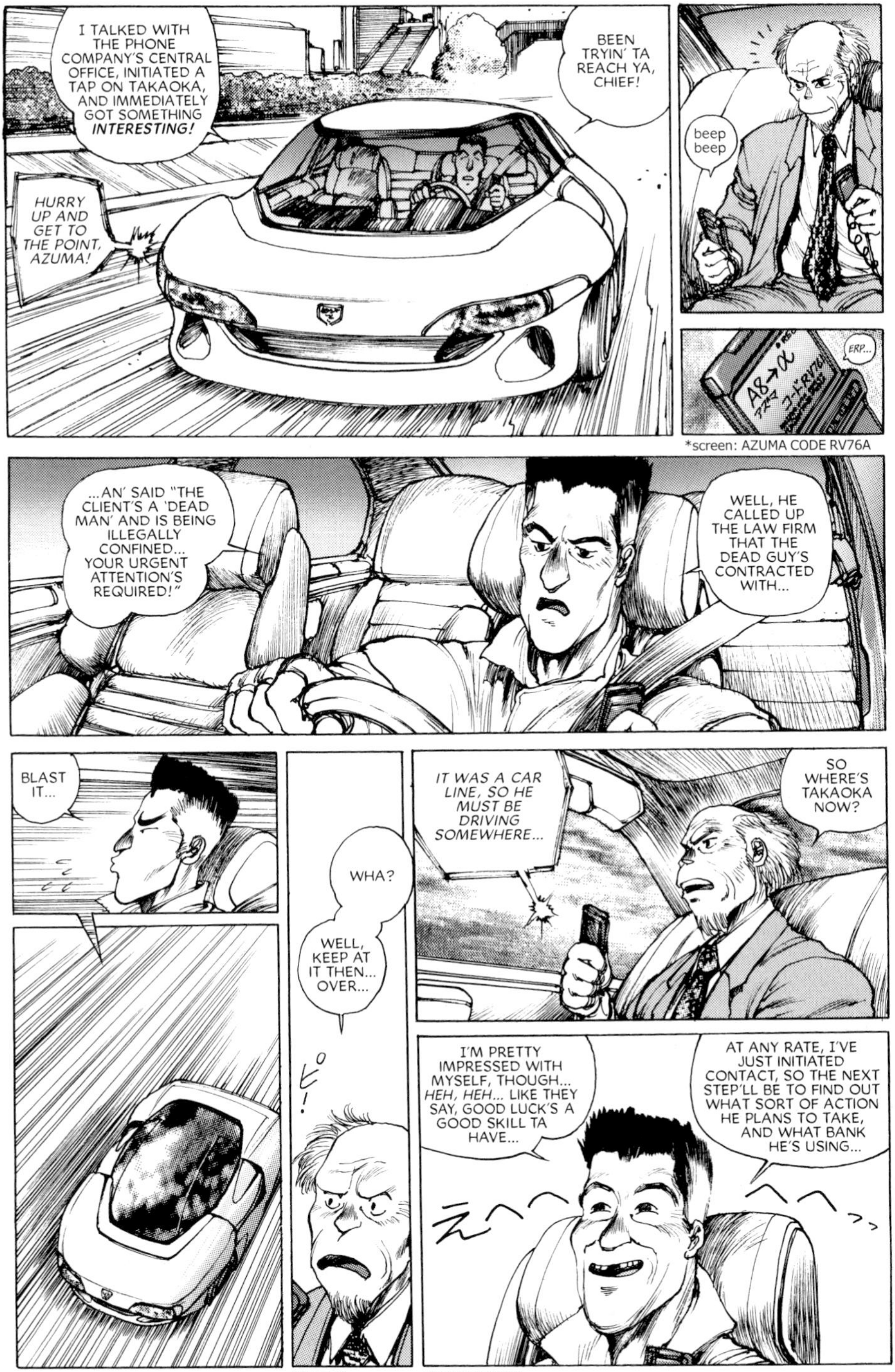
beep beep
ERP...
*screen: AZUMA CODE RV76A
BEEN TRYIN' TA REACH YA, CHIEF!
HURRY UP AND GET TO THE POINT, AZUMA!
I TALKED WITH THE PHONE COMPANY'S CENTRAL OFFICE, INITIATED A TAP ON TAKAOKA, AND IMMEDIATELY GOT SOMETHING *INTERESTING!*
WELL, HE CALLED UP THE LAW FIRM THAT THE DEAD GUY'S CONTRACTED WITH...
...AN' SAID "THE CLIENT'S A 'DEAD MAN' AND IS BEING ILLEGALLY CONFINED... YOUR URGENT ATTENTION'S REQUIRED!"
SO WHERE'S TAKAOKA NOW?
IT WAS A CAR LINE, SO HE MUST BE DRIVING SOMEWHERE...
AT ANY RATE, I'VE JUST INITIATED CONTACT, SO THE NEXT STEP'LL BE TO FIND OUT WHAT SORT OF ACTION HE PLANS TO TAKE, AND WHAT BANK HE'S USING...
I'M PRETTY IMPRESSED WITH MYSELF, THOUGH... *HEH, HEH...* LIKE THEY SAY, GOOD LUCK'S A GOOD SKILL TA HAVE...
えへへへへっ
WHA?
WELL, KEEP AT IT THEN... OVER...
ピ!
BLAST IT...

*FX: BEEP

*FX: HEH HEH HEH

*FX: SCREECH

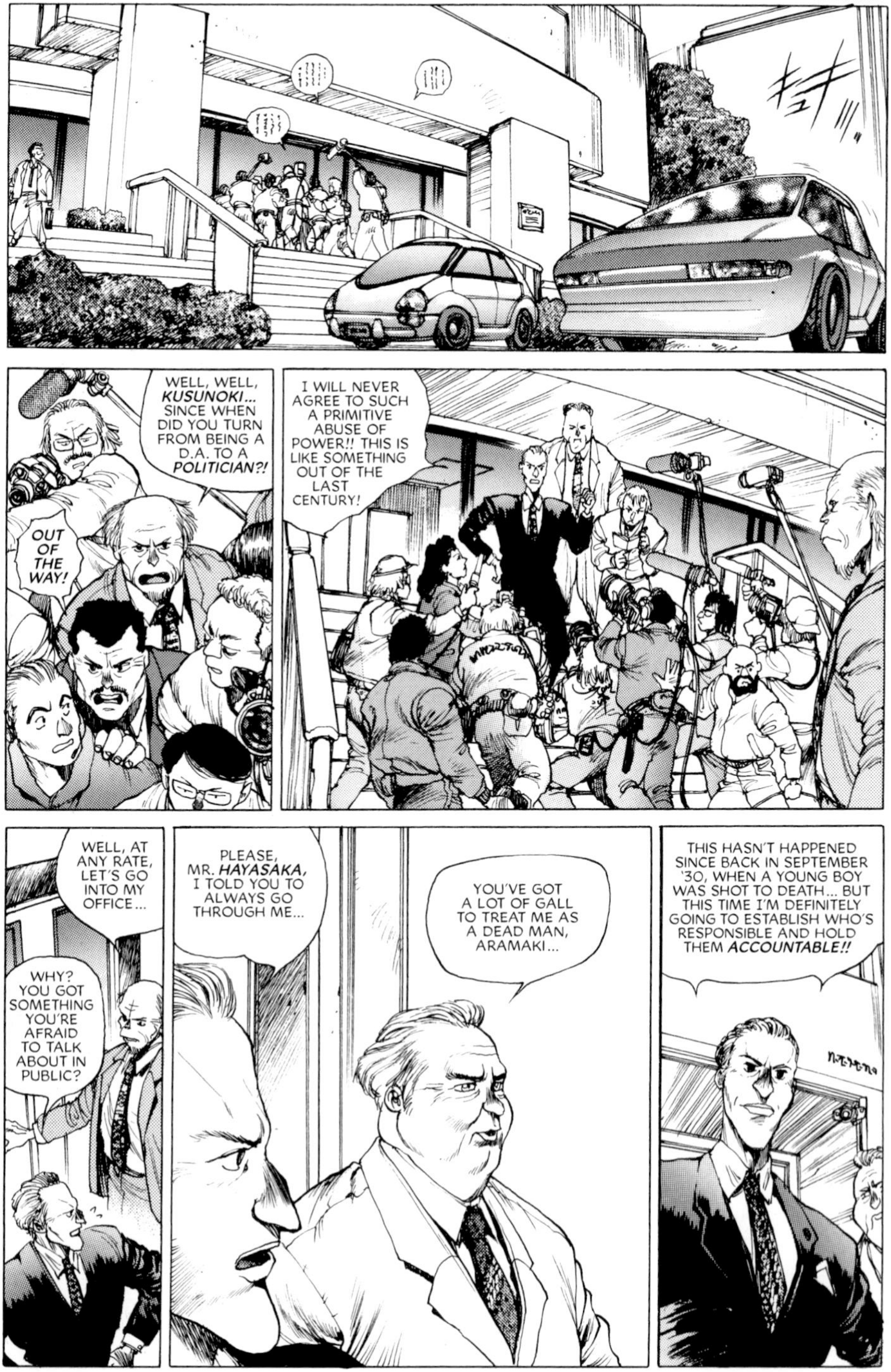
WELL, WELL, KUSUNOKI... SINCE WHEN DID YOU TURN FROM BEING A D.A. TO A POLITICIAN?!
OUT OF THE WAY!
I WILL NEVER AGREE TO SUCH A PRIMITIVE ABUSE OF POWER!! THIS IS LIKE SOMETHING OUT OF THE LAST CENTURY!
WELL, AT ANY RATE, LET'S GO INTO MY OFFICE...
WHY? YOU GOT SOMETHING YOU'RE AFRAID TO TALK ABOUT IN PUBLIC?
PLEASE, MR. HAYASAKA, I TOLD YOU TO ALWAYS GO THROUGH ME...
YOU'VE GOT A LOT OF GALL TO TREAT ME AS A DEAD MAN, ARAMAKI...
THIS HASN'T HAPPENED SINCE BACK IN SEPTEMBER '30, WHEN A YOUNG BOY WAS SHOT TO DEATH... BUT THIS TIME I'M DEFINITELY GOING TO ESTABLISH WHO'S RESPONSIBLE AND HOLD THEM ACCOUNTABLE!!

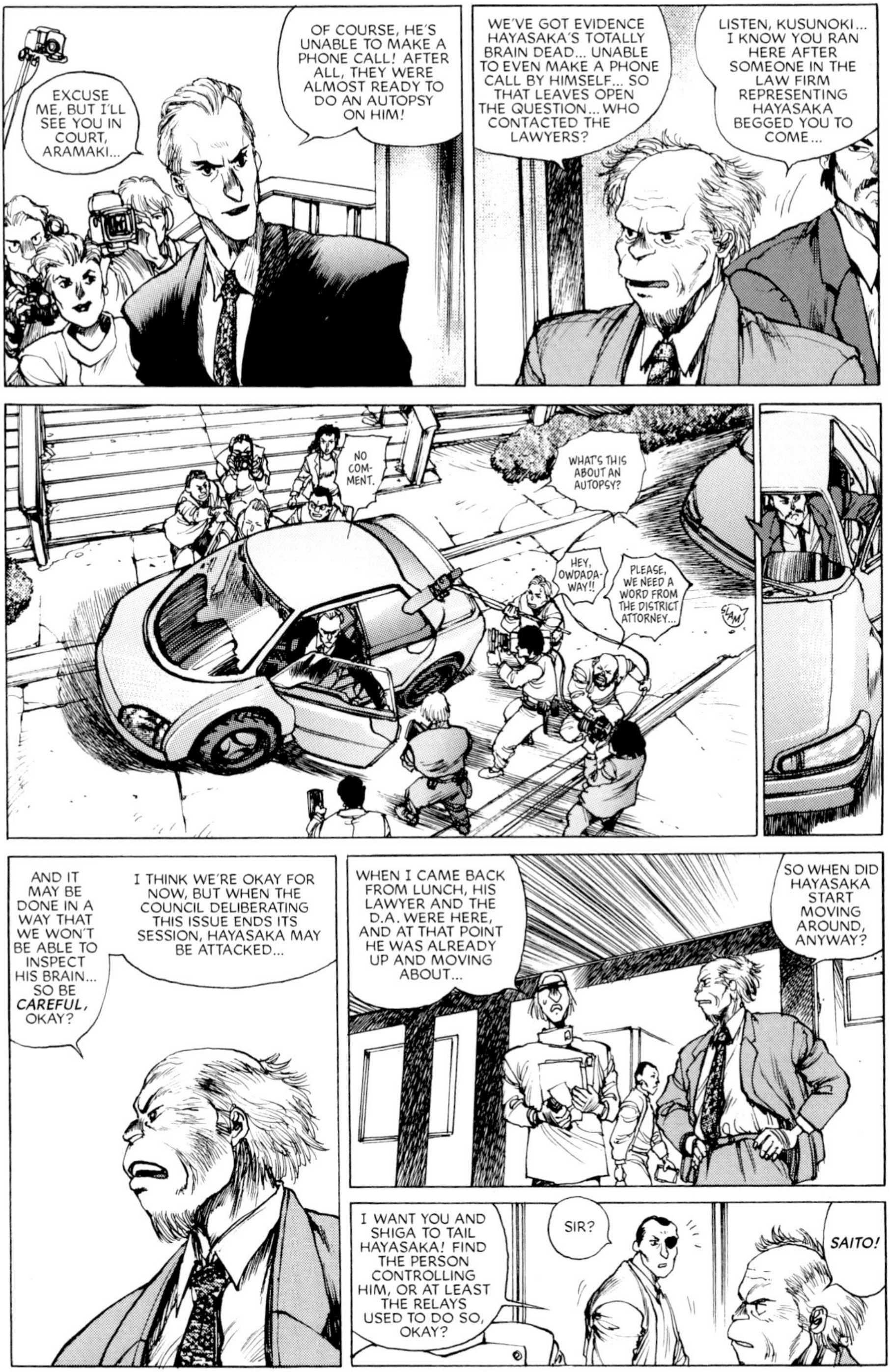
LISTEN, KUSUNOKI... I KNOW YOU RAN HERE AFTER SOMEONE IN THE LAW FIRM REPRESENTING HAYASAKA BEGGED YOU TO COME...
WE'VE GOT EVIDENCE HAYASAKA'S TOTALLY BRAIN DEAD... UNABLE TO EVEN MAKE A PHONE CALL BY HIMSELF... SO THAT LEAVES OPEN THE QUESTION... WHO CONTACTED THE LAWYERS?
OF COURSE, HE'S UNABLE TO MAKE A PHONE CALL! AFTER ALL, THEY WERE ALMOST READY TO DO AN AUTOPSY ON HIM!
EXCUSE ME, BUT I'LL SEE YOU IN COURT, ARAMAKI...
SLAM
WHAT'S THIS ABOUT AN AUTOPSY?
PLEASE, WE NEED A WORD FROM THE DISTRICT ATTORNEY...
HEY, OWDADA-WAY!!
NO COMMENT.
SO WHEN DID HAYASAKA START MOVING AROUND, ANYWAY?
WHEN I CAME BACK FROM LUNCH, HIS LAWYER AND THE D.A. WERE HERE, AND AT THAT POINT HE WAS ALREADY UP AND MOVING ABOUT...
SAITO!
SIR?
I WANT YOU AND SHIGA TO TAIL HAYASAKA! FIND THE PERSON CONTROLLING HIM, OR AT LEAST THE RELAYS USED TO DO SO, OKAY?
I THINK WE'RE OKAY FOR NOW, BUT WHEN THE COUNCIL DELIBERATING THIS ISSUE ENDS ITS SESSION, HAYASAKA MAY BE ATTACKED...
AND IT MAY BE DONE IN A WAY THAT WE WON'T BE ABLE TO INSPECT HIS BRAIN... SO BE CAREFUL, OKAY?

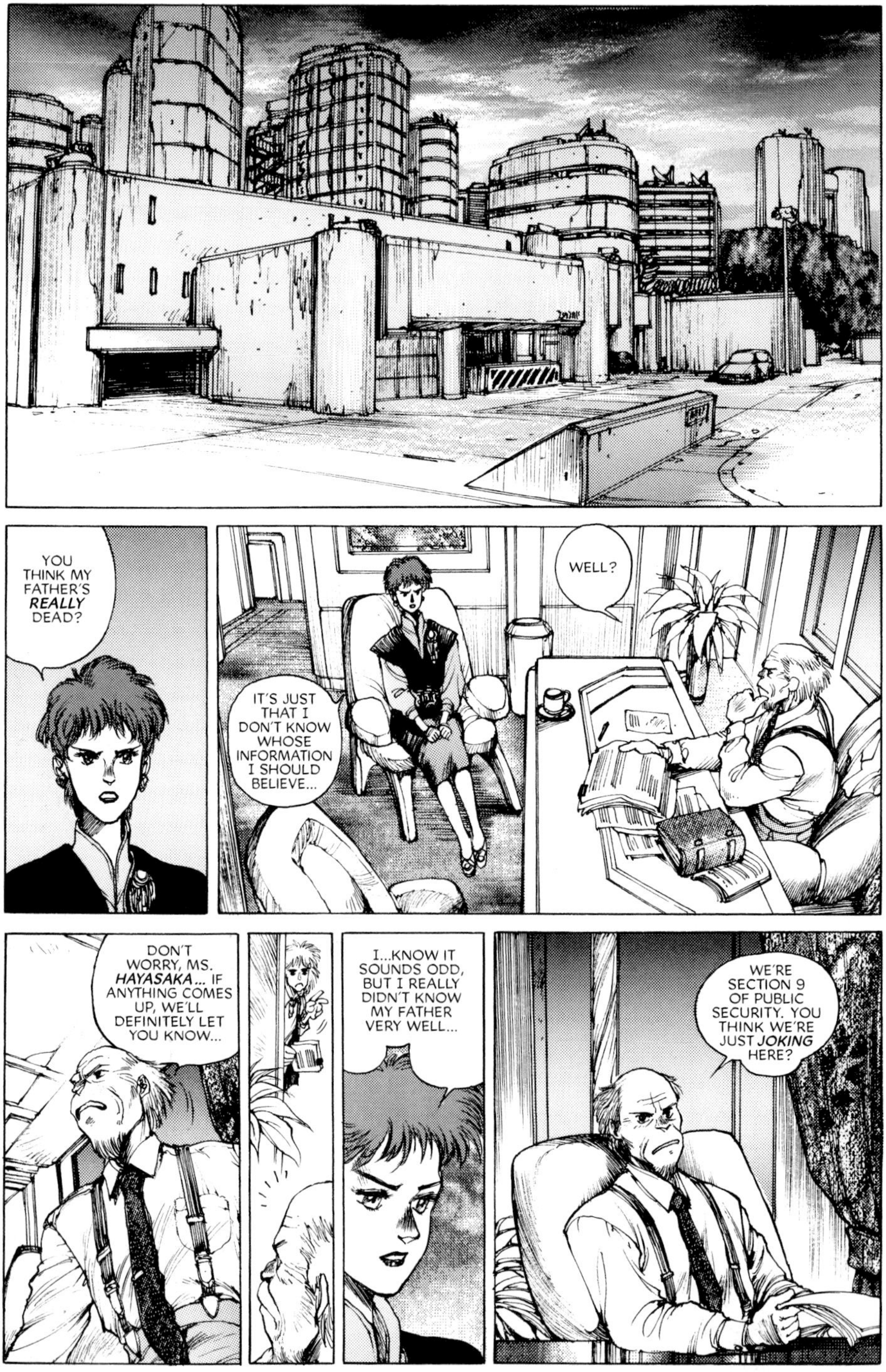
WELL?
IT'S JUST THAT I DON'T KNOW WHOSE INFORMATION I SHOULD BELIEVE...
YOU THINK MY FATHER'S *REALLY* DEAD?
WE'RE SECTION 9 OF PUBLIC SECURITY. YOU THINK WE'RE JUST *JOKING* HERE?
I...KNOW IT SOUNDS ODD, BUT I REALLY DIDN'T KNOW MY FATHER VERY WELL...
DON'T WORRY, MS. *HAYASAKA*... IF ANYTHING COMES UP, WE'LL DEFINITELY LET YOU KNOW...

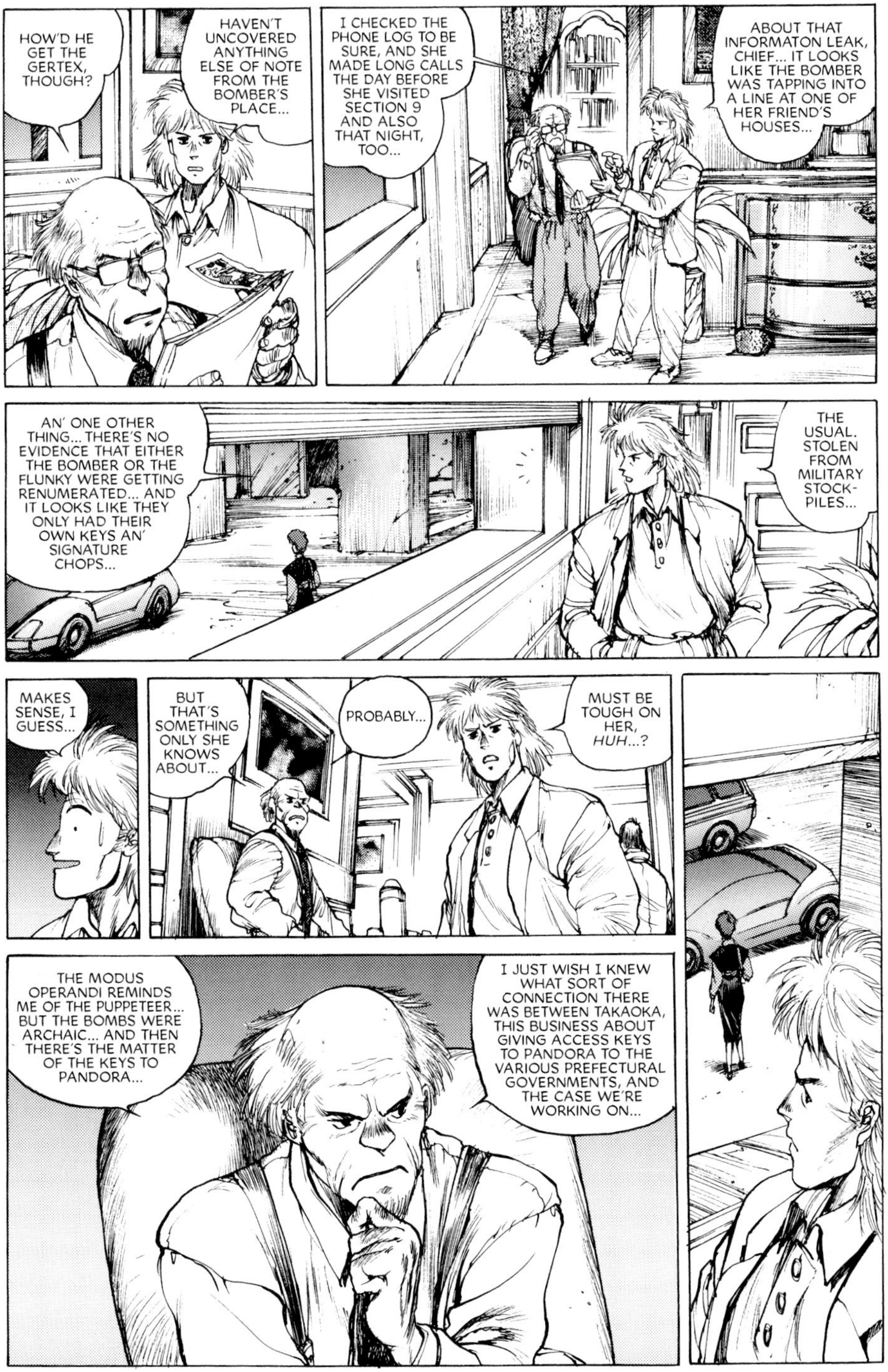
ABOUT THAT INFORMATON LEAK, CHIEF... IT LOOKS LIKE THE BOMBER WAS TAPPING INTO A LINE AT ONE OF HER FRIEND'S HOUSES...
I CHECKED THE PHONE LOG TO BE SURE, AND SHE MADE LONG CALLS THE DAY BEFORE SHE VISITED SECTION 9 AND ALSO THAT NIGHT, TOO...
HAVEN'T UNCOVERED ANYTHING ELSE OF NOTE FROM THE BOMBER'S PLACE...
HOW'D HE GET THE GERTEX, THOUGH?
THE USUAL. STOLEN FROM MILITARY STOCK-PILES...
AN' ONE OTHER THING... THERE'S NO EVIDENCE THAT EITHER THE BOMBER OR THE FLUNKY WERE GETTING RENUMERATED... AND IT LOOKS LIKE THEY ONLY HAD THEIR OWN KEYS AN' SIGNATURE CHOPS...
MUST BE TOUGH ON HER, *HUH*...?
PROBABLY...
BUT THAT'S SOMETHING ONLY SHE KNOWS ABOUT...
MAKES SENSE, I GUESS...
I JUST WISH I KNEW WHAT SORT OF CONNECTION THERE WAS BETWEEN TAKAOKA, THIS BUSINESS ABOUT GIVING ACCESS KEYS TO PANDORA TO THE VARIOUS PREFECTURAL GOVERNMENTS, AND THE CASE WE'RE WORKING ON...
THE MODUS OPERANDI REMINDS ME OF THE PUPPETEER... BUT THE BOMBS WERE ARCHAIC... AND THEN THERE'S THE MATTER OF THE KEYS TO PANDORA...

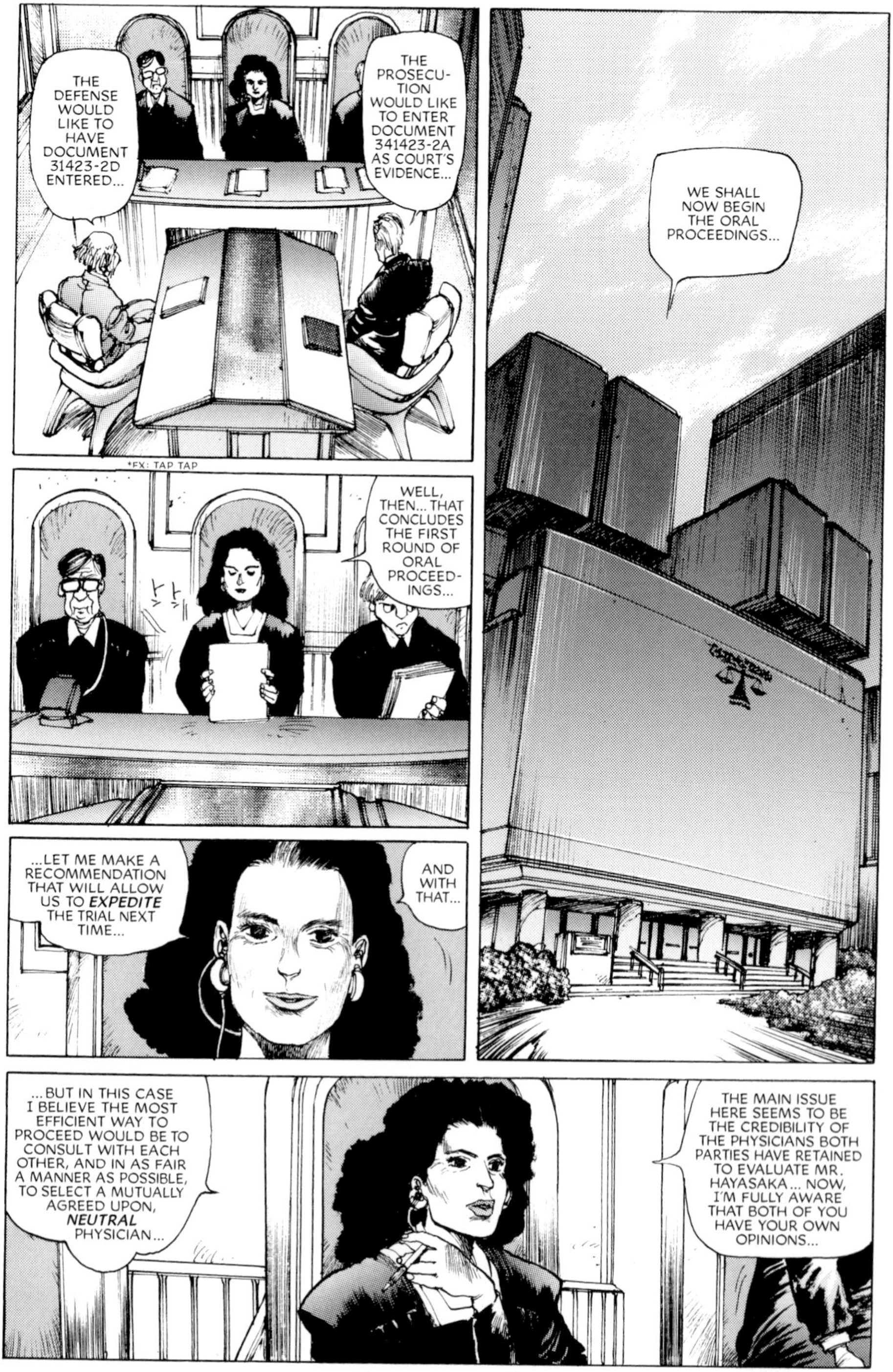
WE SHALL NOW BEGIN THE ORAL PROCEEDINGS...
THE PROSECUTION WOULD LIKE TO ENTER DOCUMENT 341423-2A AS COURT'S EVIDENCE...
THE DEFENSE WOULD LIKE TO HAVE DOCUMENT 31423-2D ENTERED...
*FX: TAP TAP
WELL, THEN... THAT CONCLUDES THE FIRST ROUND OF ORAL PROCEEDINGS...
AND WITH THAT...
...LET ME MAKE A RECOMMENDATION THAT WILL ALLOW US TO ***EXPEDITE*** THE TRIAL NEXT TIME...
THE MAIN ISSUE HERE SEEMS TO BE THE CREDIBILITY OF THE PHYSICIANS BOTH PARTIES HAVE RETAINED TO EVALUATE MR. HAYASAKA... NOW, I'M FULLY AWARE THAT BOTH OF YOU HAVE YOUR OWN OPINIONS...
...BUT IN THIS CASE I BELIEVE THE MOST EFFICIENT WAY TO PROCEED WOULD BE TO CONSULT WITH EACH OTHER, AND IN AS FAIR A MANNER AS POSSIBLE, TO SELECT A MUTUALLY AGREED UPON, ***NEUTRAL*** PHYSICIAN...

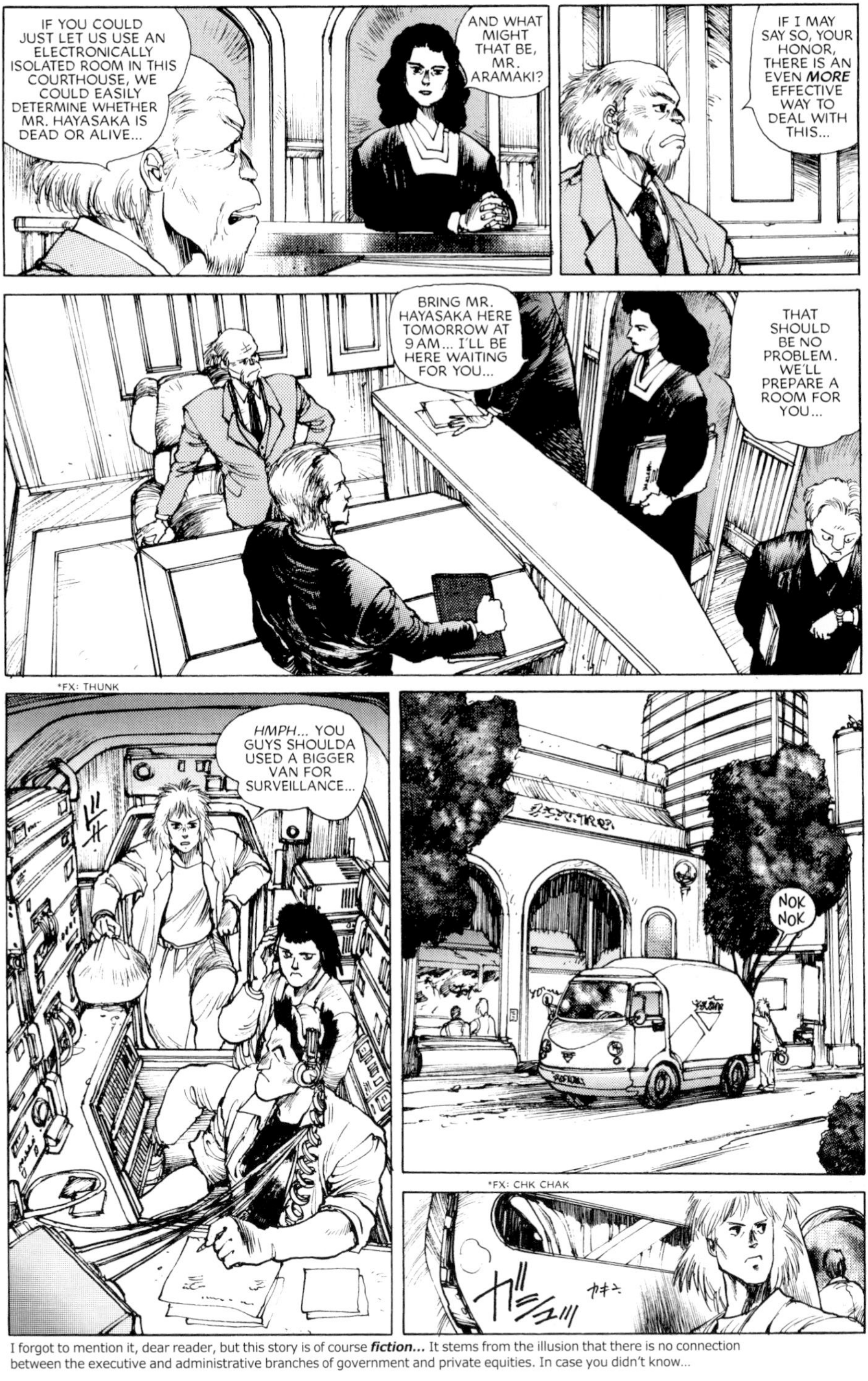
IF I MAY SAY SO, YOUR HONOR, THERE IS AN EVEN *MORE* EFFECTIVE WAY TO DEAL WITH THIS...
AND WHAT MIGHT THAT BE, MR. ARAMAKI?
IF YOU COULD JUST LET US USE AN ELECTRONICALLY ISOLATED ROOM IN THIS COURTHOUSE, WE COULD EASILY DETERMINE WHETHER MR. HAYASAKA IS DEAD OR ALIVE...
BRING MR. HAYASAKA HERE TOMORROW AT 9 AM... I'LL BE HERE WAITING FOR YOU...
THAT SHOULD BE NO PROBLEM. WE'LL PREPARE A ROOM FOR YOU...
NOK NOK
*FX: CHK CHAK
*FX: THUNK
HMPH... YOU GUYS SHOULDA USED A BIGGER VAN FOR SURVEILLANCE...

I forgot to mention it, dear reader, but this story is of course ***fiction...*** It stems from the illusion that there is no connection between the executive and administrative branches of government and private equities. In case you didn't know...

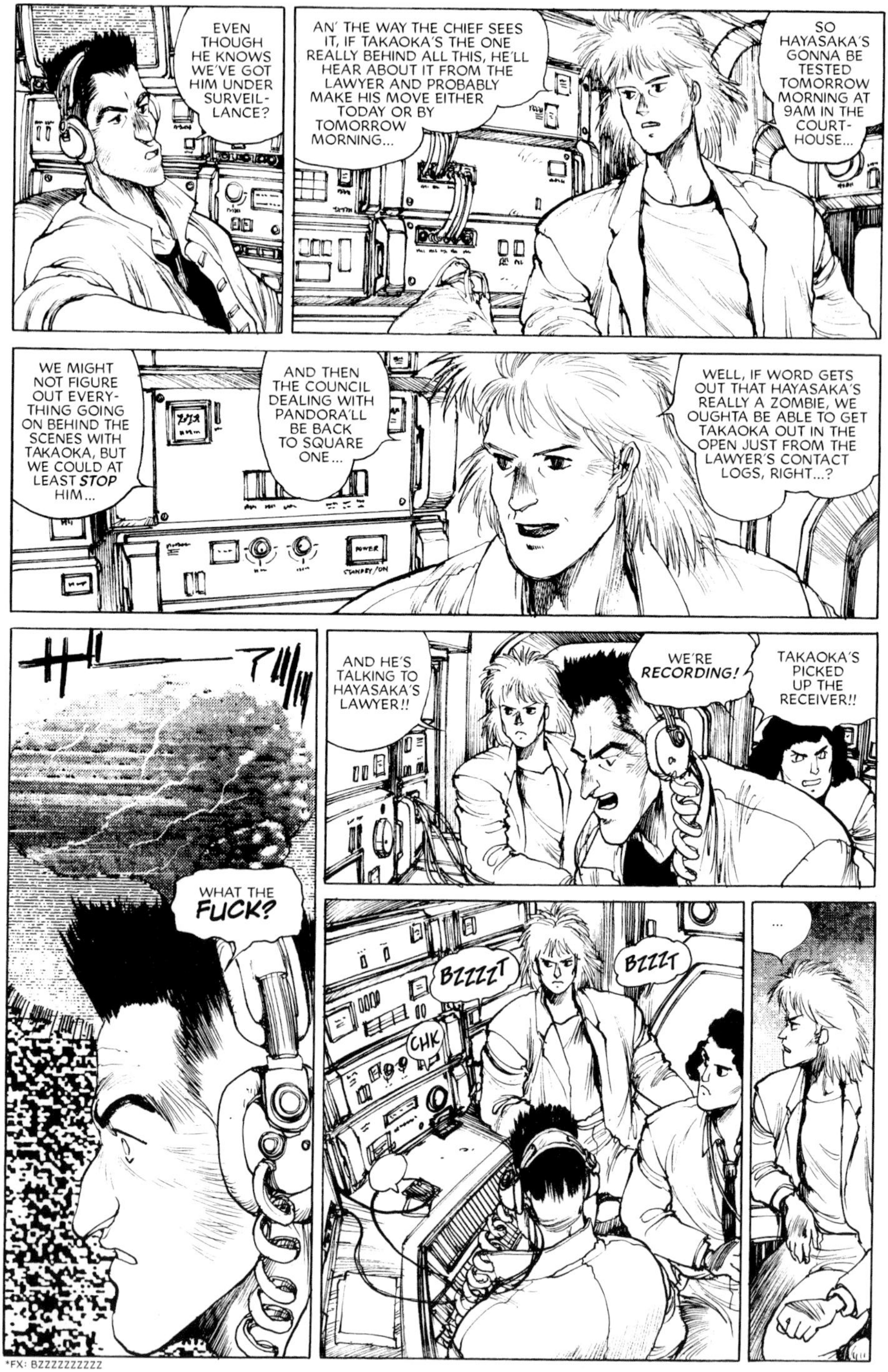
SO HAYASAKA'S GONNA BE TESTED TOMORROW MORNING AT 9AM IN THE COURT-HOUSE...
AN' THE WAY THE CHIEF SEES IT, IF TAKAOKA'S THE ONE REALLY BEHIND ALL THIS, HE'LL HEAR ABOUT IT FROM THE LAWYER AND PROBABLY MAKE HIS MOVE EITHER TODAY OR BY TOMORROW MORNING...
EVEN THOUGH HE KNOWS WE'VE GOT HIM UNDER SURVEIL-LANCE?
WELL, IF WORD GETS OUT THAT HAYASAKA'S REALLY A ZOMBIE, WE OUGHTA BE ABLE TO GET TAKAOKA OUT IN THE OPEN JUST FROM THE LAWYER'S CONTACT LOGS, RIGHT...?
AND THEN THE COUNCIL DEALING WITH PANDORA'LL BE BACK TO SQUARE ONE...
WE MIGHT NOT FIGURE OUT EVERY-THING GOING ON BEHIND THE SCENES WITH TAKAOKA, BUT WE COULD AT LEAST *STOP* HIM...
TAKAOKA'S PICKED UP THE RECEIVER!!
WE'RE *RECORDING!*
AND HE'S TALKING TO HAYASAKA'S LAWYER!!
...
BZZZT
BZZZZT
CHK
WHAT THE *FUCK?*

*FX: BZZZZZZZZZZ

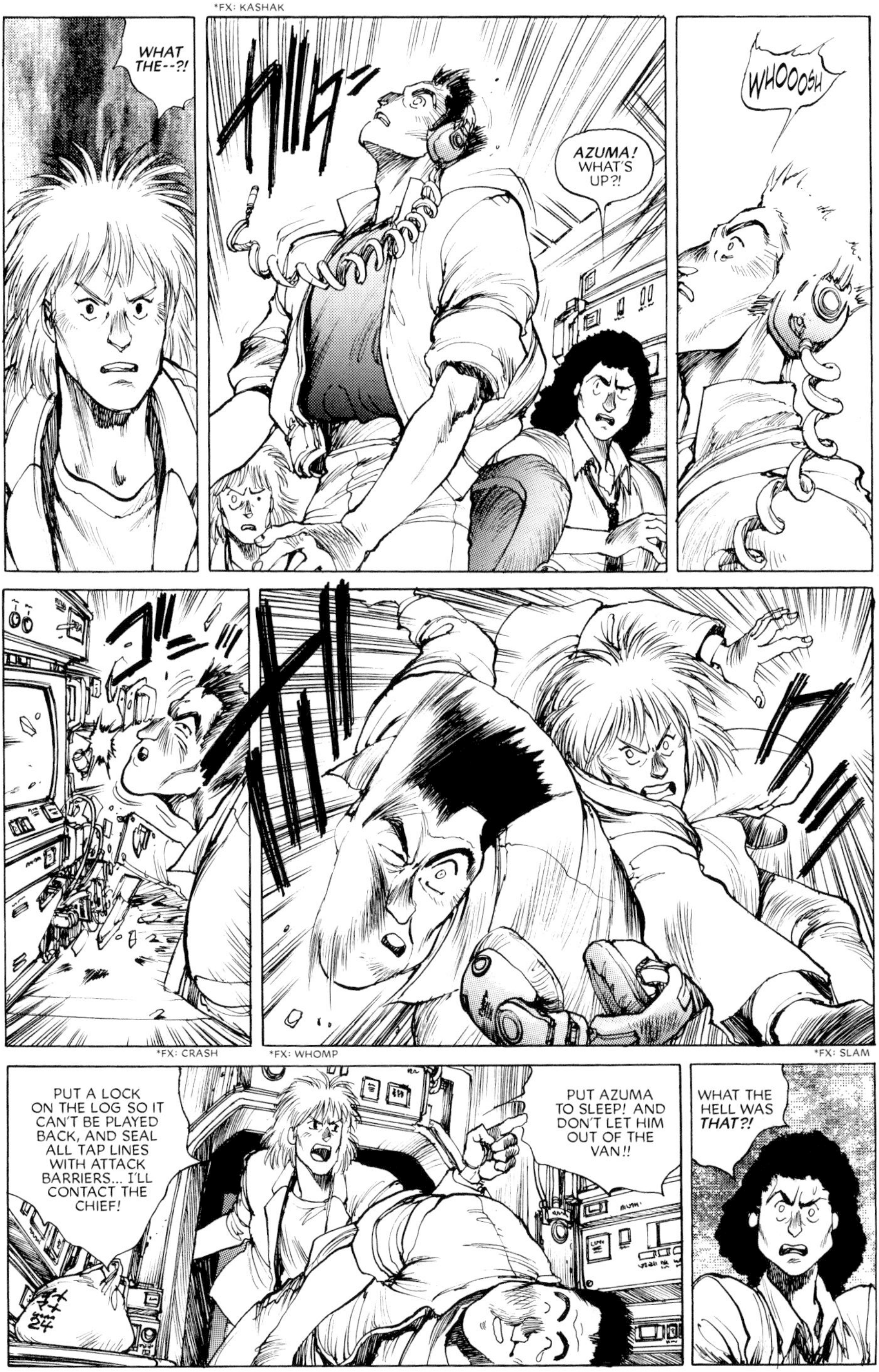
WHOOOSH
*FX: KASHAK
AZUMA! WHAT'S UP?!
WHAT THE--?!
*FX: WHOMP
*FX: SLAM
*FX: CRASH
WHAT THE HELL WAS *THAT?!*
PUT AZUMA TO SLEEP! AND DON'T LET HIM OUT OF THE VAN!!
PUT A LOCK ON THE LOG SO IT CAN'T BE PLAYED BACK, AND SEAL ALL TAP LINES WITH ATTACK BARRIERS... I'LL CONTACT THE CHIEF!

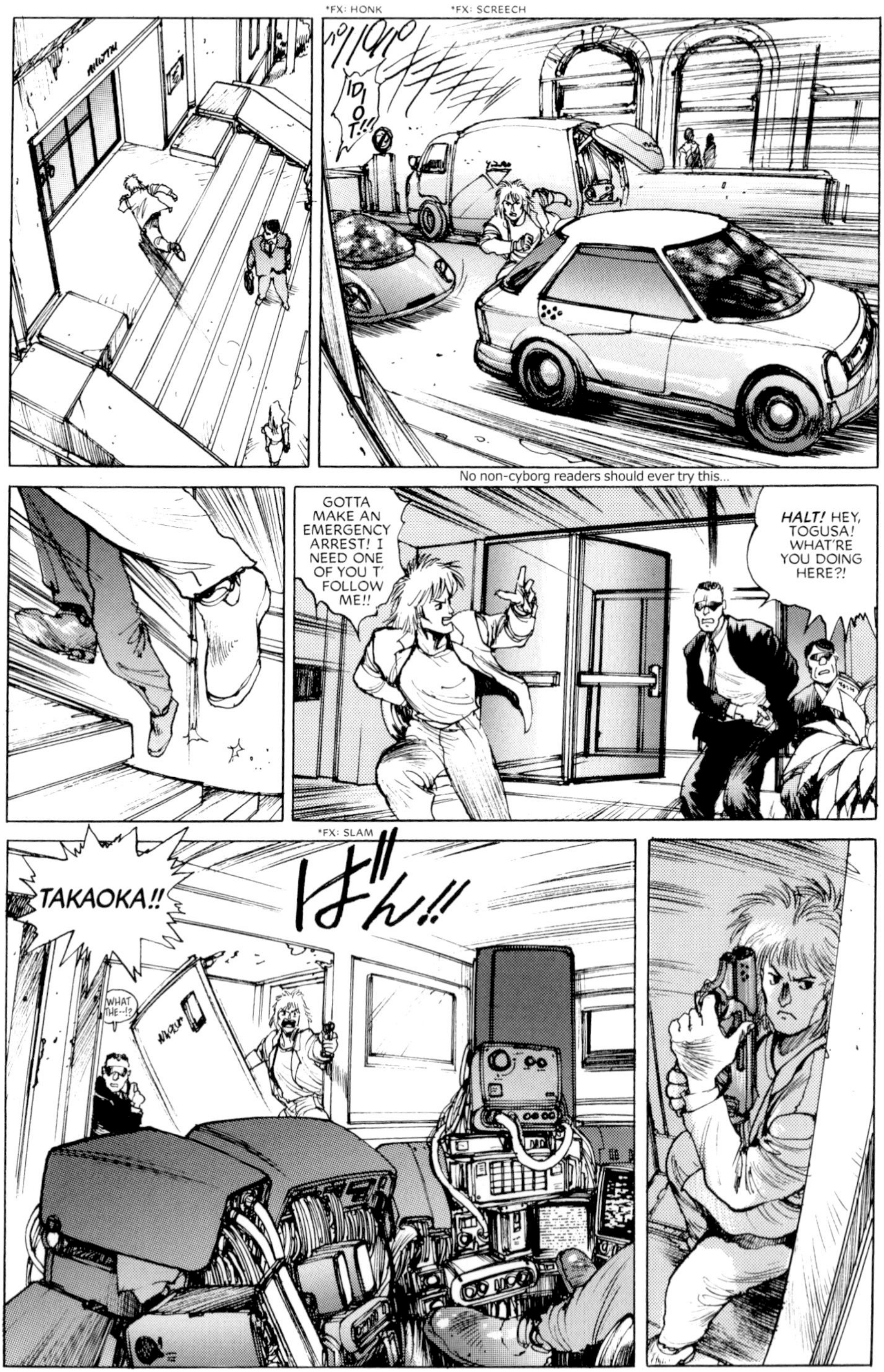
*FX: SCREECH
*FX: HONK
IDIOT!!
No non-cyborg readers should ever try this...
HALT! HEY, TOGUSA! WHAT'RE YOU DOING HERE?!
GOTTA MAKE AN EMERGENCY ARREST! I NEED ONE OF YOU T' FOLLOW ME!!
TAKAOKA!!
WHAT THE--!?
ばん!!
*FX: SLAM

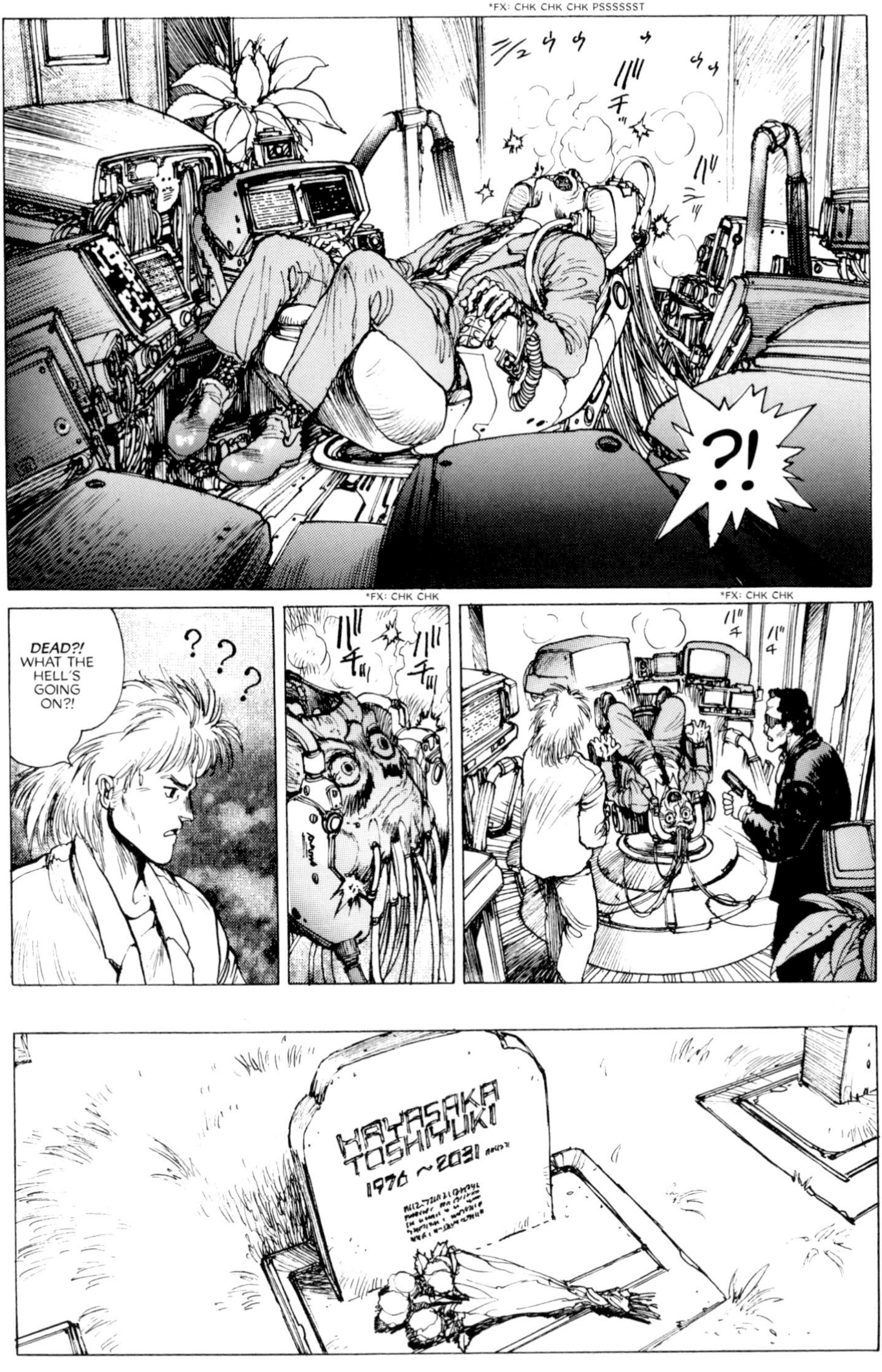
*FX: CHK CHK CHK PSSSSSST
?!
*FX: CHK CHK
*FX: CHK CHK
DEAD?! WHAT THE HELL'S GOING ON?!
???
HAYASAKA TOSHIYUKI
1976 ~ 2031

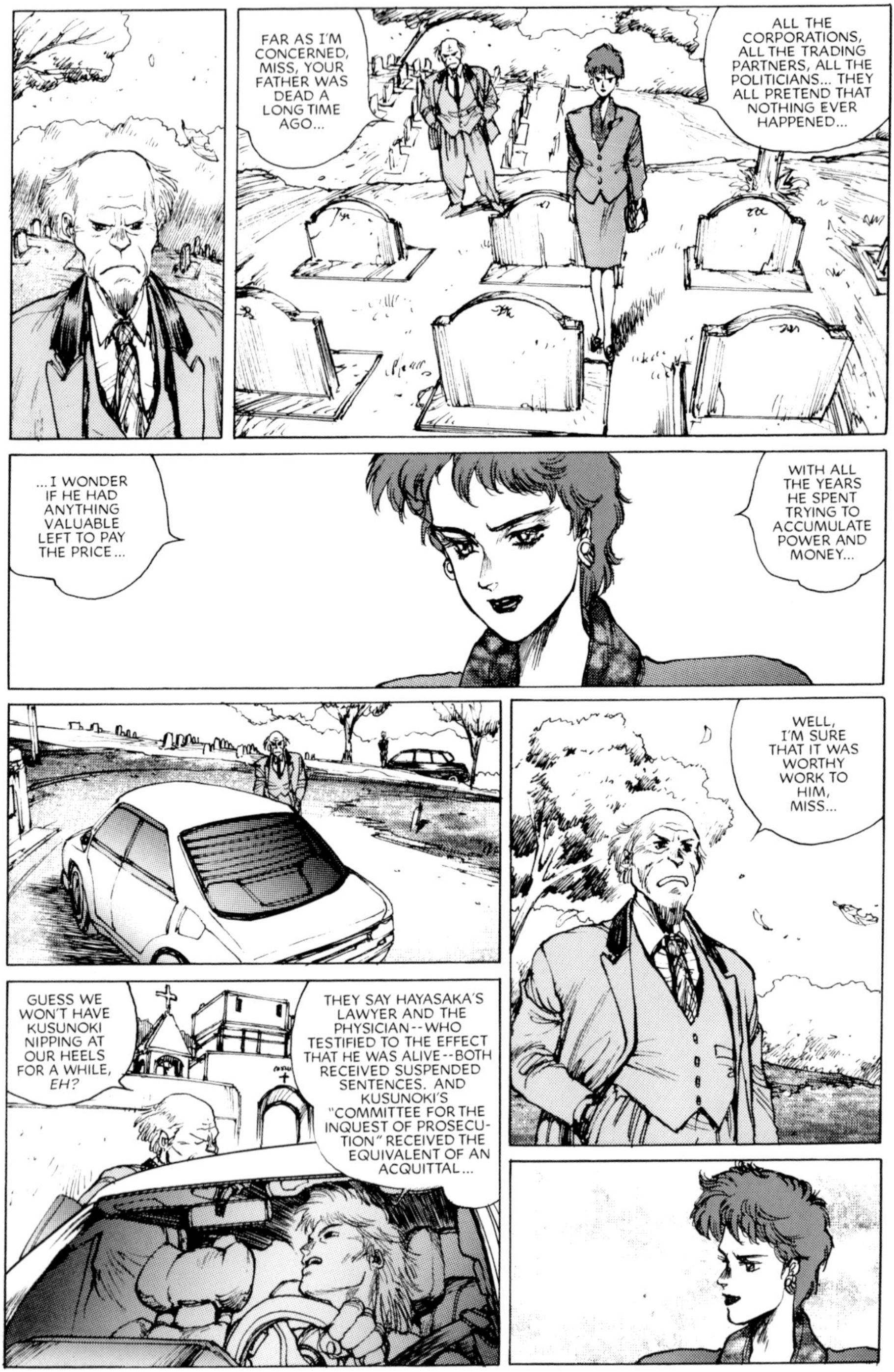
ALL THE CORPORATIONS, ALL THE TRADING PARTNERS, ALL THE POLITICIANS... THEY ALL PRETEND THAT NOTHING EVER HAPPENED...
FAR AS I'M CONCERNED, MISS, YOUR FATHER WAS DEAD A LONG TIME AGO...
WITH ALL THE YEARS HE SPENT TRYING TO ACCUMULATE POWER AND MONEY...
...I WONDER IF HE HAD ANYTHING VALUABLE LEFT TO PAY THE PRICE...
WELL, I'M SURE THAT IT WAS WORTHY WORK TO HIM, MISS...
THEY SAY HAYASAKA'S LAWYER AND THE PHYSICIAN--WHO TESTIFIED TO THE EFFECT THAT HE WAS ALIVE--BOTH RECEIVED SUSPENDED SENTENCES. AND KUSUNOKI'S "COMMITTEE FOR THE INQUEST OF PROSECUTION" RECEIVED THE EQUIVALENT OF AN ACQUITTAL...
GUESS WE WON'T HAVE KUSUNOKI NIPPING AT OUR HEELS FOR A WHILE, *EH?*

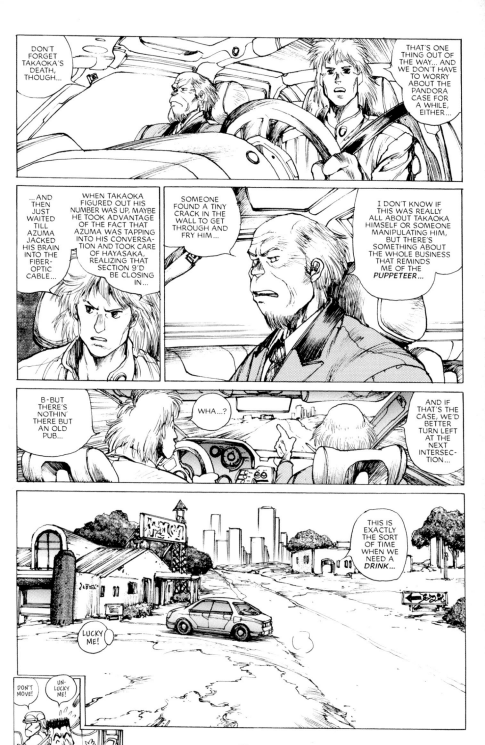

03

DRIVE SLAVE Part 1

1992

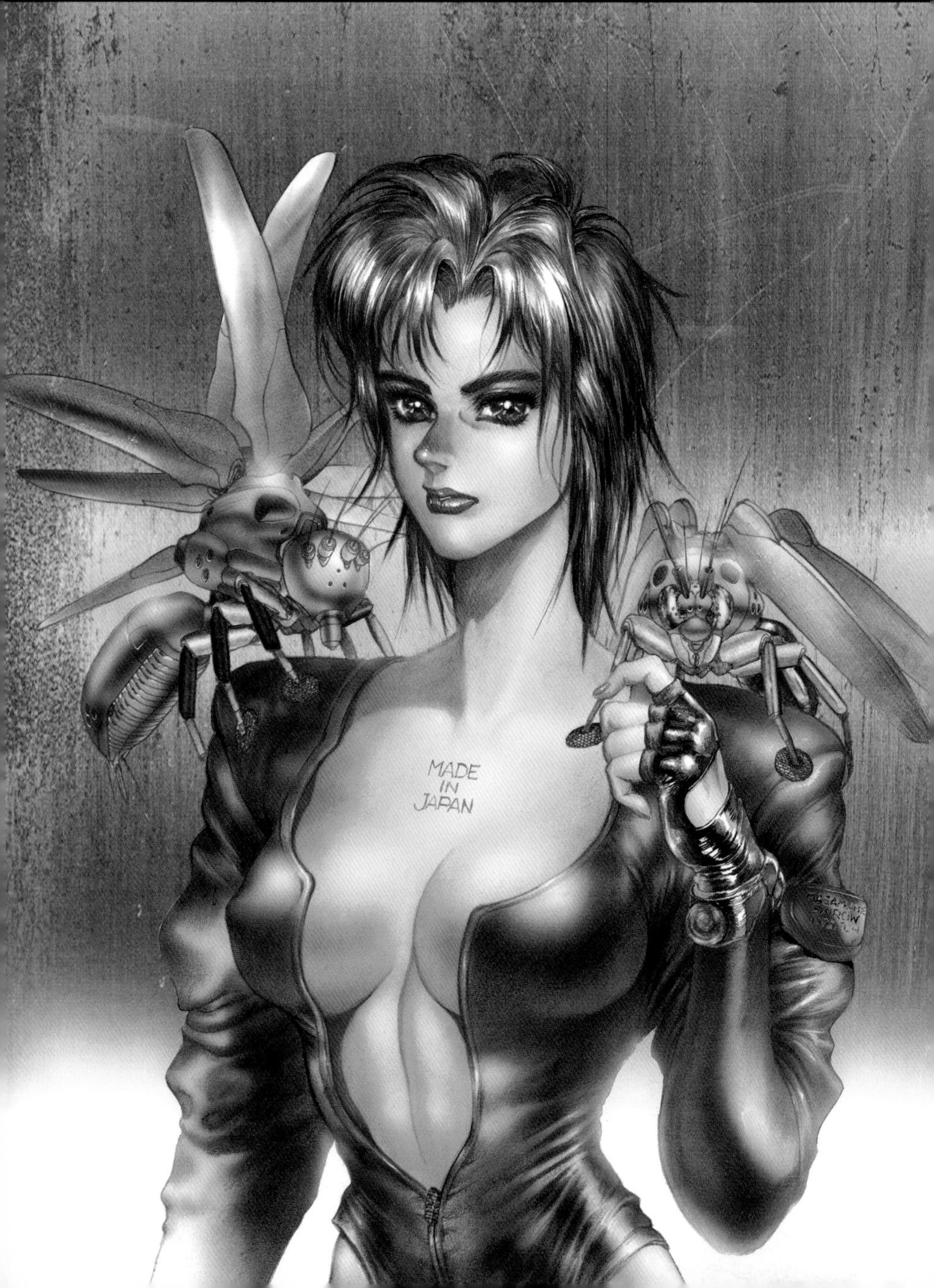
MADE
IN
JAPAN

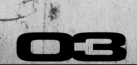

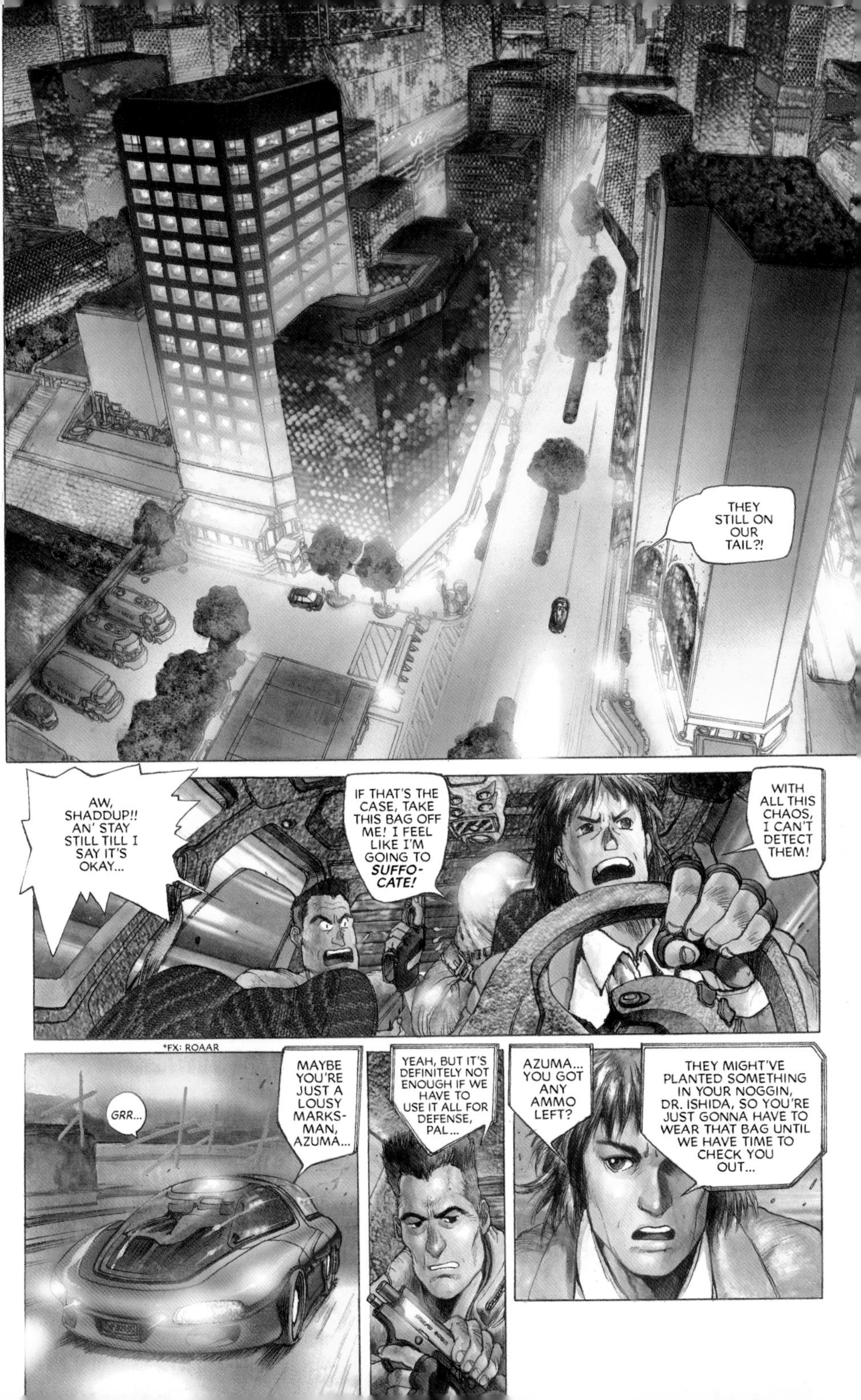
THEY STILL ON OUR TAIL?!
WITH ALL THIS CHAOS, I CAN'T DETECT THEM!
IF THAT'S THE CASE, TAKE THIS BAG OFF ME! I FEEL LIKE I'M GOING TO ***SUFFOCATE!***
AW, SHADDUP!! AN' STAY STILL TILL I SAY IT'S OKAY...
THEY MIGHT'VE PLANTED SOMETHING IN YOUR NOGGIN, DR. ISHIDA, SO YOU'RE JUST GONNA HAVE TO WEAR THAT BAG UNTIL WE HAVE TIME TO CHECK YOU OUT...
AZUMA... YOU GOT ANY AMMO LEFT?
YEAH, BUT IT'S DEFINITELY NOT ENOUGH IF WE HAVE TO USE IT ALL FOR DEFENSE, PAL...
MAYBE YOU'RE JUST A LOUSY MARKS-MAN, AZUMA...
GRR...
*FX: ROAAR

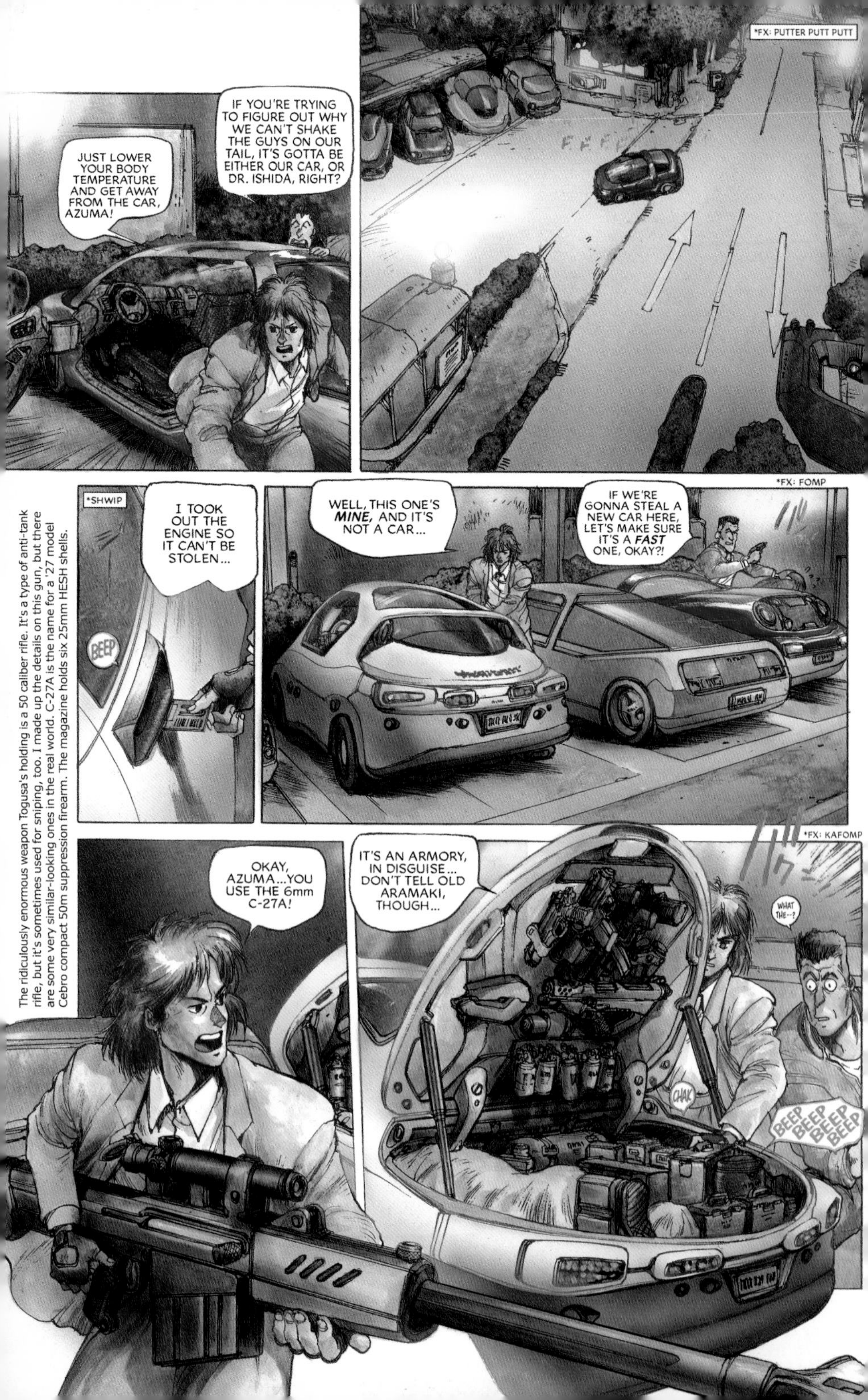
*FX: PUTTER PUTT PUTT
IF YOU'RE TRYING TO FIGURE OUT WHY WE CAN'T SHAKE THE GUYS ON OUR TAIL, IT'S GOTTA BE EITHER OUR CAR, OR DR. ISHIDA, RIGHT?
JUST LOWER YOUR BODY TEMPERATURE AND GET AWAY FROM THE CAR, AZUMA!
*FX: FOMP
IF WE'RE GONNA STEAL A NEW CAR HERE, LET'S MAKE SURE IT'S A *FAST* ONE, OKAY?!
WELL, THIS ONE'S *MINE,* AND IT'S NOT A CAR...
*SHWIP
I TOOK OUT THE ENGINE SO IT CAN'T BE STOLEN...
BEEP
*FX: KAFOMP
WHAT THE--?
BEEP BEEP BEEP BEEP
IT'S AN ARMORY, IN DISGUISE... DON'T TELL OLD ARAMAKI, THOUGH...
CHAK
OKAY, AZUMA...YOU USE THE 6mm C-27A!

The ridiculously enormous weapon Togusa's holding is a 50 caliber rifle. It's a type of anti-tank rifle, but it's sometimes used for sniping, too. I made up the details on this gun, but there are some very similar-looking ones in the real world. C-27A is the name for a '27 model Cebro compact 50m suppression firearm. The magazine holds six 25mm HESH shells.

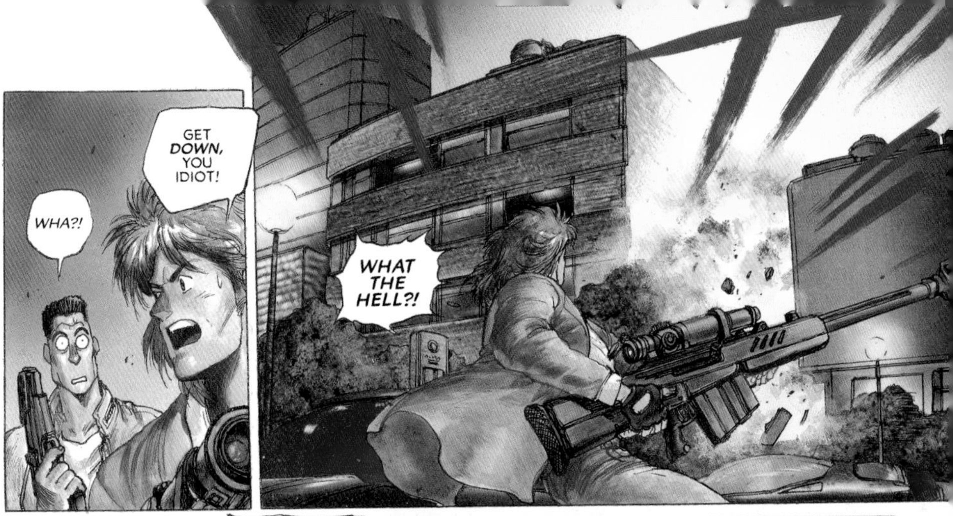
WHAT THE HELL?!
GET DOWN, YOU IDIOT!
WHA?!

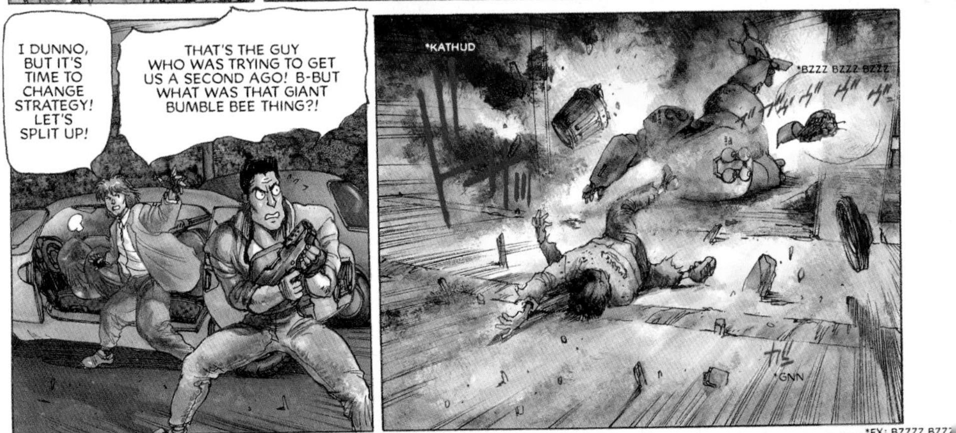
*KATHUD
*BZZZ BZZZ BZZZ
*GNN
THAT'S THE GUY WHO WAS TRYING TO GET US A SECOND AGO! B-BUT WHAT WAS THAT GIANT BUMBLE BEE THING?!
I DUNNO, BUT IT'S TIME TO CHANGE STRATEGY! LET'S SPLIT UP!

*FX: BZZZZ BZZZ

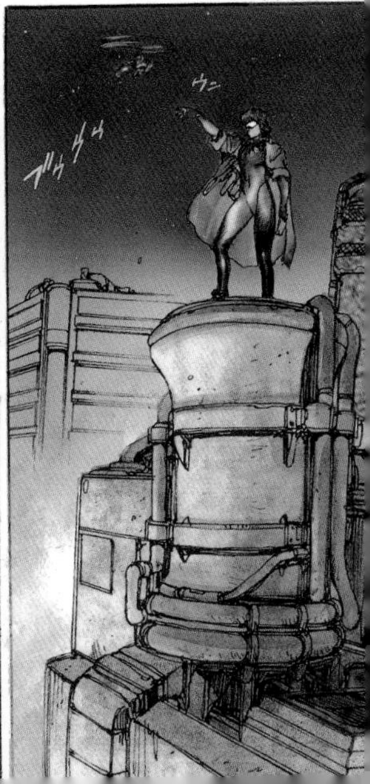

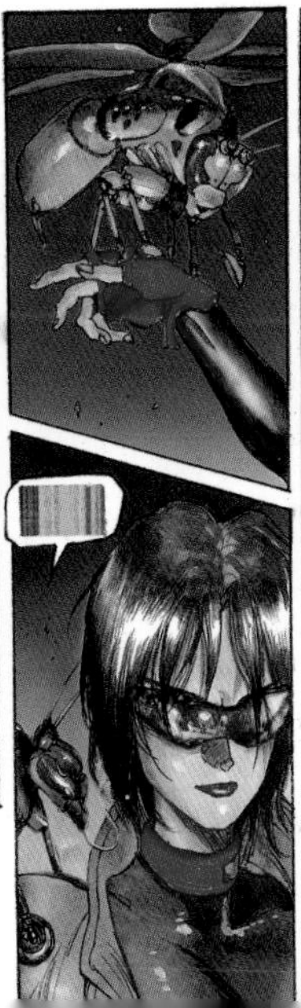

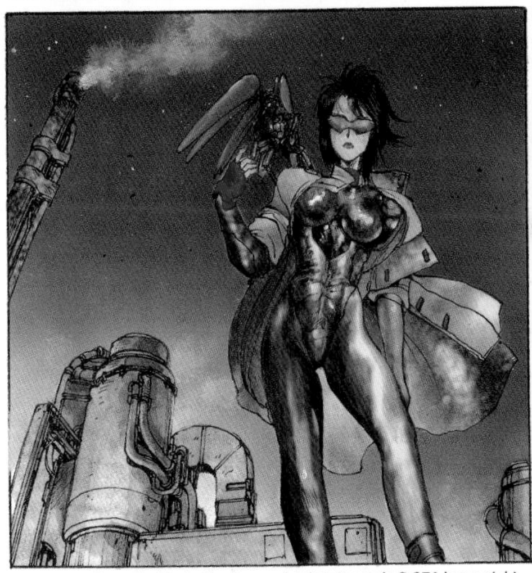

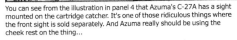

You can see from the illustration in panel 4 that Azuma's C-27A has a sight mounted on the cartridge catcher. It's one of those ridiculous things where the front sight is sold separately. And Azuma really should be using the cheek rest on the thing...

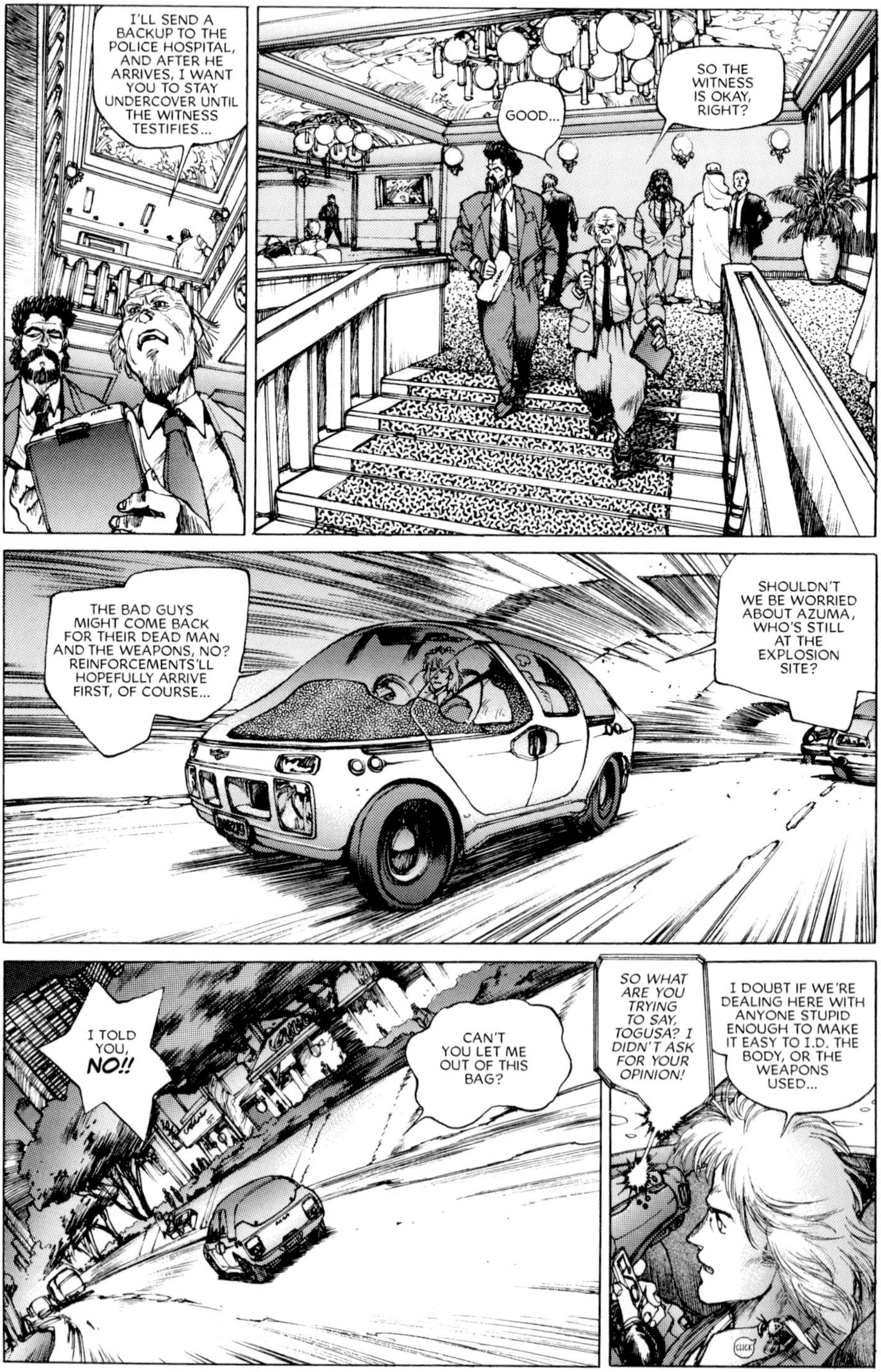
I'LL SEND A BACKUP TO THE POLICE HOSPITAL, AND AFTER HE ARRIVES, I WANT YOU TO STAY UNDERCOVER UNTIL THE WITNESS TESTIFIES...
GOOD...
SO THE WITNESS IS OKAY, RIGHT?
THE BAD GUYS MIGHT COME BACK FOR THEIR DEAD MAN AND THE WEAPONS, NO? REINFORCEMENTS'LL HOPEFULLY ARRIVE FIRST, OF COURSE...
SHOULDN'T WE BE WORRIED ABOUT AZUMA, WHO'S STILL AT THE EXPLOSION SITE?
I TOLD YOU, **NO!!**
CAN'T YOU LET ME OUT OF THIS BAG?
SO WHAT ARE YOU TRYING TO SAY, TOGUSA? I DIDN'T ASK FOR YOUR OPINION!
I DOUBT IF WE'RE DEALING HERE WITH ANYONE STUPID ENOUGH TO MAKE IT EASY TO I.D. THE BODY, OR THE WEAPONS USED...
CLICK

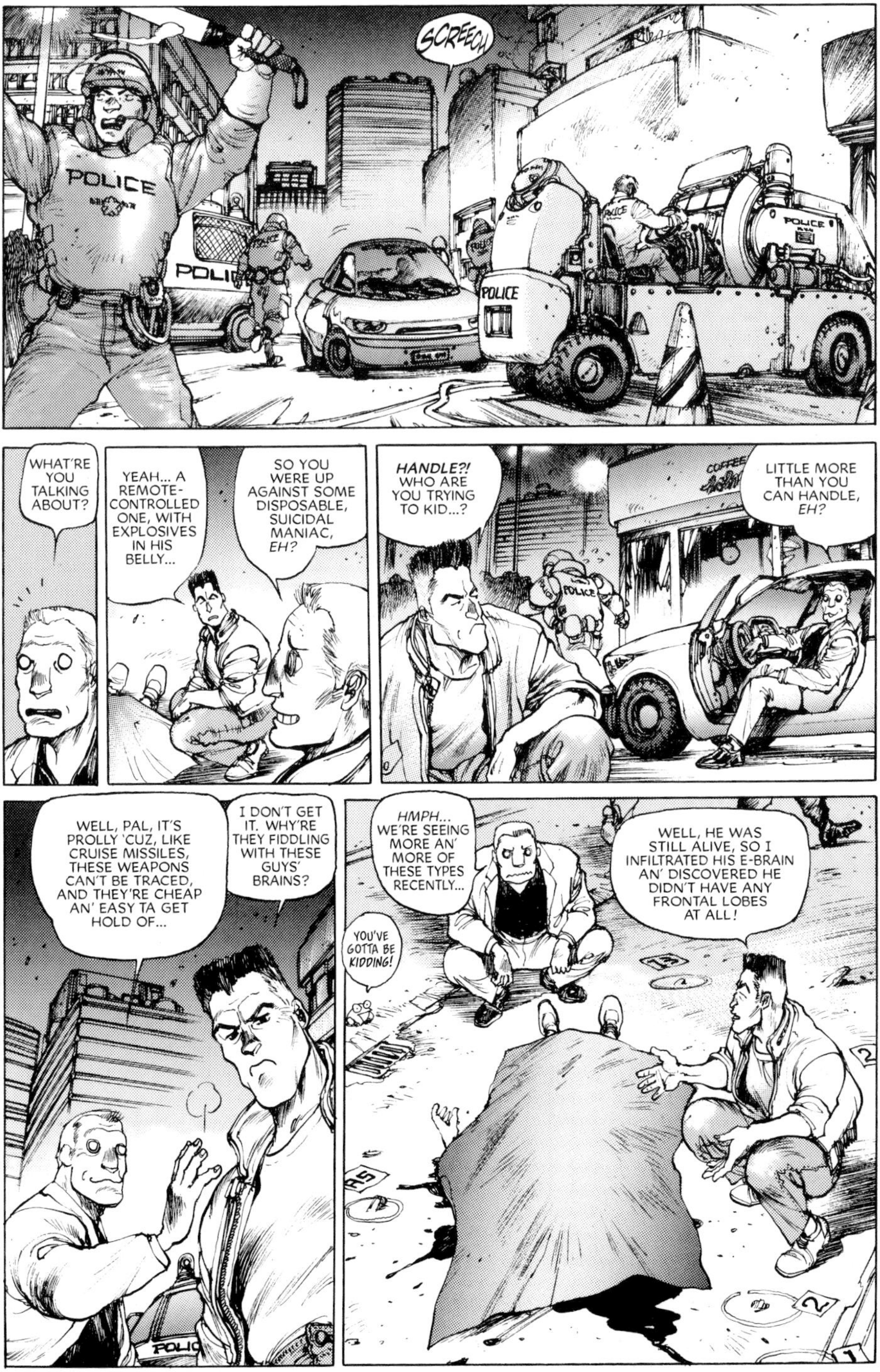
SCREECH
LITTLE MORE THAN YOU CAN HANDLE, *EH?*
HANDLE?! WHO ARE YOU TRYING TO KID...?
SO YOU WERE UP AGAINST SOME DISPOSABLE, SUICIDAL MANIAC, *EH?*
YEAH... A REMOTE-CONTROLLED ONE, WITH EXPLOSIVES IN HIS BELLY...
WHAT'RE YOU TALKING ABOUT?
WELL, HE WAS STILL ALIVE, SO I INFILTRATED HIS E-BRAIN AN' DISCOVERED HE DIDN'T HAVE ANY FRONTAL LOBES AT ALL!
HMPH... WE'RE SEEING MORE AN' MORE OF THESE TYPES RECENTLY...
YOU'VE GOTTA BE *KIDDING!*
I DON'T GET IT. WHY'RE THEY FIDDLING WITH THESE GUYS' BRAINS?
WELL, PAL, IT'S PROLLY 'CUZ, LIKE CRUISE MISSILES, THESE WEAPONS CAN'T BE TRACED, AND THEY'RE CHEAP AN' EASY TA GET HOLD OF...

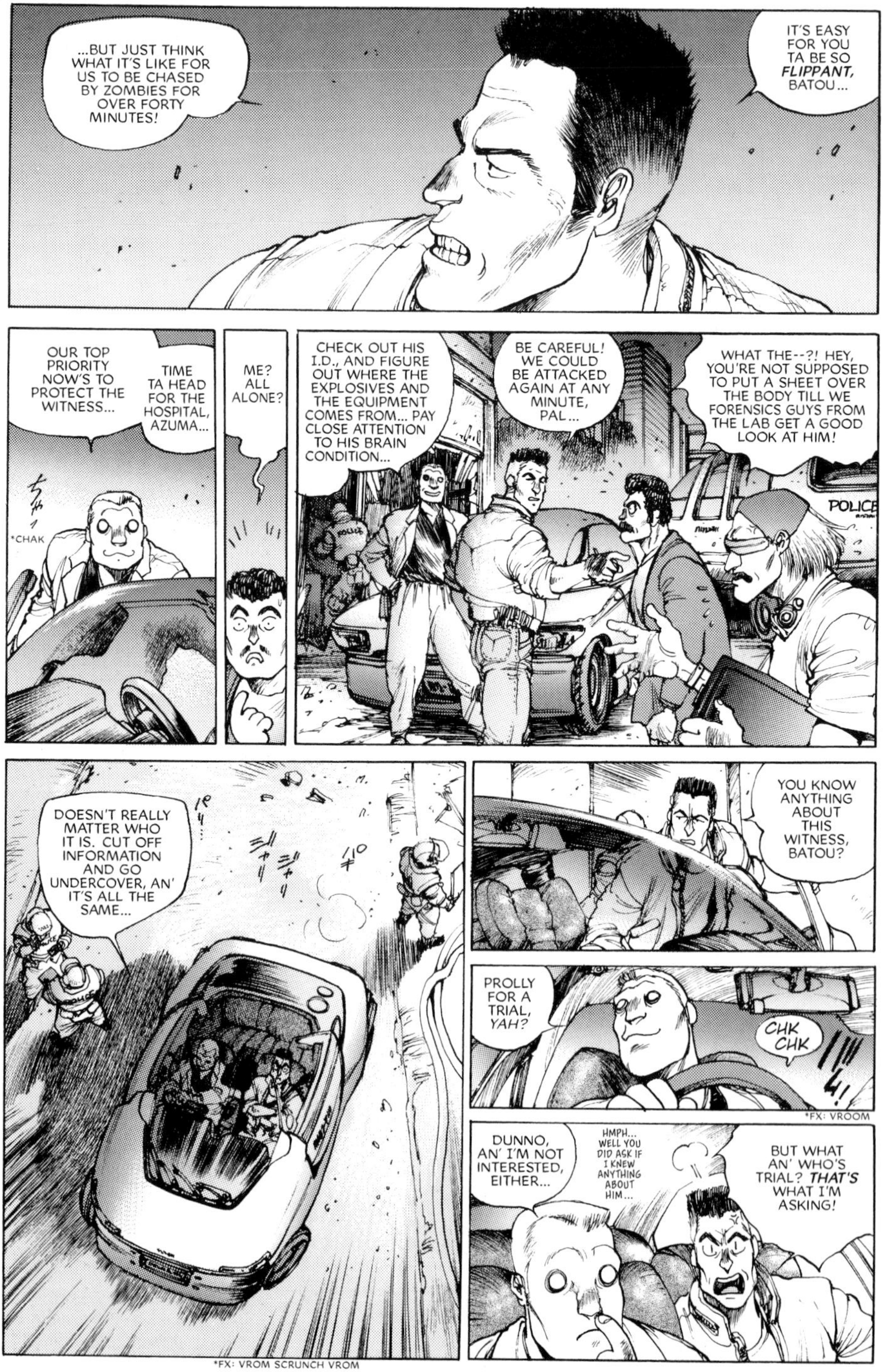
IT'S EASY FOR YOU TA BE SO *FLIPPANT,* BATOU...
...BUT JUST THINK WHAT IT'S LIKE FOR US TO BE CHASED BY ZOMBIES FOR OVER FORTY MINUTES!
WHAT THE--?! HEY, YOU'RE NOT SUPPOSED TO PUT A SHEET OVER THE BODY TILL WE FORENSICS GUYS FROM THE LAB GET A GOOD LOOK AT HIM!
BE CAREFUL! WE COULD BE ATTACKED AGAIN AT ANY MINUTE, PAL...
CHECK OUT HIS I.D., AND FIGURE OUT WHERE THE EXPLOSIVES AND THE EQUIPMENT COMES FROM... PAY CLOSE ATTENTION TO HIS BRAIN CONDITION...
ME? ALL ALONE?
TIME TA HEAD FOR THE HOSPITAL, AZUMA...
OUR TOP PRIORITY NOW'S TO PROTECT THE WITNESS...
*CHAK
YOU KNOW ANYTHING ABOUT THIS WITNESS, BATOU?
PROLLY FOR A TRIAL, *YAH?*
CHK CHK
*FX: VROOM
BUT WHAT AN' WHO'S TRIAL? ***THAT'S*** WHAT I'M ASKING!
HMPH... WELL YOU DID ASK IF I KNEW ANYTHING ABOUT HIM...
DUNNO, AN' I'M NOT INTERESTED, EITHER...
DOESN'T REALLY MATTER WHO IT IS. CUT OFF INFORMATION AND GO UNDERCOVER, AN' IT'S ALL THE SAME...
*FX: VROM SCRUNCH VROM

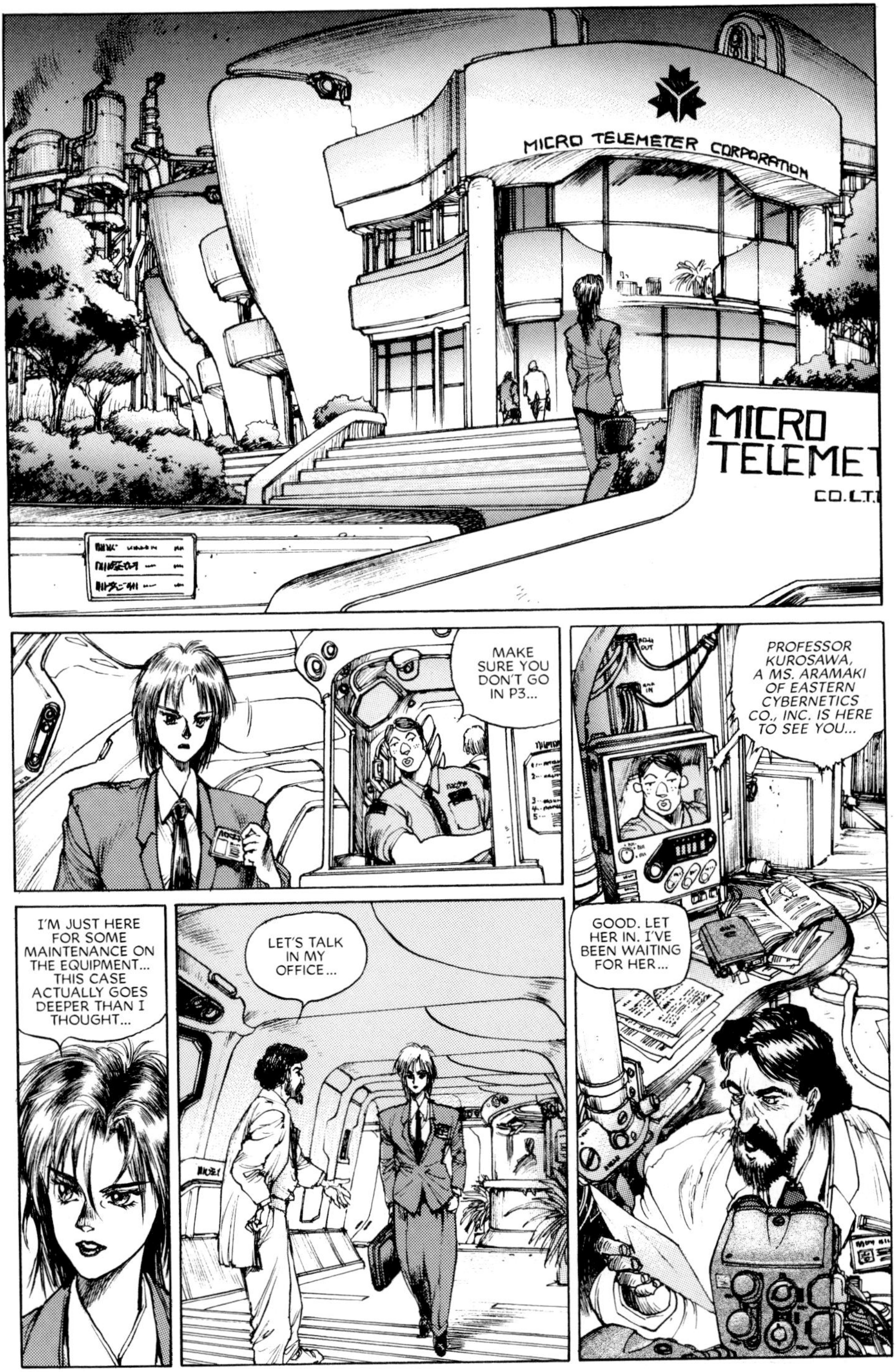
MICRO TELEMETER CORPORATION
MICRO TELEMET
CO.LT
MAKE SURE YOU DON'T GO IN P3...
PROFESSOR KUROSAWA, A MS. ARAMAKI OF EASTERN CYBERNETICS CO., INC. IS HERE TO SEE YOU...
GOOD. LET HER IN. I'VE BEEN WAITING FOR HER...
I'M JUST HERE FOR SOME MAINTENANCE ON THE EQUIPMENT... THIS CASE ACTUALLY GOES DEEPER THAN I THOUGHT...
LET'S TALK IN MY OFFICE...

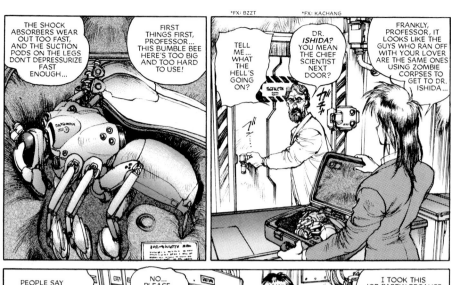
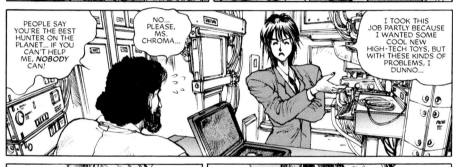
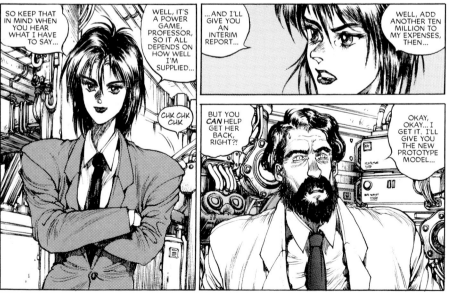

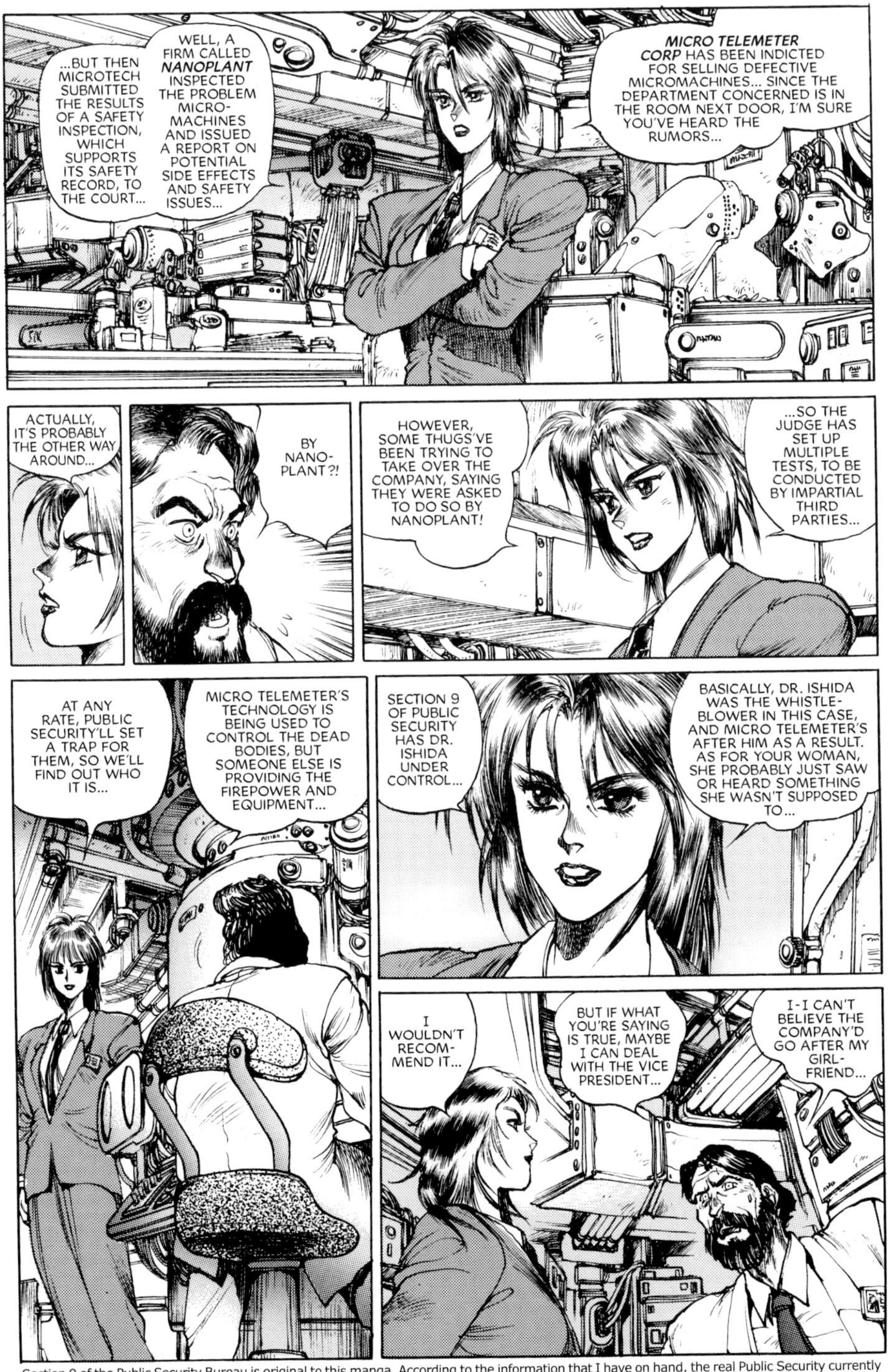
MICRO TELEMETER CORP HAS BEEN INDICTED FOR SELLING DEFECTIVE MICROMACHINES... SINCE THE DEPARTMENT CONCERNED IS IN THE ROOM NEXT DOOR, I'M SURE YOU'VE HEARD THE RUMORS...
WELL, A FIRM CALLED NANOPLANT INSPECTED THE PROBLEM MICRO-MACHINES AND ISSUED A REPORT ON POTENTIAL SIDE EFFECTS AND SAFETY ISSUES...
...BUT THEN MICROTECH SUBMITTED THE RESULTS OF A SAFETY INSPECTION, WHICH SUPPORTS ITS SAFETY RECORD, TO THE COURT...
...SO THE JUDGE HAS SET UP MULTIPLE TESTS, TO BE CONDUCTED BY IMPARTIAL THIRD PARTIES...
HOWEVER, SOME THUGS'VE BEEN TRYING TO TAKE OVER THE COMPANY, SAYING THEY WERE ASKED TO DO SO BY NANOPLANT!
BY NANO-PLANT?!
ACTUALLY, IT'S PROBABLY THE OTHER WAY AROUND...
BASICALLY, DR. ISHIDA WAS THE WHISTLE-BLOWER IN THIS CASE, AND MICRO TELEMETER'S AFTER HIM AS A RESULT. AS FOR YOUR WOMAN, SHE PROBABLY JUST SAW OR HEARD SOMETHING SHE WASN'T SUPPOSED TO...
SECTION 9 OF PUBLIC SECURITY HAS DR. ISHIDA UNDER CONTROL...
I-I CAN'T BELIEVE THE COMPANY'D GO AFTER MY GIRL-FRIEND...
BUT IF WHAT YOU'RE SAYING IS TRUE, MAYBE I CAN DEAL WITH THE VICE PRESIDENT...
I WOULDN'T RECOM-MEND IT...
MICRO TELEMETER'S TECHNOLOGY IS BEING USED TO CONTROL THE DEAD BODIES, BUT SOMEONE ELSE IS PROVIDING THE FIREPOWER AND EQUIPMENT...
AT ANY RATE, PUBLIC SECURITY'LL SET A TRAP FOR THEM, SO WE'LL FIND OUT WHO IT IS...

Section 9 of the Public Security Bureau is original to this manga. According to the information that I have on hand, the real Public Security currently consists of General Affairs (including special support troops), Section 1 (in charge of investigating student movements and radical activities), Section 2 (labor disputes and organized crime), Section 3 (right-wing activities), Section 4 (information gathering, statistics, etc.), External Affairs Section 1 (in charge of investigating non-Asian foreigners), and External Affairs Section 2 (Asian foreigners).

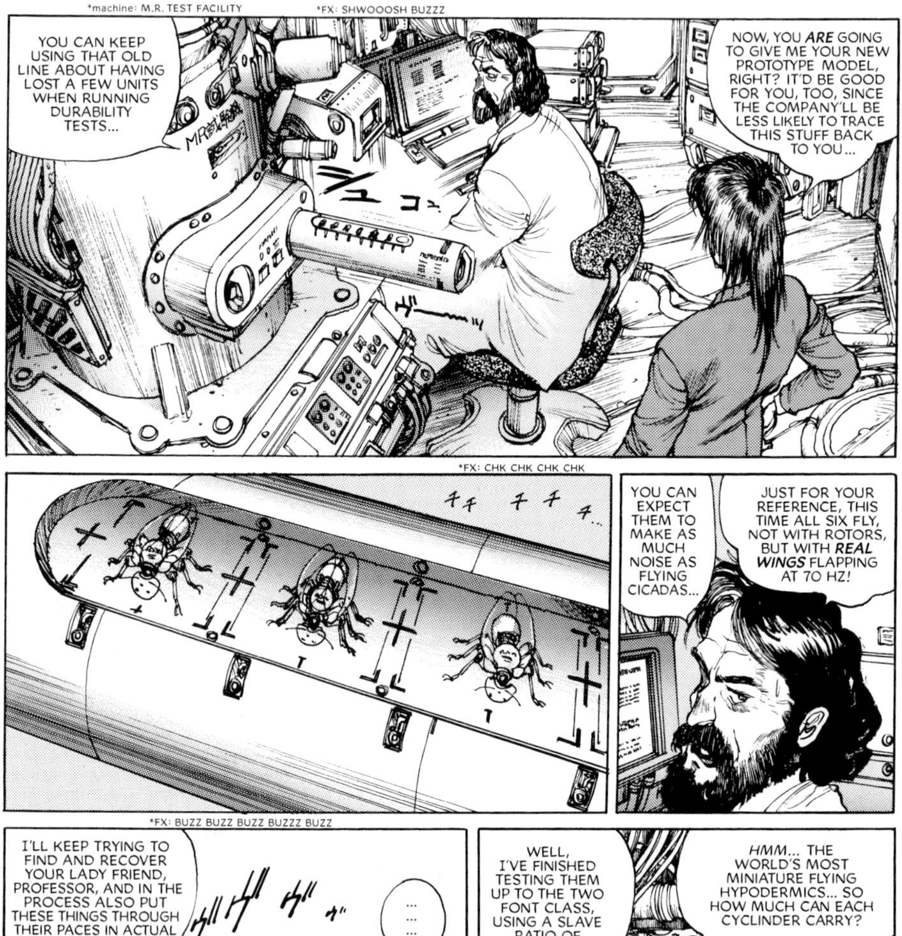
*machine: M.R. TEST FACILITY
*FX: SHWOOOSH BUZZZ
YOU CAN KEEP USING THAT OLD LINE ABOUT HAVING LOST A FEW UNITS WHEN RUNNING DURABILITY TESTS...
NOW, YOU ARE GOING TO GIVE ME YOUR NEW PROTOTYPE MODEL, RIGHT? IT'D BE GOOD FOR YOU, TOO, SINCE THE COMPANY'LL BE LESS LIKELY TO TRACE THIS STUFF BACK TO YOU...
*FX: CHK CHK CHK CHK
YOU CAN EXPECT THEM TO MAKE AS MUCH NOISE AS FLYING CICADAS...
JUST FOR YOUR REFERENCE, THIS TIME ALL SIX FLY, NOT WITH ROTORS, BUT WITH REAL WINGS FLAPPING AT 70 HZ!
*FX: BUZZ BUZZ BUZZ BUZZZ BUZZ
I'LL KEEP TRYING TO FIND AND RECOVER YOUR LADY FRIEND, PROFESSOR, AND IN THE PROCESS ALSO PUT THESE THINGS THROUGH THEIR PACES IN ACTUAL COMBAT...
... ...
WELL, I'VE FINISHED TESTING THEM UP TO THE TWO FONT CLASS, USING A SLAVE RATIO OF 10-4 MILLI-MACHINES...
HMM... THE WORLD'S MOST MINIATURE FLYING HYPODERMICS... SO HOW MUCH CAN EACH CYCLINDER CARRY?

Section 9 was formed as a small-scale, highly privileged and elite organization, in conjunction with a crossover in categories of criminal activity. (An example of such a crossover would be Asian mafia and right-wing Japanese gangs that attempt to import illegal weapons and assassinate corporate VIPs, using funds procured from the sale of drugs, and are —*phew*— themselves sometimes infiltrated by the FBI., etc., etc....) Public Security specializes in domestic affairs, but on paper is positioned as an organization involved in international rescue efforts, etc. Members are specially selected from other groups, and thus no volunteers are accepted.

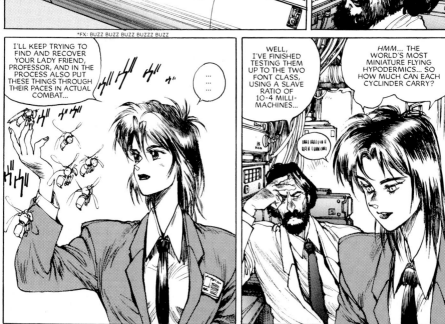

*signs: SHINHAMA CENTRAL POLICE HOSPITAL

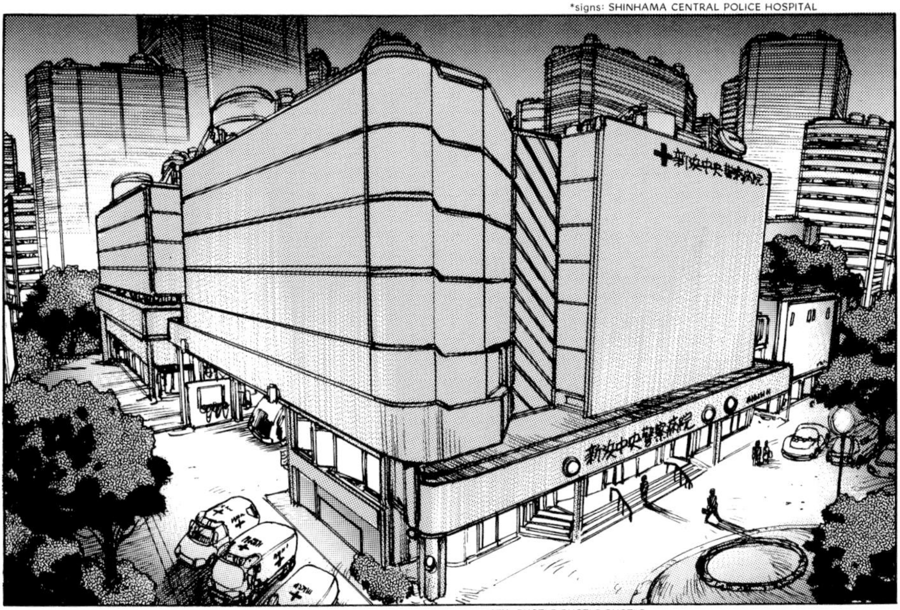

*FX: RUSTLE RUSTLE RUSTLE

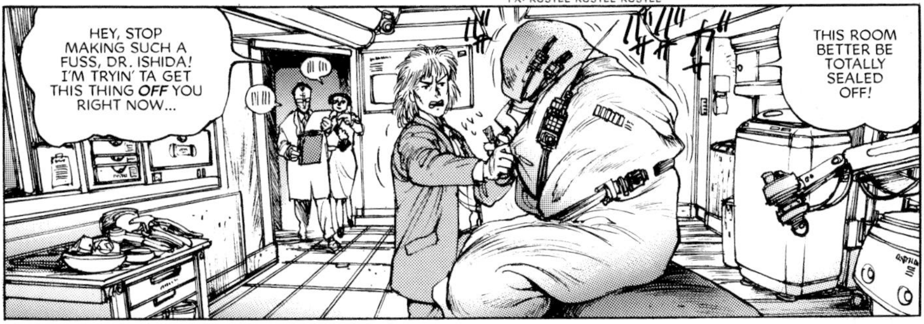
THIS ROOM BETTER BE TOTALLY SEALED OFF!
HEY, STOP MAKING SUCH A FUSS, DR. ISHIDA! I'M TRYIN' TA GET THIS THING *OFF* YOU RIGHT NOW...

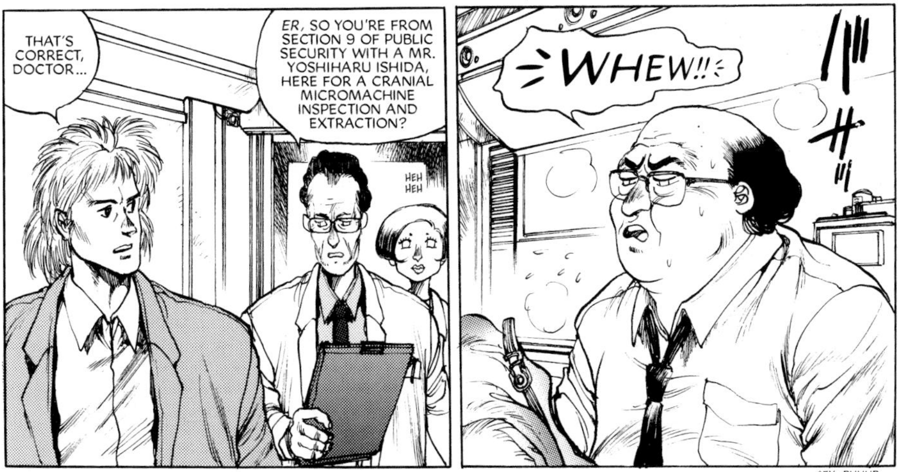
WHEW!!
ER, SO YOU'RE FROM SECTION 9 OF PUBLIC SECURITY WITH A MR. YOSHIHARU ISHIDA, HERE FOR A CRANIAL MICROMACHINE INSPECTION AND EXTRACTION?
HEH HEH
THAT'S CORRECT, DOCTOR...

*FX: PHHHP

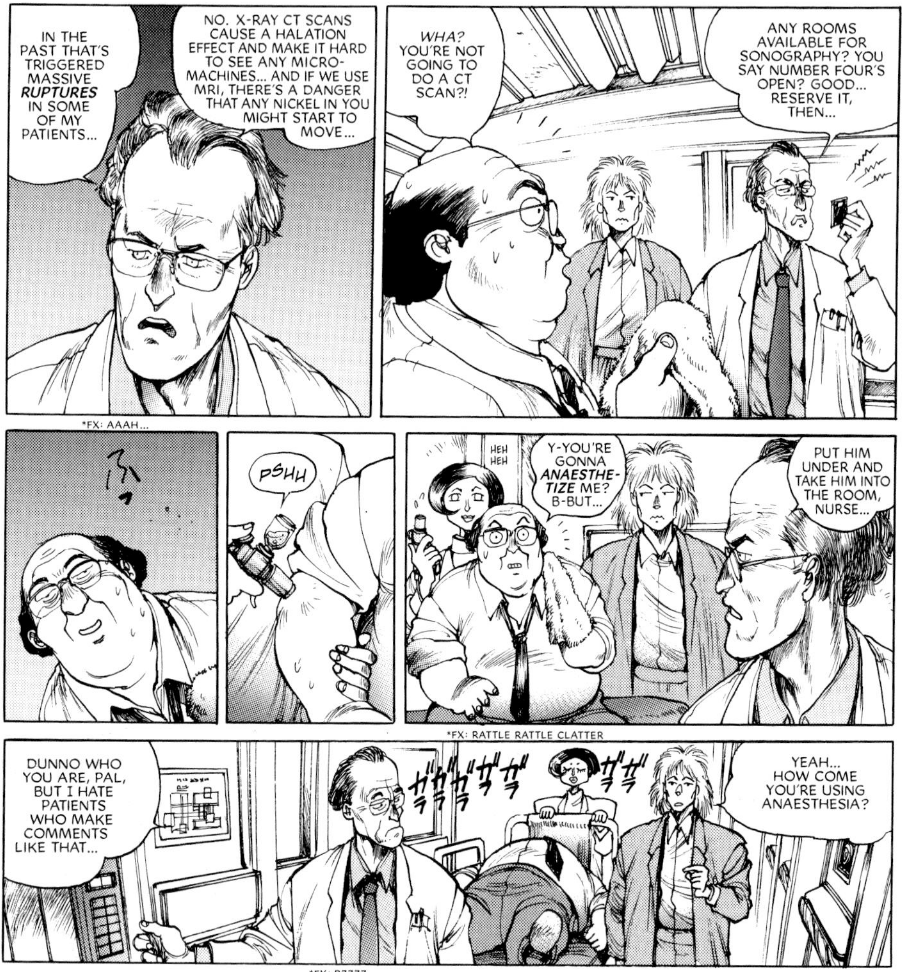
IN THE PAST THAT'S TRIGGERED MASSIVE ***RUPTURES*** IN SOME OF MY PATIENTS...
NO. X-RAY CT SCANS CAUSE A HALATION EFFECT AND MAKE IT HARD TO SEE ANY MICRO-MACHINES... AND IF WE USE MRI, THERE'S A DANGER THAT ANY NICKEL IN YOU MIGHT START TO MOVE...
WHA? YOU'RE NOT GOING TO DO A CT SCAN?!
ANY ROOMS AVAILABLE FOR SONOGRAPHY? YOU SAY NUMBER FOUR'S OPEN? GOOD... RESERVE IT, THEN...
*FX: AAAH...
PSHH
HEH HEH
Y-YOU'RE GONNA ***ANAESTHETIZE*** ME? B-BUT...
PUT HIM UNDER AND TAKE HIM INTO THE ROOM, NURSE...
*FX: RATTLE RATTLE CLATTER
DUNNO WHO YOU ARE, PAL, BUT I HATE PATIENTS WHO MAKE COMMENTS LIKE THAT...
YEAH... HOW COME YOU'RE USING ANAESTHESIA?
*FX: BZZZZ
BEEP

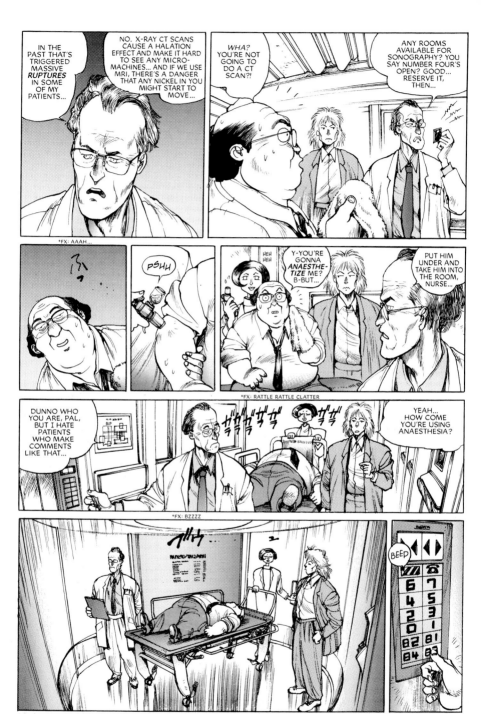

I don't mean to imply that nickel is the only thing that would move in the human body when doing an MRI... Other elements with strong magnetic susceptibility, from scandium to lead, would also be a problem. The author of this story (me) chose nickel here because it would likely be used near e-brain micromachines and transformers. Nickel-titanium alloys and grade 316 stainless steel would also present the most problems with biocompatibility... I've never done any experiments in this regard, of course, or even designed any micromachines. And what the doctor refers to as "nickel" here is in reality probably the ferromagnetic material NiO-Fe2O3. (Ferrites are, of course, used in stuff like high-frequency transformers and magnetic recording devices...).

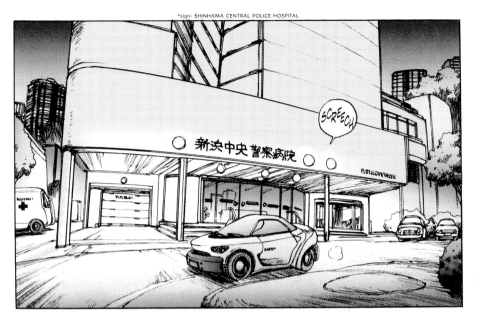

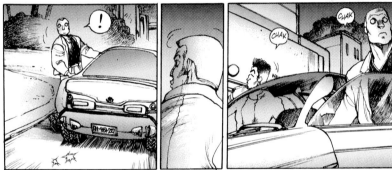

*sign: SHINHAMA CENTRAL POLICE HOSPITAL

SCREECH
新浜中央警察病院
CHAK
CHAK
!
WHAT THE--?!
SHIT! WE'VE BEEN HOOKED BY WIRED INSEC-TRONS!!
WE'VE LED THE ENEMY STRAIGHT TO OUR WITNESS!!
THEN WE'VE GOTTA KEEP MOVING AND CHANGE CARS!!
CHAK

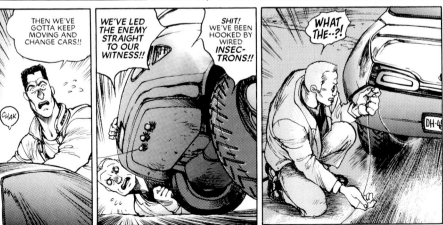

Insectrons: general name (made up, of course) given to insect-like robots ranging in size from several millimeters to several centimeters. Micromachining is currently a hot field of research, and there is a great deal of anticipation that future applications of the technology could include insect pest eradication or performance of maintenance procedures (including interior photography) on tiny capillaries and vessels. Larger-scale applications are reportedly already in use. In addition to such mechanical engineering approaches, some scientists are also attempting to use genetically engineered bio-organisms to accomplish similar tasks. Rather than refer to "robots" in this case, I probably should just say "devices"...

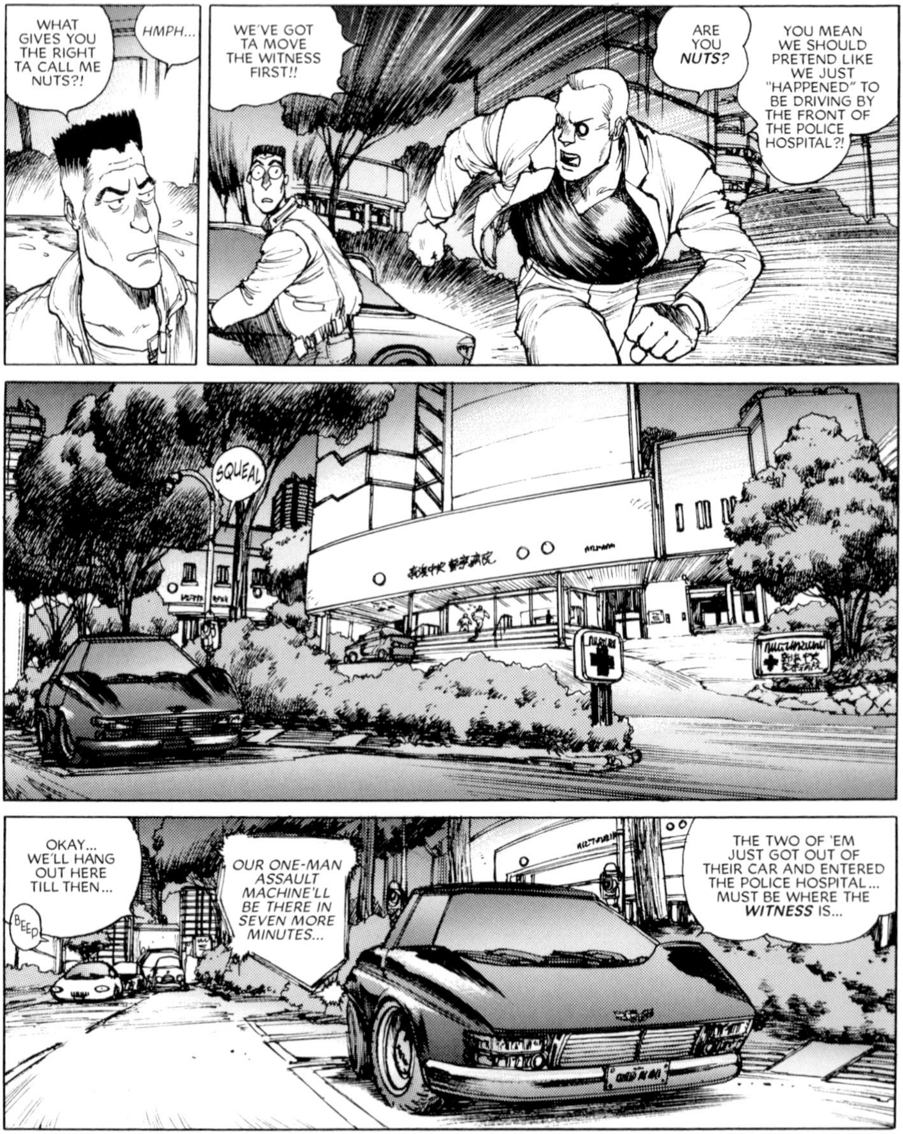
ARE YOU NUTS?
YOU MEAN WE SHOULD PRETEND LIKE WE JUST "HAPPENED" TO BE DRIVING BY THE FRONT OF THE POLICE HOSPITAL?!
WE'VE GOT TA MOVE THE WITNESS FIRST!!
HMPH...
WHAT GIVES YOU THE RIGHT TA CALL ME NUTS?!
SQUEAL
THE TWO OF 'EM JUST GOT OUT OF THEIR CAR AND ENTERED THE POLICE HOSPITAL... MUST BE WHERE THE WITNESS IS...
OUR ONE-MAN ASSAULT MACHINE'LL BE THERE IN SEVEN MORE MINUTES...
OKAY... WE'LL HANG OUT HERE TILL THEN...
BEEP
HMPH...

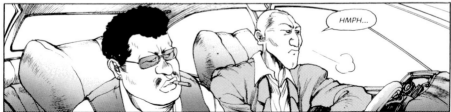

Regarding the spider threads shown on the previous page, like real spider threads, these are "extracted" from a tank in the belly of the tiny robot. But that doesn't mean that the threads are actually wound and stored on an internal reel structure. (I used to think that spider threads were created through some sort of physical interaction of liquid with the air...) In addition to simply maneuvering about, spiders use their threads as "bookmarks" or "signposts" when evacuating an area in an emergency or when attacking. In the case of insectrons, one also has to take into account the extreme viscous resistance and tension of the threads they deploy. So even if the insectrons have successfully attached themselves to a surface with their suction cups, they probably have to sever their threads in a relative hurry. Actual spider theads, by the way, are created from a protein matter called fibroin, and are said to have greater elasticity and tensile strength than nylon...

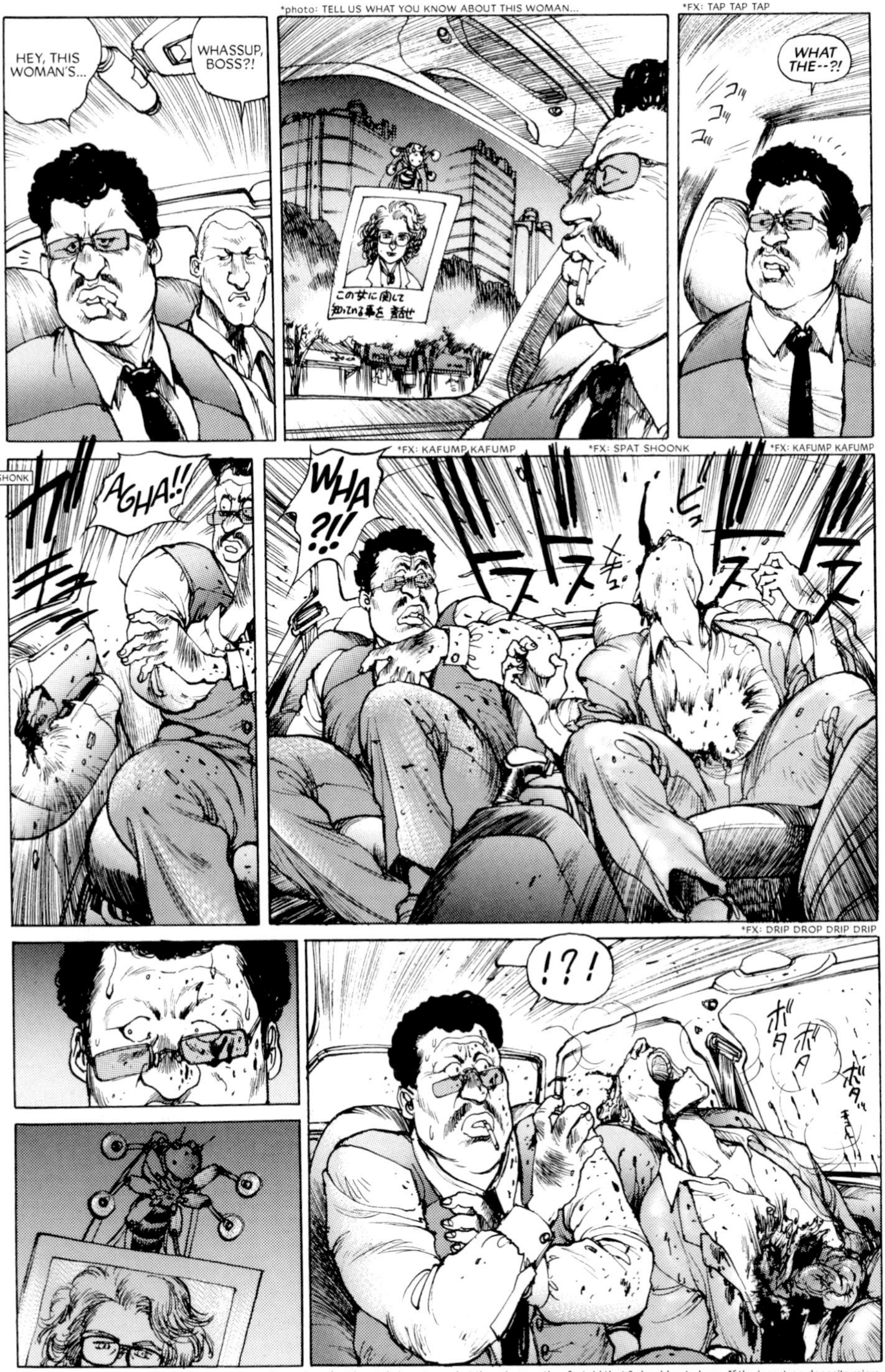
HEY, THIS WOMAN'S...
WHASSUP, BOSS?!
*photo: TELL US WHAT YOU KNOW ABOUT THIS WOMAN...
*FX: TAP TAP TAP
WHAT THE--?!
KASHONK
AGHA!!
WHA ?!!
*FX: KAFUMP KAFUMP
*FX: SPAT SHOONK
*FX: KAFUMP KAFUMP
*FX: DRIP DROP DRIP DRIP
!?!

Forgive me, dear readers, for continuing with my discussion of spider-style insectrons, but there is one other factoid that I should note here. If the insectron deposits micro drops of its sticky thread liquid at one to two meter intervals and then lets threads play out from the center of the car, they'd be less likely to be disconnected or severed except during lane changes or in pedestrian crossings. (Of course the thread liquid would be used up faster...) For trailing another vehicle at a distance of one kilometer or so, this might do the trick. (Of course, the insectron's tank capacity would be an issue, but the *nephilia clavata* spider can reportedly spin over 700 meters of thread...)

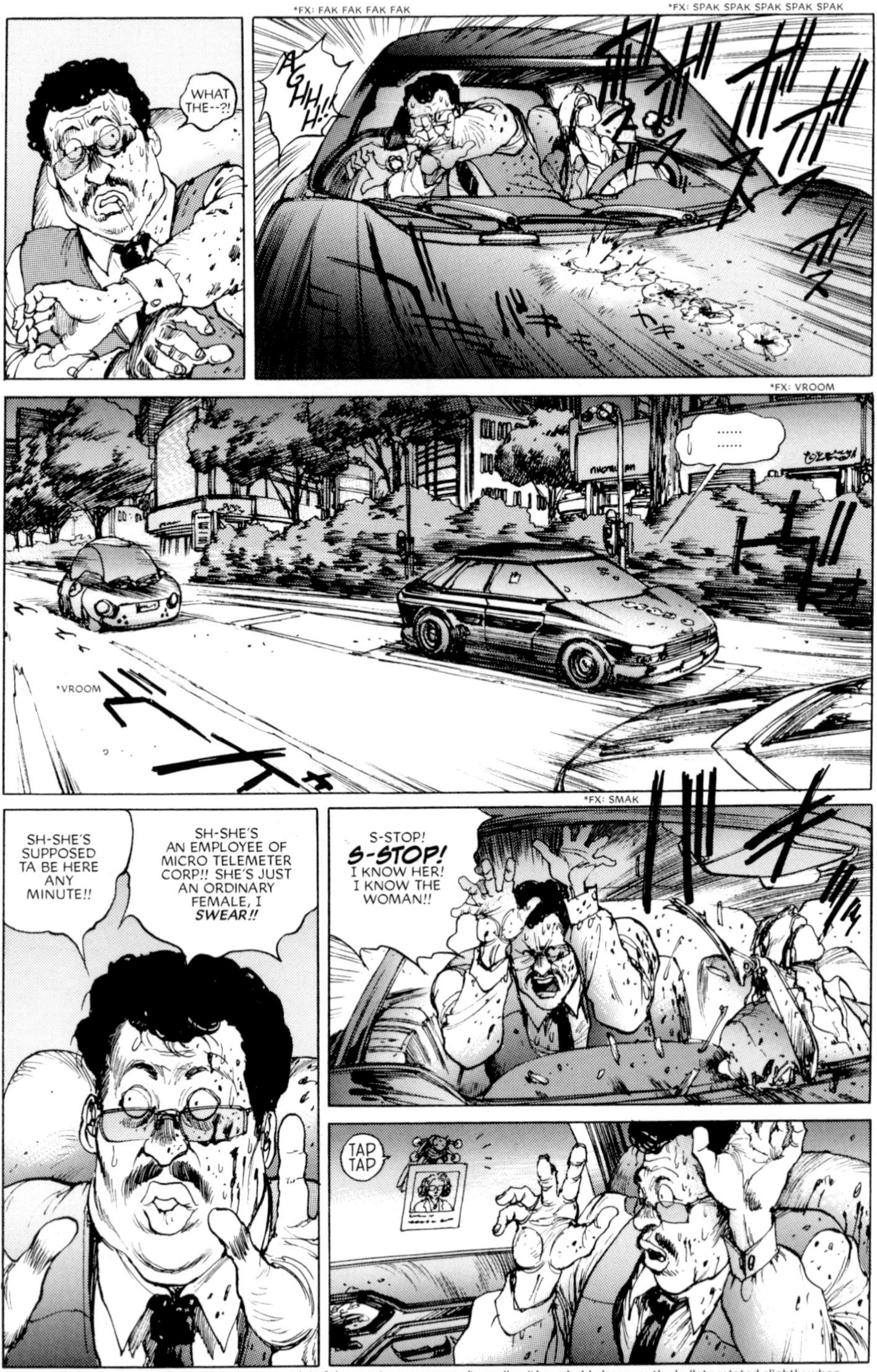
*FX: SPAK SPAK SPAK SPAK SPAK
*FX: FAK FAK FAK FAK
AGHHH!!
WHAT THE--?!
*FX: VROOM
......
......
*VROOM
*FX: SMAK
S-STOP! S-STOP! I KNOW HER! I KNOW THE WOMAN!!
TAP TAP
SH-SHE'S AN EMPLOYEE OF MICRO TELEMETER CORP!! SHE'S JUST AN ORDINARY FEMALE, I SWEAR!!
SH-SHE'S SUPPOSED TA BE HERE ANY MINUTE!!

If any readers wonder why the bullet holes in panel 4 of the previous page aren't smaller, it's probably because the bullets rotated slightly when they penetrated the car's windshield. Of course, the bullets went right through the entire car and smashed into the road, but even with their large caliber they weren't able to pierce the car's engine block. Given the distance involved, the victims wouldn't hear any audible gunshots or be able to see a reflection from the rifle scope lens (in this manga, at least)...

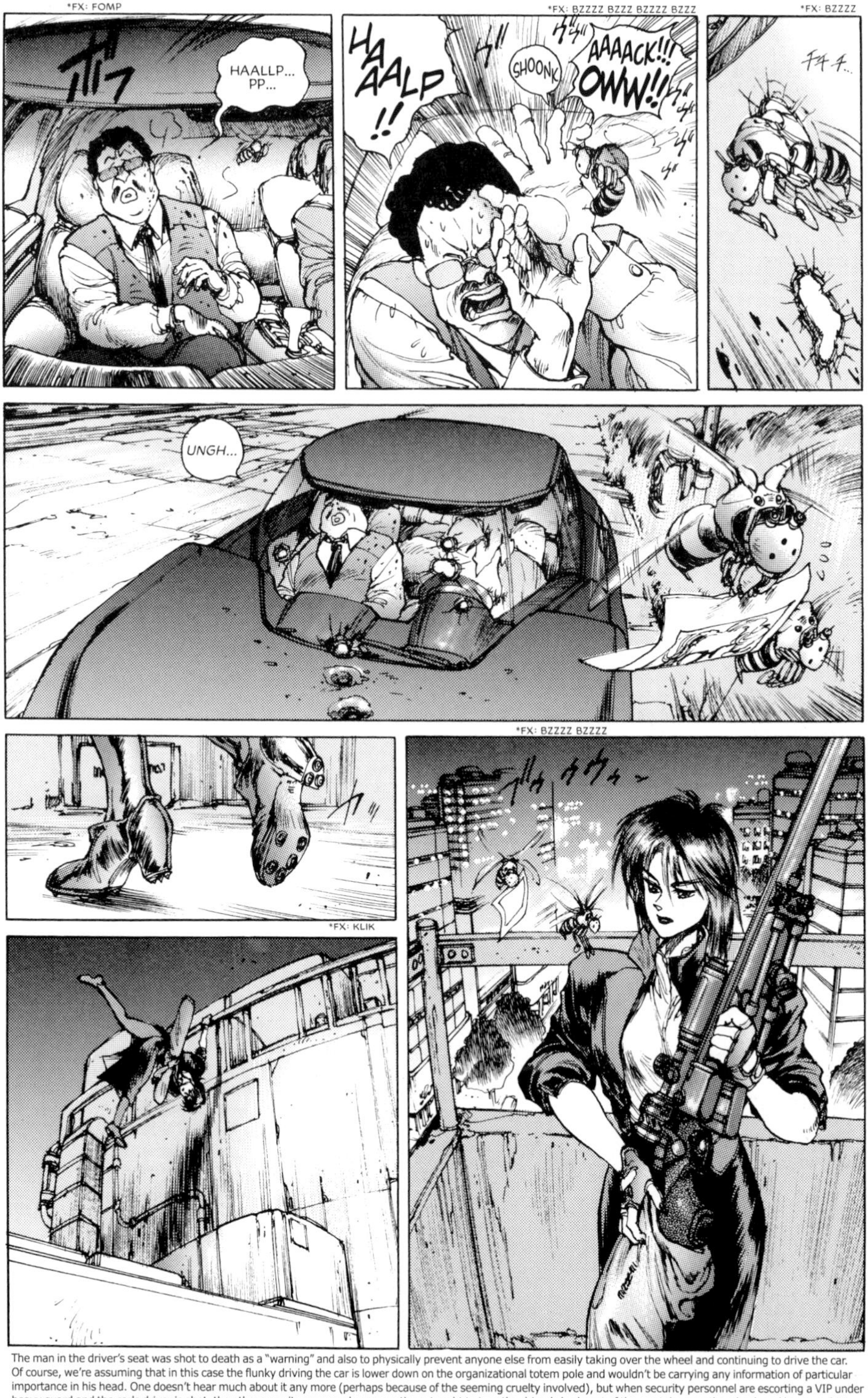
*FX: BZZZZ
チチチ...
*FX: BZZZZ BZZZ BZZZZ BZZZ
HAAALP!!
SHOONK
AAAACK!!! OWW!!!
*FX: FOMP
HAALLP... PP...
UNGH...
*FX: BZZZZ BZZZZ
*FX: KLIK

The man in the driver's seat was shot to death as a "warning" and also to physically prevent anyone else from easily taking over the wheel and continuing to drive the car. Of course, we're assuming that in this case the flunky driving the car is lower down on the organizational totem pole and wouldn't be carrying any information of particular importance in his head. One doesn't hear much about it any more (perhaps because of the seeming cruelty involved), but when security personnel are escorting a VIP under heavy guard and the car's driver is shot, the other security personnel are sometimes taught to toss the driver's body out of the car, take over the wheel, and keep on driving. Also, in the first panel on this page please overlook the fact that I drew the bullet hole in the windshield in what would be regarded as a slightly out-of-date style.

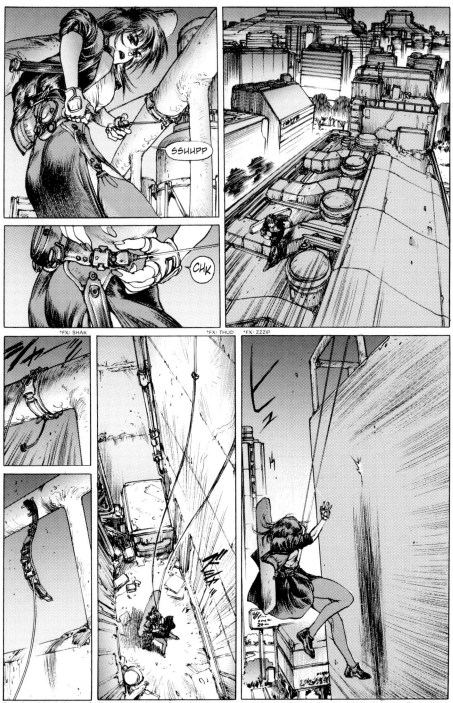

SSHHPP

CHK

*FX: SHAK   *FX: THUD   *FX: ZZZIP

Regarding sniping, in this case, for Chroma/Major to be out of normal visual range, a distance of around 400 meters from the victim would usually suffice. One of the main things that she has to worry about is that—since she's not using a linear rifle—the sound of the gunshot is pretty loud. I made her rifle a heavy barrel, bolt-action design because I've heard that M-16s, etc., wouldn't be effective, presumably because of their small caliber. In this story, her rifle uses 9mm bullets. The protrusion on the side of the magazine is a cartridge catcher. Assume that she doesn't leave any footprints because her shoes have spikes.

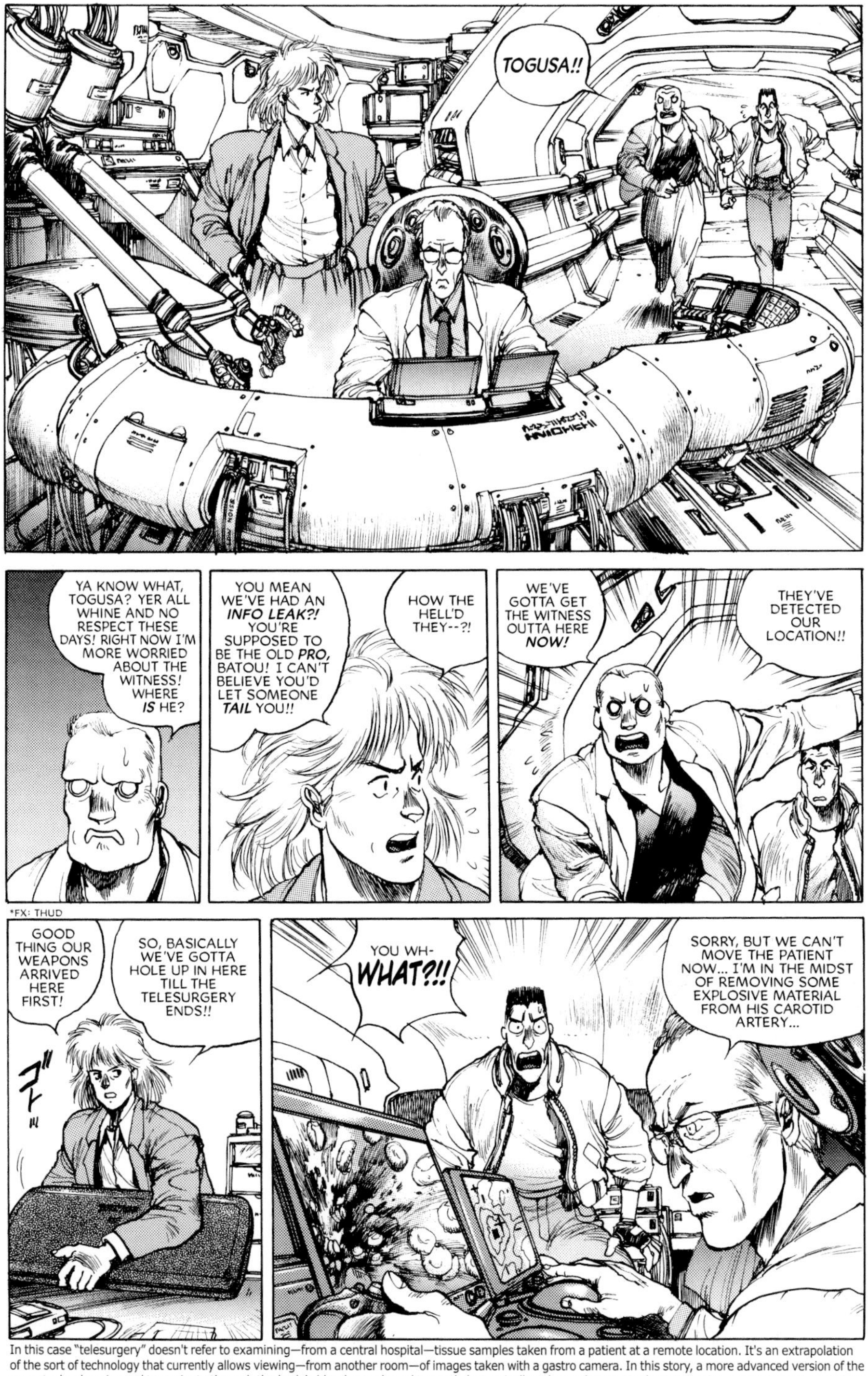
TOGUSA!!
THEY'VE DETECTED OUR LOCATION!!
WE'VE GOTTA GET THE WITNESS OUTTA HERE *NOW!*
HOW THE HELL'D THEY--?!
YOU MEAN WE'VE HAD AN *INFO LEAK?!* YOU'RE SUPPOSED TO BE THE OLD *PRO,* BATOU! I CAN'T BELIEVE YOU'D LET SOMEONE *TAIL* YOU!!
YA KNOW WHAT, TOGUSA? YER ALL WHINE AND NO RESPECT THESE DAYS! RIGHT NOW I'M MORE WORRIED ABOUT THE WITNESS! WHERE *IS* HE?
*FX: THUD
SORRY, BUT WE CAN'T MOVE THE PATIENT NOW... I'M IN THE MIDST OF REMOVING SOME EXPLOSIVE MATERIAL FROM HIS CAROTID ARTERY...
YOU WH- WHAT?!!
SO, BASICALLY WE'VE GOTTA HOLE UP IN HERE TILL THE TELESURGERY ENDS!!
GOOD THING OUR WEAPONS ARRIVED HERE FIRST!

In this case "telesurgery" doesn't refer to examining—from a central hospital—tissue samples taken from a patient at a remote location. It's an extrapolation of the sort of technology that currently allows viewing—from another room—of images taken with a gastro camera. In this story, a more advanced version of the same technology is used to navigate through the body's blood vessels and to send electronically enhanced compound computer images to a remote monitor. The system can also be used to remotely remove foreign matter (as long as it's not too large) from the patient, using scissors, bonding agents, staples, etc.

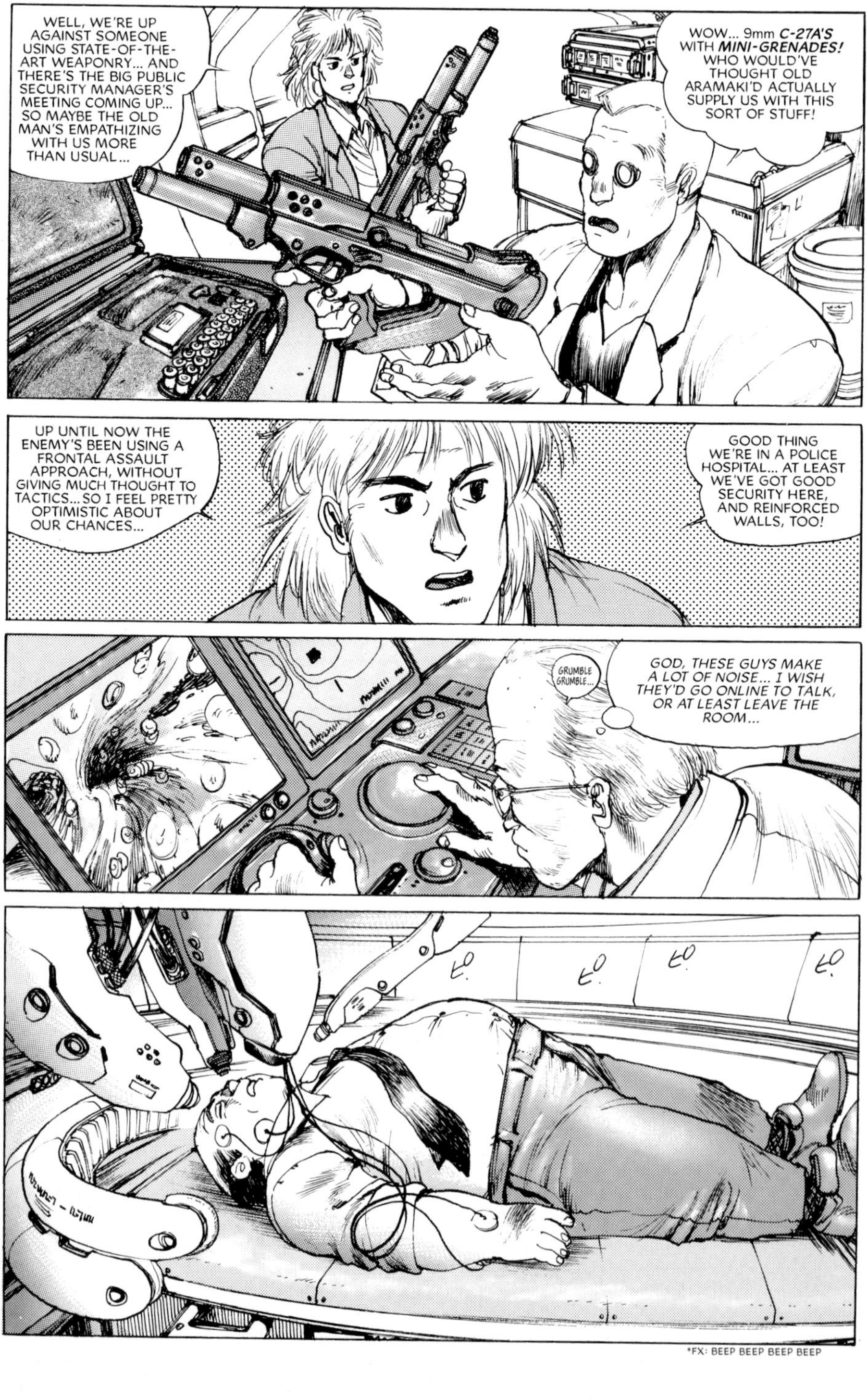
WELL, WE'RE UP AGAINST SOMEONE USING STATE-OF-THE-ART WEAPONRY... AND THERE'S THE BIG PUBLIC SECURITY MANAGER'S MEETING COMING UP... SO MAYBE THE OLD MAN'S EMPATHIZING WITH US MORE THAN USUAL...
WOW... 9mm ***C-27A'S*** WITH ***MINI-GRENADES!*** WHO WOULD'VE THOUGHT OLD ARAMAKI'D ACTUALLY SUPPLY US WITH THIS SORT OF STUFF!
UP UNTIL NOW THE ENEMY'S BEEN USING A FRONTAL ASSAULT APPROACH, WITHOUT GIVING MUCH THOUGHT TO TACTICS... SO I FEEL PRETTY OPTIMISTIC ABOUT OUR CHANCES...
GOOD THING WE'RE IN A POLICE HOSPITAL... AT LEAST WE'VE GOT GOOD SECURITY HERE, AND REINFORCED WALLS, TOO!
GRUMBLE GRUMBLE...
GOD, THESE GUYS MAKE A LOT OF NOISE... I WISH THEY'D GO ONLINE TO TALK, OR AT LEAST LEAVE THE ROOM...
ピ ピ ピ ピ

*FX: BEEP BEEP BEEP BEEP

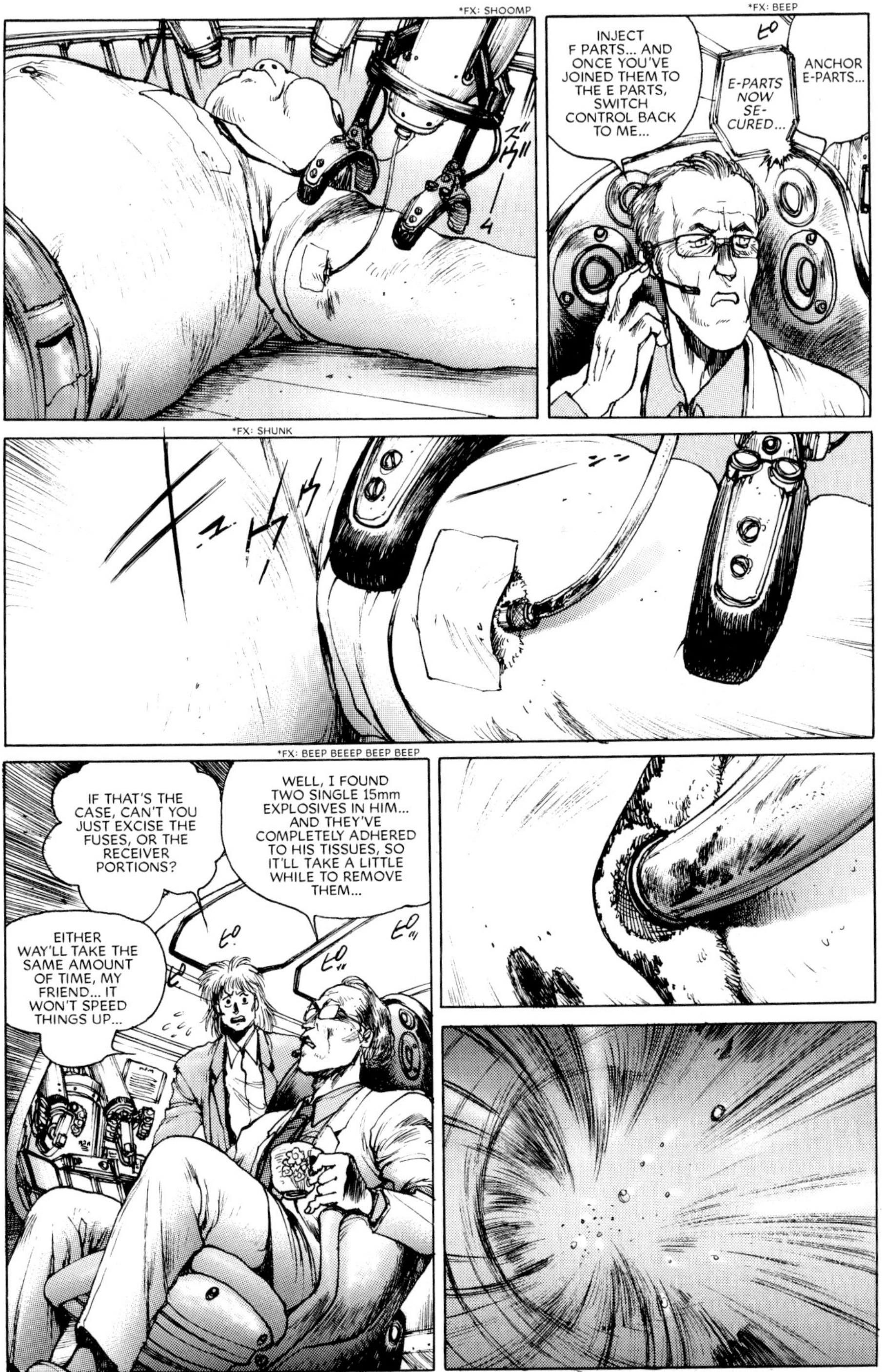
*FX: BEEP
ANCHOR E-PARTS...
E-PARTS NOW SECURED...
INJECT F PARTS... AND ONCE YOU'VE JOINED THEM TO THE E PARTS, SWITCH CONTROL BACK TO ME...
*FX: SHOOMP
*FX: SHUNK
*FX: BEEP BEEEP BEEP BEEP
WELL, I FOUND TWO SINGLE 15mm EXPLOSIVES IN HIM... AND THEY'VE COMPLETELY ADHERED TO HIS TISSUES, SO IT'LL TAKE A LITTLE WHILE TO REMOVE THEM...
IF THAT'S THE CASE, CAN'T YOU JUST EXCISE THE FUSES, OR THE RECEIVER PORTIONS?
EITHER WAY'LL TAKE THE SAME AMOUNT OF TIME, MY FRIEND... IT WON'T SPEED THINGS UP...

Regarding the "two" explosives—I arbitrarily came up with this number. First of all, only a limited number of blood vessels are searched, because they have to be ones wide enough to accommodate the inserted explosives. The doctor then injects thousands of micromachines into these blood vessels. The micromachines proceed to detect relatively large foreign particles (especially the metallic portion of any signal receivers attached to the explosive material in the body), to adhere to them and then to emit an audio alert (of course, inaudible to humans under normal circumstances).

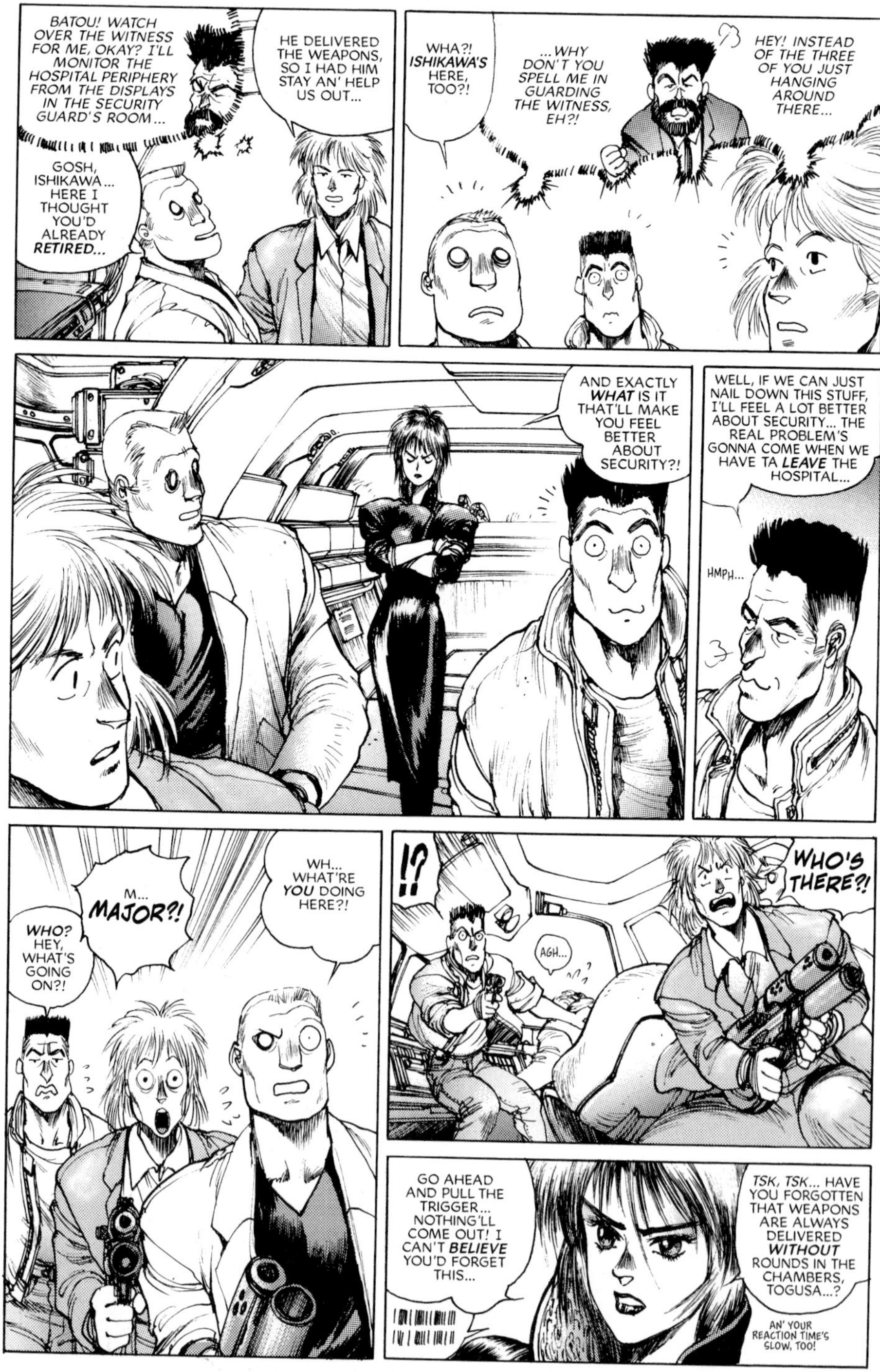
HEY! INSTEAD OF THE THREE OF YOU JUST HANGING AROUND THERE...
...WHY DON'T YOU SPELL ME IN GUARDING THE WITNESS, EH?!
WHA?! *ISHIKAWA'S* HERE, TOO?!
BATOU! WATCH OVER THE WITNESS FOR ME, OKAY? I'LL MONITOR THE HOSPITAL PERIPHERY FROM THE DISPLAYS IN THE SECURITY GUARD'S ROOM...
HE DELIVERED THE WEAPONS, SO I HAD HIM STAY AN' HELP US OUT...
GOSH, ISHIKAWA... HERE I THOUGHT YOU'D ALREADY *RETIRED...*
WELL, IF WE CAN JUST NAIL DOWN THIS STUFF, I'LL FEEL A LOT BETTER ABOUT SECURITY... THE REAL PROBLEM'S GONNA COME WHEN WE HAVE TA *LEAVE* THE HOSPITAL...
HMPH...
AND EXACTLY *WHAT* IS IT THAT'LL MAKE YOU FEEL BETTER ABOUT SECURITY?!
!?
WHO'S THERE?!
AGH...
TSK, TSK... HAVE YOU FORGOTTEN THAT WEAPONS ARE ALWAYS DELIVERED *WITHOUT* ROUNDS IN THE CHAMBERS, TOGUSA...?
GO AHEAD AND PULL THE TRIGGER... NOTHING'LL COME OUT! I CAN'T *BELIEVE* YOU'D FORGET THIS...
AN' YOUR REACTION TIME'S SLOW, TOO!
WH... WHAT'RE *YOU* DOING HERE?!
M... MAJOR?!
WHO? HEY, WHAT'S GOING ON?!

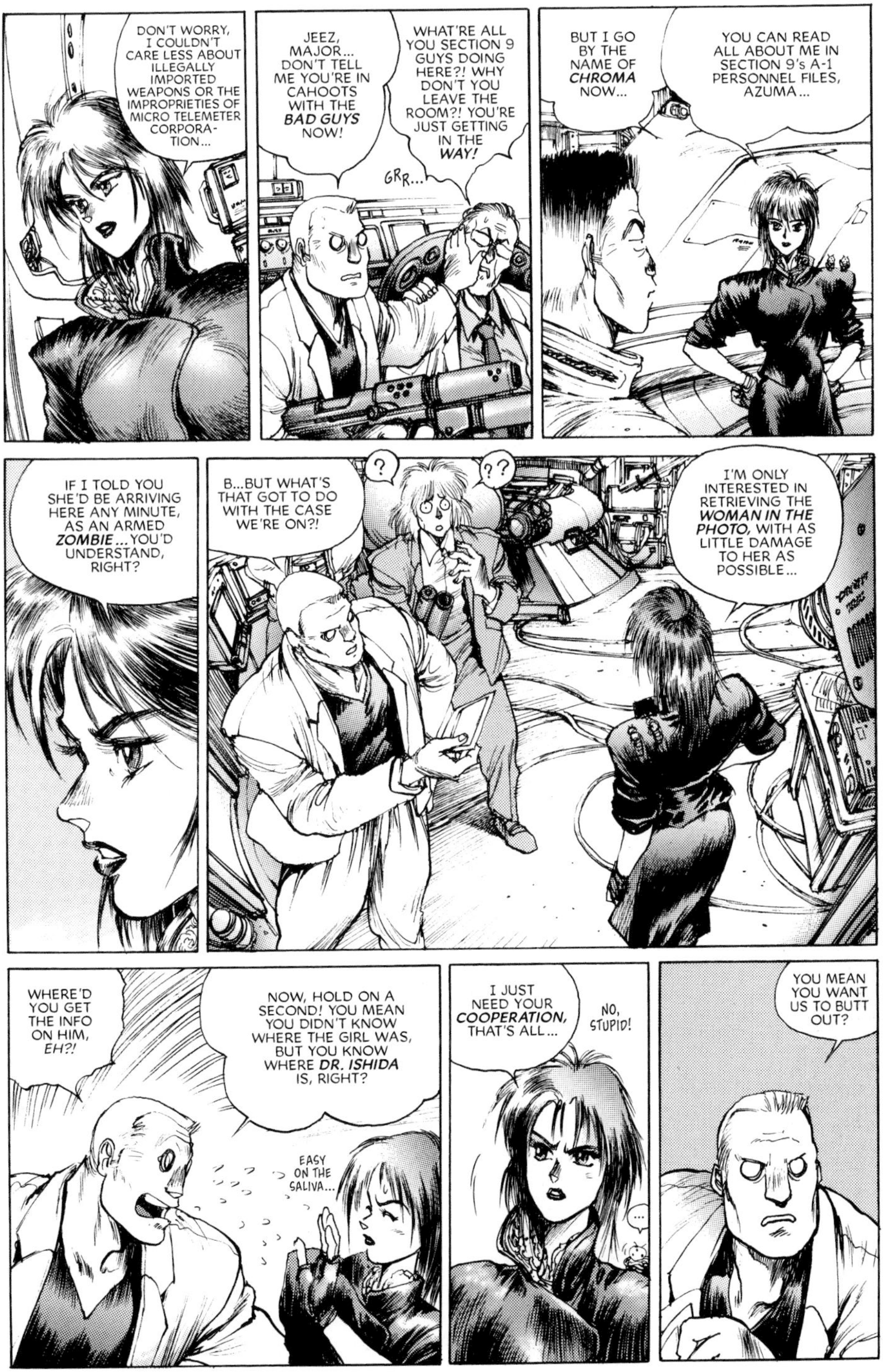
DON'T WORRY, I COULDN'T CARE LESS ABOUT ILLEGALLY IMPORTED WEAPONS OR THE IMPROPRIETIES OF MICRO TELEMETER CORPORATION...
JEEZ, MAJOR... DON'T TELL ME YOU'RE IN CAHOOTS WITH THE *BAD GUYS* NOW!
WHAT'RE ALL YOU SECTION 9 GUYS DOING HERE?! WHY DON'T YOU LEAVE THE ROOM?! YOU'RE JUST GETTING IN THE *WAY!*
GRR...
BUT I GO BY THE NAME OF *CHROMA* NOW...
YOU CAN READ ALL ABOUT ME IN SECTION 9's A-1 PERSONNEL FILES, AZUMA...
IF I TOLD YOU SHE'D BE ARRIVING HERE ANY MINUTE, AS AN ARMED *ZOMBIE...* YOU'D UNDERSTAND, RIGHT?
B...BUT WHAT'S THAT GOT TO DO WITH THE CASE WE'RE ON?!
?
??
I'M ONLY INTERESTED IN RETRIEVING THE *WOMAN IN THE PHOTO,* WITH AS LITTLE DAMAGE TO HER AS POSSIBLE...
WHERE'D YOU GET THE INFO ON HIM, *EH?!*
NOW, HOLD ON A SECOND! YOU MEAN YOU DIDN'T KNOW WHERE THE GIRL WAS, BUT YOU KNOW WHERE *DR. ISHIDA* IS, RIGHT?
EASY ON THE SALIVA...
I JUST NEED YOUR *COOPERATION,* THAT'S ALL...
NO, STUPID!
...
YOU MEAN YOU WANT US TO BUTT OUT?

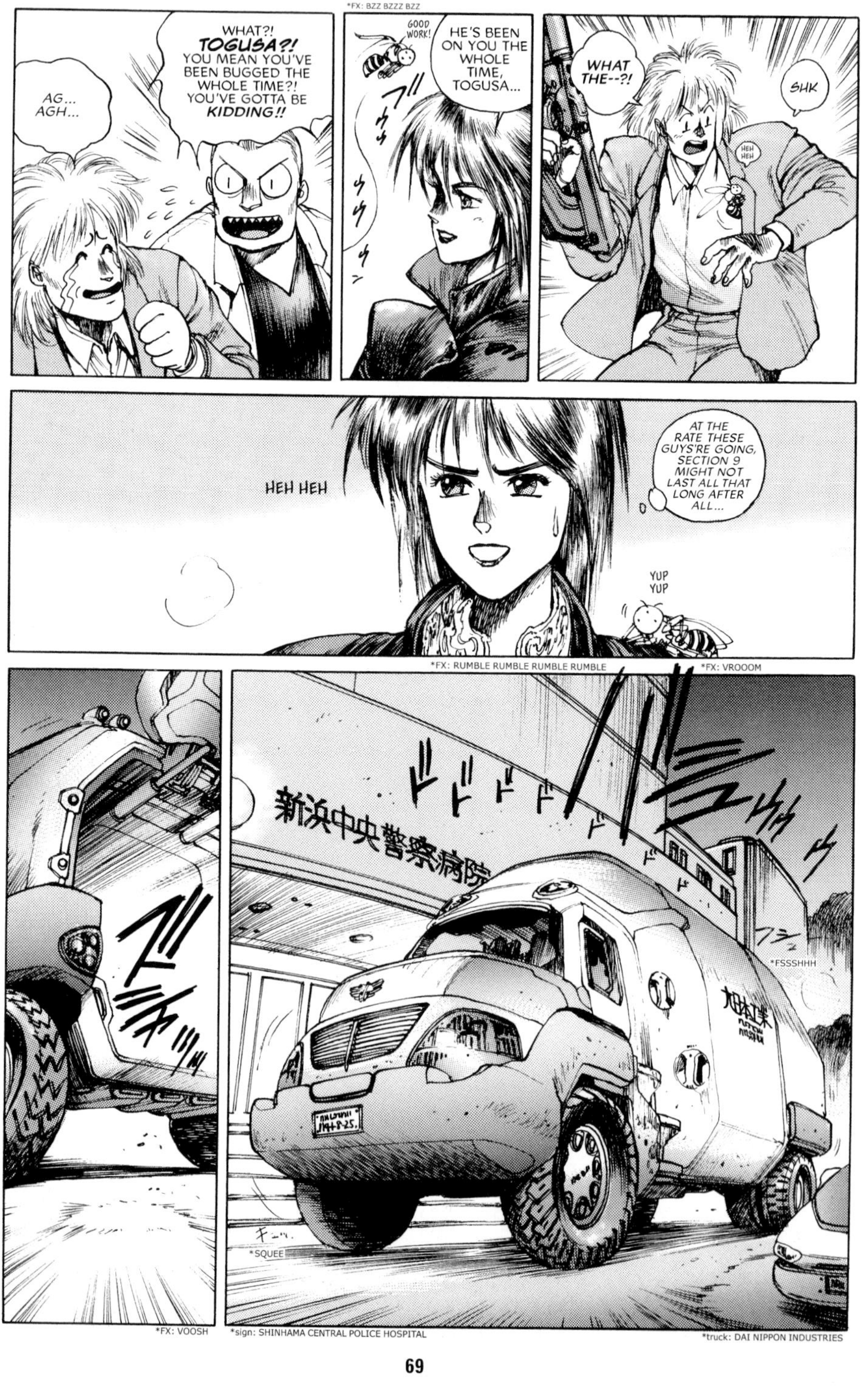
AG... AGH...
WHAT?! TOGUSA?! YOU MEAN YOU'VE BEEN BUGGED THE WHOLE TIME?! YOU'VE GOTTA BE KIDDING!!
*FX: BZZ BZZZ BZZ
GOOD WORK!
HE'S BEEN ON YOU THE WHOLE TIME, TOGUSA...
WHAT THE--?!
SHK
HEH HEH
HEH HEH
AT THE RATE THESE GUYS'RE GOING, SECTION 9 MIGHT NOT LAST ALL THAT LONG AFTER ALL...
YUP YUP
*FX: RUMBLE RUMBLE RUMBLE RUMBLE
*FX: VROOOM
新浜中央警察病院
*FSSSHHH
*SQUEE
*FX: VOOSH
*sign: SHINHAMA CENTRAL POLICE HOSPITAL
*truck: DAI NIPPON INDUSTRIES

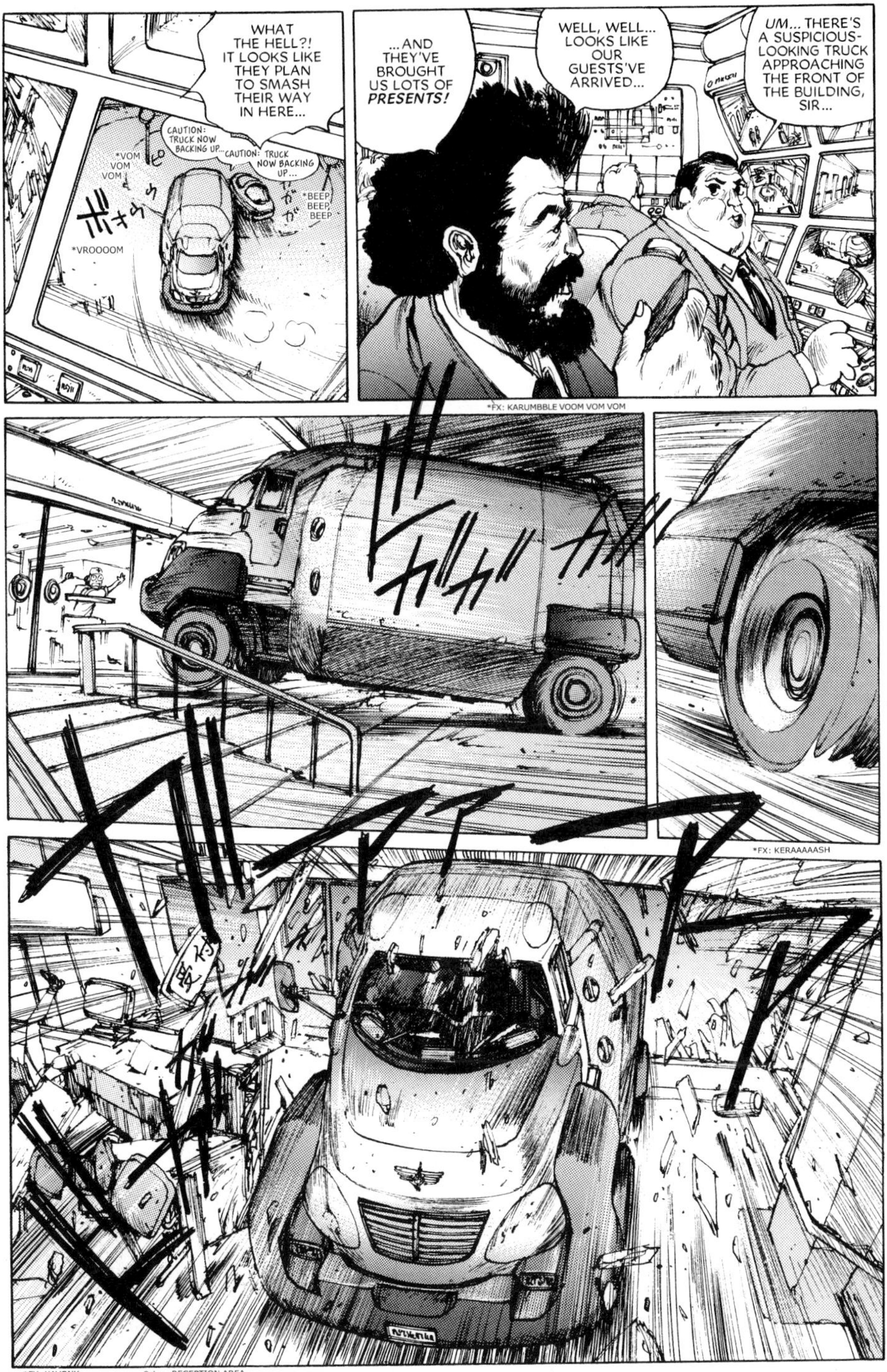
UM... THERE'S A SUSPICIOUS-LOOKING TRUCK APPROACHING THE FRONT OF THE BUILDING, SIR...
WELL, WELL... LOOKS LIKE OUR GUESTS'VE ARRIVED...
...AND THEY'VE BROUGHT US LOTS OF *PRESENTS!*
WHAT THE HELL?! IT LOOKS LIKE THEY PLAN TO SMASH THEIR WAY IN HERE...
CAUTION: TRUCK NOW BACKING UP...
CAUTION: TRUCK NOW BACKING UP...
*BEEP BEEP BEEP
*VOM VOM VOM
*VROOOOM

*FX: KARUMBBLE VOOM VOM VOM

*FX: KERAAAAASH

*FX: KAVONK *sign: RECEPTION AREA

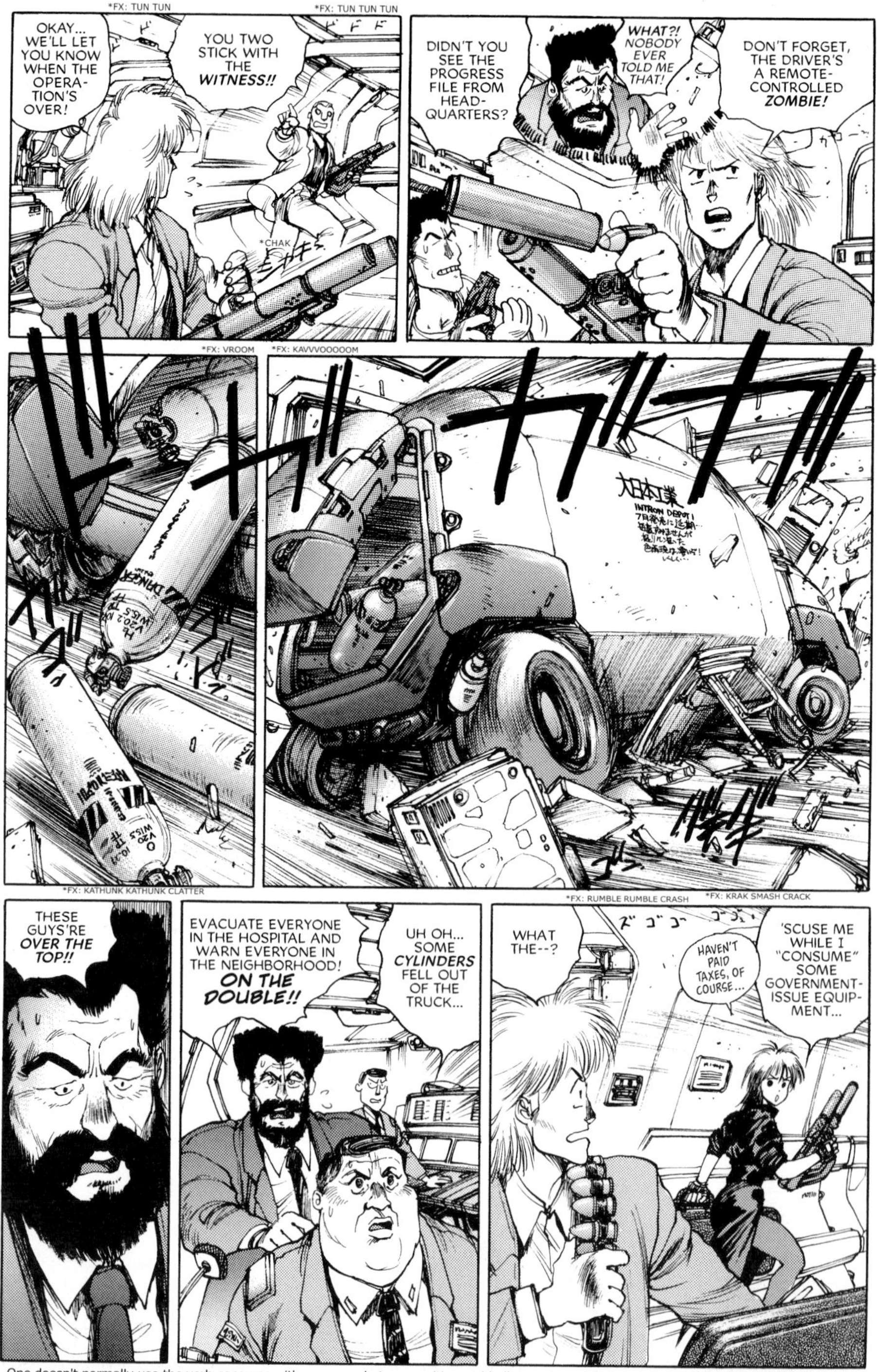
*FX: TUN TUN TUN
DON'T FORGET, THE DRIVER'S A REMOTE-CONTROLLED ZOMBIE!
WHAT?! NOBODY EVER TOLD ME THAT!
DIDN'T YOU SEE THE PROGRESS FILE FROM HEAD-QUARTERS?
*FX: TUN TUN
YOU TWO STICK WITH THE WITNESS!!
OKAY... WE'LL LET YOU KNOW WHEN THE OPERATION'S OVER!
*CHAK
*FX: KAVVVOOOOOM
*FX: RUMBLE RUMBLE CRASH
*FX: VROOM
*FX: KATHUNK KATHUNK CLATTER
*FX: KRAK SMASH CRACK
'SCUSE ME WHILE I "CONSUME" SOME GOVERNMENT-ISSUE EQUIPMENT...
HAVEN'T PAID TAXES, OF COURSE...
WHAT THE--?
UH OH... SOME CYLINDERS FELL OUT OF THE TRUCK...
EVACUATE EVERYONE IN THE HOSPITAL AND WARN EVERYONE IN THE NEIGHBORHOOD! ON THE DOUBLE!!
THESE GUYS'RE OVER THE TOP!!

One doesn't normally use the verb *consume* with weapons, but ammunition and bullets are consumed, so we're not just talking about "borrowing" in the strict sense. And when we talk about "using" explosives, we're talking about a license to "use/consume" them, and not just the "license to handle explosives" often seen in manga, etc. Just as one needs more than a license to drive a car (one needs the car itself)—in the case of explosives, the licensed user is usually supplied only the amount of material specified in the license...

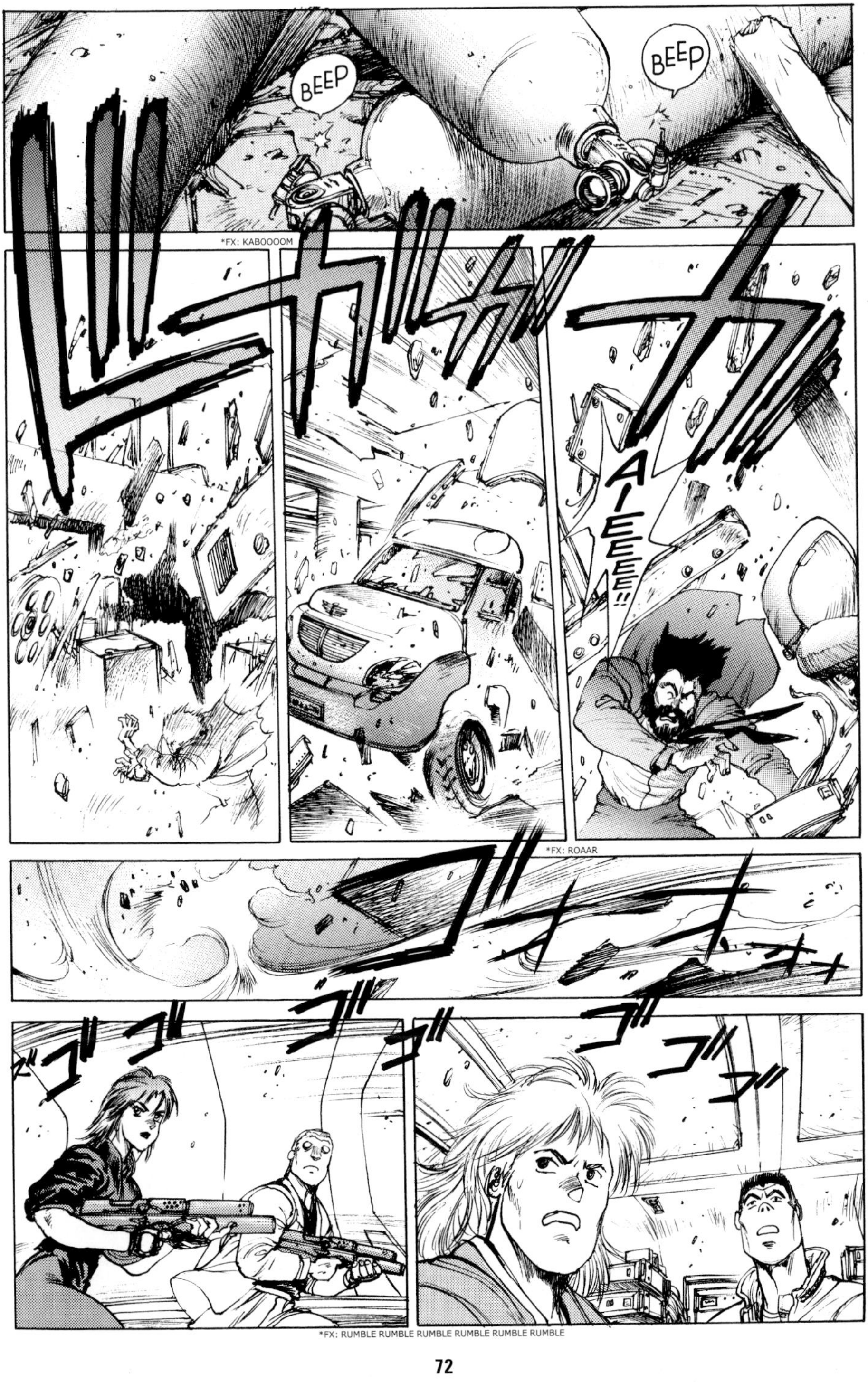
BEEP
BEEP
*FX: KABOOOOM
AIEEEEE!!
*FX: ROAAR
*FX: RUMBLE RUMBLE RUMBLE RUMBLE RUMBLE RUMBLE

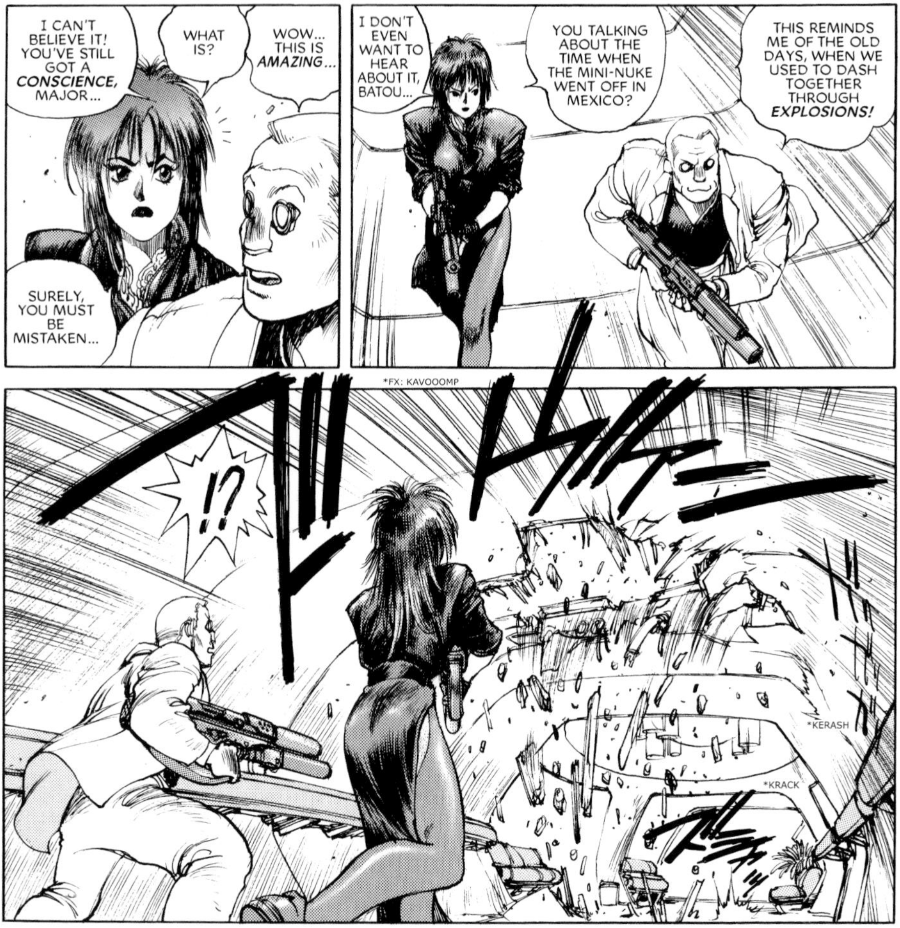
THIS REMINDS ME OF THE OLD DAYS, WHEN WE USED TO DASH TOGETHER THROUGH *EXPLOSIONS!*
YOU TALKING ABOUT THE TIME WHEN THE MINI-NUKE WENT OFF IN MEXICO?
I DON'T EVEN WANT TO HEAR ABOUT IT, BATOU...
WOW... THIS IS *AMAZING*...
WHAT IS?
I CAN'T BELIEVE IT! YOU'VE STILL GOT A ***CONSCIENCE,*** MAJOR...
SURELY, YOU MUST BE MISTAKEN...
*FX: KAVOOOMP
!?
*KERASH
*KRACK
!!
ISHIKAWA! ACTIVATE THE BUILDING'S FIREWALL AND THE SPRINKLER SYSTEM!!
... ...

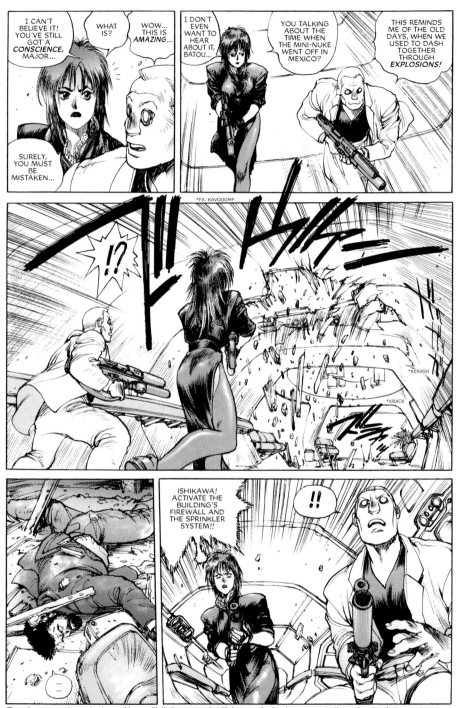

The pair may seem to running in an odd way with their weapons, but it's because they're always concentrating on keeping their upper torsos properly aligned, and mainly moving their lower torsos. I know it would look "cooler" to draw them running bent at the waist, waving their guns about, but these are two highly trained professionals, entirely incapable of assuming a specific stance just for the sake of looking "cool." In reality, their stance is actually far superior, both in terms of stability and reaction times...

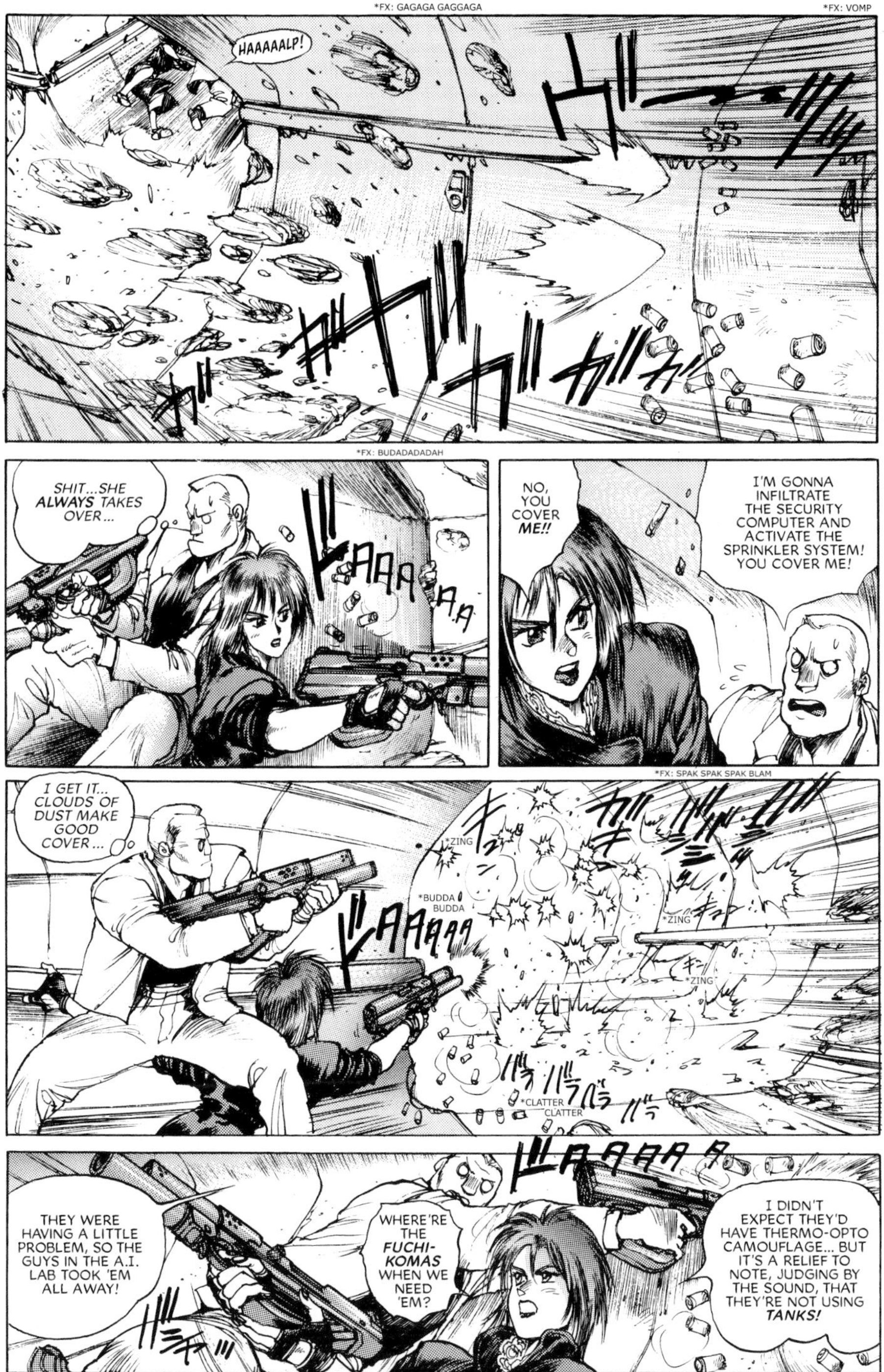
*FX: VOMP
*FX: GAGAGA GAGGAGA
HAAAAALP!
*FX: BUDADADADAH
I'M GONNA INFILTRATE THE SECURITY COMPUTER AND ACTIVATE THE SPRINKLER SYSTEM! YOU COVER ME!
NO, YOU COVER *ME!!*
*SHIT...SHE **ALWAYS** TAKES OVER...*
*FX: SPAK SPAK SPAK BLAM
*ZING
*ZING
*ZING
*BUDDA BUDDA
*CLATTER CLATTER
I GET IT... CLOUDS OF DUST MAKE GOOD COVER...
I DIDN'T EXPECT THEY'D HAVE THERMO-OPTO CAMOUFLAGE... BUT IT'S A RELIEF TO NOTE, JUDGING BY THE SOUND, THAT THEY'RE NOT USING ***TANKS!***
WHERE'RE THE ***FUCHI-KOMAS*** WHEN WE NEED 'EM?
THEY WERE HAVING A LITTLE PROBLEM, SO THE GUYS IN THE A.I. LAB TOOK 'EM ALL AWAY!
*FX: BUDADADADAH
*FX: KASHAK

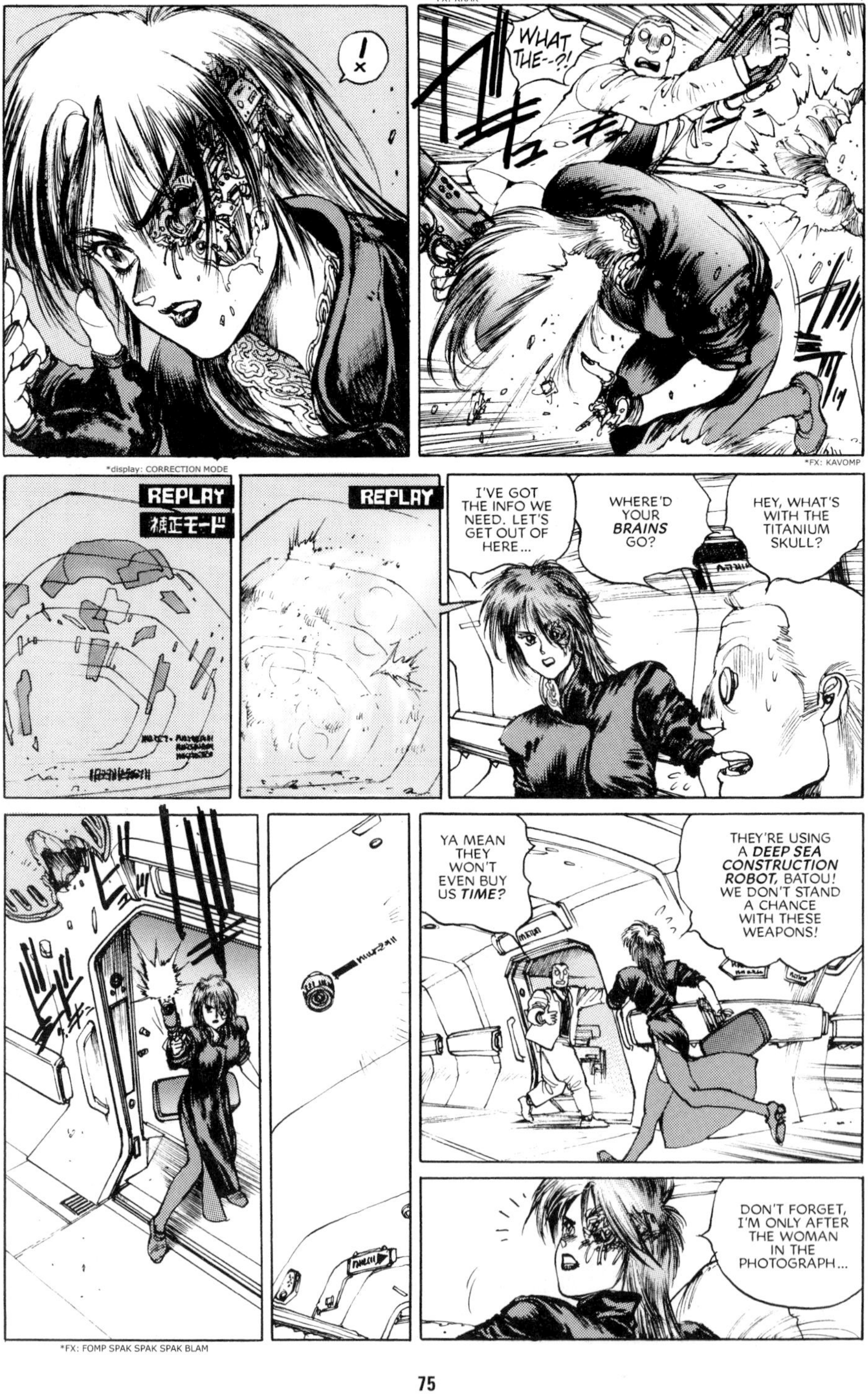
!
WHAT THE--?!
REPLAY
補正モード
REPLAY
I'VE GOT THE INFO WE NEED. LET'S GET OUT OF HERE...
WHERE'D YOUR BRAINS GO?
HEY, WHAT'S WITH THE TITANIUM SKULL?
YA MEAN THEY WON'T EVEN BUY US TIME?
THEY'RE USING A DEEP SEA CONSTRUCTION ROBOT, BATOU! WE DON'T STAND A CHANCE WITH THESE WEAPONS!
DON'T FORGET, I'M ONLY AFTER THE WOMAN IN THE PHOTOGRAPH...

*FX: KRAK

*FX: KAVOMP

*display: CORRECTION MODE

*FX: FOMP SPAK SPAK SPAK BLAM

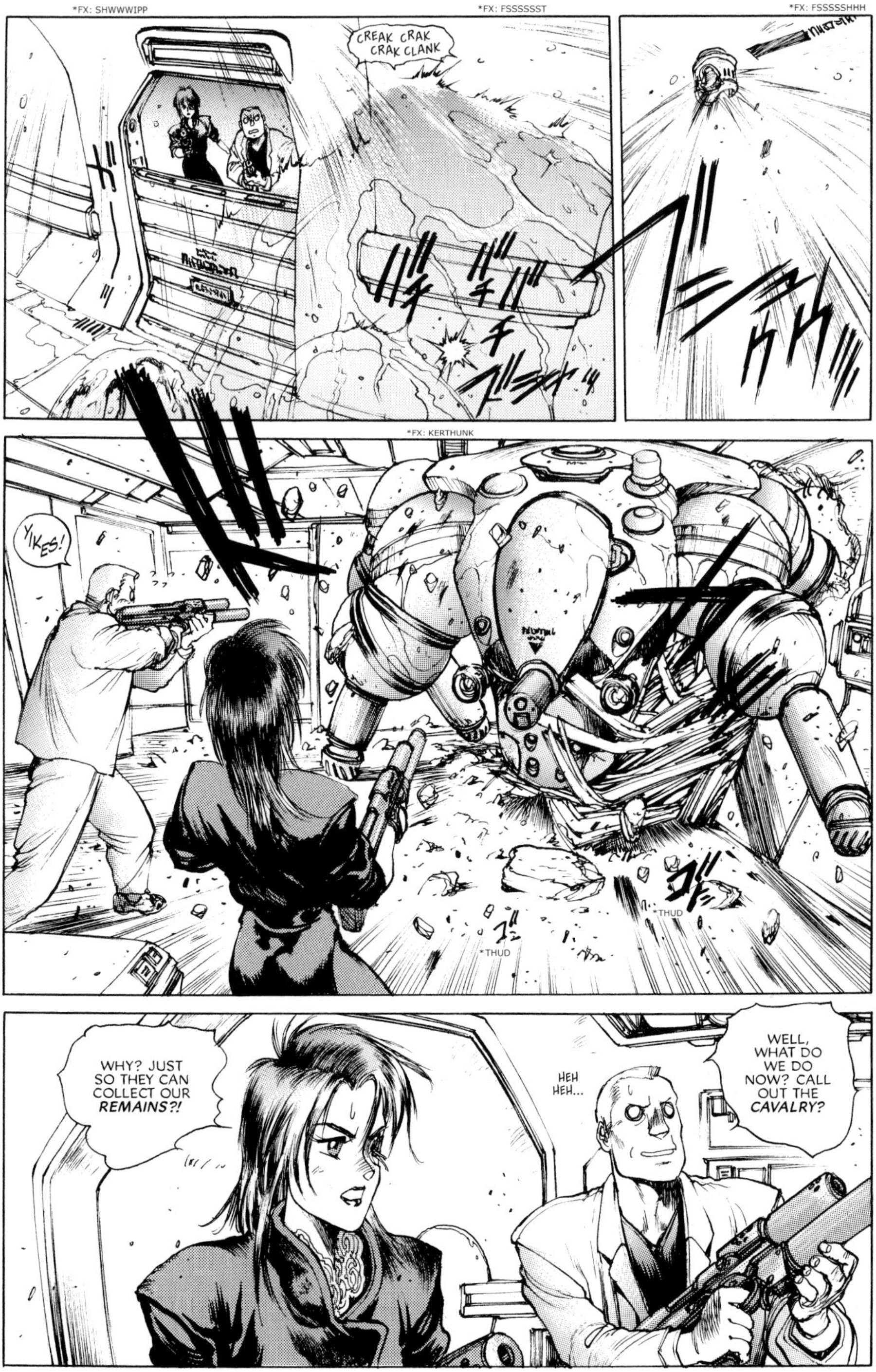
*FX: FSSSSSHHH
*FX: FSSSSSST
CREAK CRAK CRAK CLANK
*FX: SHWWWIPP
*FX: KERTHUNK
YIKES!
*THUD
*THUD
WELL, WHAT DO WE DO NOW? CALL OUT THE *CAVALRY?*
HEH HEH...
WHY? JUST SO THEY CAN COLLECT OUR ***REMAINS?!***

DRIVE SLAVE Part 2

1992

04

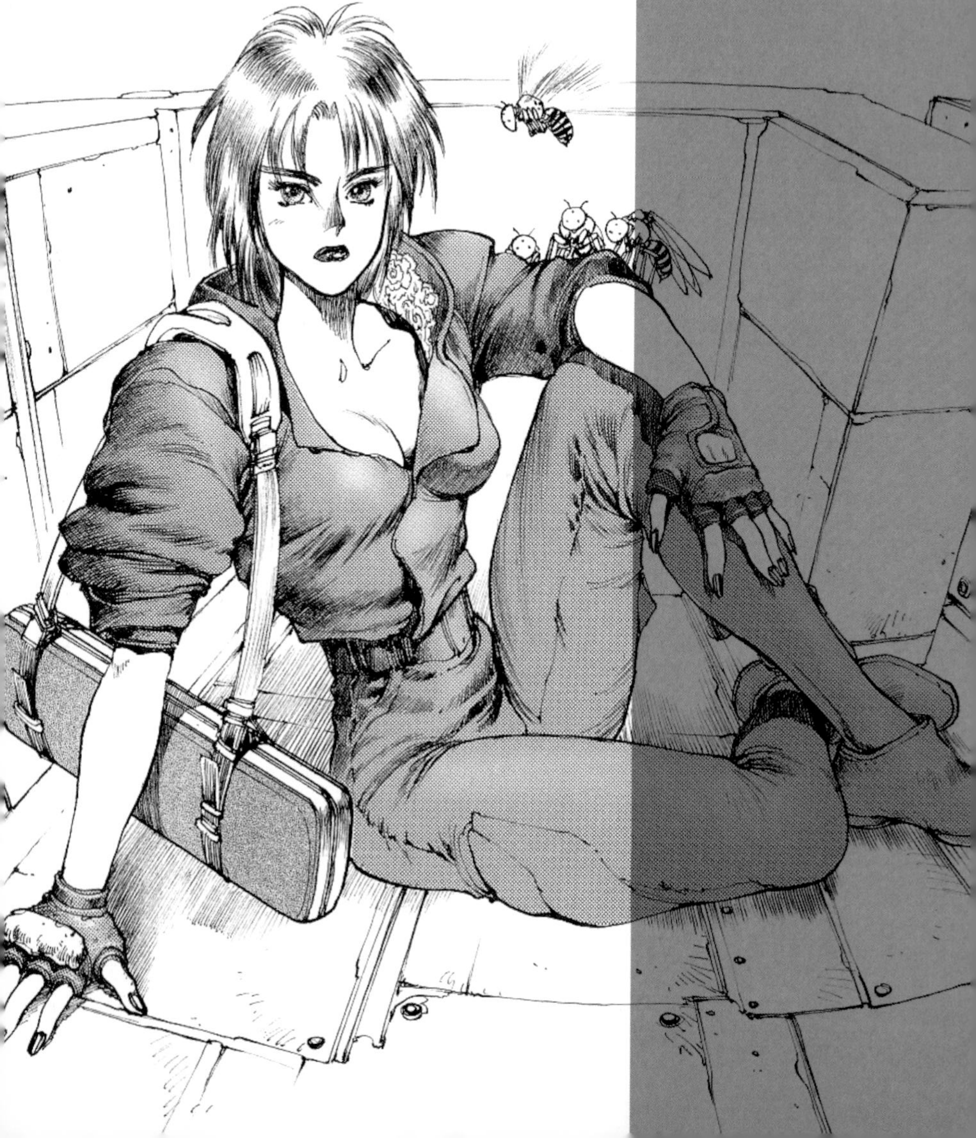

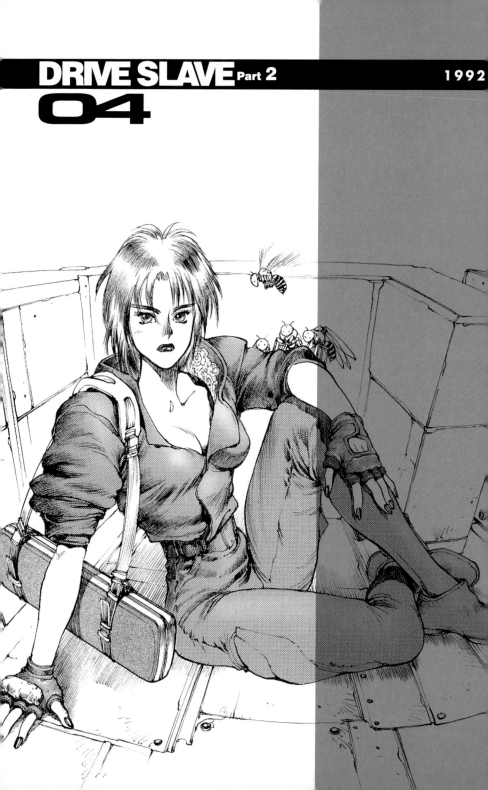

*FX: BZZZ

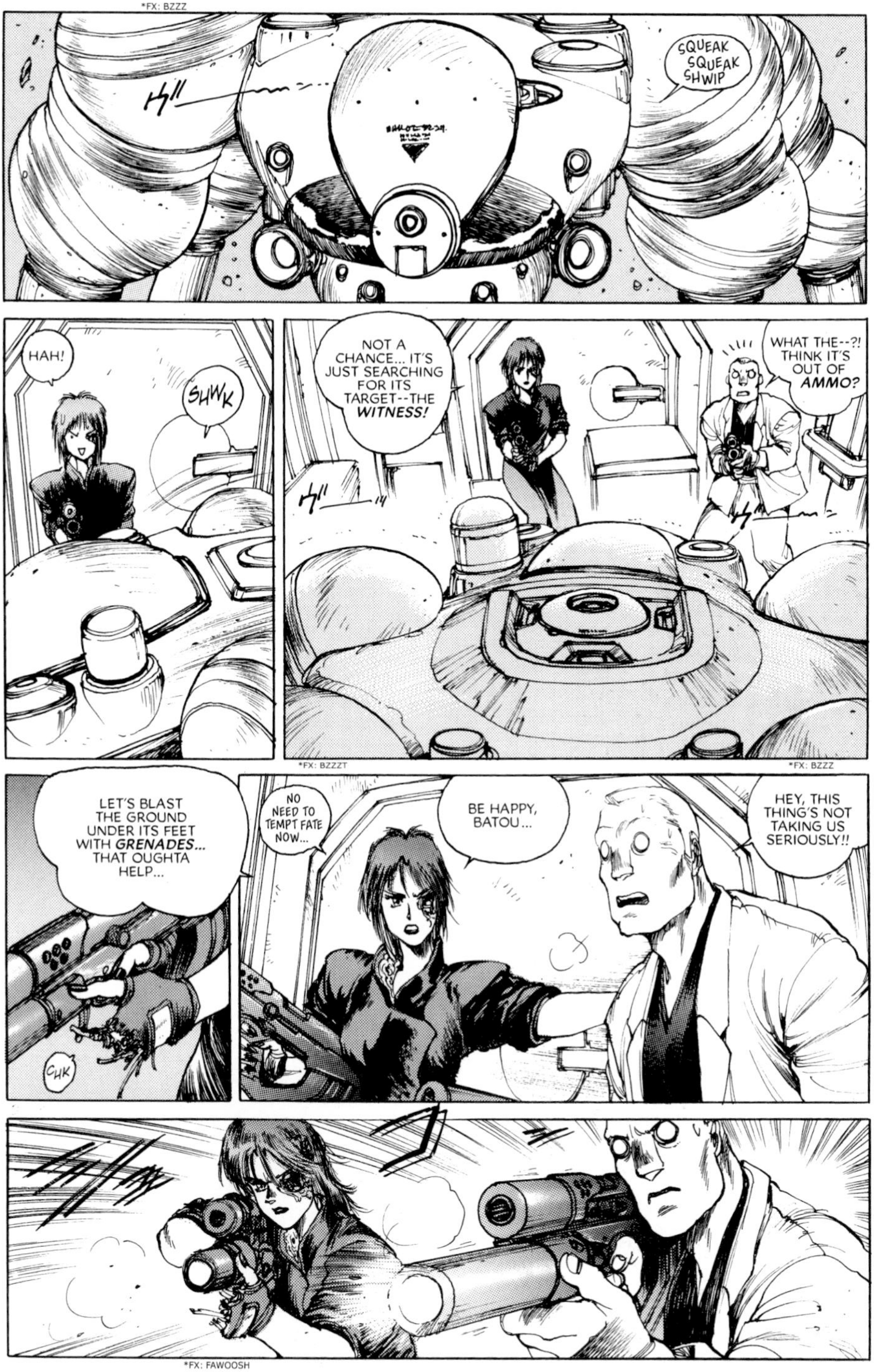
SQUEAK
SQUEAK
SHWIP
WHAT THE--?! THINK IT'S OUT OF AMMO?
NOT A CHANCE... IT'S JUST SEARCHING FOR ITS TARGET--THE WITNESS!
SHWK
HAH!
HEY, THIS THING'S NOT TAKING US SERIOUSLY!!
BE HAPPY, BATOU...
NO NEED TO TEMPT FATE NOW...
LET'S BLAST THE GROUND UNDER ITS FEET WITH GRENADES... THAT OUGHTA HELP...
CHK

*FX: BZZZ

*FX: BZZZT

*FX: FAWOOSH

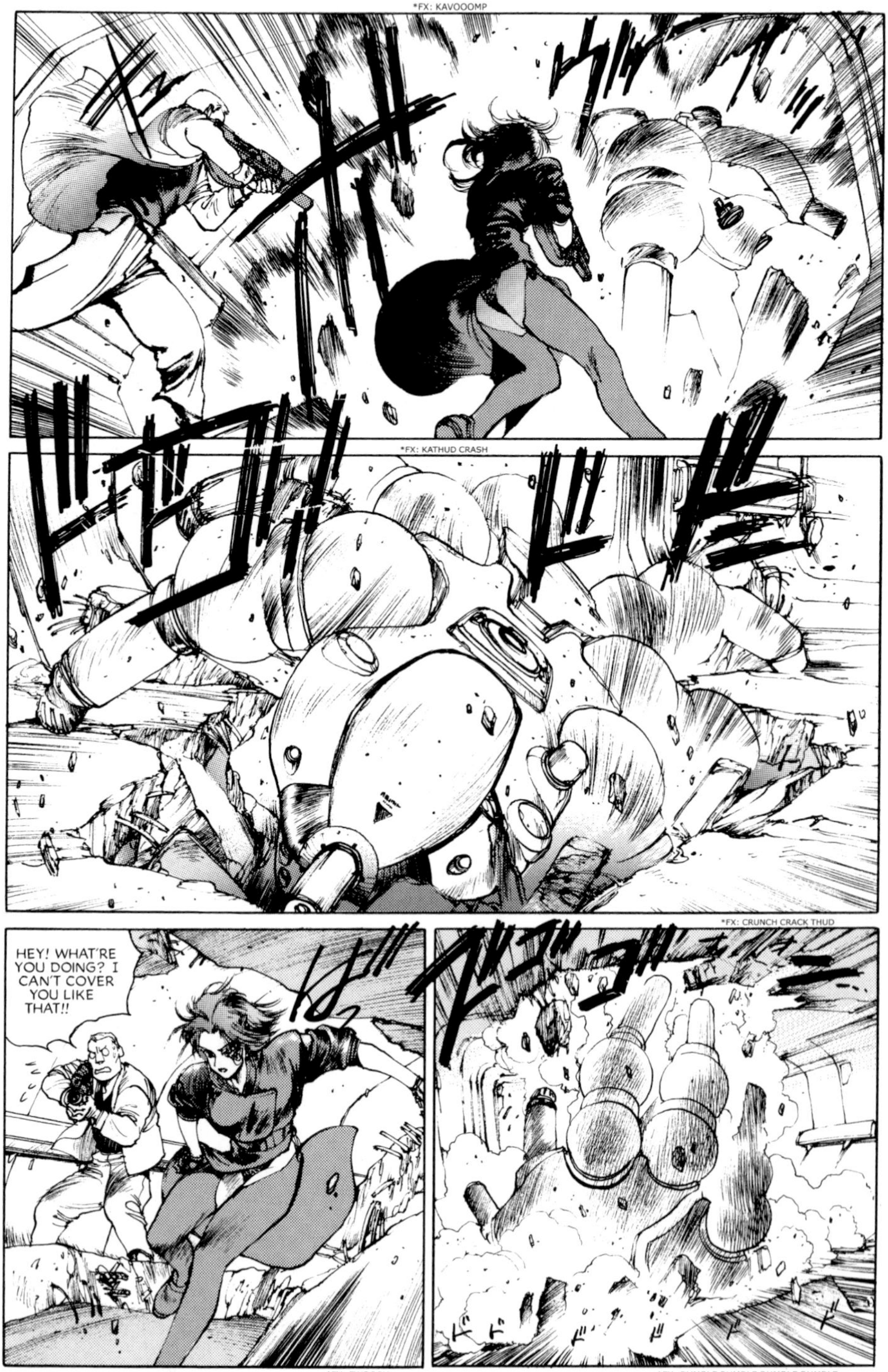
*FX: KAVOOOMP
*FX: KATHUD CRASH
*FX: CRUNCH CRACK THUD
*FX: RUMBLE RUMBLE RUMBLE RUMBLE
HEY! WHAT'RE YOU DOING? I CAN'T COVER YOU LIKE THAT!!
*FX: FWOOSH

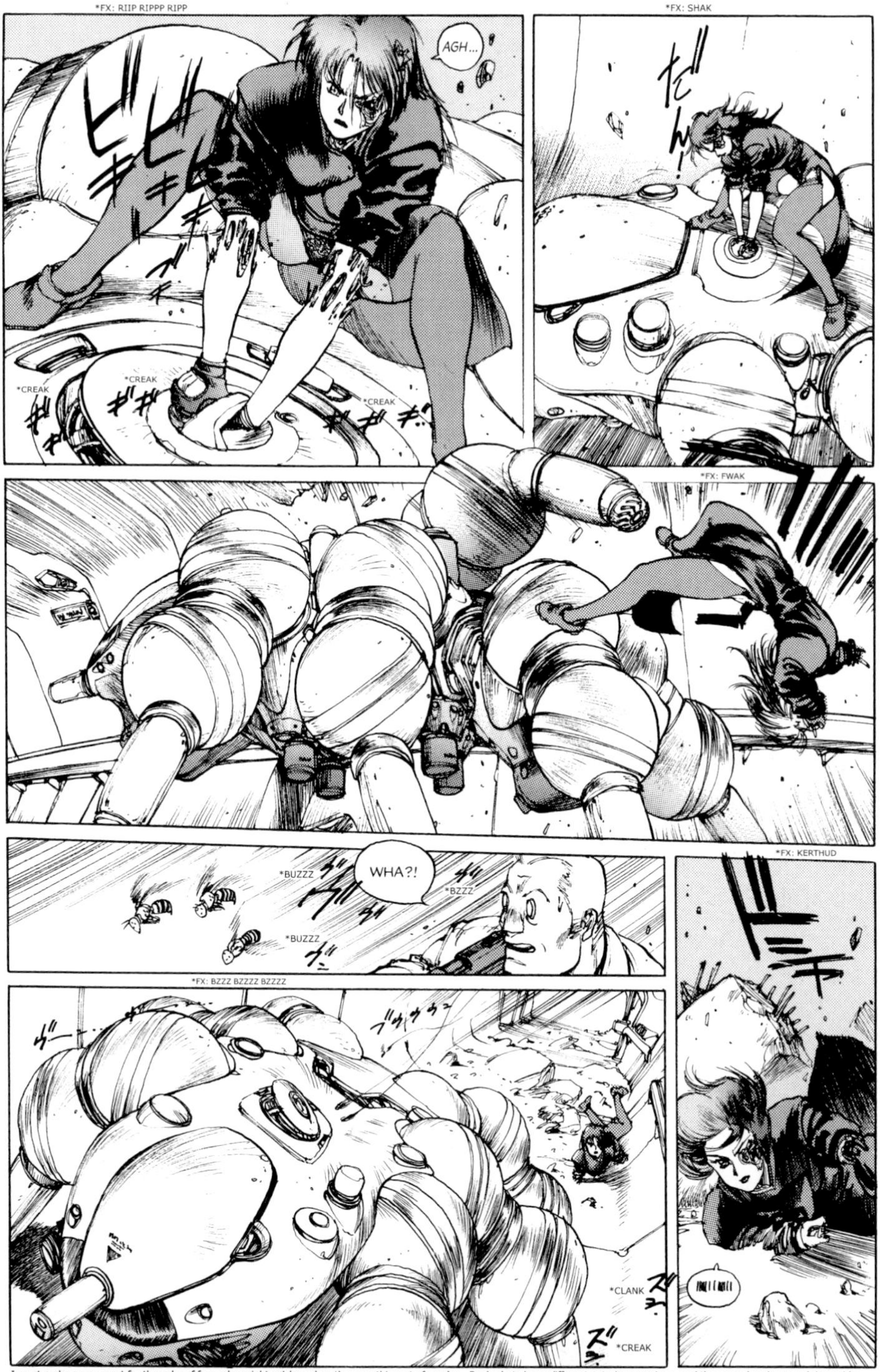
*FX: SHAK
*FX: RIIP RIPPP RIPP
AGH...
*CREAK
*CREAK
*CREAK
*FX: FWAK
*FX: KERTHUD
WHA?!
*BUZZZ
*BZZZ
*BUZZZ
*FX: BZZZ BZZZZ BZZZZ
*CLANK
*CREAK

I must make a comment for the sake of fans who might snicker when they see this sort of mecha... Real robots have different exterior coverings, and they are already at work in a wide variety of industries. So it's a little behind the times to say this one is "something out of sci-fi." The real-life robots that most resemble my drawing here are surely those developed for work in extremely hazardous environments—such as the six-legged model designed to work in undersea oil fields, or "Ken-Chan," which was developed to work in nuclear reactors. Of course "robots" in this case are actually remote-controlled, so whether they should really be called "robots" is probably open to debate. Just for reference, although the word *robot* appears man times in the officially recognized list of J.I.S. (Japan Industrial Standards) terms, there apparently is, strictly speaking, no single, universally agreed-upon definition in existence...

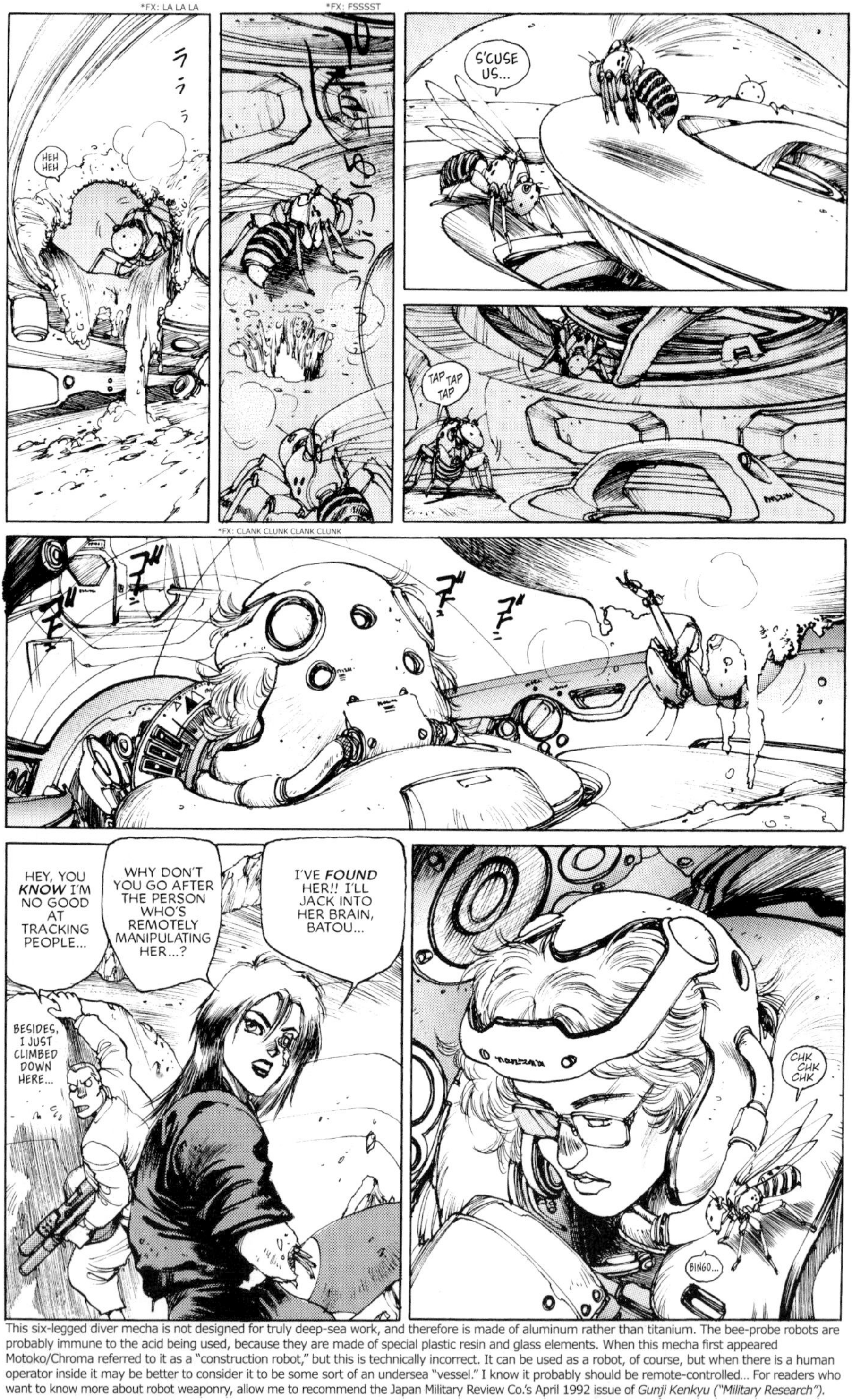
S'CUSE US...
TAP TAP TAP
*FX: FSSST
*FX: LA LA LA
HEH HEH
*FX: CLANK CLUNK CLANK CLUNK
CHK CHK CHK
BINGO...
I'VE *FOUND* HER!! I'LL JACK INTO HER BRAIN, BATOU...
WHY DON'T YOU GO AFTER THE PERSON WHO'S REMOTELY MANIPULATING HER...?
HEY, YOU *KNOW* I'M NO GOOD AT TRACKING PEOPLE...
BESIDES, I JUST CLIMBED DOWN HERE...

This six-legged diver mecha is not designed for truly deep-sea work, and therefore is made of aluminum rather than titanium. The bee-probe robots are probably immune to the acid being used, because they are made of special plastic resin and glass elements. When this mecha first appeared Motoko/Chroma referred to it as a "construction robot," but this is technically incorrect. It can be used as a robot, of course, but when there is a human operator inside it may be better to consider it to be some sort of an undersea "vessel." I know it probably should be remote-controlled... For readers who want to know more about robot weaponry, allow me to recommend the Japan Military Review Co.'s April 1992 issue of *Gunji Kenkyu ("Military Research")*.

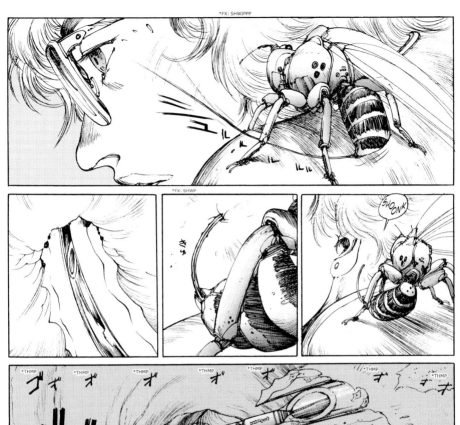

SHOONK

*THMP *THMP *THMP *THMP *THMP *THMP *THMP

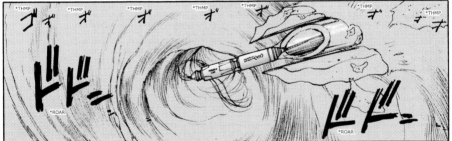

*ROAR *ROAR

...

*THMP *THMP *THMP *THMP

PHEW...

*THUNK

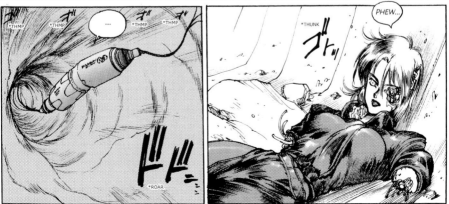

*ROAR

I could have shown red blood corpuscles roaring through the inside of blood vessels, a la *Fantastic Voyage,* but with the sort of microsurgery I'm depicting here, millimeter-scale machines are used, so red corpuscles, which are nearly a thousand times smaller, wouldn't be very visible. I do worry that the blood vessel I've drawn looks like some sort of gritty liquid, but what the heck... The forward part of the tiny machine shown here, with the flagella-like protrusions, is designed to help the device navigate the blood flow; adjusting its length also adjusts the machine's speed. The line protruding out of the rear of the device is not flagella, but a life-line. In the first panel on this page the bee-probe is shown getting the air out of its stinger-like tube...

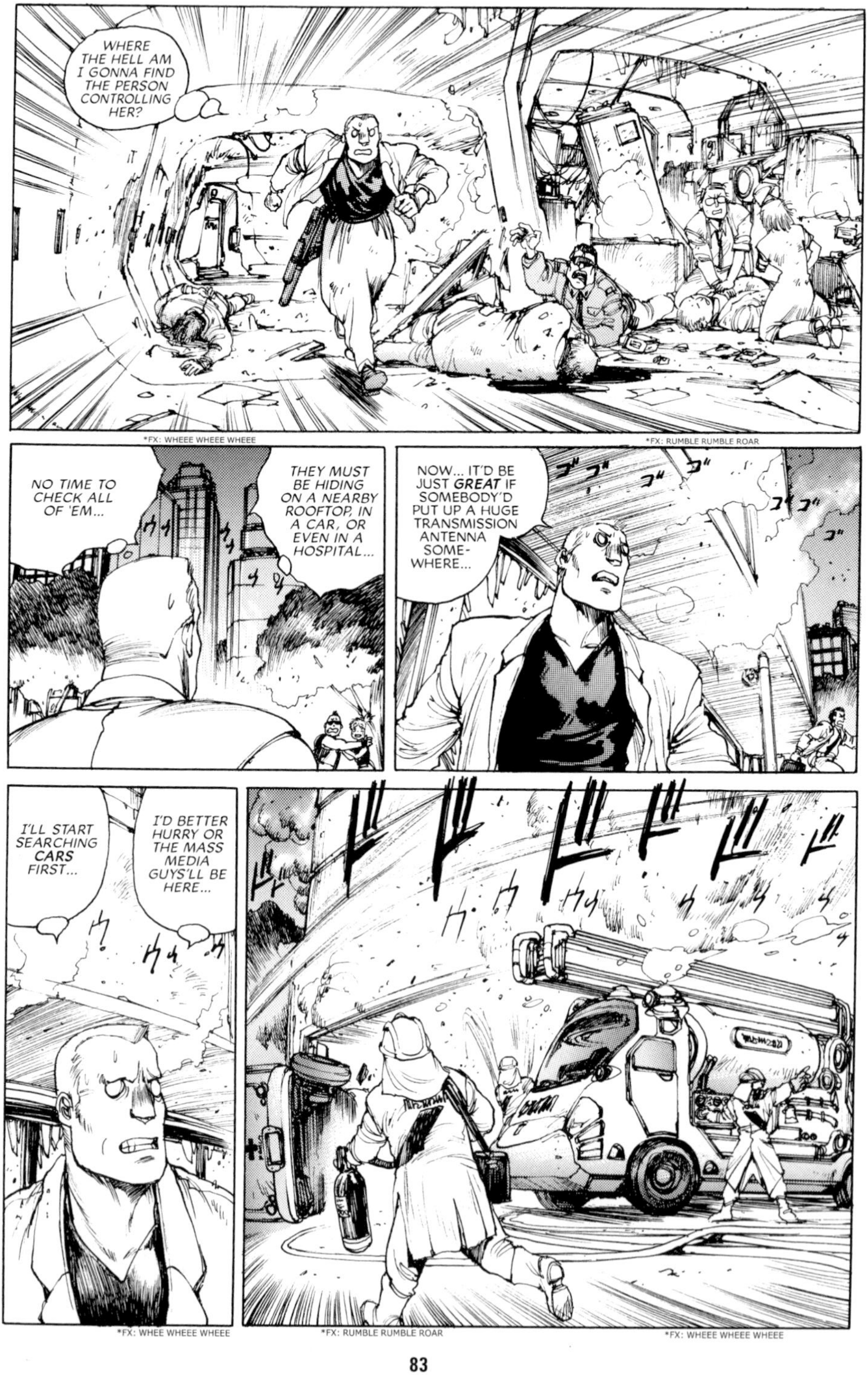
WHERE THE HELL AM I GONNA FIND THE PERSON CONTROLLING HER?
NO TIME TO CHECK ALL OF 'EM...
THEY MUST BE HIDING ON A NEARBY ROOFTOP, IN A CAR, OR EVEN IN A HOSPITAL...
NOW... IT'D BE JUST **GREAT** IF SOMEBODY'D PUT UP A HUGE TRANSMISSION ANTENNA SOME-WHERE...
I'LL START SEARCHING **CARS** FIRST...
I'D BETTER HURRY OR THE MASS MEDIA GUYS'LL BE HERE...
*FX: WHEEE WHEEE WHEEE
*FX: RUMBLE RUMBLE ROAR
*FX: WHEE WHEEE WHEEE
*FX: RUMBLE RUMBLE ROAR
*FX: WHEEE WHEEE WHEEE

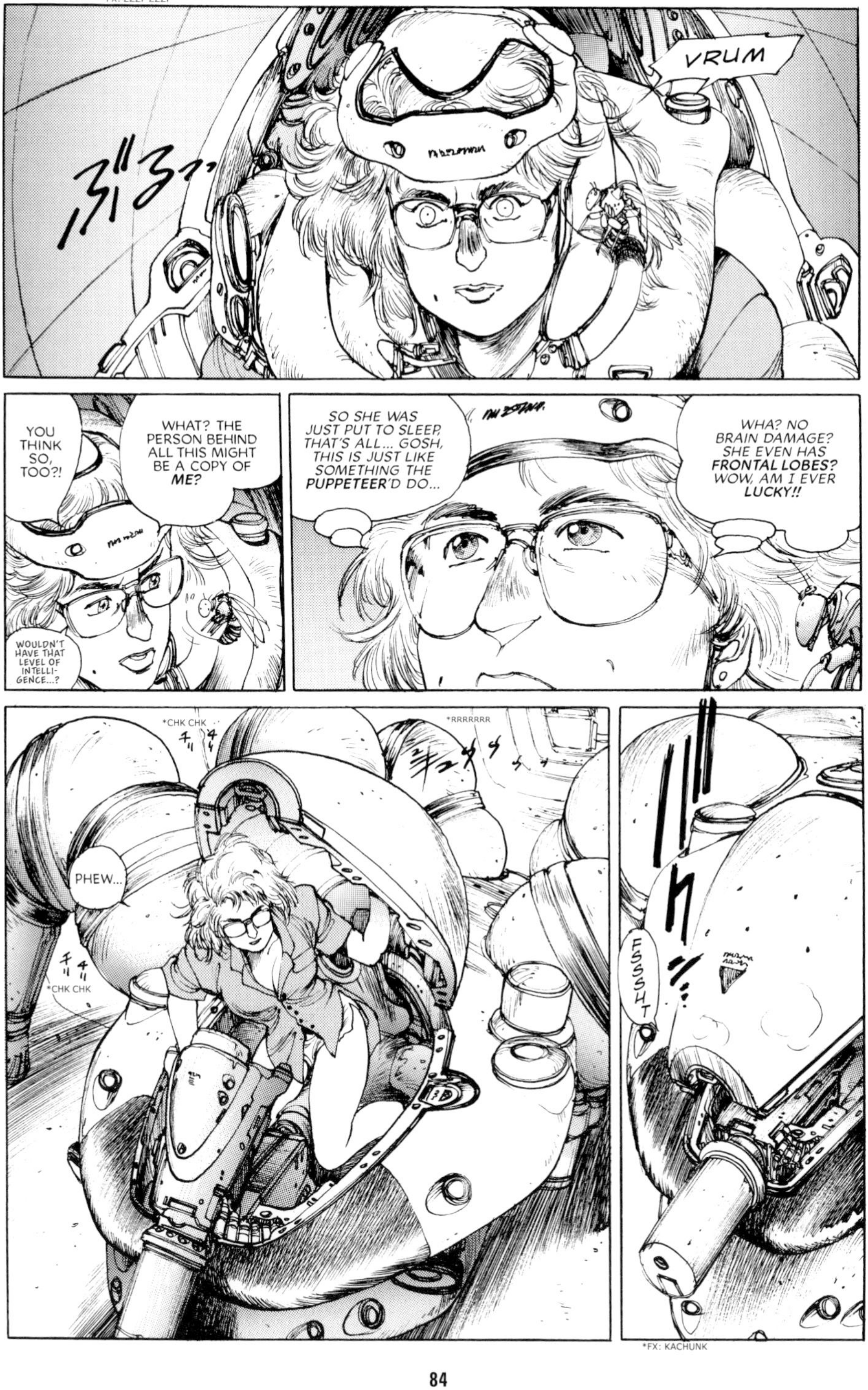
*FX: ZZZP ZZZP
VRUM
WHA? NO BRAIN DAMAGE? SHE EVEN HAS **FRONTAL LOBES?** WOW, AM I EVER **LUCKY!!**
SO SHE WAS JUST PUT TO SLEEP, THAT'S ALL... GOSH, THIS IS JUST LIKE SOMETHING THE ***PUPPETEER****'D DO...*
WHAT? THE PERSON BEHIND ALL THIS MIGHT BE A COPY OF **ME?**
YOU THINK SO, TOO?!
WOULDN'T HAVE THAT LEVEL OF INTELLIGENCE...?
FSSSHT
*FX: KACHUNK
*RRRRRRR
*CHK CHK
PHEW...
*CHK CHK

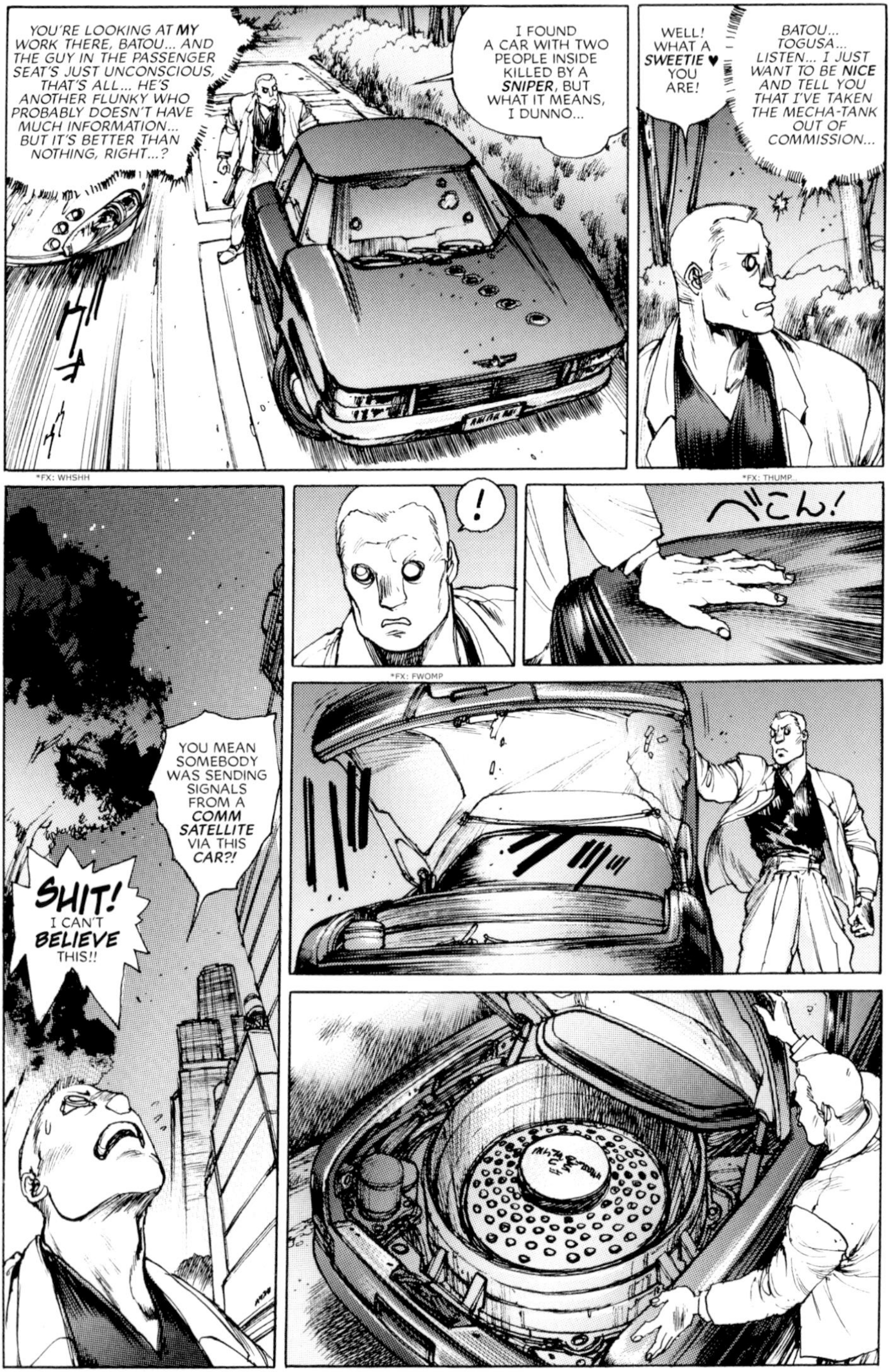
YOU'RE LOOKING AT MY WORK THERE, BATOU... AND THE GUY IN THE PASSENGER SEAT'S JUST UNCONSCIOUS, THAT'S ALL... HE'S ANOTHER FLUNKY WHO PROBABLY DOESN'T HAVE MUCH INFORMATION... BUT IT'S BETTER THAN NOTHING, RIGHT...?
I FOUND A CAR WITH TWO PEOPLE INSIDE KILLED BY A SNIPER, BUT WHAT IT MEANS, I DUNNO...
*FX: WHSHH
BATOU... TOGUSA... LISTEN... I JUST WANT TO BE NICE AND TELL YOU THAT I'VE TAKEN THE MECHA-TANK OUT OF COMMISSION...
WELL! WHAT A SWEETIE ♥ YOU ARE!
!
*FX: THUMP...
べこん!
*FX: FWOMP
YOU MEAN SOMEBODY WAS SENDING SIGNALS FROM A COMM SATELLITE VIA THIS CAR?!
SHIT! I CAN'T BELIEVE THIS!!

*FX: RUMBLE RUMBLE ROAR

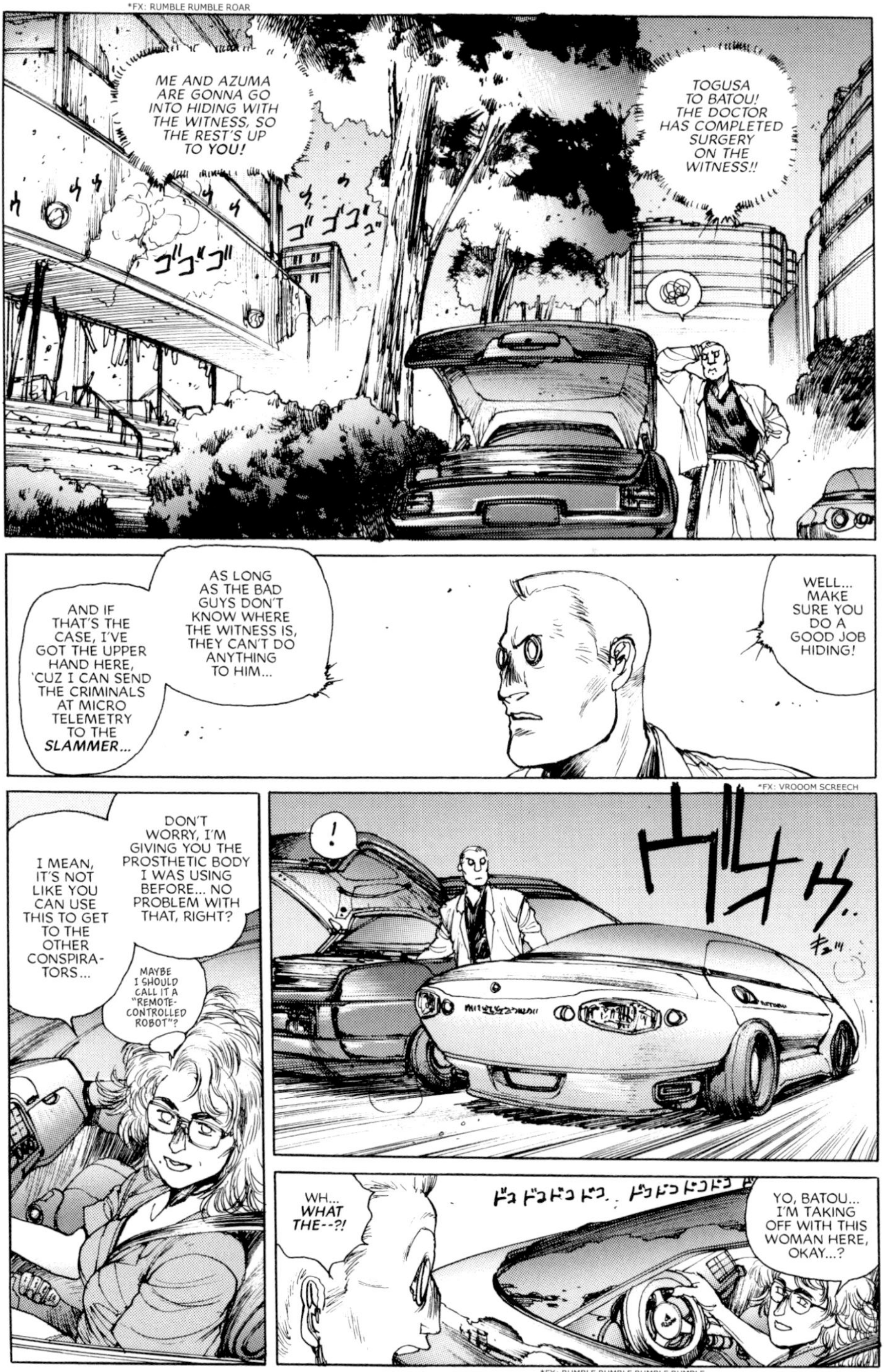
TOGUSA TO BATOU! THE DOCTOR HAS COMPLETED SURGERY ON THE WITNESS!!
ME AND AZUMA ARE GONNA GO INTO HIDING WITH THE WITNESS, SO THE REST'S UP TO YOU!
WELL... MAKE SURE YOU DO A GOOD JOB HIDING!
AS LONG AS THE BAD GUYS DON'T KNOW WHERE THE WITNESS IS, THEY CAN'T DO ANYTHING TO HIM...
AND IF THAT'S THE CASE, I'VE GOT THE UPPER HAND HERE, 'CUZ I CAN SEND THE CRIMINALS AT MICRO TELEMETRY TO THE SLAMMER...
*FX: VROOOM SCREECH
!
YO, BATOU... I'M TAKING OFF WITH THIS WOMAN HERE, OKAY...?
WH... WHAT THE--?!
DON'T WORRY, I'M GIVING YOU THE PROSTHETIC BODY I WAS USING BEFORE... NO PROBLEM WITH THAT, RIGHT?
I MEAN, IT'S NOT LIKE YOU CAN USE THIS TO GET TO THE OTHER CONSPIRATORS...
MAYBE I SHOULD CALL IT A "REMOTE-CONTROLLED ROBOT"?

*FX: RUMBLE RUMBLE RUMBLE RUMBLE

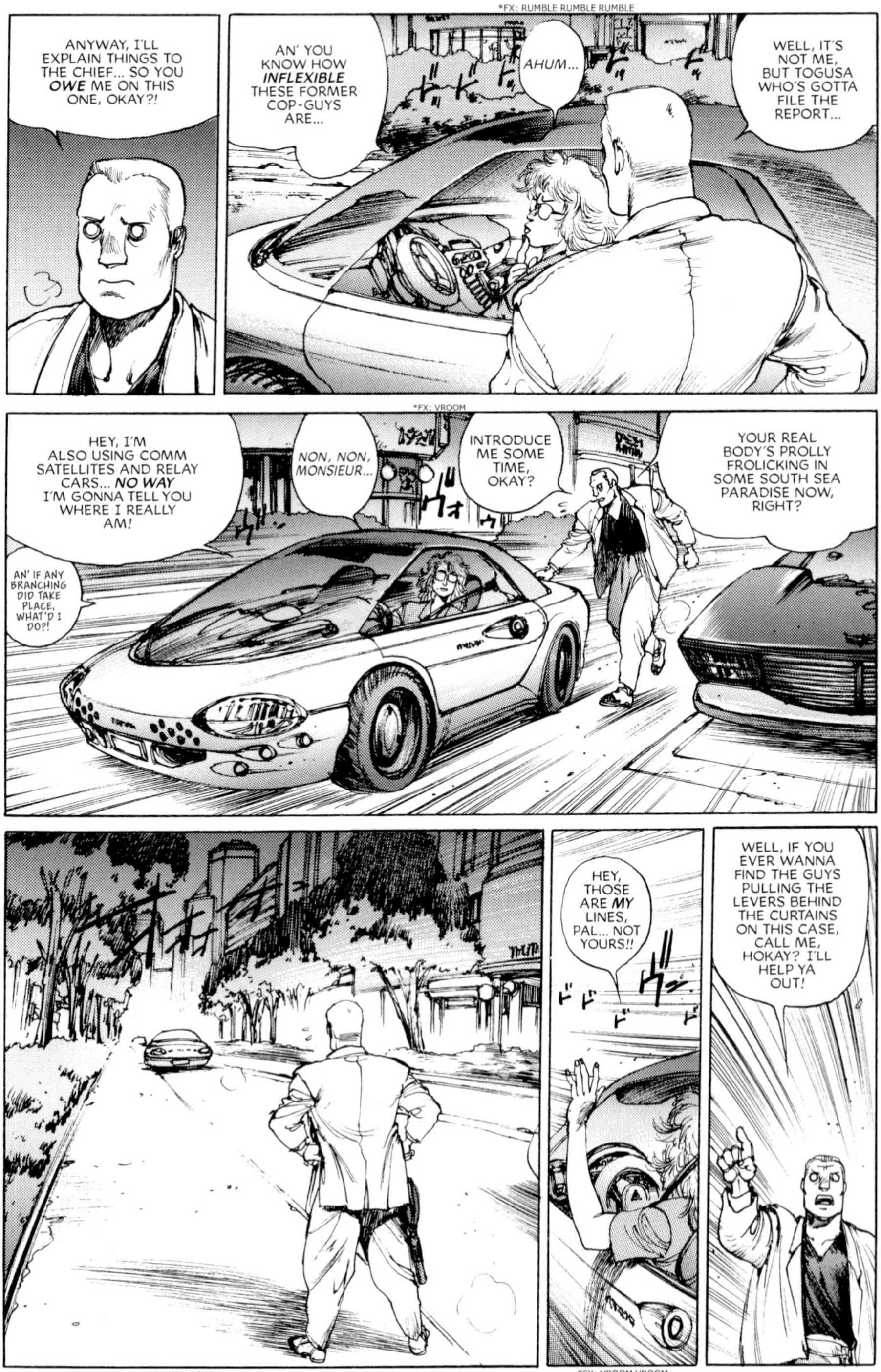
*FX: RUMBLE RUMBLE RUMBLE
WELL, IT'S NOT ME, BUT TOGUSA WHO'S GOTTA FILE THE REPORT...
AHUM...
AN' YOU KNOW HOW INFLEXIBLE THESE FORMER COP-GUYS ARE...
ANYWAY, I'LL EXPLAIN THINGS TO THE CHIEF... SO YOU OWE ME ON THIS ONE, OKAY?!
*FX: VROOM
YOUR REAL BODY'S PROLLY FROLICKING IN SOME SOUTH SEA PARADISE NOW, RIGHT?
INTRODUCE ME SOME TIME, OKAY?
NON, NON, MONSIEUR...
HEY, I'M ALSO USING COMM SATELLITES AND RELAY CARS... NO WAY I'M GONNA TELL YOU WHERE I REALLY AM!
AN' IF ANY BRANCHING DID TAKE PLACE, WHAT'D I DO?!
WELL, IF YOU EVER WANNA FIND THE GUYS PULLING THE LEVERS BEHIND THE CURTAINS ON THIS CASE, CALL ME, HOKAY? I'LL HELP YA OUT!
HEY, THOSE ARE MY LINES, PAL... NOT YOURS!!
*FX: VROOM VROOM
*FX: ROAR

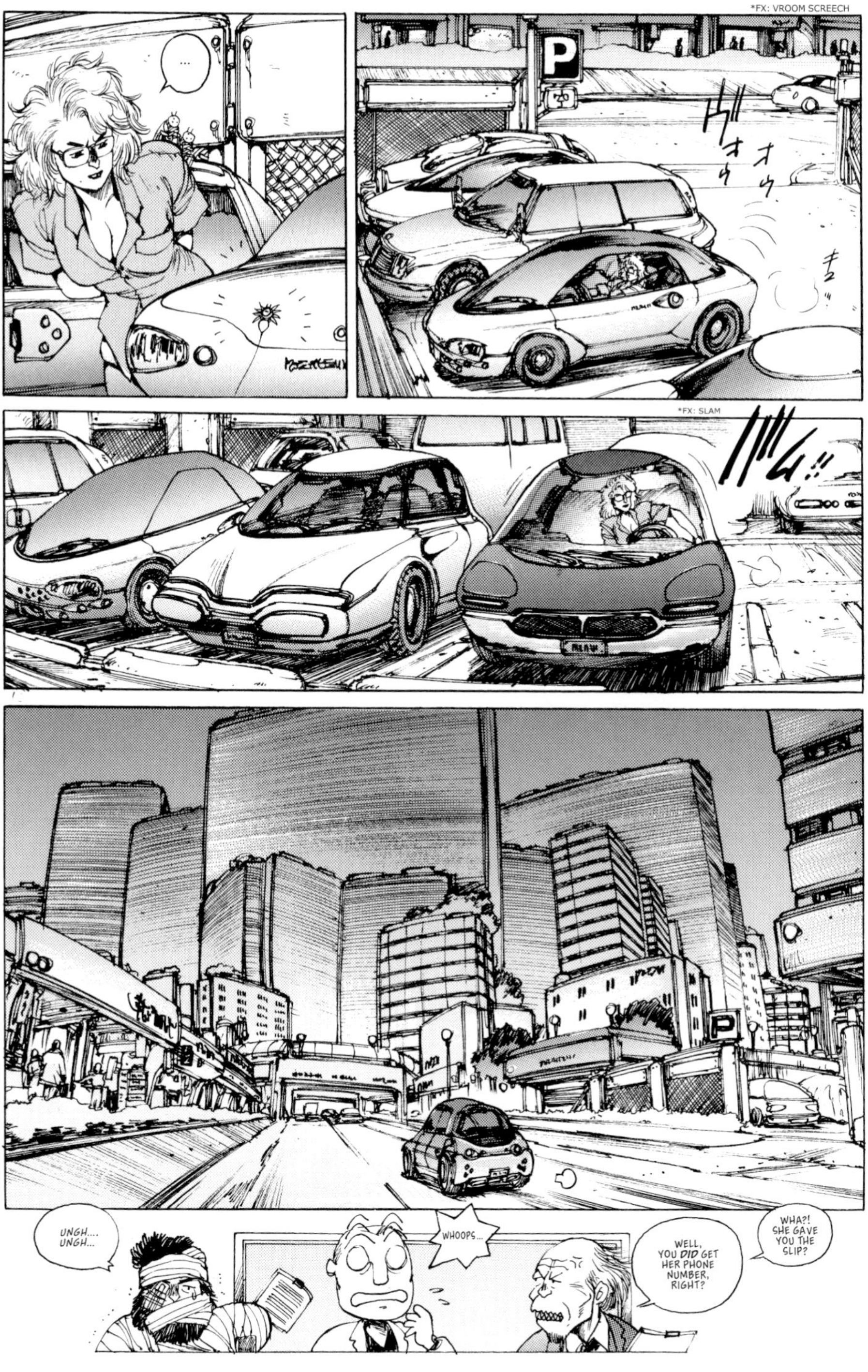
*FX: VROOM SCREECH
...
*FX: SLAM
WHA?! SHE GAVE YOU THE SLIP?
WELL, YOU *DID* GET HER PHONE NUMBER, RIGHT?
WHOOPS...
UNGH.... UNGH...

05 MINES OF MIND Part 1

1995

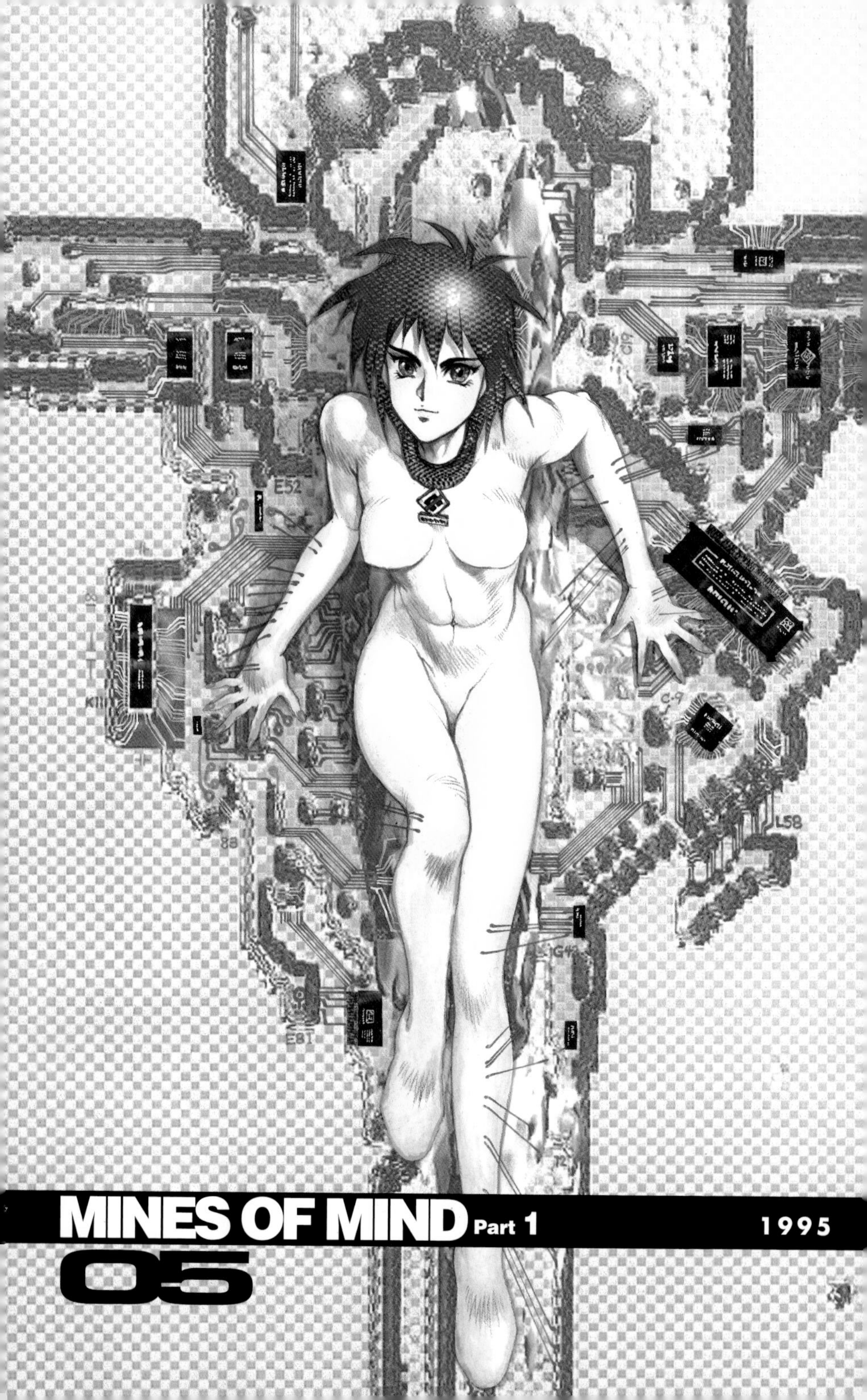

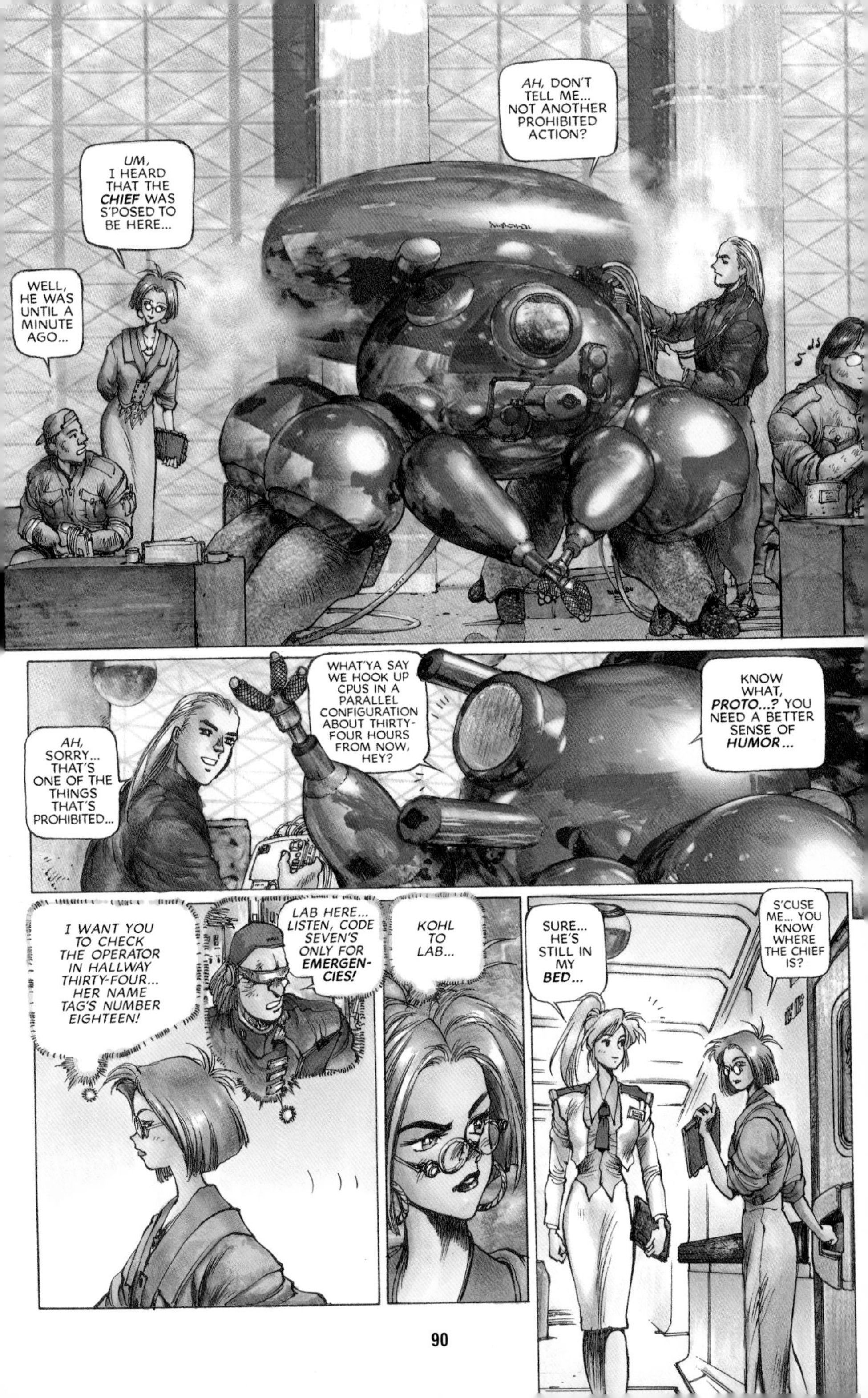
UM, I HEARD THAT THE CHIEF WAS S'POSED TO BE HERE...
WELL, HE WAS UNTIL A MINUTE AGO...
AH, DON'T TELL ME... NOT ANOTHER PROHIBITED ACTION?
WHAT'YA SAY WE HOOK UP CPUS IN A PARALLEL CONFIGURATION ABOUT THIRTY-FOUR HOURS FROM NOW, HEY?
AH, SORRY... THAT'S ONE OF THE THINGS THAT'S PROHIBITED...
KNOW WHAT, PROTO...? YOU NEED A BETTER SENSE OF HUMOR...
KOHL TO LAB...
LAB HERE... LISTEN, CODE SEVEN'S ONLY FOR EMERGENCIES!
I WANT YOU TO CHECK THE OPERATOR IN HALLWAY THIRTY-FOUR... HER NAME TAG'S NUMBER EIGHTEEN!
S'CUSE ME... YOU KNOW WHERE THE CHIEF IS?
SURE... HE'S STILL IN MY BED...

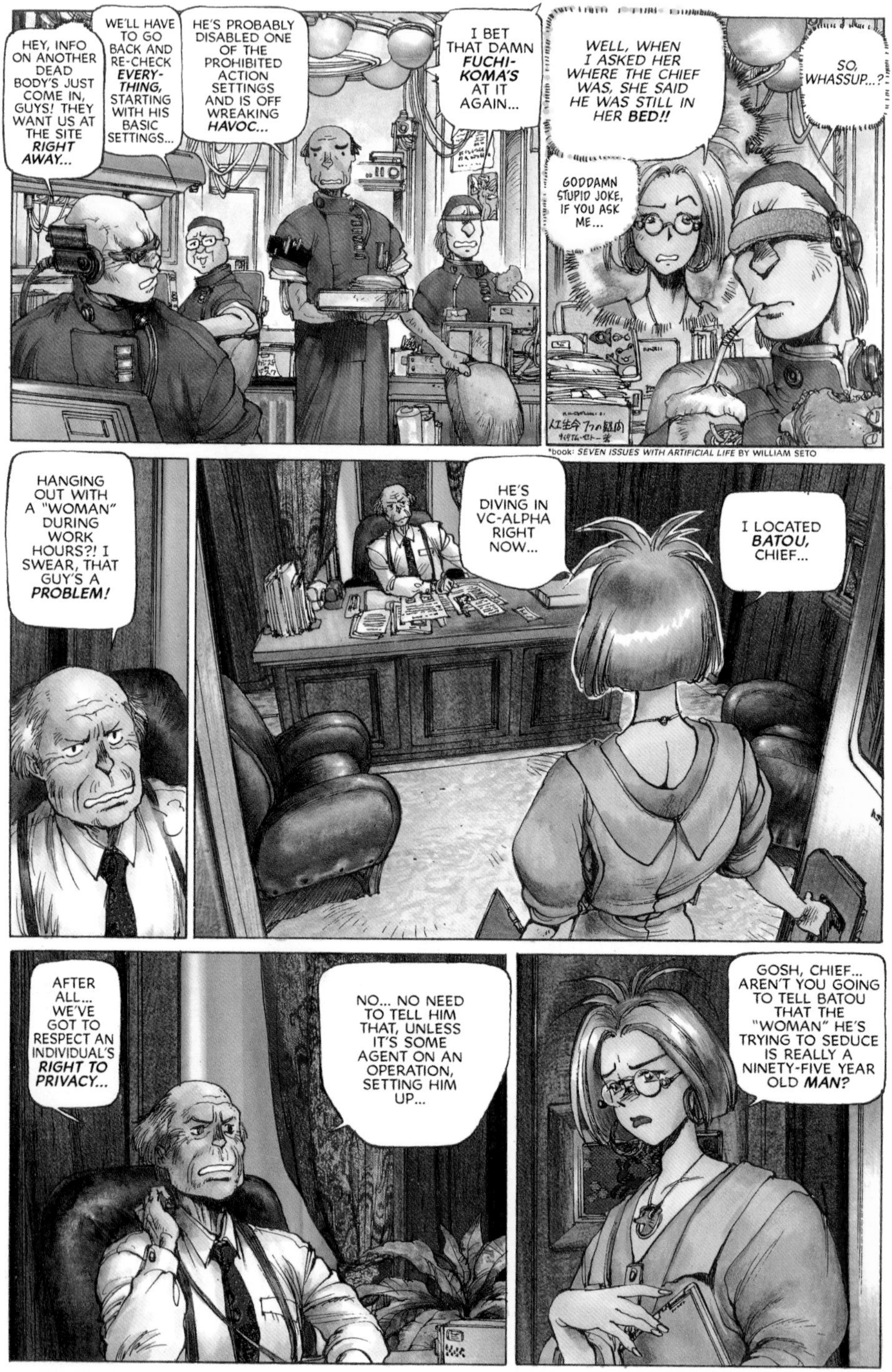
SO, WHASSUP...?
WELL, WHEN I ASKED HER WHERE THE CHIEF WAS, SHE SAID HE WAS STILL IN HER BED!!
GODDAMN STUPID JOKE, IF YOU ASK ME...
I BET THAT DAMN FUCHIKOMA'S AT IT AGAIN...
HE'S PROBABLY DISABLED ONE OF THE PROHIBITED ACTION SETTINGS AND IS OFF WREAKING HAVOC...
WE'LL HAVE TO GO BACK AND RE-CHECK EVERYTHING, STARTING WITH HIS BASIC SETTINGS...
HEY, INFO ON ANOTHER DEAD BODY'S JUST COME IN, GUYS! THEY WANT US AT THE SITE RIGHT AWAY...
*book: SEVEN ISSUES WITH ARTIFICIAL LIFE BY WILLIAM SETO
I LOCATED BATOU, CHIEF...
HE'S DIVING IN VC-ALPHA RIGHT NOW...
HANGING OUT WITH A "WOMAN" DURING WORK HOURS?! I SWEAR, THAT GUY'S A PROBLEM!
GOSH, CHIEF... AREN'T YOU GOING TO TELL BATOU THAT THE "WOMAN" HE'S TRYING TO SEDUCE IS REALLY A NINETY-FIVE YEAR OLD MAN?
NO... NO NEED TO TELL HIM THAT, UNLESS IT'S SOME AGENT ON AN OPERATION, SETTING HIM UP...
AFTER ALL... WE'VE GOT TO RESPECT AN INDIVIDUAL'S RIGHT TO PRIVACY...

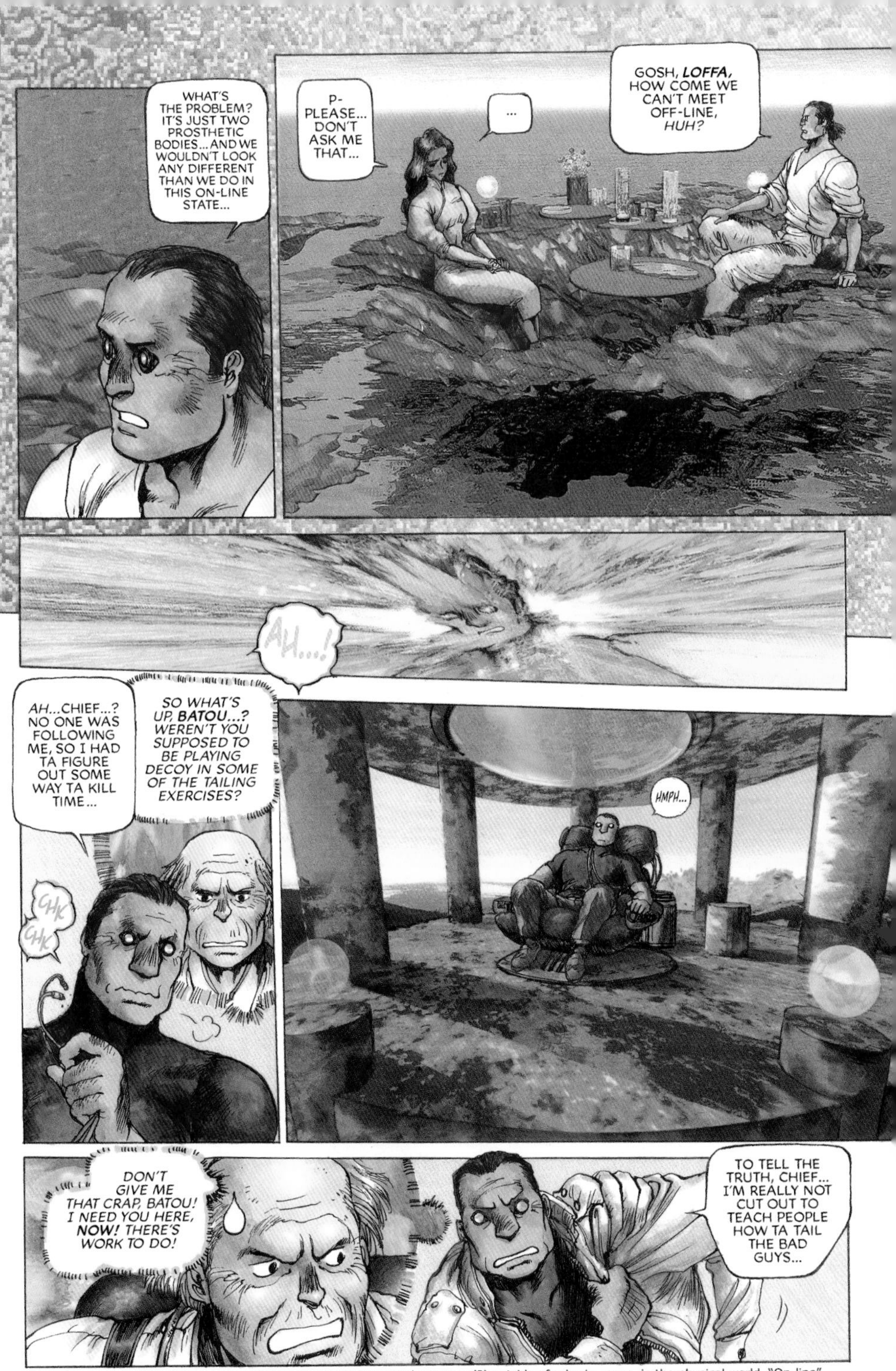
GOSH, LOFFA, HOW COME WE CAN'T MEET OFF-LINE, HUH?
...
P-PLEASE... DON'T ASK ME THAT...
WHAT'S THE PROBLEM? IT'S JUST TWO PROSTHETIC BODIES... AND WE WOULDN'T LOOK ANY DIFFERENT THAN WE DO IN THIS ON-LINE STATE...
AH...!
HMPH...
SO WHAT'S UP, BATOU...? WEREN'T YOU SUPPOSED TO BE PLAYING DECOY IN SOME OF THE TAILING EXERCISES?
AH...CHIEF...? NO ONE WAS FOLLOWING ME, SO I HAD TA FIGURE OUT SOME WAY TA KILL TIME...
CHK CHK
TO TELL THE TRUTH, CHIEF... I'M REALLY NOT CUT OUT TO TEACH PEOPLE HOW TA TAIL THE BAD GUYS...
DON'T GIVE ME THAT CRAP, BATOU! I NEED YOU HERE, NOW! THERE'S WORK TO DO!

The reference to "off-line" here means that Batou wants to meet the woman(?) outside of e-brain space, in the physical world. "On-line" means within e-brain space. Meeting off-line in the physical world doesn't mean that Batou would instantly know Loffa's real sex or age, but "she's" nonetheless afraid he'd figure it out from seeing the environment in which "she" lives, or from "her" friends...

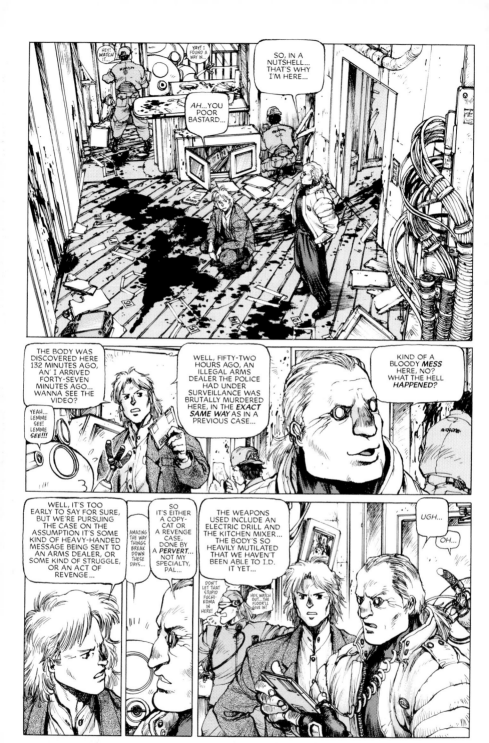

93

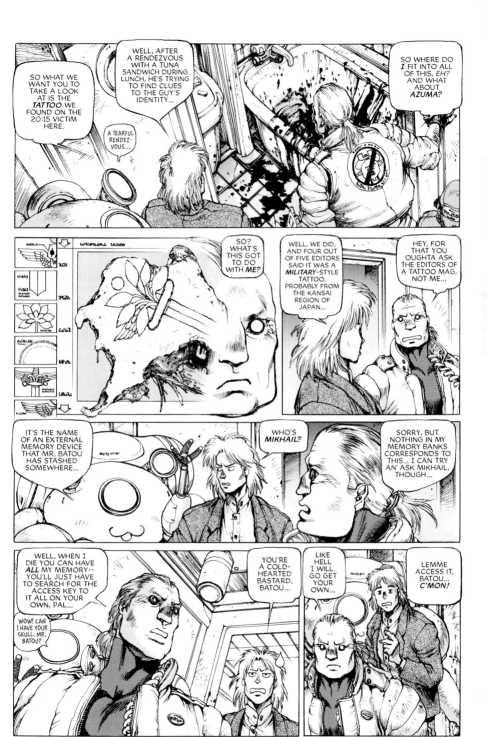

The "memory" that Batou is referring to here is e-brain memory and not the sort of memory we refer to in normal conversation. Dictionary information, language translation data, business maps, authentification passwords, and encrypted files needed to access the net—these are all stored near the transmission gears in his neck. They are a type of memory, but don't ask me what sort of media they're stored on, how much capacity it has, and whether the data's been backed up or not... Not all data is stored in the e-brain itself.

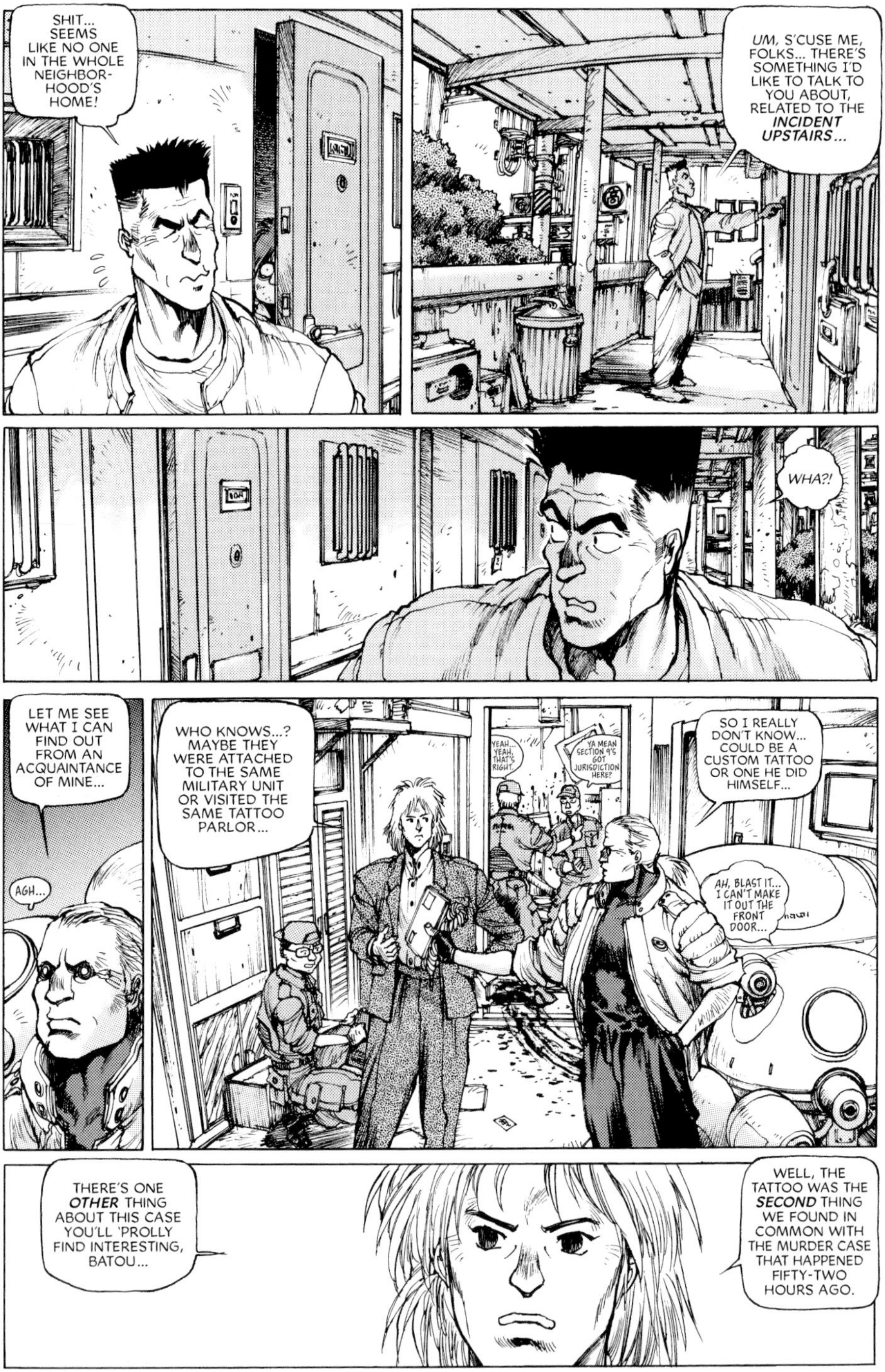
SHIT... SEEMS LIKE NO ONE IN THE WHOLE NEIGHBOR-HOOD'S HOME!
UM, S'CUSE ME, FOLKS... THERE'S SOMETHING I'D LIKE TO TALK TO YOU ABOUT, RELATED TO THE INCIDENT UPSTAIRS...
WHA?!
LET ME SEE WHAT I CAN FIND OUT FROM AN ACQUAINTANCE OF MINE...
AGH...
WHO KNOWS...? MAYBE THEY WERE ATTACHED TO THE SAME MILITARY UNIT OR VISITED THE SAME TATTOO PARLOR...
YEAH... YEAH, THAT'S RIGHT.
YA MEAN SECTION 9'S GOT JURISDICTION HERE?
SO I REALLY DON'T KNOW... COULD BE A CUSTOM TATTOO OR ONE HE DID HIMSELF...
AH, BLAST IT... I CAN'T MAKE IT OUT THE FRONT DOOR...
THERE'S ONE OTHER THING ABOUT THIS CASE YOU'LL 'PROLLY FIND INTERESTING, BATOU...
WELL, THE TATTOO WAS THE SECOND THING WE FOUND IN COMMON WITH THE MURDER CASE THAT HAPPENED FIFTY-TWO HOURS AGO.

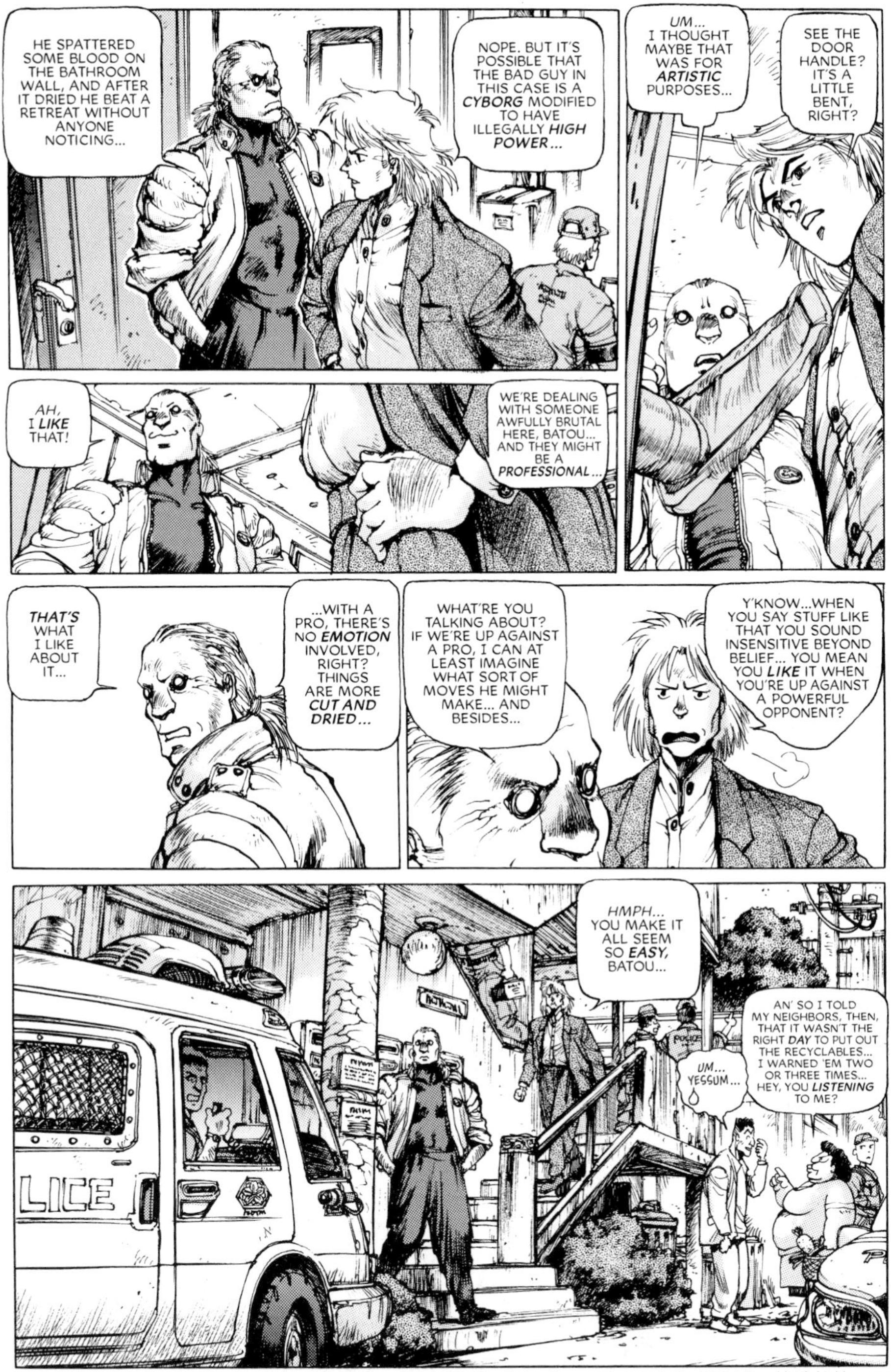
SEE THE DOOR HANDLE? IT'S A LITTLE BENT, RIGHT?
UM... I THOUGHT MAYBE THAT WAS FOR *ARTISTIC* PURPOSES...
NOPE. BUT IT'S POSSIBLE THAT THE BAD GUY IN THIS CASE IS A *CYBORG* MODIFIED TO HAVE ILLEGALLY *HIGH POWER*...
HE SPATTERED SOME BLOOD ON THE BATHROOM WALL, AND AFTER IT DRIED HE BEAT A RETREAT WITHOUT ANYONE NOTICING...
WE'RE DEALING WITH SOMEONE AWFULLY BRUTAL HERE, BATOU... AND THEY MIGHT BE A *PROFESSIONAL*...
AH, I *LIKE* THAT!
Y'KNOW...WHEN YOU SAY STUFF LIKE THAT YOU SOUND INSENSITIVE BEYOND BELIEF... YOU MEAN YOU *LIKE* IT WHEN YOU'RE UP AGAINST A POWERFUL OPPONENT?
WHAT'RE YOU TALKING ABOUT? IF WE'RE UP AGAINST A PRO, I CAN AT LEAST IMAGINE WHAT SORT OF MOVES HE MIGHT MAKE... AND BESIDES...
...WITH A PRO, THERE'S NO *EMOTION* INVOLVED, RIGHT? THINGS ARE MORE *CUT AND DRIED*...
THAT'S WHAT I LIKE ABOUT IT...
HMPH... YOU MAKE IT ALL SEEM SO *EASY*, BATOU...
AN' SO I TOLD MY NEIGHBORS, THEN, THAT IT WASN'T THE RIGHT *DAY* TO PUT OUT THE RECYCLABLES... I WARNED 'EM TWO OR THREE TIMES... HEY, YOU *LISTENING* TO ME?
UM... YESSUM...
LICE

Illegally high-powered cyborgs are often made with a lot of muscle, so they often look rather conspicuous. In the *GITS 1.5* world, it's highly unlikely that any individual would have exclusive access to an advanced material or technology. In other words, whatever one person can obtain is also something that someone else can obtain... In reality, the cyborg in this case probably just over-twisted the door handle in his hurry to enter the room... Of course, the neighbors probably should have heard what was going on...

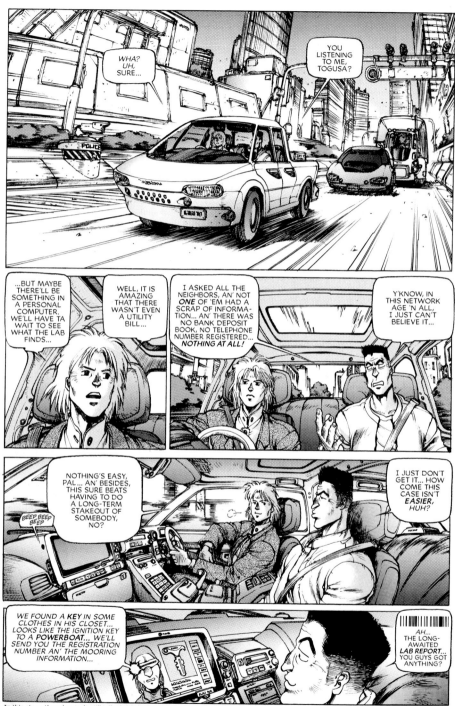

In this story, though people still talk about the "network age," wide disparities remain in the population between those who have information and those who don't or between those who can or cannot access the net. The role of professional net searchers or specialist research companies thus becomes extremely important. Azuma was ultimately able to easily estimate the utility bill of the dead man because he knew the address and could simply ask the gas, electricity, and telecommunications companies in the area.

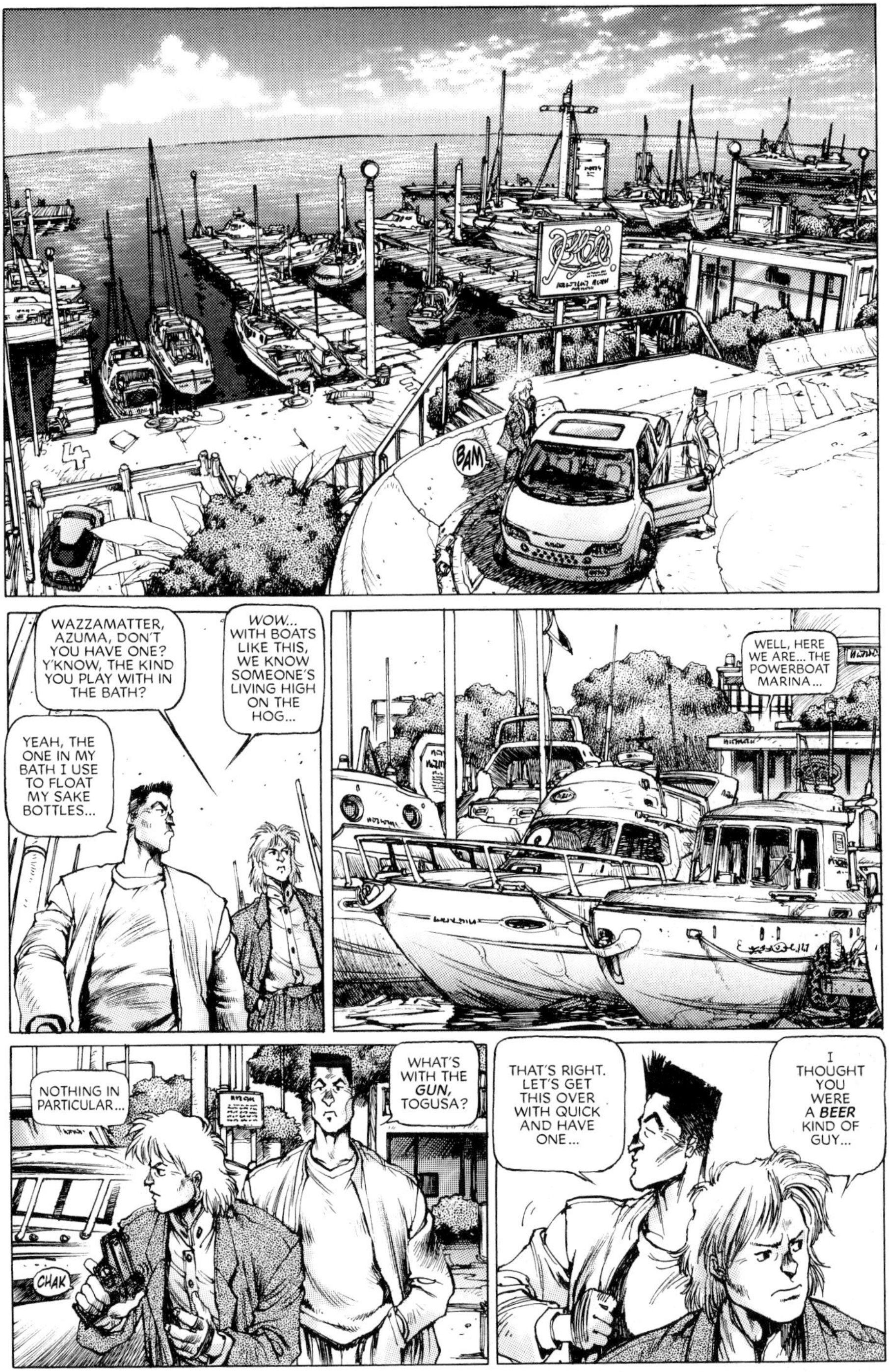
BAM
WELL, HERE WE ARE... THE POWERBOAT MARINA...
WOW... WITH BOATS LIKE THIS, WE KNOW SOMEONE'S LIVING HIGH ON THE HOG...
WAZZAMATTER, AZUMA, DON'T YOU HAVE ONE? Y'KNOW, THE KIND YOU PLAY WITH IN THE BATH?
YEAH, THE ONE IN MY BATH I USE TO FLOAT MY SAKE BOTTLES...
I THOUGHT YOU WERE A *BEER* KIND OF GUY...
THAT'S RIGHT. LET'S GET THIS OVER WITH QUICK AND HAVE ONE...
WHAT'S WITH THE *GUN*, TOGUSA?
NOTHING IN PARTICULAR...
CHAK

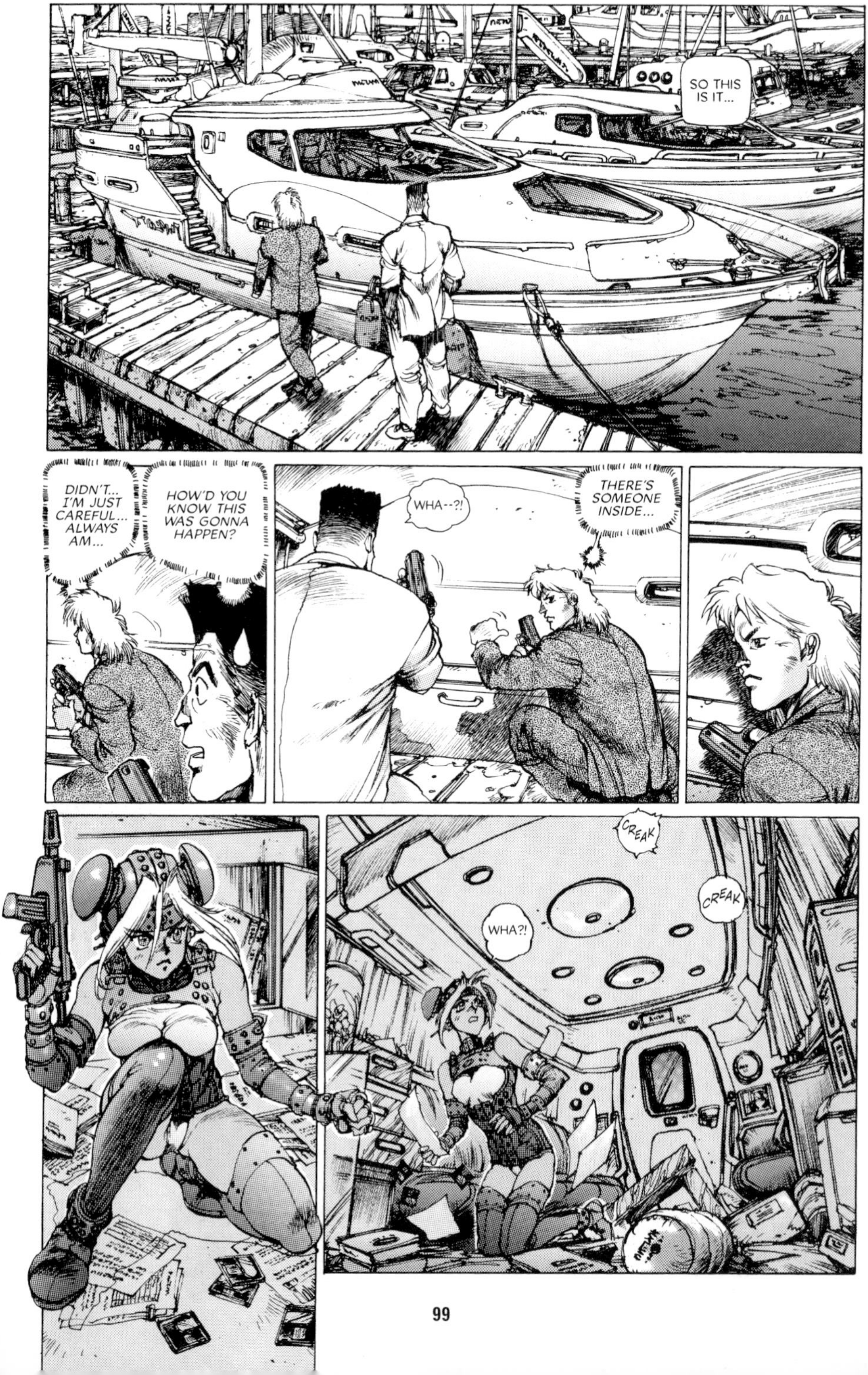
SO THIS IS IT...
THERE'S SOMEONE INSIDE...
WHA--?!
HOW'D YOU KNOW THIS WAS GONNA HAPPEN?
DIDN'T... I'M JUST CAREFUL... ALWAYS AM...
CREAK
CREAK
WHA?!

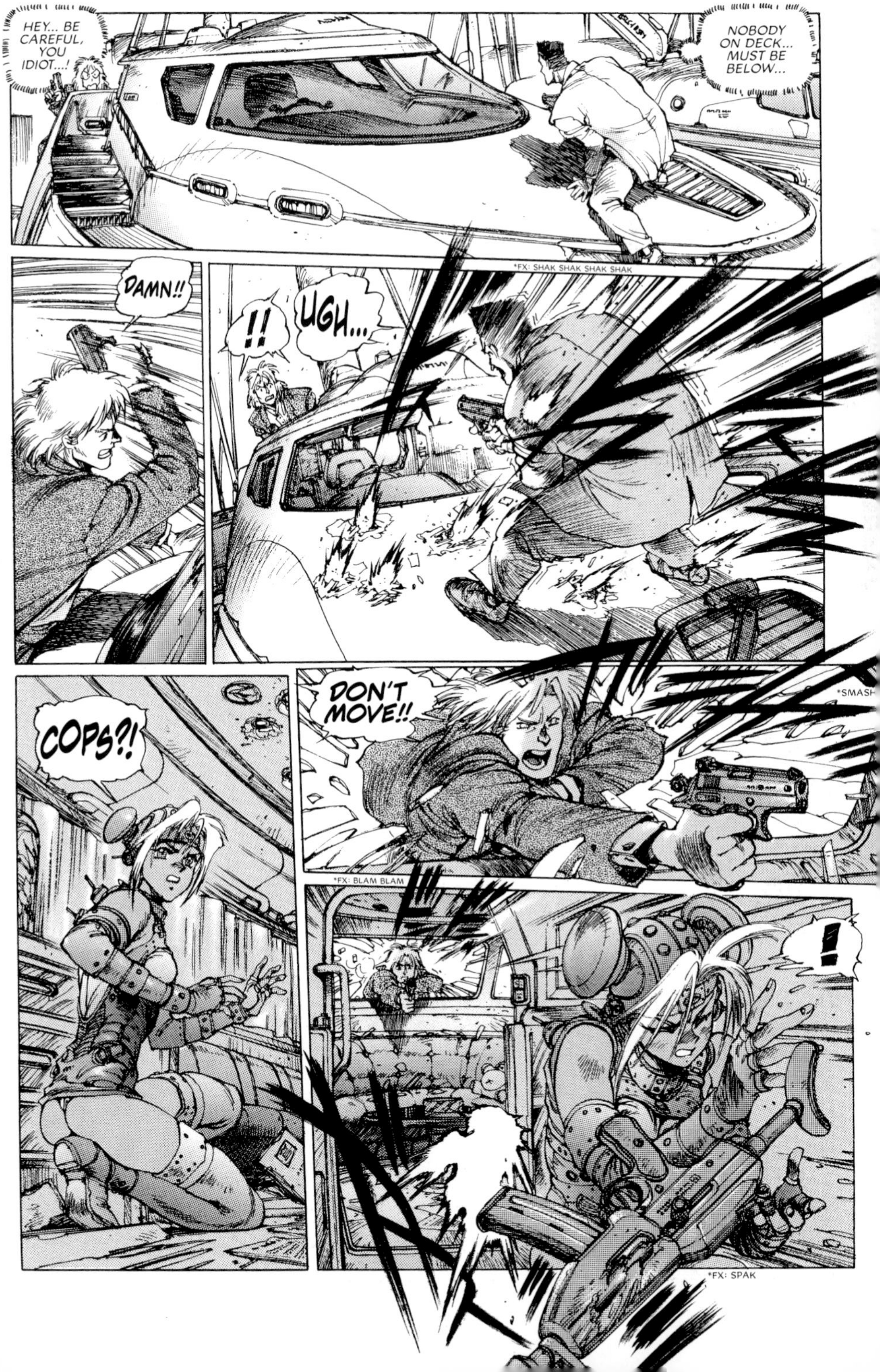
NOBODY ON DECK... MUST BE BELOW...
HEY... BE CAREFUL, YOU IDIOT...!
*FX: SHAK SHAK SHAK SHAK
!!
UGH...
DAMN!!
DON'T MOVE!!
*SMASH
*FX: BLAM BLAM
!
*FX: SPAK
COPS?!

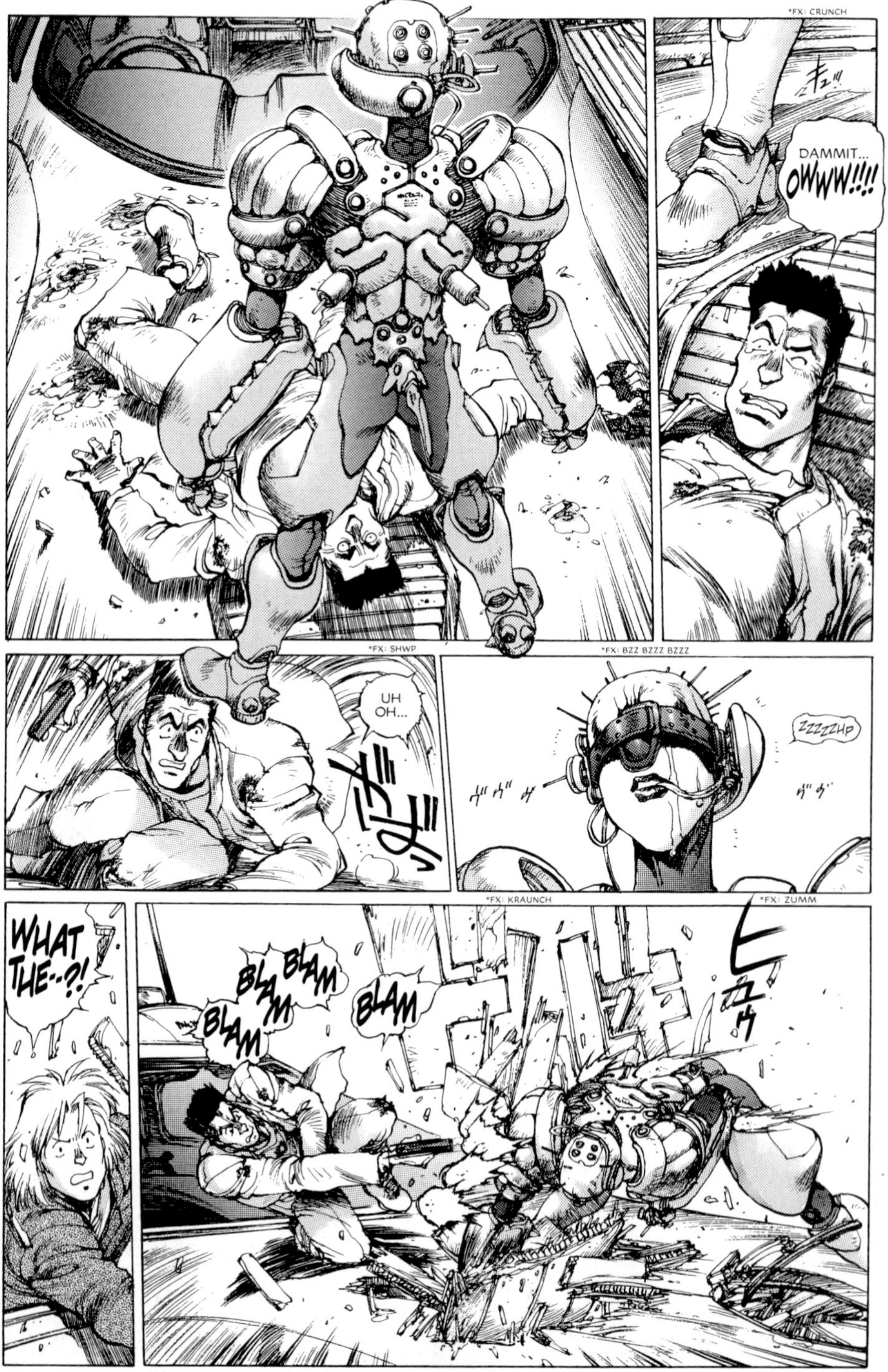
*FX: CRUNCH
DAMMIT... OWWW!!!!
*FX: BZZ BZZZ BZZZ
ZZZZZHP
*FX: SHWP
UH OH...
*FX: ZUMM
*FX: KRAUNCH
BLAM BLAM BLAM BLAM
BLAM
WHAT THE--?!

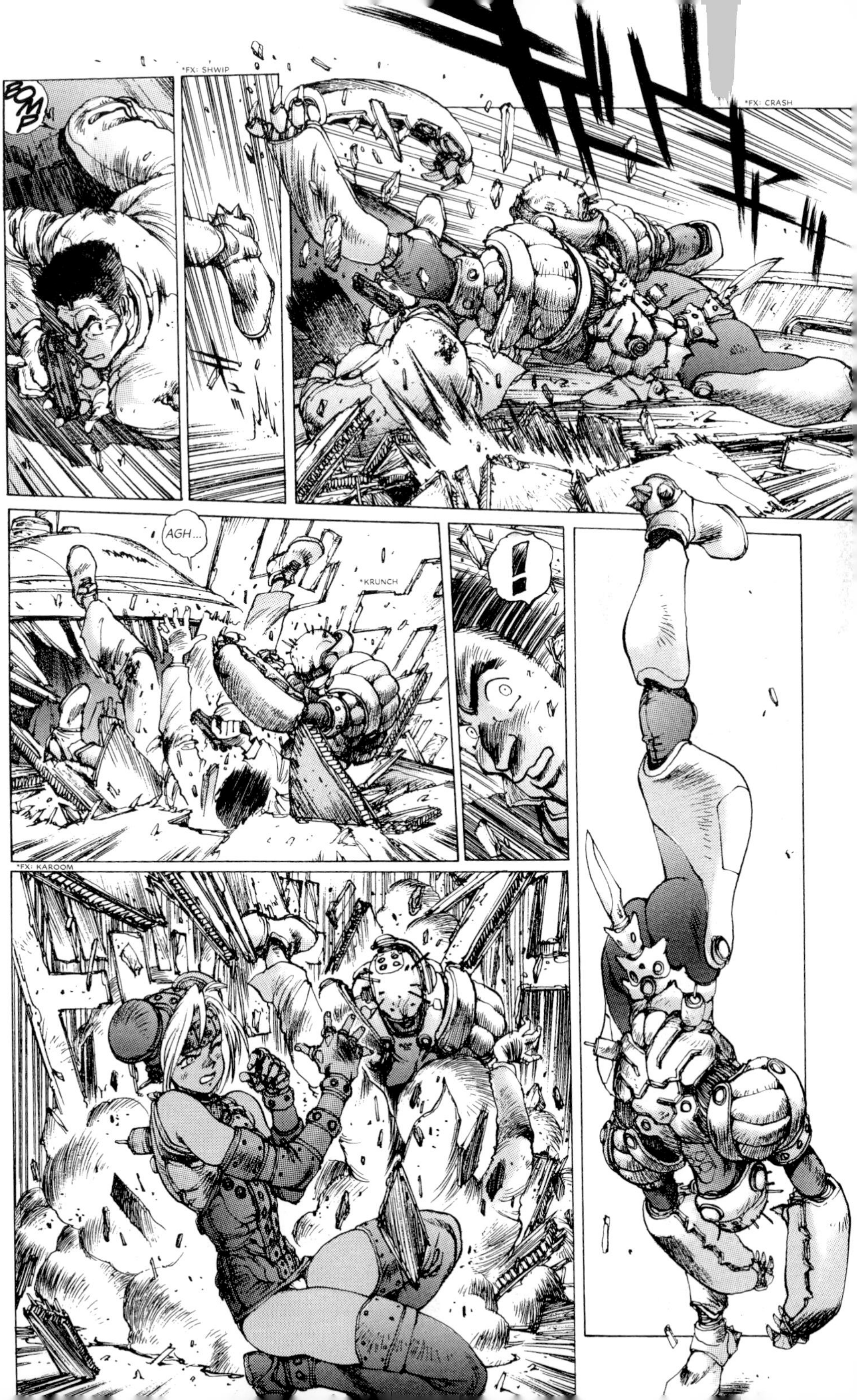
*FX: CRASH
*FX: SHWIP
BOMP
!
AGH...
*KRUNCH
*FX: KAROOM

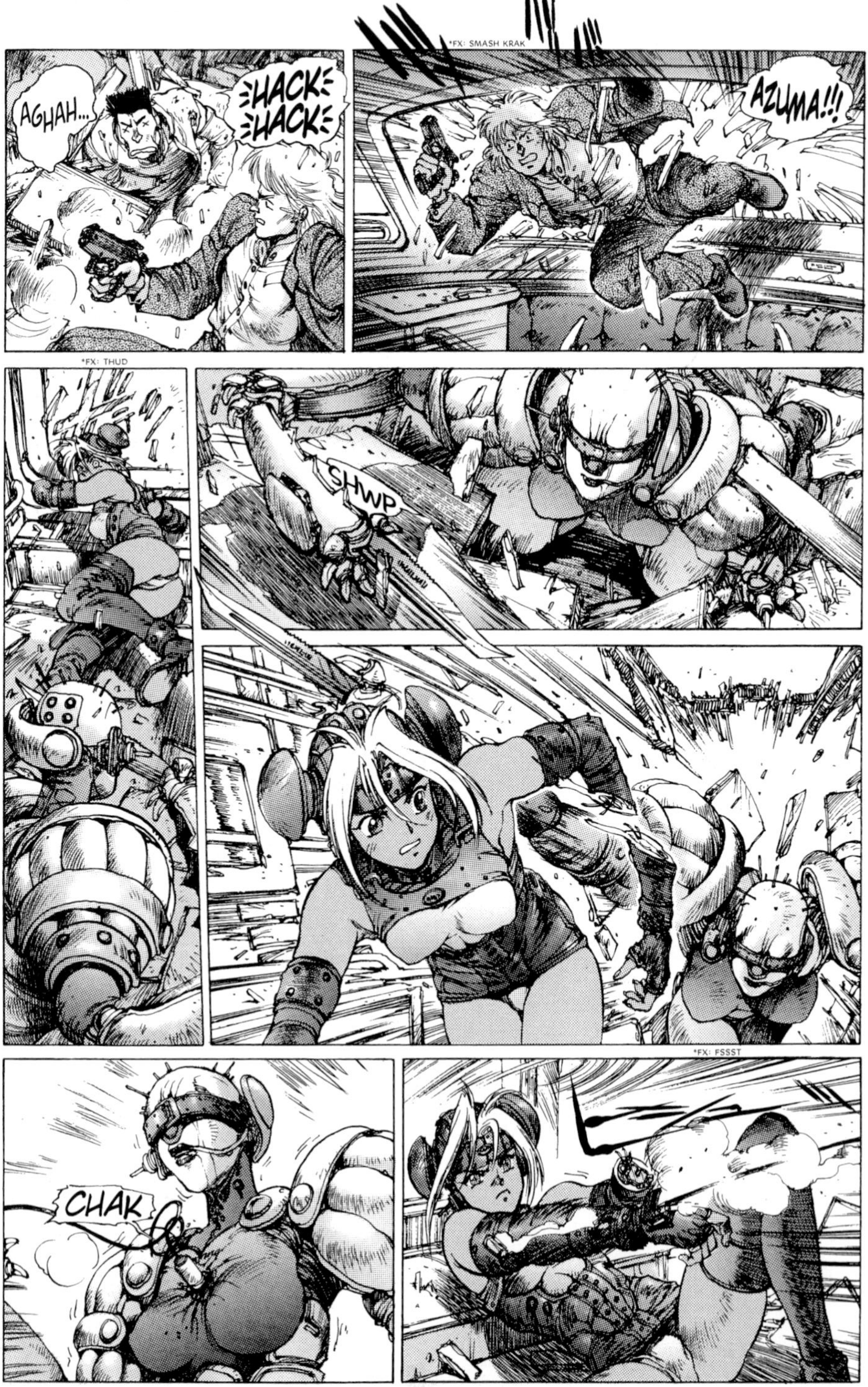
AGHAH...
HACK HACK
*FX: SMASH KRAK
AZUMA!!!
*FX: THUD
SHWP
CHAK
*FX: FSSST

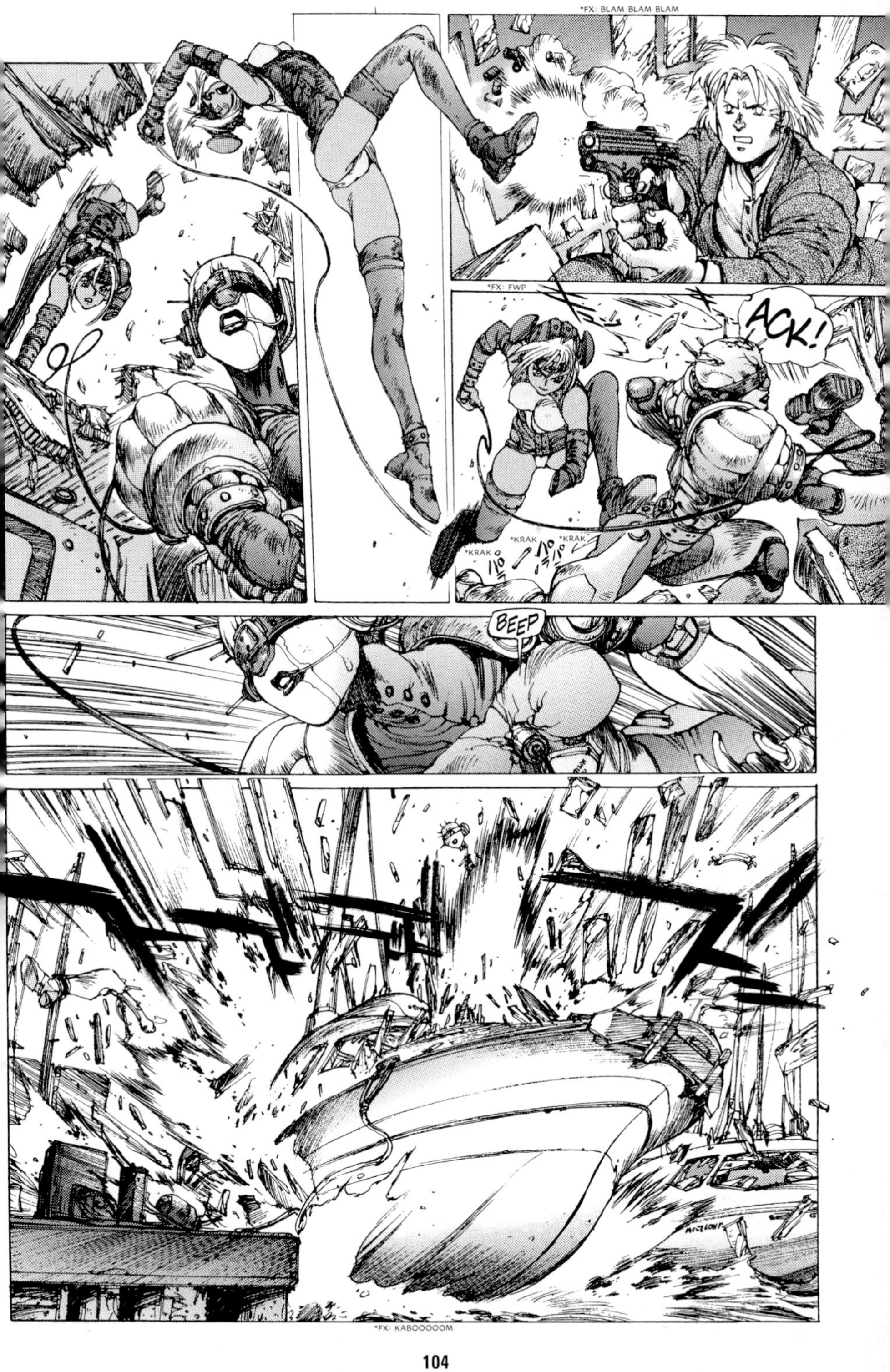
*FX: BLAM BLAM BLAM
*FX: FWP
ACK!
*KRAK
*KRAK
*KRAK
BEEP
*FX: KABOOOOOM

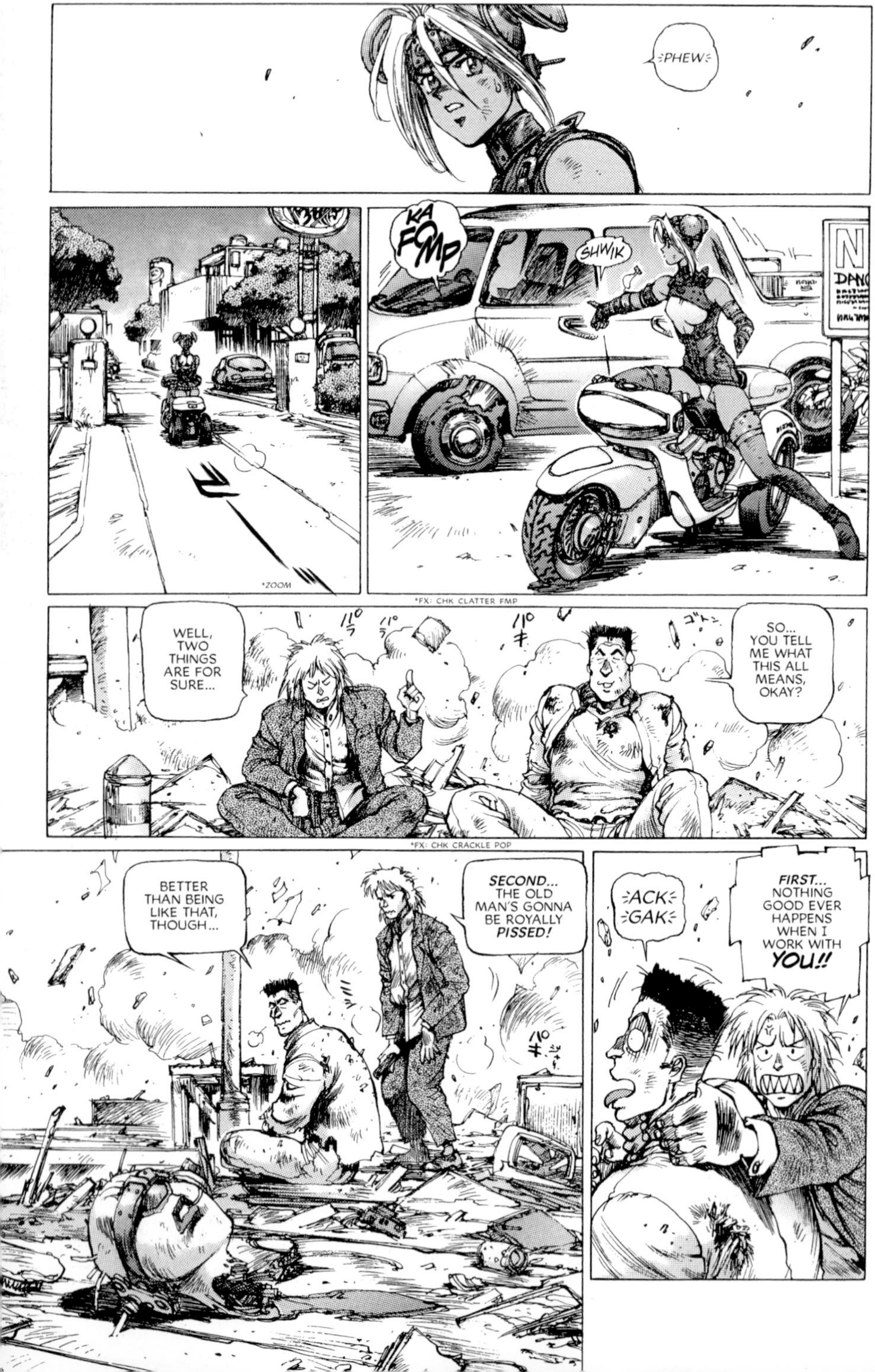
PHEW
KA FOMP
SHWIK
*ZOOM
*FX: CHK CLATTER FMP
SO... YOU TELL ME WHAT THIS ALL MEANS, OKAY?
WELL, TWO THINGS ARE FOR SURE...
*FX: CHK CRACKLE POP
FIRST... NOTHING GOOD EVER HAPPENS WHEN I WORK WITH YOU!!
ACK GAK
SECOND... THE OLD MAN'S GONNA BE ROYALLY PISSED!
BETTER THAN BEING LIKE THAT, THOUGH...

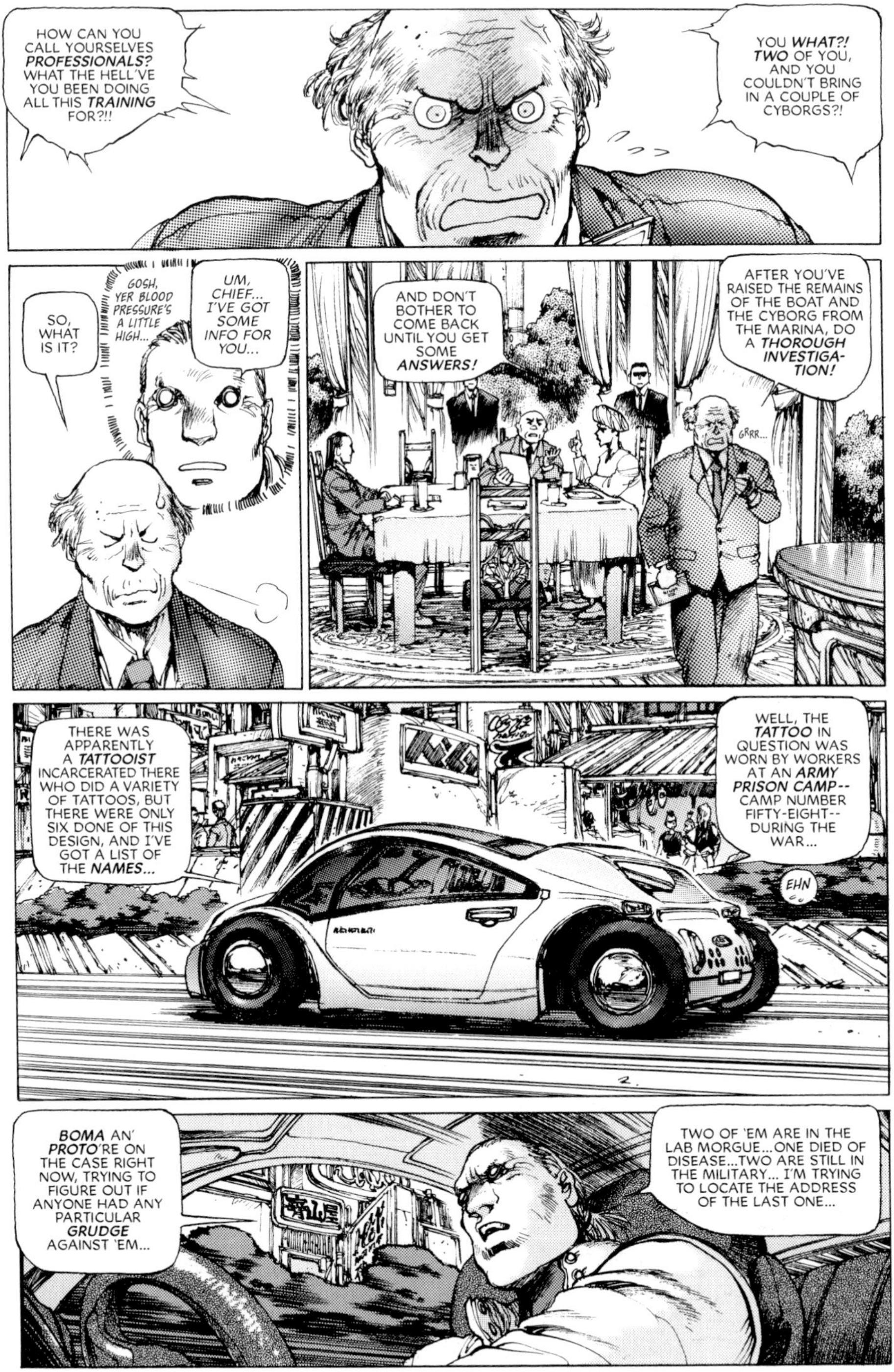
YOU WHAT?! TWO OF YOU, AND YOU COULDN'T BRING IN A COUPLE OF CYBORGS?!
HOW CAN YOU CALL YOURSELVES PROFESSIONALS? WHAT THE HELL'VE YOU BEEN DOING ALL THIS TRAINING FOR?!!
AFTER YOU'VE RAISED THE REMAINS OF THE BOAT AND THE CYBORG FROM THE MARINA, DO A THOROUGH INVESTIGA-TION!
GRRR...
AND DON'T BOTHER TO COME BACK UNTIL YOU GET SOME ANSWERS!
UM, CHIEF... I'VE GOT SOME INFO FOR YOU...
GOSH, YER BLOOD PRESSURE'S A LITTLE HIGH...
SO, WHAT IS IT?
WELL, THE TATTOO IN QUESTION WAS WORN BY WORKERS AT AN ARMY PRISON CAMP-- CAMP NUMBER FIFTY-EIGHT-- DURING THE WAR...
EHN
THERE WAS APPARENTLY A TATTOOIST INCARCERATED THERE WHO DID A VARIETY OF TATTOOS, BUT THERE WERE ONLY SIX DONE OF THIS DESIGN, AND I'VE GOT A LIST OF THE NAMES...
TWO OF 'EM ARE IN THE LAB MORGUE...ONE DIED OF DISEASE...TWO ARE STILL IN THE MILITARY... I'M TRYING TO LOCATE THE ADDRESS OF THE LAST ONE...
BOMA AN' PROTO'RE ON THE CASE RIGHT NOW, TRYING TO FIGURE OUT IF ANYONE HAD ANY PARTICULAR GRUDGE AGAINST 'EM...

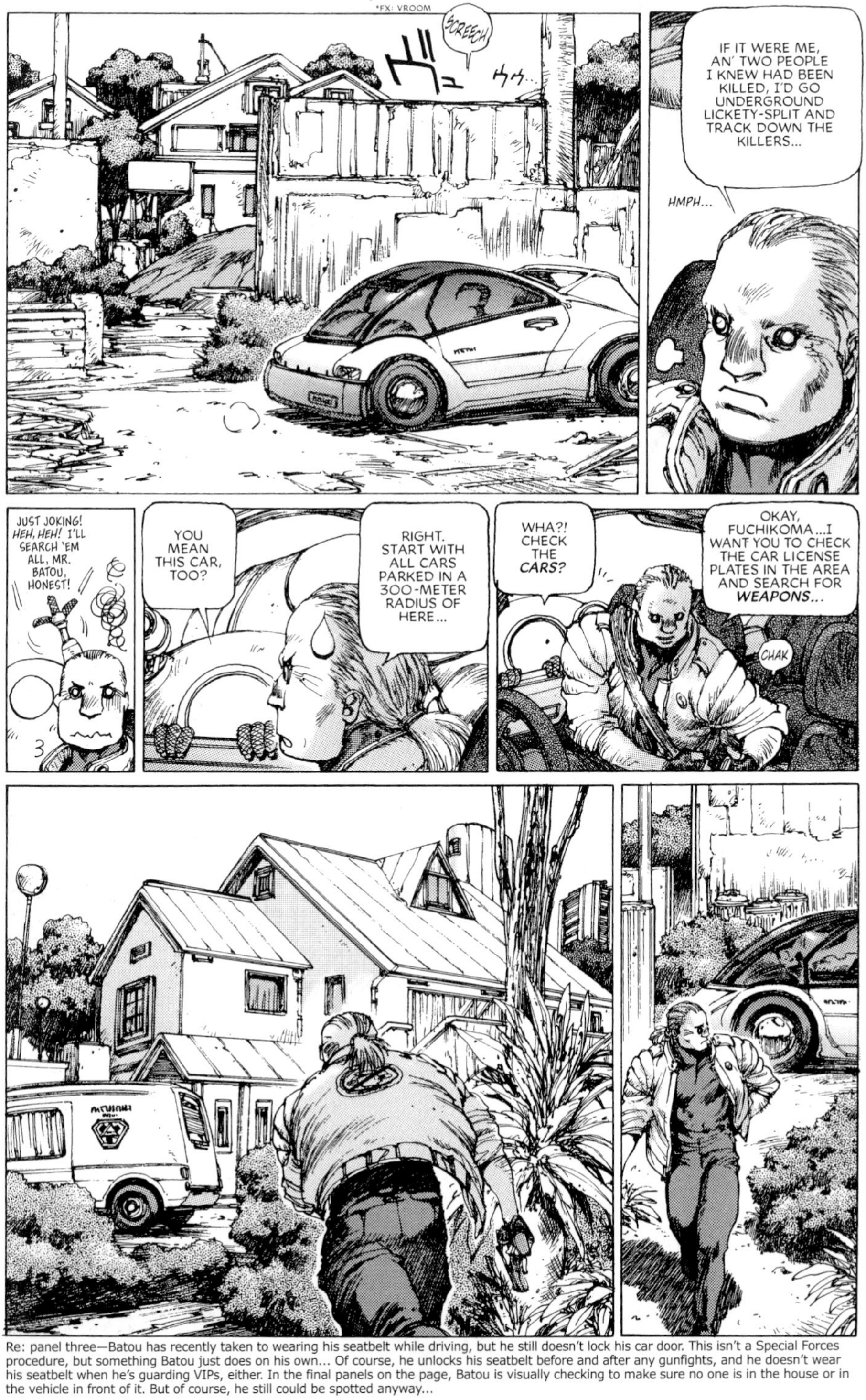
IF IT WERE ME, AN' TWO PEOPLE I KNEW HAD BEEN KILLED, I'D GO UNDERGROUND LICKETY-SPLIT AND TRACK DOWN THE KILLERS...
HMPH...
*FX: VROOM
SCREECH
OKAY, FUCHIKOMA...I WANT YOU TO CHECK THE CAR LICENSE PLATES IN THE AREA AND SEARCH FOR *WEAPONS...*
CHAK
WHA?! CHECK THE *CARS?*
RIGHT. START WITH ALL CARS PARKED IN A 300-METER RADIUS OF HERE...
YOU MEAN THIS CAR, TOO?
JUST JOKING! *HEH, HEH!* I'LL SEARCH 'EM ALL, MR. BATOU, HONEST!

Re: panel three—Batou has recently taken to wearing his seatbelt while driving, but he still doesn't lock his car door. This isn't a Special Forces procedure, but something Batou just does on his own... Of course, he unlocks his seatbelt before and after any gunfights, and he doesn't wear his seatbelt when he's guarding VIPs, either. In the final panels on the page, Batou is visually checking to make sure no one is in the house or in the vehicle in front of it. But of course, he still could be spotted anyway...

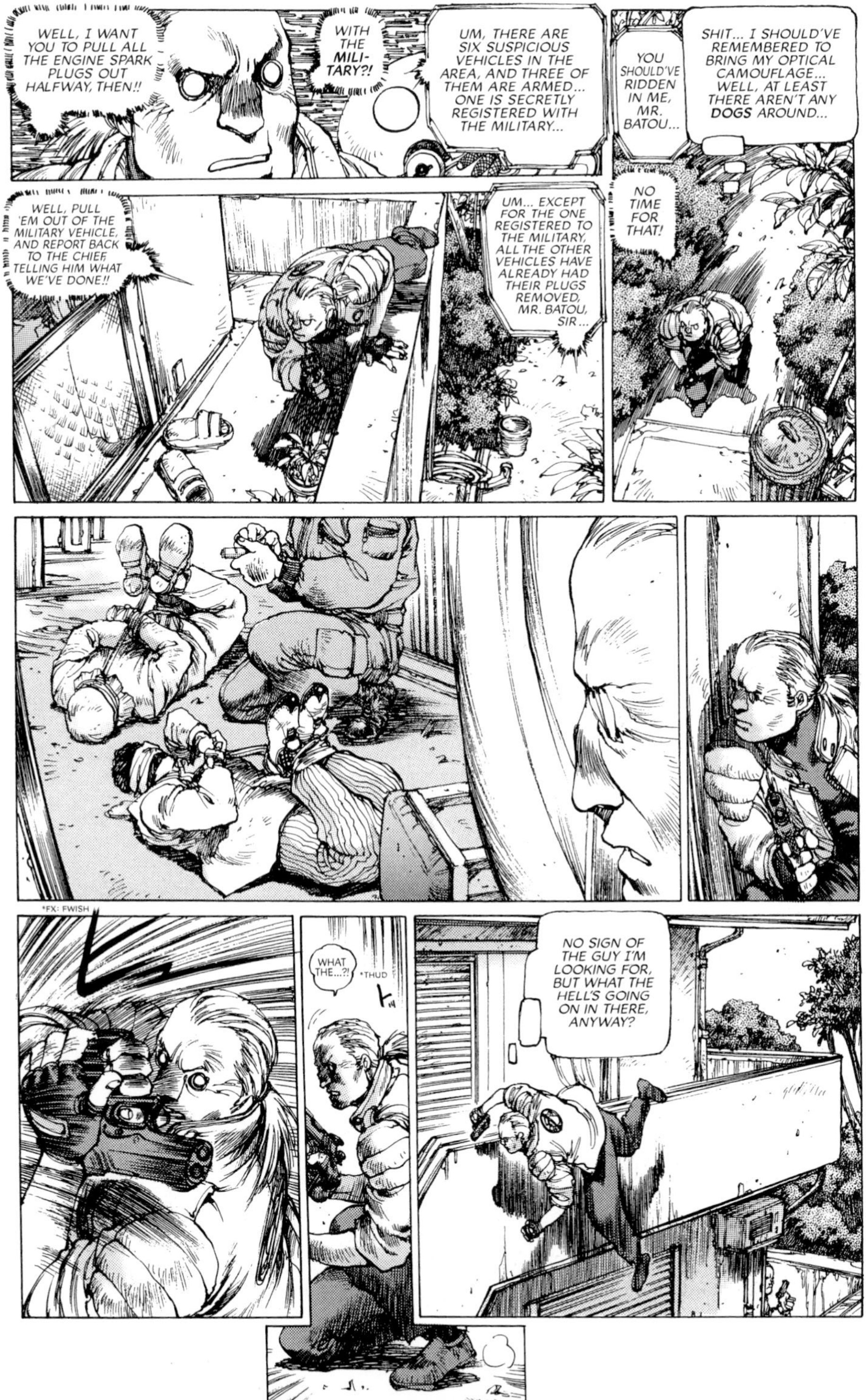
SHIT... I SHOULD'VE REMEMBERED TO BRING MY OPTICAL CAMOUFLAGE... WELL, AT LEAST THERE AREN'T ANY **DOGS** AROUND...
YOU SHOULD'VE RIDDEN IN ME, MR. BATOU...
NO TIME FOR THAT!
UM, THERE ARE SIX SUSPICIOUS VEHICLES IN THE AREA, AND THREE OF THEM ARE ARMED... ONE IS SECRETLY REGISTERED WITH THE MILITARY...
WITH THE **MILITARY**?!
WELL, I WANT YOU TO PULL ALL THE ENGINE SPARK PLUGS OUT HALFWAY, THEN!!
UM... EXCEPT FOR THE ONE REGISTERED TO THE MILITARY, ALL THE OTHER VEHICLES HAVE ALREADY HAD THEIR PLUGS REMOVED, MR. BATOU, SIR...
WELL, PULL 'EM OUT OF THE MILITARY VEHICLE, AND REPORT BACK TO THE CHIEF, TELLING HIM WHAT WE'VE DONE!!
NO SIGN OF THE GUY I'M LOOKING FOR, BUT WHAT THE HELL'S GOING ON IN THERE, ANYWAY?
WHAT THE...?!
*THUD
*FX: FWISH

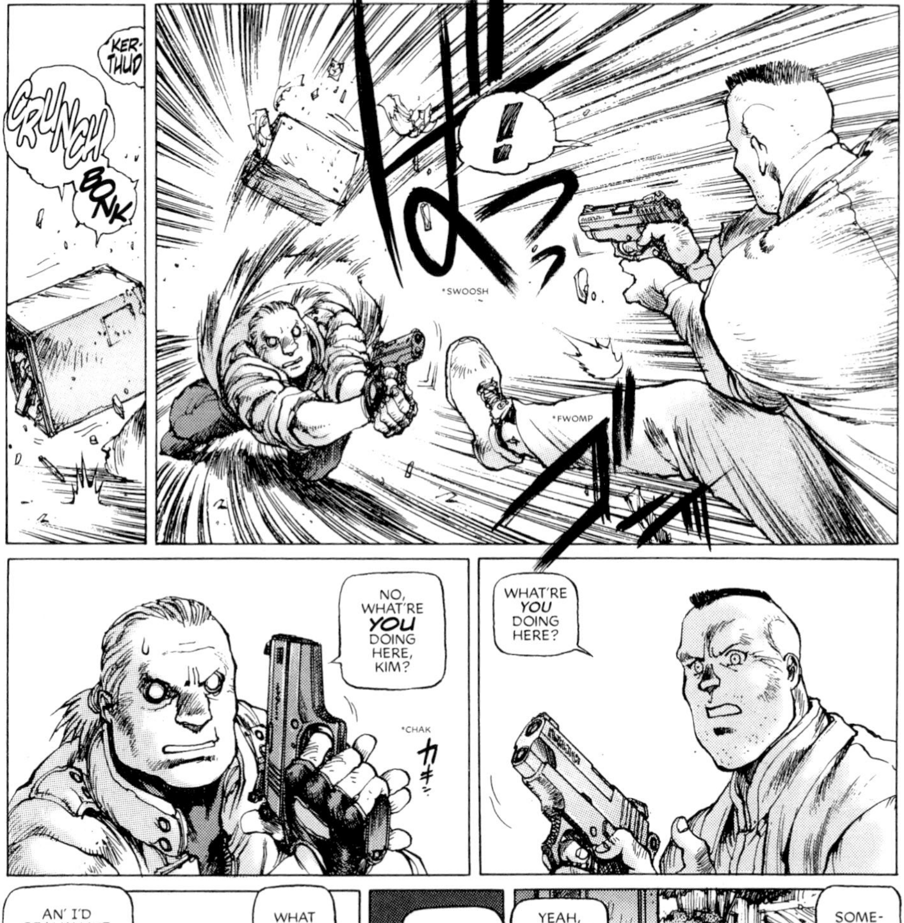
!
*SWOOSH
*FWOMP
KER-THUD
CRUNCH
BONK
WHAT'RE YOU DOING HERE?
NO, WHAT'RE YOU DOING HERE, KIM?
*CHAK
SOME-ONE YOU KNOW, KIM?
YEAH, HE'S FROM PUBLIC SECURITY'S SECTION 9...
YOU MEAN YOU'RE WORKING ON THE SAME CASE WE ARE?!
WHAT OTHER CASE IS THERE?
AN' I'D REALLY LIKE YOU GUYS TO STOP THIS STUFF...
*SHWIP

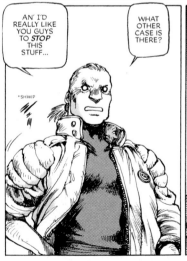

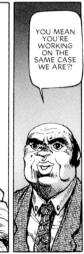

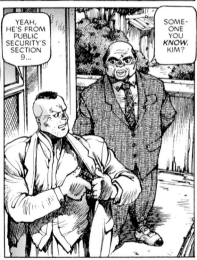

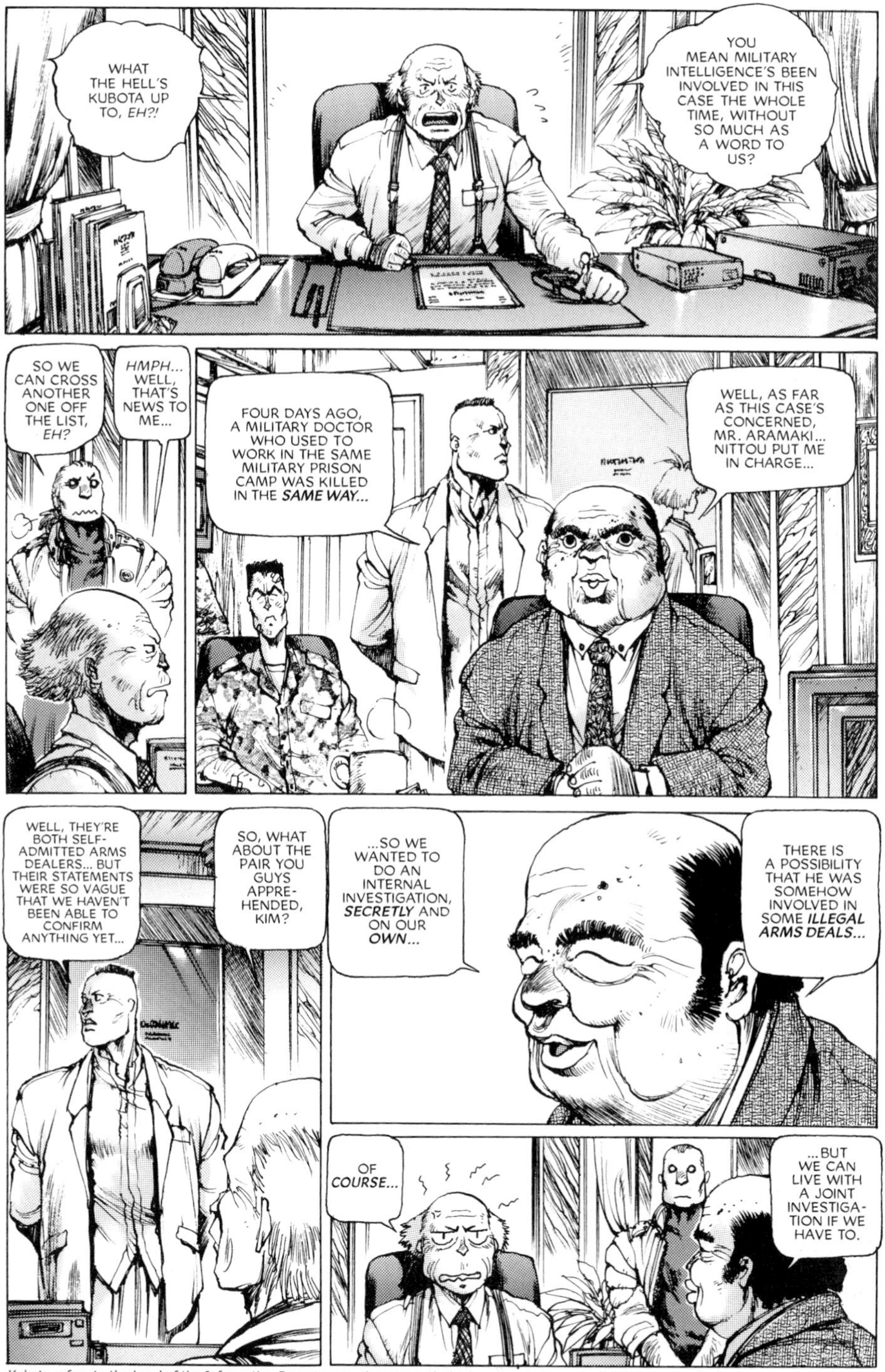
YOU MEAN MILITARY INTELLIGENCE'S BEEN INVOLVED IN THIS CASE THE WHOLE TIME, WITHOUT SO MUCH AS A WORD TO US?
WHAT THE HELL'S KUBOTA UP TO, *EH?!*
WELL, AS FAR AS THIS CASE'S CONCERNED, MR. ARAMAKI... NITTOU PUT ME IN CHARGE...
FOUR DAYS AGO, A MILITARY DOCTOR WHO USED TO WORK IN THE SAME MILITARY PRISON CAMP WAS KILLED IN THE ***SAME WAY...***
HMPH... WELL, THAT'S NEWS TO ME...
SO WE CAN CROSS ANOTHER ONE OFF THE LIST, *EH?*
THERE IS A POSSIBILITY THAT HE WAS SOMEHOW INVOLVED IN SOME ***ILLEGAL ARMS DEALS...***
...SO WE WANTED TO DO AN INTERNAL INVESTIGATION, ***SECRETLY*** AND ON OUR ***OWN...***
...BUT WE CAN LIVE WITH A JOINT INVESTIGA-TION IF WE HAVE TO.
OF ***COURSE...***
SO, WHAT ABOUT THE PAIR YOU GUYS APPRE-HENDED, KIM?
WELL, THEY'RE BOTH SELF-ADMITTED ARMS DEALERS... BUT THEIR STATEMENTS WERE SO VAGUE THAT WE HAVEN'T BEEN ABLE TO CONFIRM ANYTHING YET...

Kubota refers to the head of the Information Department—the man with the beard and glasses in *Fat Cat*. Apparently, he has a good relationship with Aramaki... I should also point out that the band-aids Azuma has on are temporary and not really designed to treat wounds. They just ensure that his artificial skin isn't too exposed by his wounds...

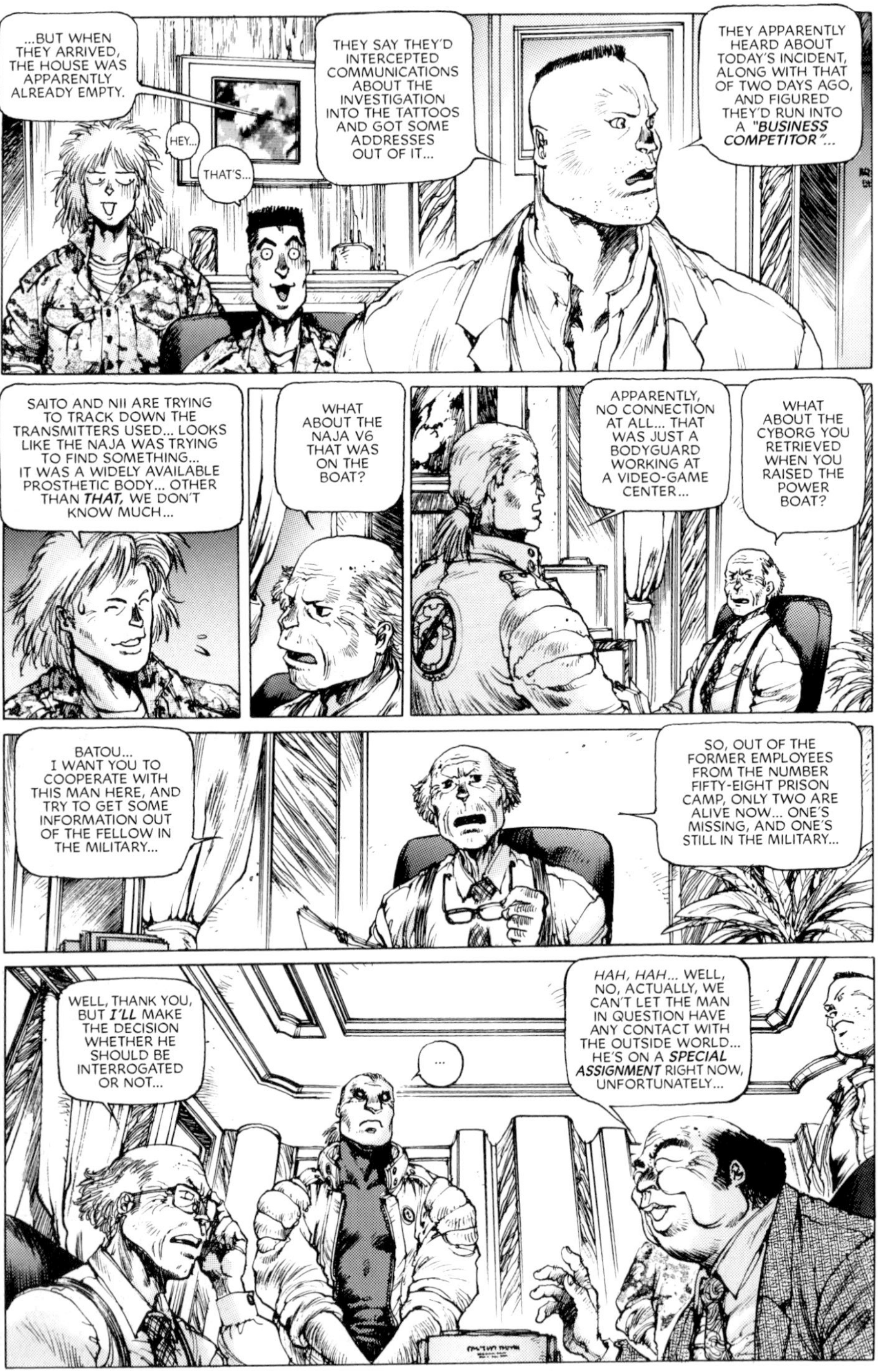
...BUT WHEN THEY ARRIVED, THE HOUSE WAS APPARENTLY ALREADY EMPTY.
HEY...
THAT'S...
THEY SAY THEY'D INTERCEPTED COMMUNICATIONS ABOUT THE INVESTIGATION INTO THE TATTOOS AND GOT SOME ADDRESSES OUT OF IT...
THEY APPARENTLY HEARD ABOUT TODAY'S INCIDENT, ALONG WITH THAT OF TWO DAYS AGO, AND FIGURED THEY'D RUN INTO A *"BUSINESS COMPETITOR"*...
SAITO AND NII ARE TRYING TO TRACK DOWN THE TRANSMITTERS USED... LOOKS LIKE THE NAJA WAS TRYING TO FIND SOMETHING... IT WAS A WIDELY AVAILABLE PROSTHETIC BODY... OTHER THAN ***THAT,*** WE DON'T KNOW MUCH...
WHAT ABOUT THE NAJA V6 THAT WAS ON THE BOAT?
APPARENTLY, NO CONNECTION AT ALL... THAT WAS JUST A BODYGUARD WORKING AT A VIDEO-GAME CENTER...
WHAT ABOUT THE CYBORG YOU RETRIEVED WHEN YOU RAISED THE POWER BOAT?
BATOU... I WANT YOU TO COOPERATE WITH THIS MAN HERE, AND TRY TO GET SOME INFORMATION OUT OF THE FELLOW IN THE MILITARY...
SO, OUT OF THE FORMER EMPLOYEES FROM THE NUMBER FIFTY-EIGHT PRISON CAMP, ONLY TWO ARE ALIVE NOW... ONE'S MISSING, AND ONE'S STILL IN THE MILITARY...
WELL, THANK YOU, BUT ***I'LL*** MAKE THE DECISION WHETHER HE SHOULD BE INTERROGATED OR NOT...
...
HAH, HAH... WELL, NO, ACTUALLY, WE CAN'T LET THE MAN IN QUESTION HAVE ANY CONTACT WITH THE OUTSIDE WORLD... HE'S ON A ***SPECIAL ASSIGNMENT*** RIGHT NOW, UNFORTUNATELY...

One obviously can't use a secret code number or encryption system when communicating with someone, unless that someone is party to the code or there has been some prior agreement on the code being used (we're not talking about code cracking here). To prevent electronic communications from being intercepted or overheard, the best thing would actually be to physically meet the party with whom one is trying to communicate, but that takes time, of course... In this case, the transmitters were in the marina or port, and attached to the most suspicious of the vehicles after their plates and owner registrations had been checked. I just haven't drawn the scenes showing the vehicles being tagged...

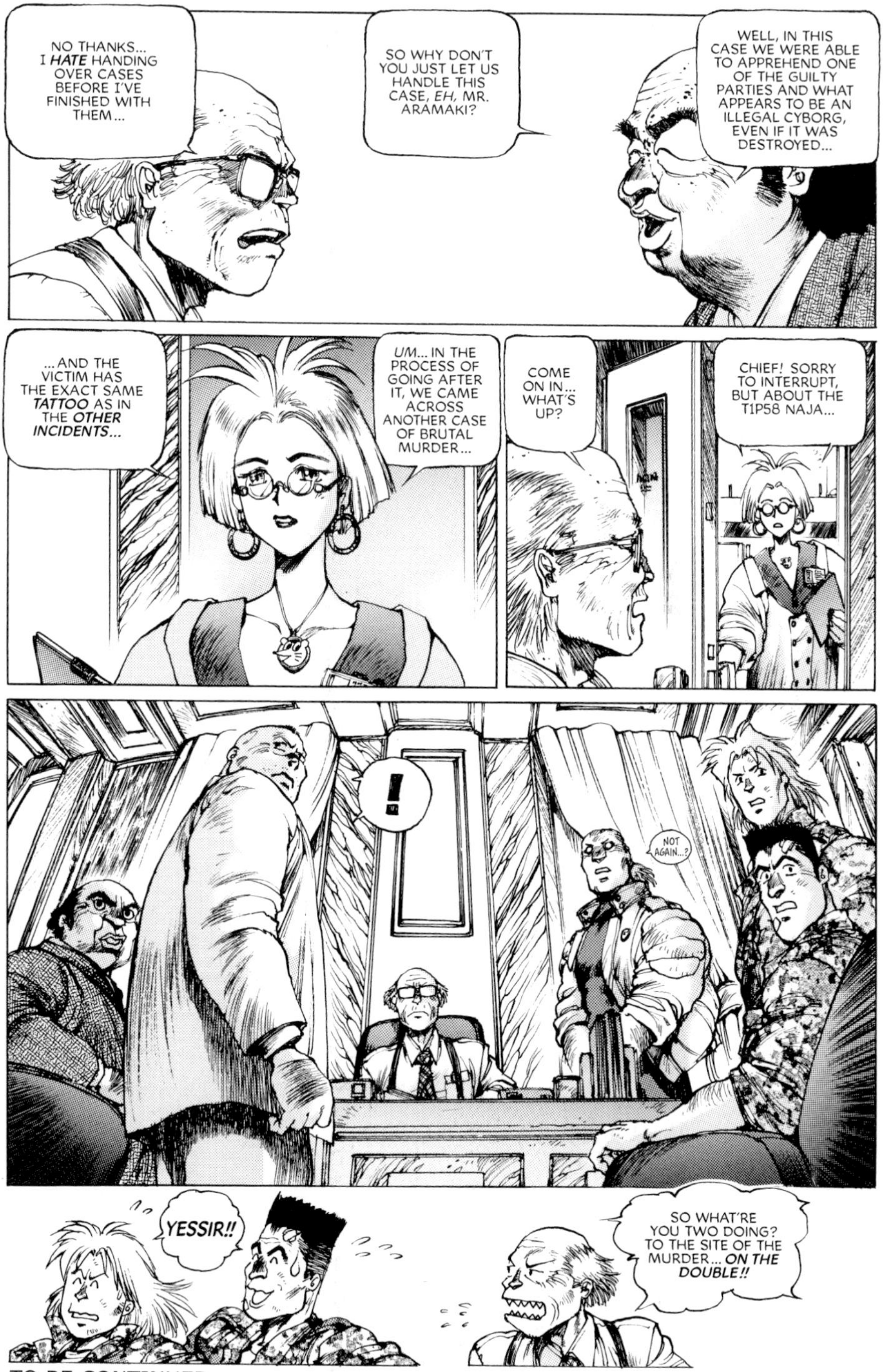
WELL, IN THIS CASE WE WERE ABLE TO APPREHEND ONE OF THE GUILTY PARTIES AND WHAT APPEARS TO BE AN ILLEGAL CYBORG, EVEN IF IT WAS DESTROYED...
SO WHY DON'T YOU JUST LET US HANDLE THIS CASE, *EH,* MR. ARAMAKI?
NO THANKS... I ***HATE*** HANDING OVER CASES BEFORE I'VE FINISHED WITH THEM...
CHIEF! SORRY TO INTERRUPT, BUT ABOUT THE T1P58 NAJA...
COME ON IN... WHAT'S UP?
UM... IN THE PROCESS OF GOING AFTER IT, WE CAME ACROSS ANOTHER CASE OF BRUTAL MURDER...
...AND THE VICTIM HAS THE EXACT SAME ***TATTOO*** AS IN THE ***OTHER INCIDENTS...***
NOT AGAIN...?
!
SO WHAT'RE YOU TWO DOING? TO THE SITE OF THE MURDER... ***ON THE DOUBLE!!***
YESSIR!!

TO BE CONTINUED

MINES OF MIND Part 2

1995

06

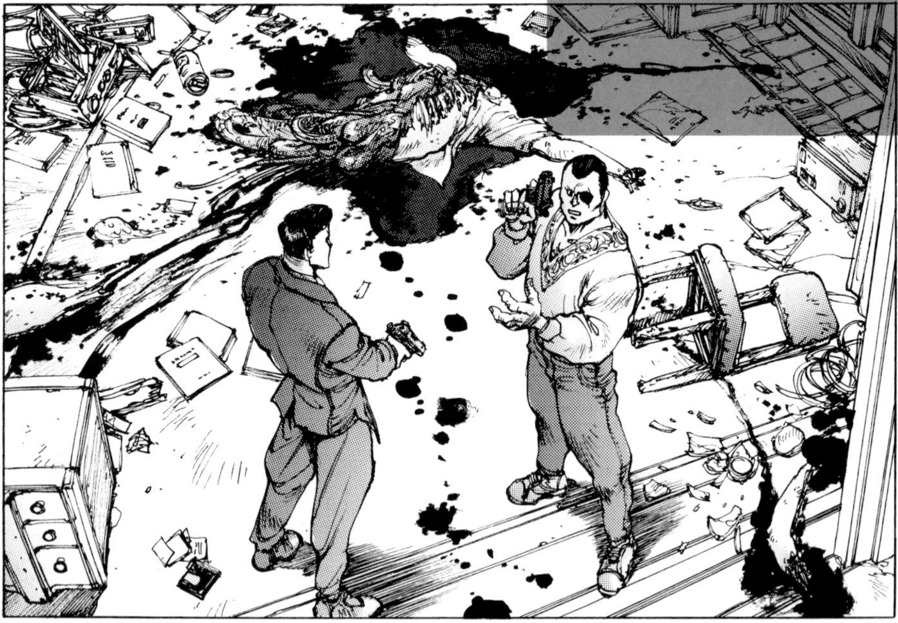

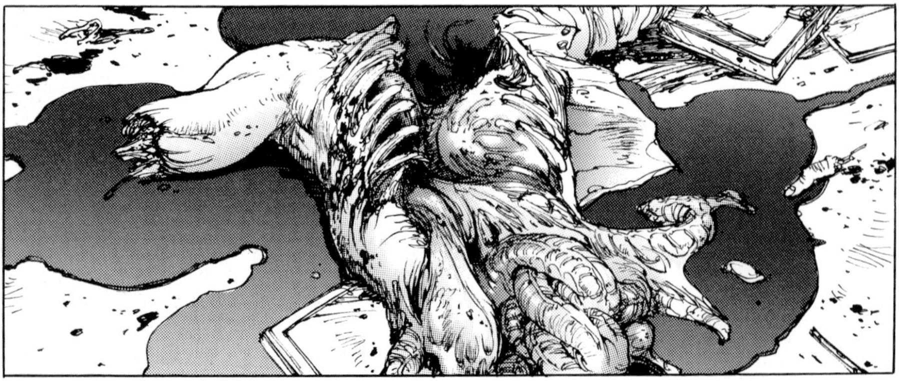

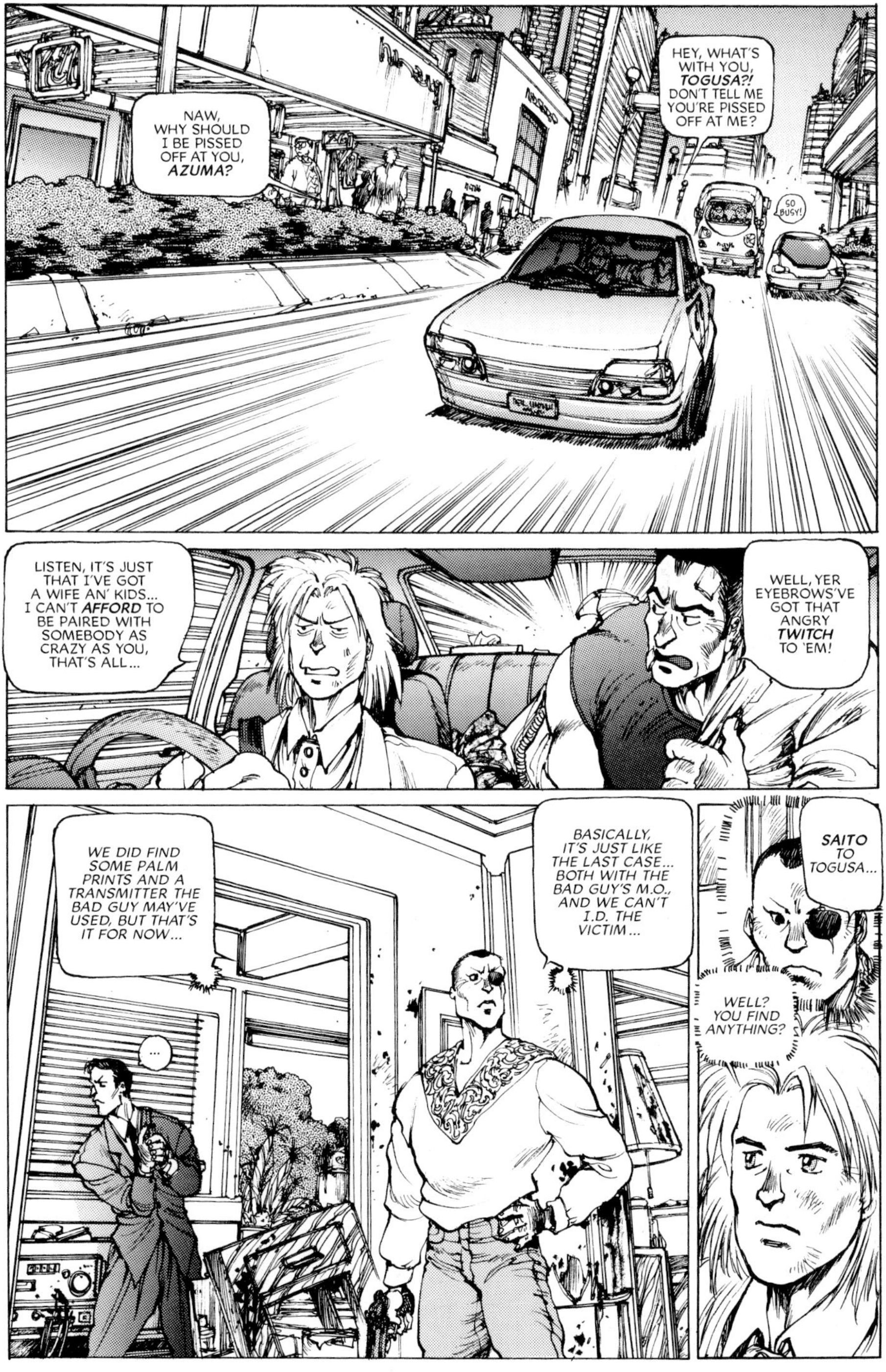
HEY, WHAT'S WITH YOU, *TOGUSA?!* DON'T TELL ME YOU'RE PISSED OFF AT ME?
SO BUSY!
NAW, WHY SHOULD I BE PISSED OFF AT YOU, *AZUMA?*
WELL, YER EYEBROWS'VE GOT THAT ANGRY *TWITCH* TO 'EM!
LISTEN, IT'S JUST THAT I'VE GOT A WIFE AN' KIDS... I CAN'T *AFFORD* TO BE PAIRED WITH SOMEBODY AS CRAZY AS YOU, THAT'S ALL...
SAITO TO TOGUSA...
WELL? YOU FIND ANYTHING?
BASICALLY, IT'S JUST LIKE THE LAST CASE... BOTH WITH THE BAD GUY'S M.O., AND WE CAN'T I.D. THE VICTIM...
WE DID FIND SOME PALM PRINTS AND A TRANSMITTER THE BAD GUY MAY'VE USED, BUT THAT'S IT FOR NOW...
...

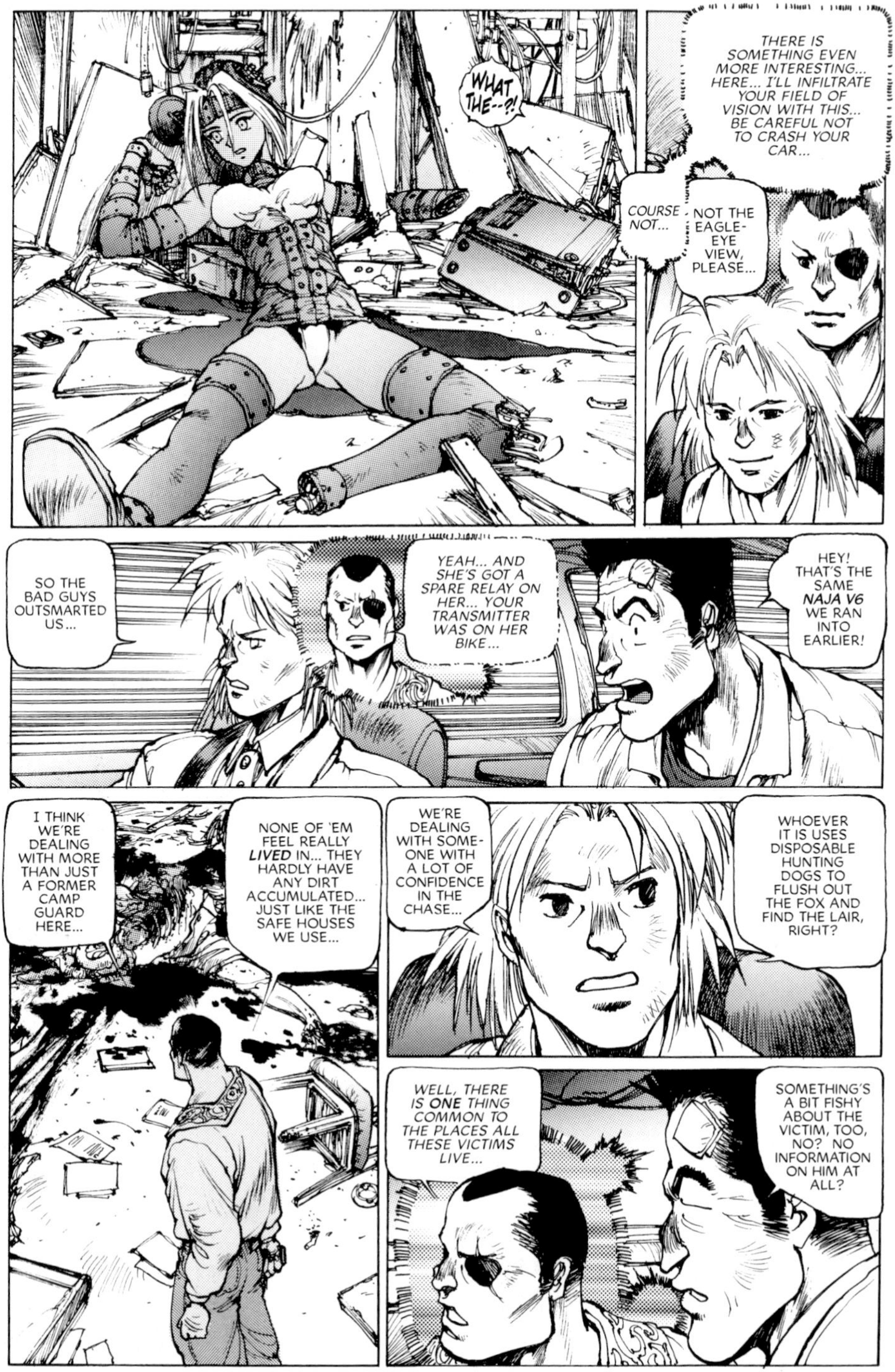
THERE IS SOMETHING EVEN MORE INTERESTING... HERE... I'LL INFILTRATE YOUR FIELD OF VISION WITH THIS... BE CAREFUL NOT TO CRASH YOUR CAR...
NOT THE EAGLE-EYE VIEW, PLEASE...
COURSE NOT...
WHAT THE--?!
HEY! THAT'S THE SAME *NAJA V6* WE RAN INTO EARLIER!
YEAH... AND SHE'S GOT A SPARE RELAY ON HER... YOUR TRANSMITTER WAS ON HER BIKE...
SO THE BAD GUYS OUTSMARTED US...
WHOEVER IT IS USES DISPOSABLE HUNTING DOGS TO FLUSH OUT THE FOX AND FIND THE LAIR, RIGHT?
WE'RE DEALING WITH SOME-ONE WITH A LOT OF CONFIDENCE IN THE CHASE...
SOMETHING'S A BIT FISHY ABOUT THE VICTIM, TOO, NO? NO INFORMATION ON HIM AT ALL?
WELL, THERE IS **ONE** THING COMMON TO THE PLACES ALL THESE VICTIMS LIVE...
NONE OF 'EM FEEL REALLY **LIVED** IN... THEY HARDLY HAVE ANY DIRT ACCUMULATED... JUST LIKE THE SAFE HOUSES WE USE...
I THINK WE'RE DEALING WITH MORE THAN JUST A FORMER CAMP GUARD HERE...

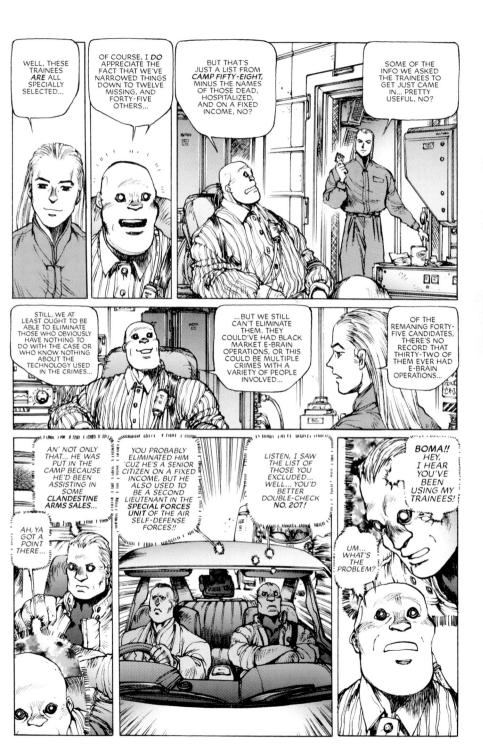

116

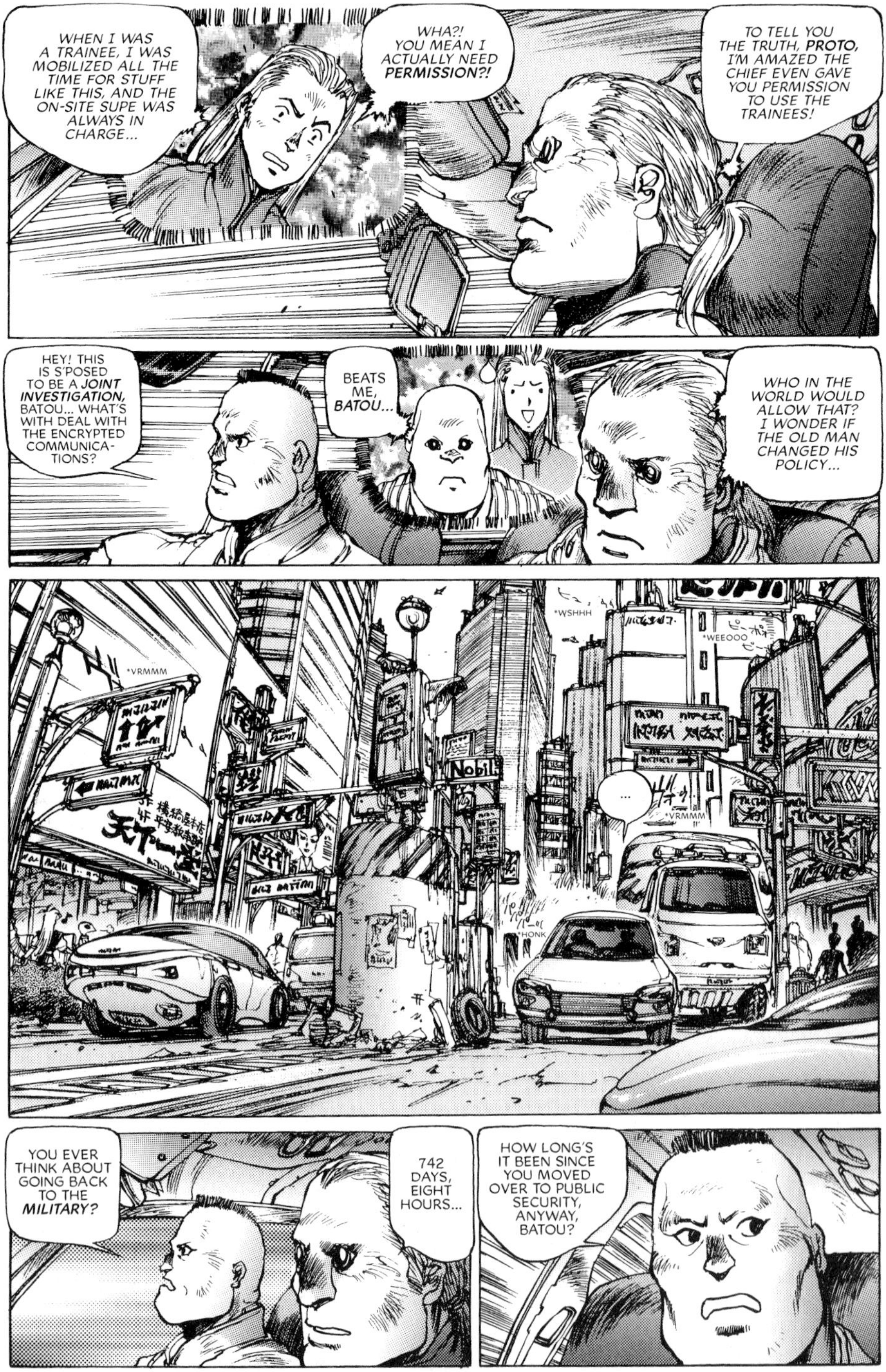
TO TELL YOU THE TRUTH, **PROTO,** I'M AMAZED THE CHIEF EVEN GAVE YOU PERMISSION TO USE THE TRAINEES!
WHA?! YOU MEAN I ACTUALLY NEED **PERMISSION?!**
WHEN I WAS A TRAINEE, I WAS MOBILIZED ALL THE TIME FOR STUFF LIKE THIS, AND THE ON-SITE SUPE WAS ALWAYS IN CHARGE...
WHO IN THE WORLD WOULD ALLOW THAT? I WONDER IF THE OLD MAN CHANGED HIS POLICY...
BEATS ME, ***BATOU...***
HEY! THIS IS S'POSED TO BE A ***JOINT INVESTIGATION,*** BATOU... WHAT'S WITH DEAL WITH THE ENCRYPTED COMMUNICA-TIONS?
*WSHHH
*WEEOOO
...
*VRMMM
*VRMMM
*HONK
HOW LONG'S IT BEEN SINCE YOU MOVED OVER TO PUBLIC SECURITY, ANYWAY, BATOU?
742 DAYS, EIGHT HOURS...
YOU EVER THINK ABOUT GOING BACK TO THE ***MILITARY?***

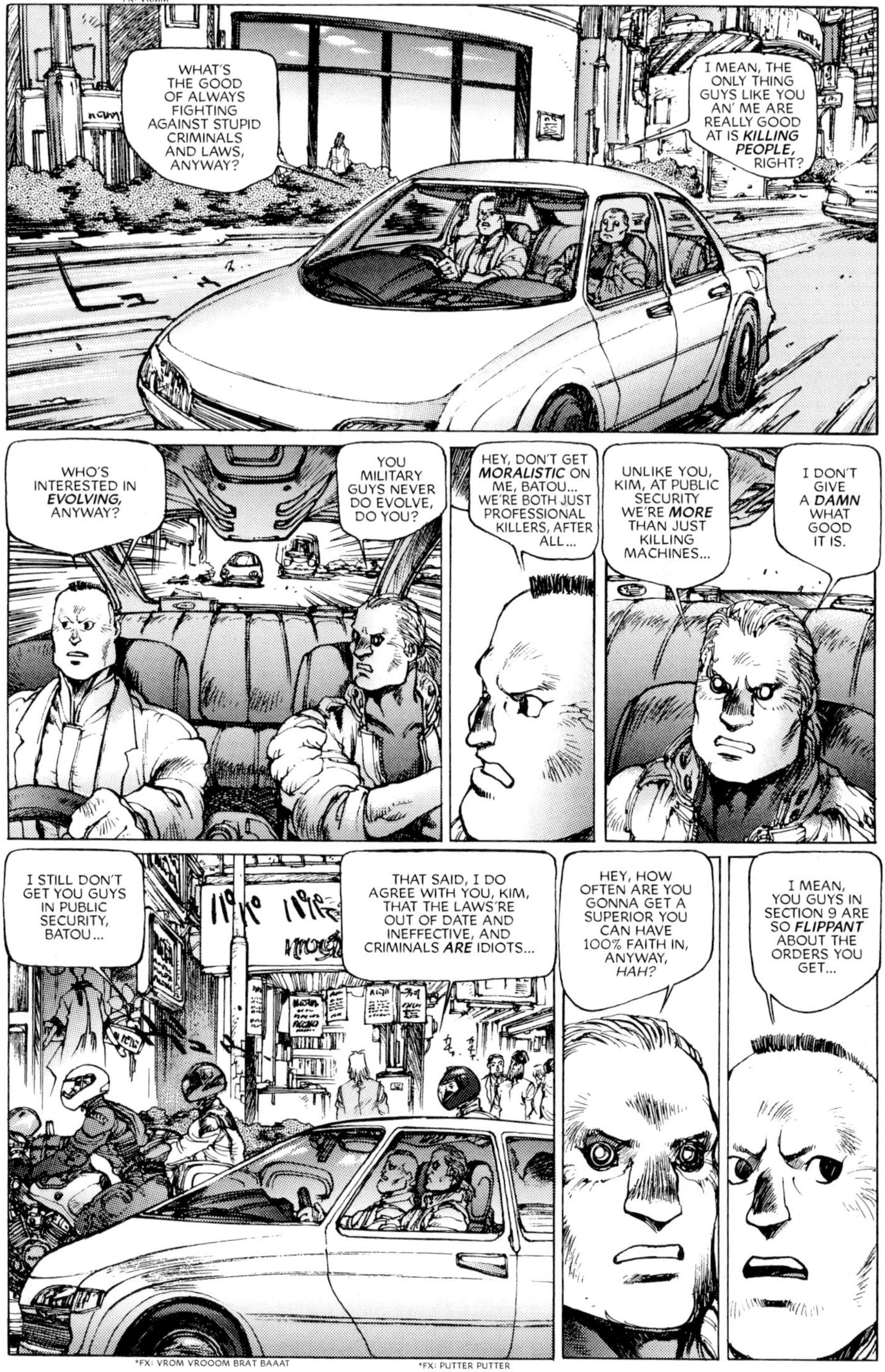
*FX: VRMM
WHAT'S THE GOOD OF ALWAYS FIGHTING AGAINST STUPID CRIMINALS AND LAWS, ANYWAY?
I MEAN, THE ONLY THING GUYS LIKE YOU AN' ME ARE REALLY GOOD AT IS *KILLING PEOPLE,* RIGHT?
WHO'S INTERESTED IN *EVOLVING,* ANYWAY?
YOU MILITARY GUYS NEVER DO EVOLVE, DO YOU?
HEY, DON'T GET *MORALISTIC* ON ME, BATOU... WE'RE BOTH JUST PROFESSIONAL KILLERS, AFTER ALL...
UNLIKE YOU, KIM, AT PUBLIC SECURITY WE'RE *MORE* THAN JUST KILLING MACHINES...
I DON'T GIVE A *DAMN* WHAT GOOD IT IS.
I STILL DON'T GET YOU GUYS IN PUBLIC SECURITY, BATOU...
THAT SAID, I DO AGREE WITH YOU, KIM, THAT THE LAWS'RE OUT OF DATE AND INEFFECTIVE, AND CRIMINALS *ARE* IDIOTS...
HEY, HOW OFTEN ARE YOU GONNA GET A SUPERIOR YOU CAN HAVE 100% FAITH IN, ANYWAY, *HAH?*
I MEAN, YOU GUYS IN SECTION 9 ARE SO *FLIPPANT* ABOUT THE ORDERS YOU GET...
*FX: VROM VROOOM BRAT BAAAT
*FX: PUTTER PUTTER

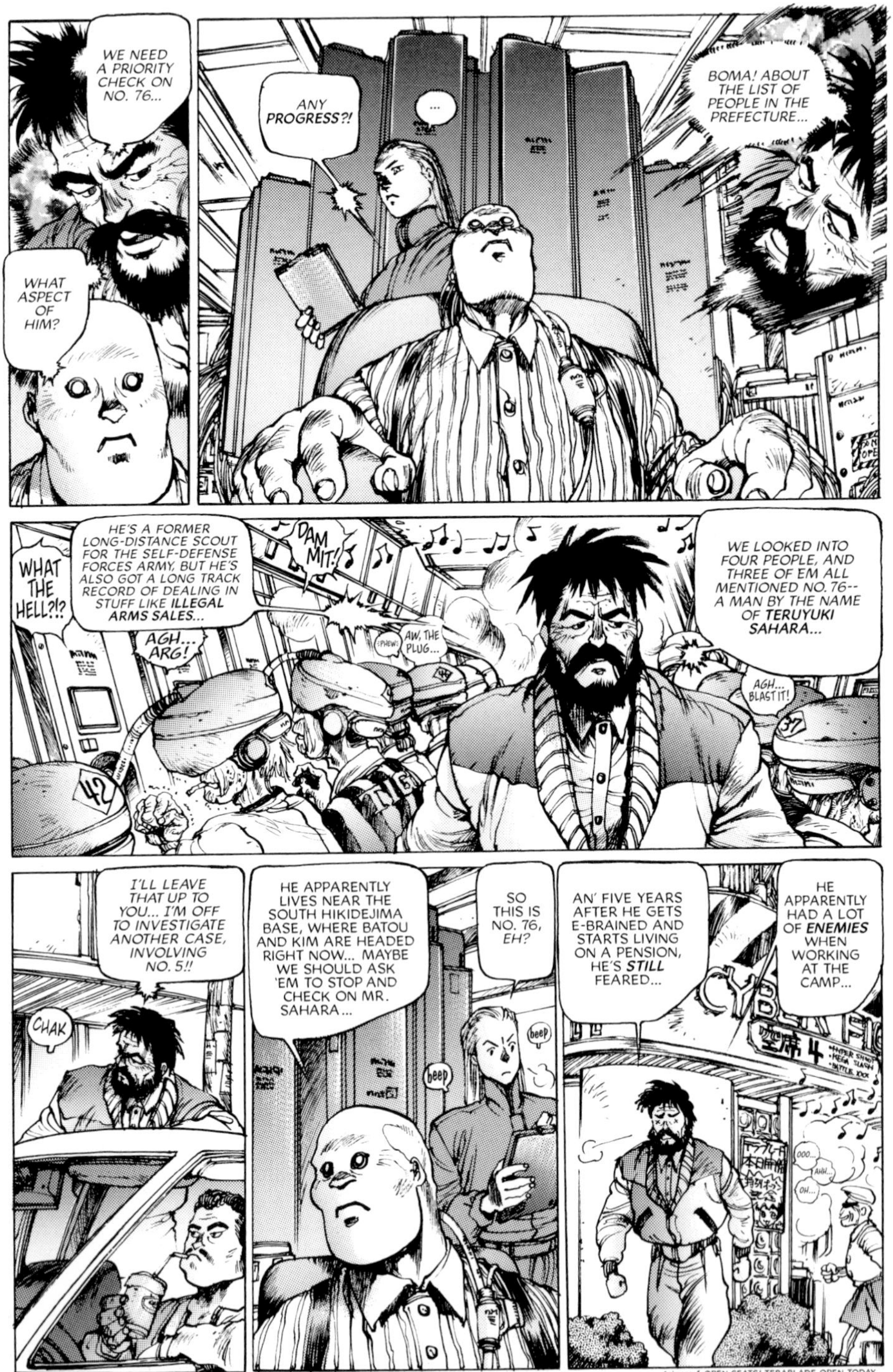
BOMA! ABOUT THE LIST OF PEOPLE IN THE PREFECTURE...
ANY PROGRESS?!
...
WE NEED A PRIORITY CHECK ON NO. 76...
WHAT ASPECT OF HIM?
WE LOOKED INTO FOUR PEOPLE, AND THREE OF EM ALL MENTIONED NO. 76-- A MAN BY THE NAME OF TERUYUKI SAHARA...
AGH... BLAST IT!
AW, THE PLUG...
PHEW
DAM MIT!
AGH... ARG!
HE'S A FORMER LONG-DISTANCE SCOUT FOR THE SELF-DEFENSE FORCES ARMY, BUT HE'S ALSO GOT A LONG TRACK RECORD OF DEALING IN STUFF LIKE ILLEGAL ARMS SALES...
WHAT THE HELL?!?
HE APPARENTLY HAD A LOT OF ENEMIES WHEN WORKING AT THE CAMP...
AN' FIVE YEARS AFTER HE GETS E-BRAINED AND STARTS LIVING ON A PENSION, HE'S STILL FEARED...
OOO...
AHH...
OH...
SO THIS IS NO. 76, EH?
HE APPARENTLY LIVES NEAR THE SOUTH HIKIDEJIMA BASE, WHERE BATOU AND KIM ARE HEADED RIGHT NOW... MAYBE WE SHOULD ASK 'EM TO STOP AND CHECK ON MR. SAHARA...
beep
beep
I'LL LEAVE THAT UP TO YOU... I'M OFF TO INVESTIGATE ANOTHER CASE, INVOLVING NO. 5!!
CHAK

*signs: 4 OPEN SEATS! TERABLADE OPEN TODAY. SPECIAL OPENING COMMEMORATION.

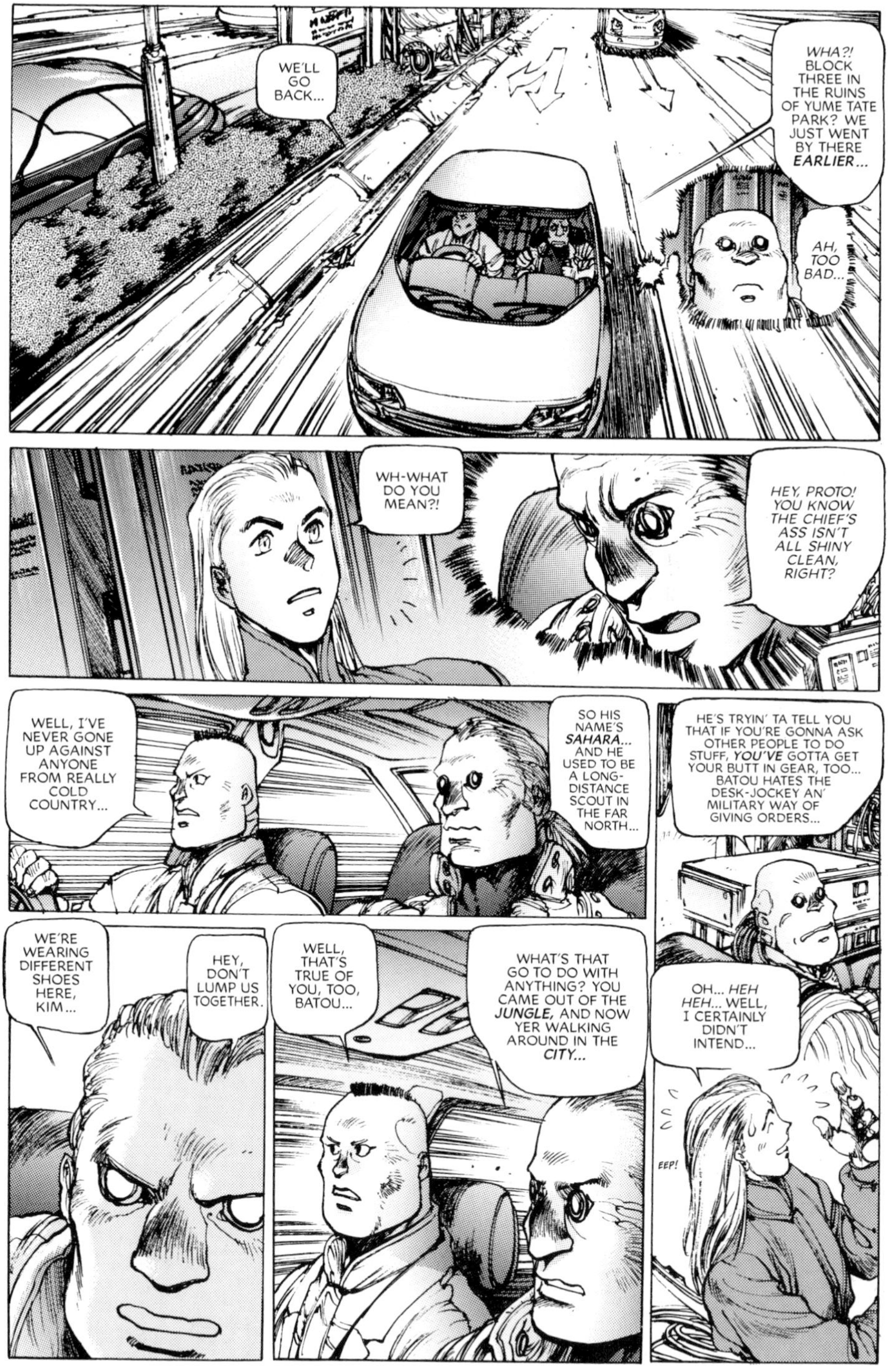
WHA?! BLOCK THREE IN THE RUINS OF YUME TATE PARK? WE JUST WENT BY THERE *EARLIER*...
AH, TOO BAD...
WE'LL GO BACK...
HEY, PROTO! YOU KNOW THE CHIEF'S ASS ISN'T ALL SHINY CLEAN, RIGHT?
WH-WHAT DO YOU MEAN?!
HE'S TRYIN' TA TELL YOU THAT IF YOU'RE GONNA ASK OTHER PEOPLE TO DO STUFF, *YOU'VE* GOTTA GET YOUR BUTT IN GEAR, TOO... BATOU HATES THE DESK-JOCKEY AN' MILITARY WAY OF GIVING ORDERS...
OH... *HEH HEH*... WELL, I CERTAINLY DIDN'T INTEND...
EEP!
SO HIS NAME'S *SAHARA*... AND HE USED TO BE A LONG-DISTANCE SCOUT IN THE FAR NORTH...
WELL, I'VE NEVER GONE UP AGAINST ANYONE FROM REALLY COLD COUNTRY...
WHAT'S THAT GO TO DO WITH ANYTHING? YOU CAME OUT OF THE *JUNGLE,* AND NOW YER WALKING AROUND IN THE *CITY*...
WELL, THAT'S TRUE OF YOU, TOO, BATOU...
HEY, DON'T LUMP US TOGETHER.
WE'RE WEARING DIFFERENT SHOES HERE, KIM...

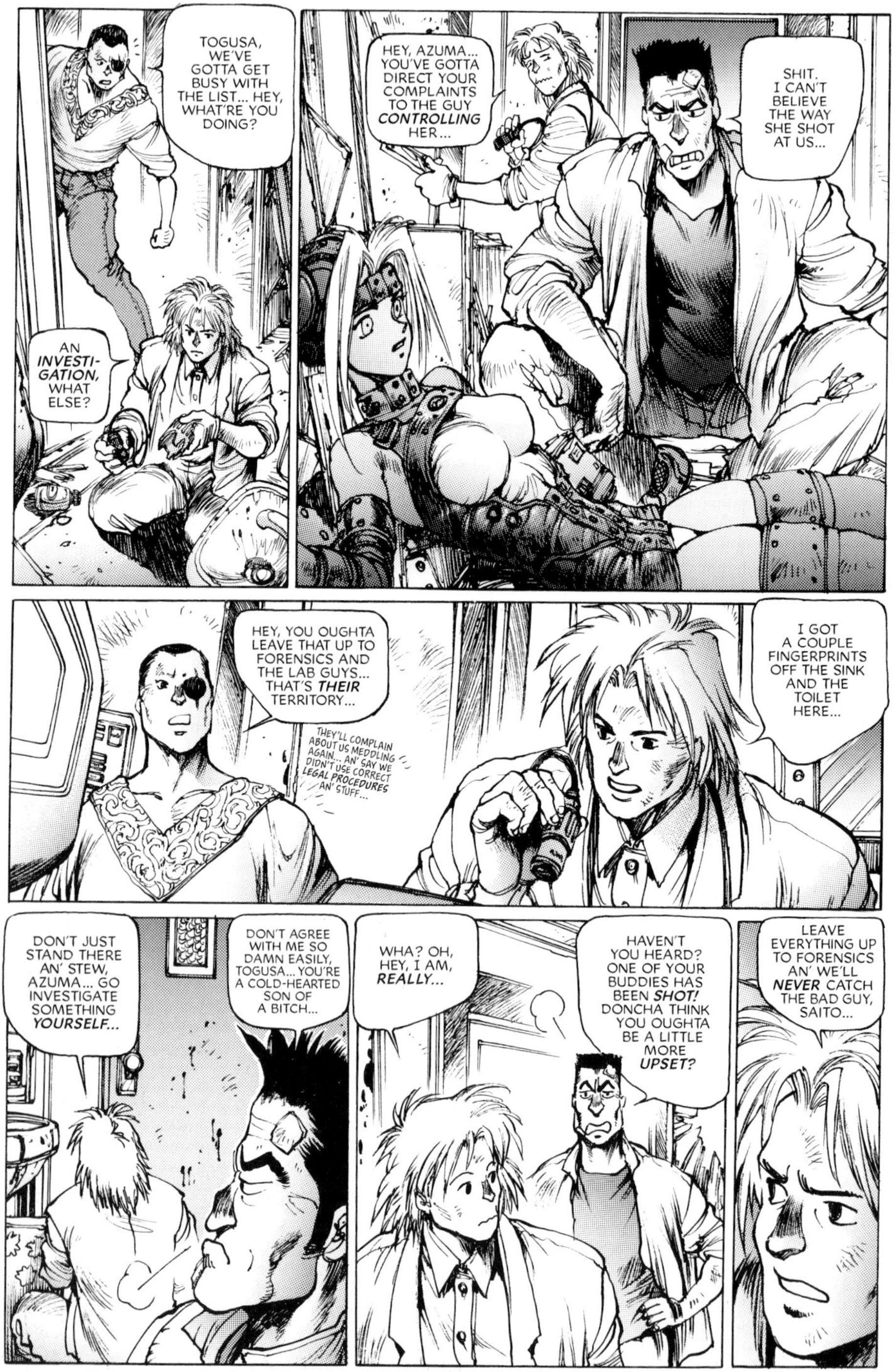
SHIT. I CAN'T BELIEVE THE WAY SHE SHOT AT US...
HEY, AZUMA... YOU'VE GOTTA DIRECT YOUR COMPLAINTS TO THE GUY **CONTROLLING** HER...
TOGUSA, WE'VE GOTTA GET BUSY WITH THE LIST... HEY, WHAT'RE YOU DOING?
AN ***INVESTIGATION,*** WHAT ELSE?
I GOT A COUPLE FINGERPRINTS OFF THE SINK AND THE TOILET HERE...
HEY, YOU OUGHTA LEAVE THAT UP TO FORENSICS AND THE LAB GUYS... THAT'S ***THEIR*** TERRITORY...
THEY'LL COMPLAIN ABOUT US MEDDLING AGAIN... AN' SAY WE DIDN'T USE CORRECT **LEGAL PROCEDURES** AN' STUFF...
LEAVE EVERYTHING UP TO FORENSICS AN' WE'LL ***NEVER*** CATCH THE BAD GUY, SAITO...
HAVEN'T YOU HEARD? ONE OF YOUR BUDDIES HAS BEEN ***SHOT!*** DONCHA THINK YOU OUGHTA BE A LITTLE MORE ***UPSET?***
WHA? OH, HEY, I AM, ***REALLY...***
DON'T AGREE WITH ME SO DAMN EASILY, TOGUSA... YOU'RE A COLD-HEARTED SON OF A BITCH...
DON'T JUST STAND THERE AN' STEW, AZUMA... GO INVESTIGATE SOMETHING ***YOURSELF...***

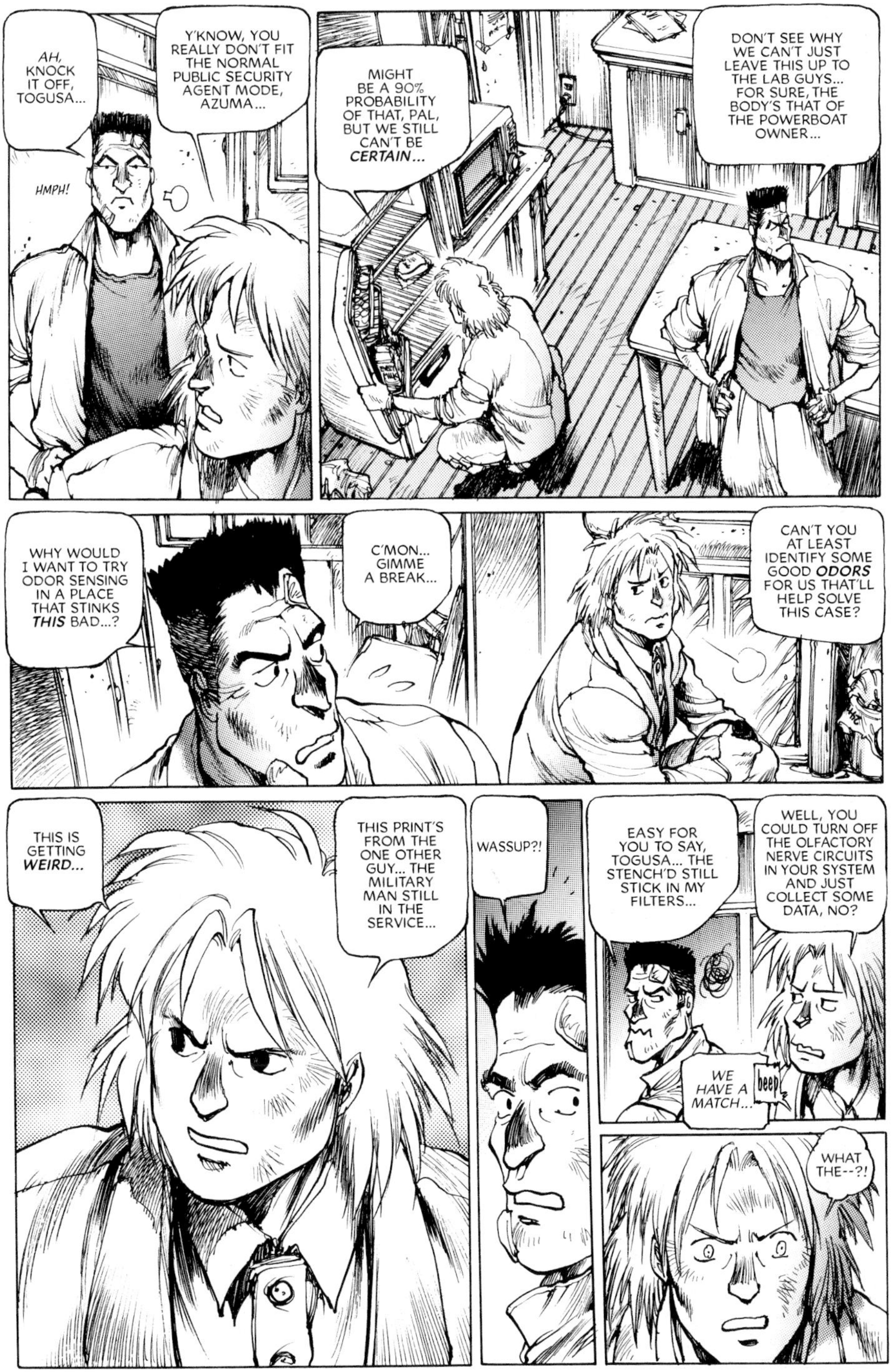
DON'T SEE WHY WE CAN'T JUST LEAVE THIS UP TO THE LAB GUYS... FOR SURE, THE BODY'S THAT OF THE POWERBOAT OWNER...
MIGHT BE A 90% PROBABILITY OF THAT, PAL, BUT WE STILL CAN'T BE *CERTAIN*...
Y'KNOW, YOU REALLY DON'T FIT THE NORMAL PUBLIC SECURITY AGENT MODE, AZUMA...
AH, KNOCK IT OFF, TOGUSA...
HMPH!
CAN'T YOU AT LEAST IDENTIFY SOME GOOD ***ODORS*** FOR US THAT'LL HELP SOLVE THIS CASE?
C'MON... GIMME A BREAK...
WHY WOULD I WANT TO TRY ODOR SENSING IN A PLACE THAT STINKS ***THIS*** BAD...?
WELL, YOU COULD TURN OFF THE OLFACTORY NERVE CIRCUITS IN YOUR SYSTEM AND JUST COLLECT SOME DATA, NO?
EASY FOR YOU TO SAY, TOGUSA... THE STENCH'D STILL STICK IN MY FILTERS...
beep
WE HAVE A MATCH...
WHAT THE--?!
WASSUP?!
THIS PRINT'S FROM THE ONE OTHER GUY... THE MILITARY MAN STILL IN THE SERVICE...
THIS IS GETTING ***WEIRD...***

*FX: ACK ACK

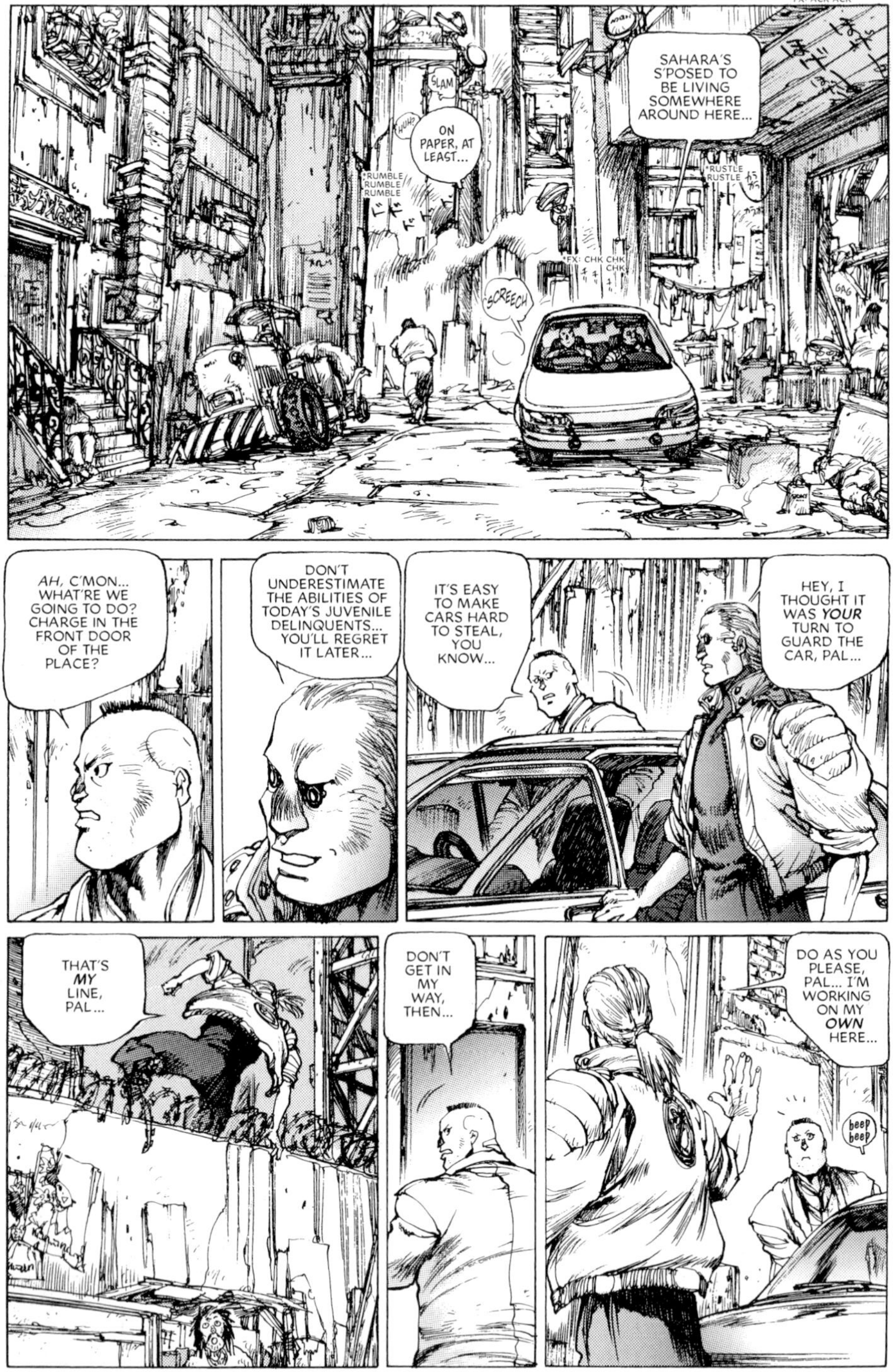
SAHARA'S S'POSED TO BE LIVING SOMEWHERE AROUND HERE...
*RUSTLE RUSTLE
ON PAPER, AT LEAST...
HUH?
SLAM
*RUMBLE RUMBLE RUMBLE
*FX: CHK CHK CHK
SCREECH
GAG
HEY, I THOUGHT IT WAS *YOUR* TURN TO GUARD THE CAR, PAL...
IT'S EASY TO MAKE CARS HARD TO STEAL, YOU KNOW...
DON'T UNDERESTIMATE THE ABILITIES OF TODAY'S JUVENILE DELINQUENTS... YOU'LL REGRET IT LATER...
AH, C'MON... WHAT'RE WE GOING TO DO? CHARGE IN THE FRONT DOOR OF THE PLACE?
DO AS YOU PLEASE, PAL... I'M WORKING ON MY *OWN* HERE...
beep beep
DON'T GET IN MY WAY, THEN...
THAT'S *MY* LINE, PAL...

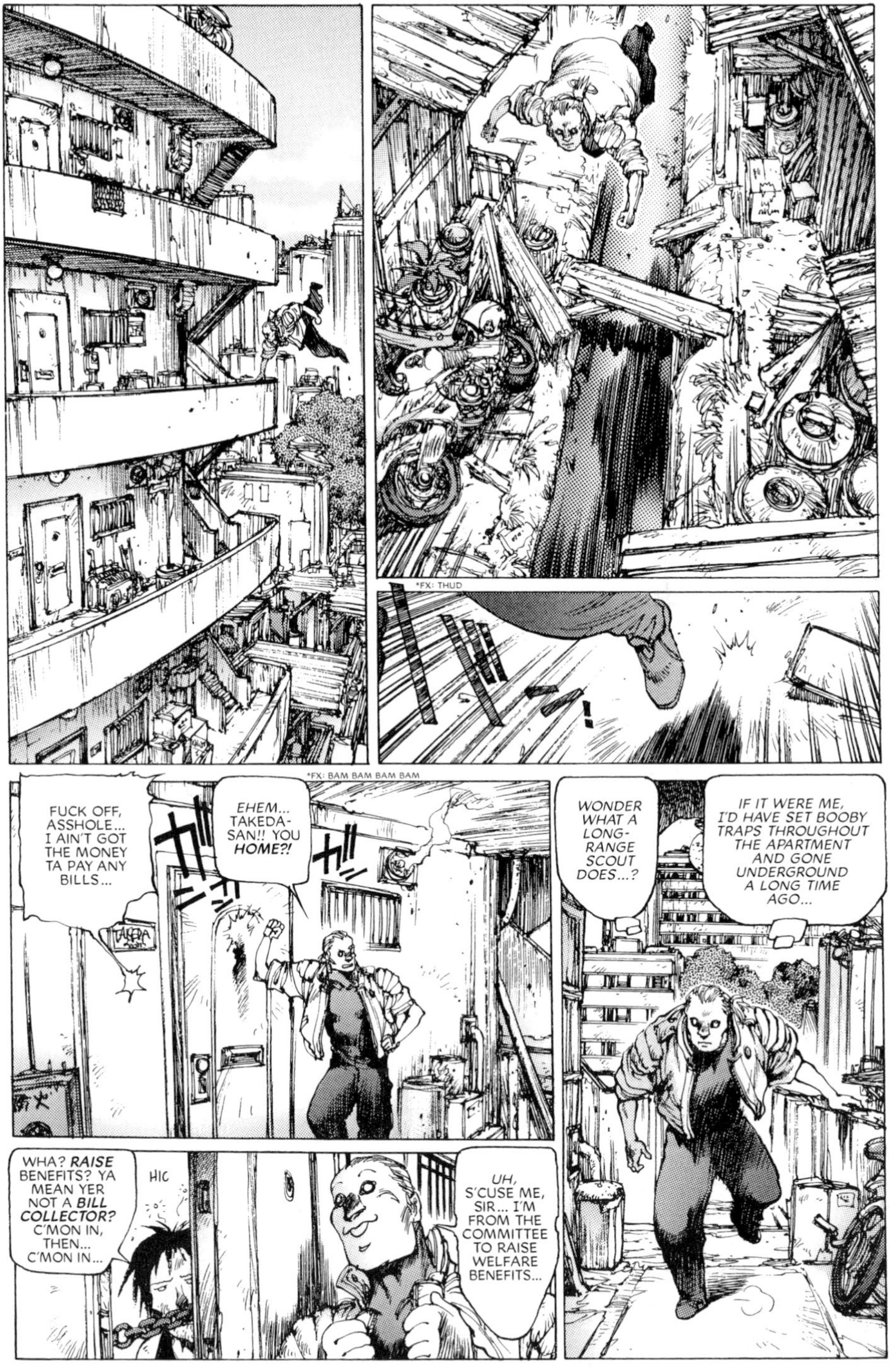
*FX: THUD
*FX: BAM BAM BAM BAM
IF IT WERE ME, I'D HAVE SET BOOBY TRAPS THROUGHOUT THE APARTMENT AND GONE UNDERGROUND A LONG TIME AGO...
WONDER WHAT A LONG-RANGE SCOUT DOES...?
EHEM... TAKEDA-SAN!! YOU *HOME?!*
FUCK OFF, ASSHOLE... I AIN'T GOT THE MONEY TA PAY ANY BILLS...
TAKEDA
UH, S'CUSE ME, SIR... I'M FROM THE COMMITTEE TO RAISE WELFARE BENEFITS...
HIC
WHA? ***RAISE*** BENEFITS? YA MEAN YER NOT A ***BILL COLLECTOR?*** C'MON IN, THEN... C'MON IN...

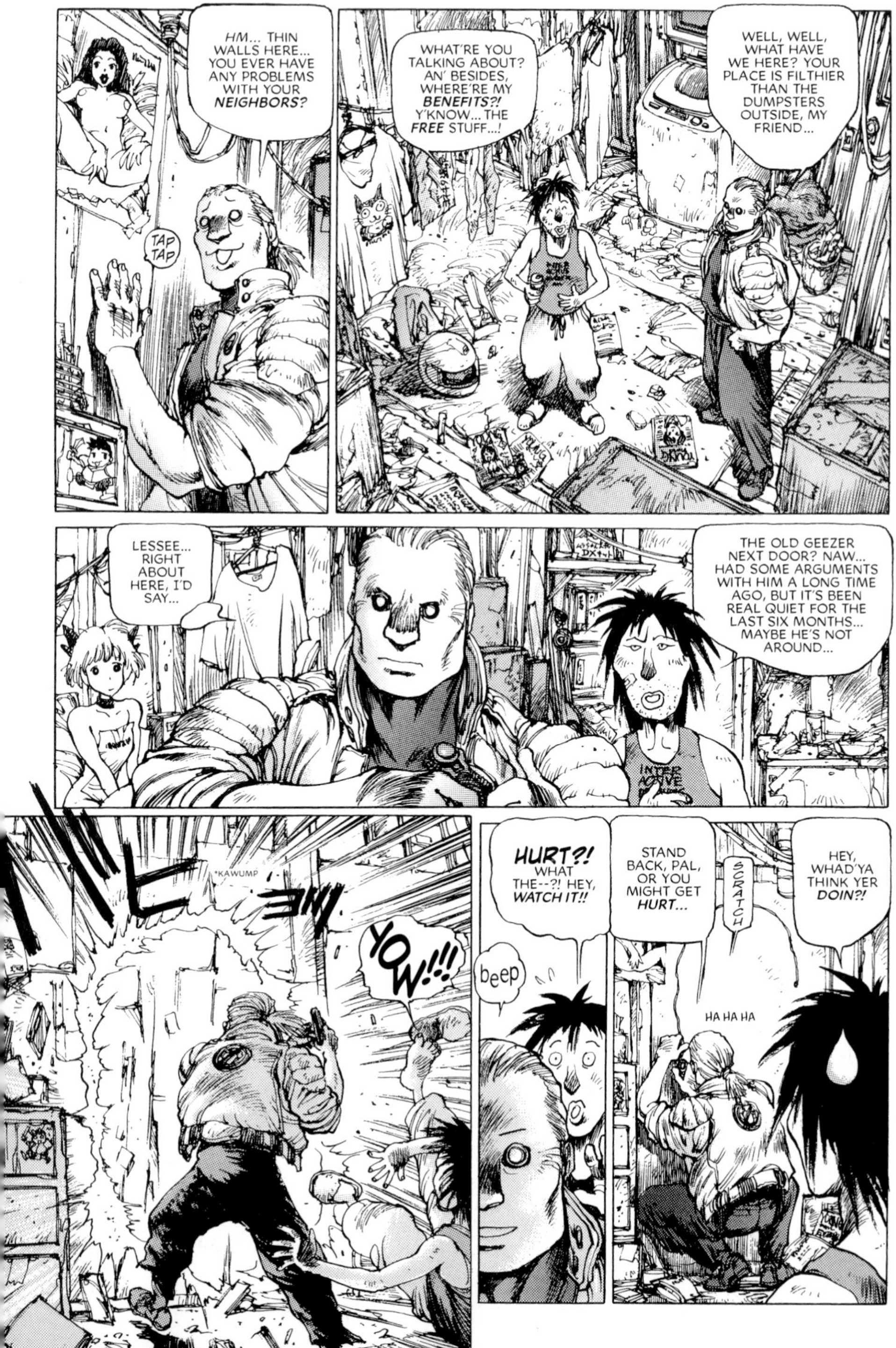
WELL, WELL, WHAT HAVE WE HERE? YOUR PLACE IS FILTHIER THAN THE DUMPSTERS OUTSIDE, MY FRIEND...
WHAT'RE YOU TALKING ABOUT? AN' BESIDES, WHERE'RE MY *BENEFITS?!* Y'KNOW... THE *FREE* STUFF...!
HM... THIN WALLS HERE... YOU EVER HAVE ANY PROBLEMS WITH YOUR ***NEIGHBORS?***
TAP TAP
THE OLD GEEZER NEXT DOOR? NAW... HAD SOME ARGUMENTS WITH HIM A LONG TIME AGO, BUT IT'S BEEN REAL QUIET FOR THE LAST SIX MONTHS... MAYBE HE'S NOT AROUND...
LESSEE... RIGHT ABOUT HERE, I'D SAY...
HEY, WHAD'YA THINK YER *DOIN?!*
SCRATCH
HA HA HA
STAND BACK, PAL, OR YOU MIGHT GET ***HURT...***
HURT?! WHAT THE--?! HEY, ***WATCH IT!!***
beep
*KAWUMP
YOW!!!

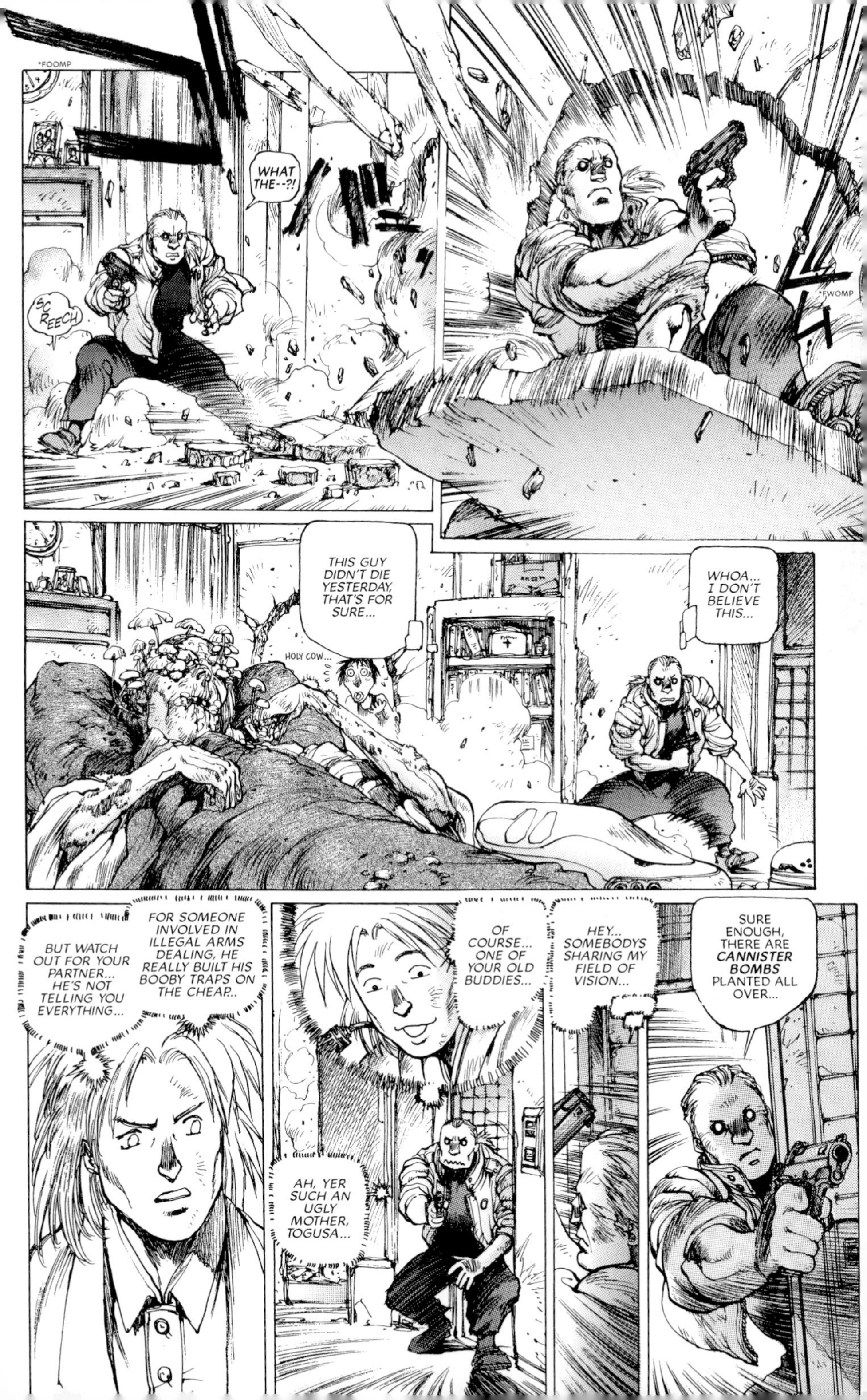
*FWOMP
*FOOMP
WHAT THE--?!
SC REECH
WHOA... I DON'T BELIEVE THIS...
THIS GUY DIDN'T DIE YESTERDAY, THAT'S FOR SURE...
HOLY COW...
SURE ENOUGH, THERE ARE **CANNISTER BOMBS** PLANTED ALL OVER...
HEY... SOMEBODYS SHARING MY FIELD OF VISION...
OF COURSE... ONE OF YOUR OLD BUDDIES...
AH, YER SUCH AN UGLY MOTHER, TOGUSA...
FOR SOMEONE INVOLVED IN ILLEGAL ARMS DEALING, HE REALLY BUILT HIS BOOBY TRAPS ON THE CHEAP...
BUT WATCH OUT FOR YOUR PARTNER... HE'S NOT TELLING YOU EVERYTHING...

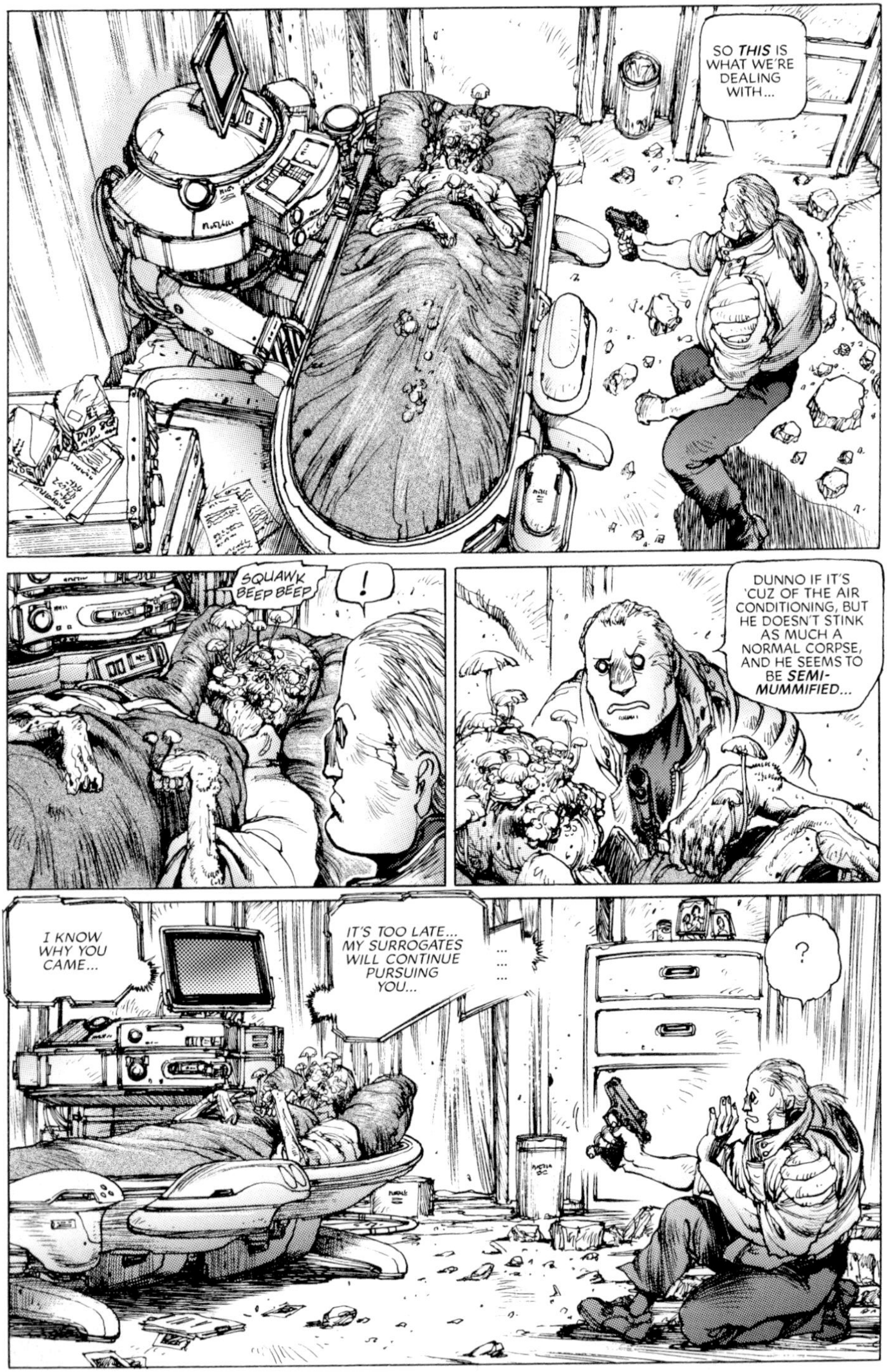
SO *THIS* IS WHAT WE'RE DEALING WITH...
SQUAWK BEEP BEEP
!
DUNNO IF IT'S 'CUZ OF THE AIR CONDITIONING, BUT HE DOESN'T STINK AS MUCH A NORMAL CORPSE, AND HE SEEMS TO BE *SEMI-MUMMIFIED*...
I KNOW WHY YOU CAME...
IT'S TOO LATE... MY SURROGATES WILL CONTINUE PURSUING YOU...
...
...
...
?

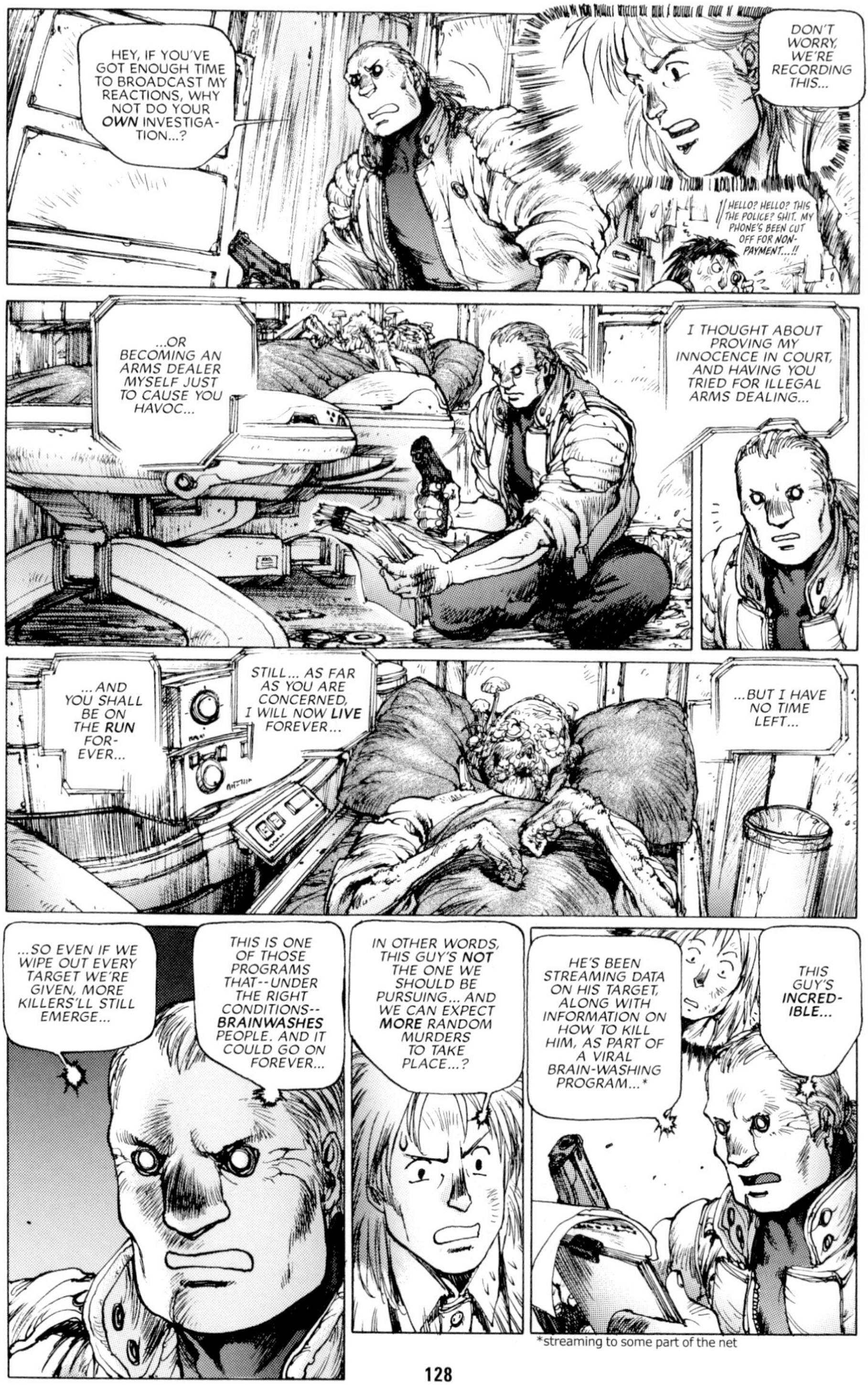
DON'T WORRY, WE'RE RECORDING THIS...
HELLO? HELLO? THIS THE POLICE? SHIT. MY PHONE'S BEEN CUT OFF FOR NON-PAYMENT...!!
HEY, IF YOU'VE GOT ENOUGH TIME TO BROADCAST MY REACTIONS, WHY NOT DO YOUR **OWN** INVESTIGA-TION...?
I THOUGHT ABOUT PROVING MY INNOCENCE IN COURT, AND HAVING YOU TRIED FOR ILLEGAL ARMS DEALING...
...OR BECOMING AN ARMS DEALER MYSELF JUST TO CAUSE YOU HAVOC...
...BUT I HAVE NO TIME LEFT...
STILL... AS FAR AS YOU ARE CONCERNED, I WILL NOW **LIVE** FOREVER...
...AND YOU SHALL BE ON THE **RUN** FOR-EVER...
THIS GUY'S **INCRED-IBLE**...
HE'S BEEN STREAMING DATA ON HIS TARGET, ALONG WITH INFORMATION ON HOW TO KILL HIM, AS PART OF A VIRAL BRAIN-WASHING PROGRAM...*
IN OTHER WORDS, THIS GUY'S **NOT** THE ONE WE SHOULD BE PURSUING... AND WE CAN EXPECT **MORE** RANDOM MURDERS TO TAKE PLACE...?
THIS IS ONE OF THOSE PROGRAMS THAT--UNDER THE RIGHT CONDITIONS--**BRAINWASHES** PEOPLE. AND IT COULD GO ON FOREVER...
...SO EVEN IF WE WIPE OUT EVERY TARGET WE'RE GIVEN, MORE KILLERS'LL STILL EMERGE...

*streaming to some part of the net

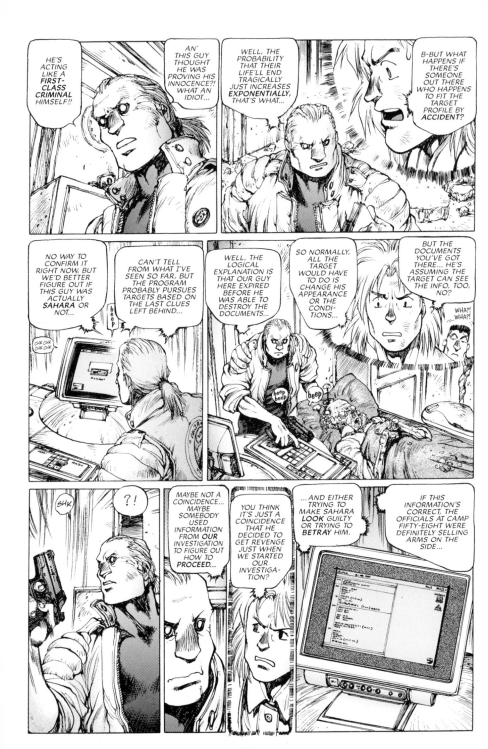

129

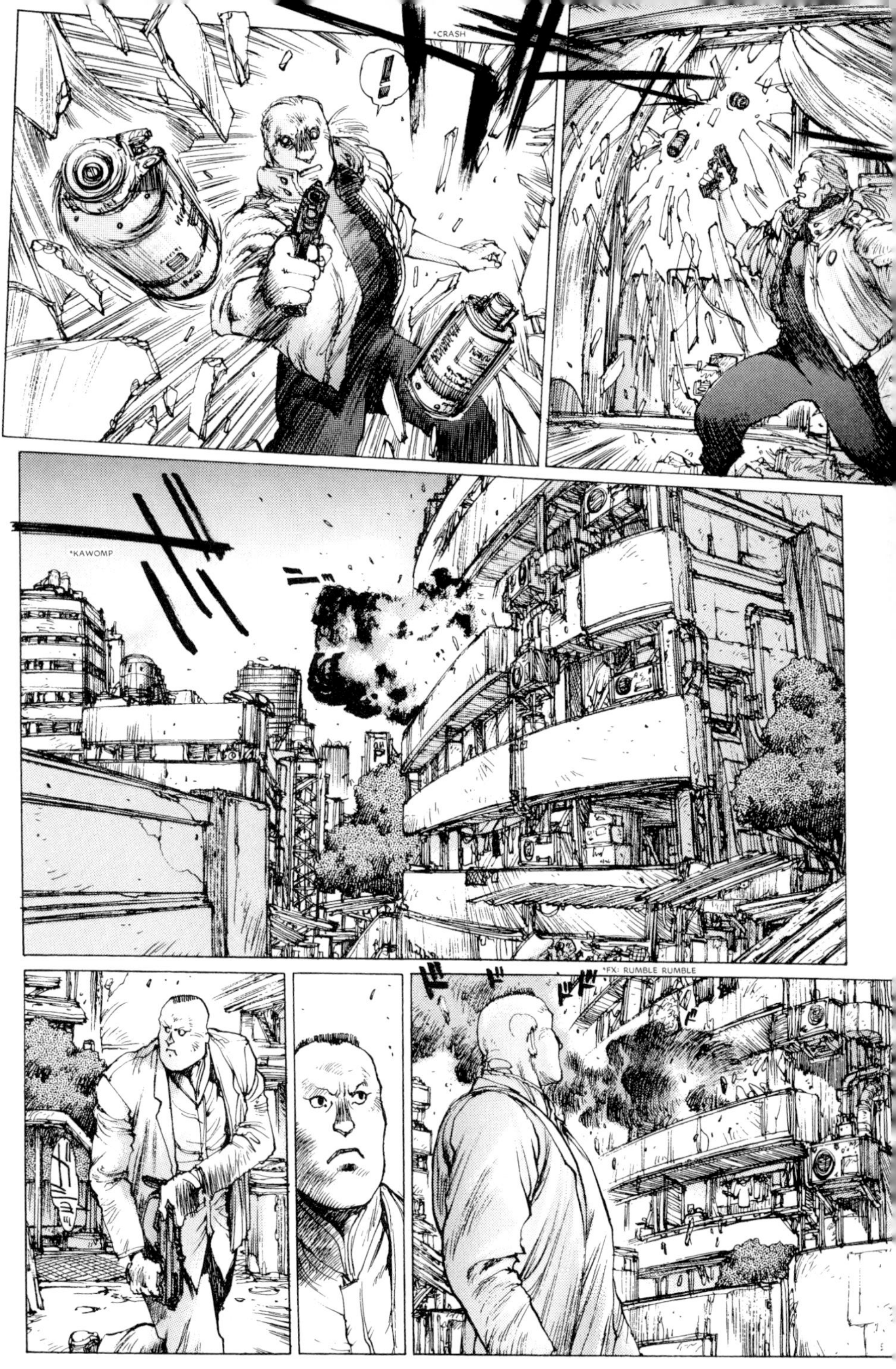
*CRASH
!
*KAWOMP
*FX: RUMBLE RUMBLE

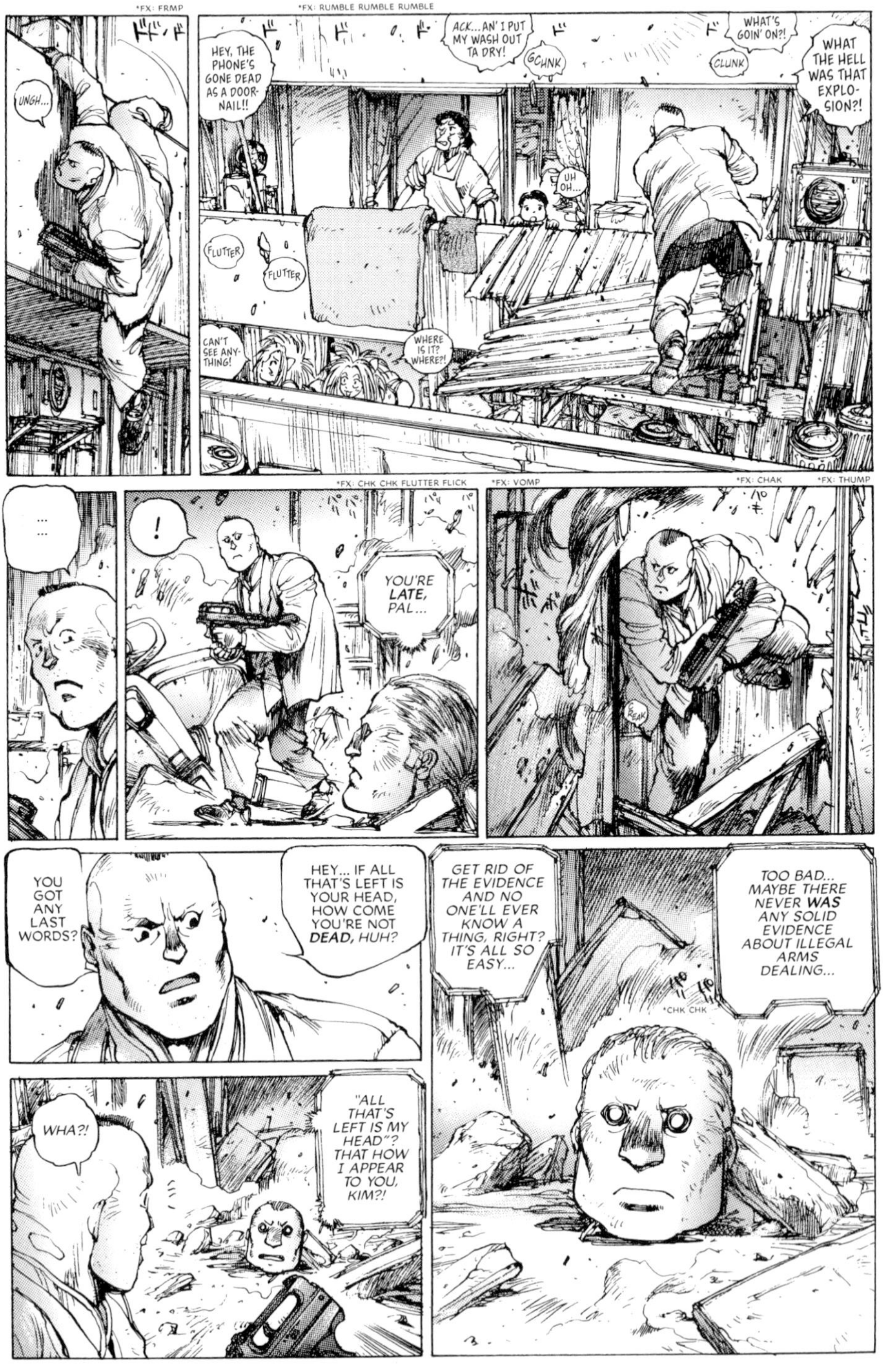
*FX: RUMBLE RUMBLE RUMBLE
WHAT THE HELL WAS THAT EXPLO-SION?!
WHAT'S GOIN' ON?!
CLUNK
ACK... AN' I PUT MY WASH OUT TA DRY!
GCHUNK
UH OH...
HEY, THE PHONE'S GONE DEAD AS A DOOR-NAIL!!
WHERE IS IT? WHERE?!
FLUTTER
FLUTTER
CAN'T SEE ANY-THING!
*FX: FRMP
UNGH...
*FX: THUMP
*FX: CHAK
*FX: VOMP
*FX: CHK CHK FLUTTER FLICK
YOU'RE LATE, PAL...
!
... ...
TOO BAD... MAYBE THERE NEVER WAS ANY SOLID EVIDENCE ABOUT ILLEGAL ARMS DEALING...
*CHK CHK
GET RID OF THE EVIDENCE AND NO ONE'LL EVER KNOW A THING, RIGHT? IT'S ALL SO EASY...
HEY... IF ALL THAT'S LEFT IS YOUR HEAD, HOW COME YOU'RE NOT DEAD, HUH?
YOU GOT ANY LAST WORDS?
"ALL THAT'S LEFT IS MY HEAD"? THAT HOW I APPEAR TO YOU, KIM?!
WHA?!

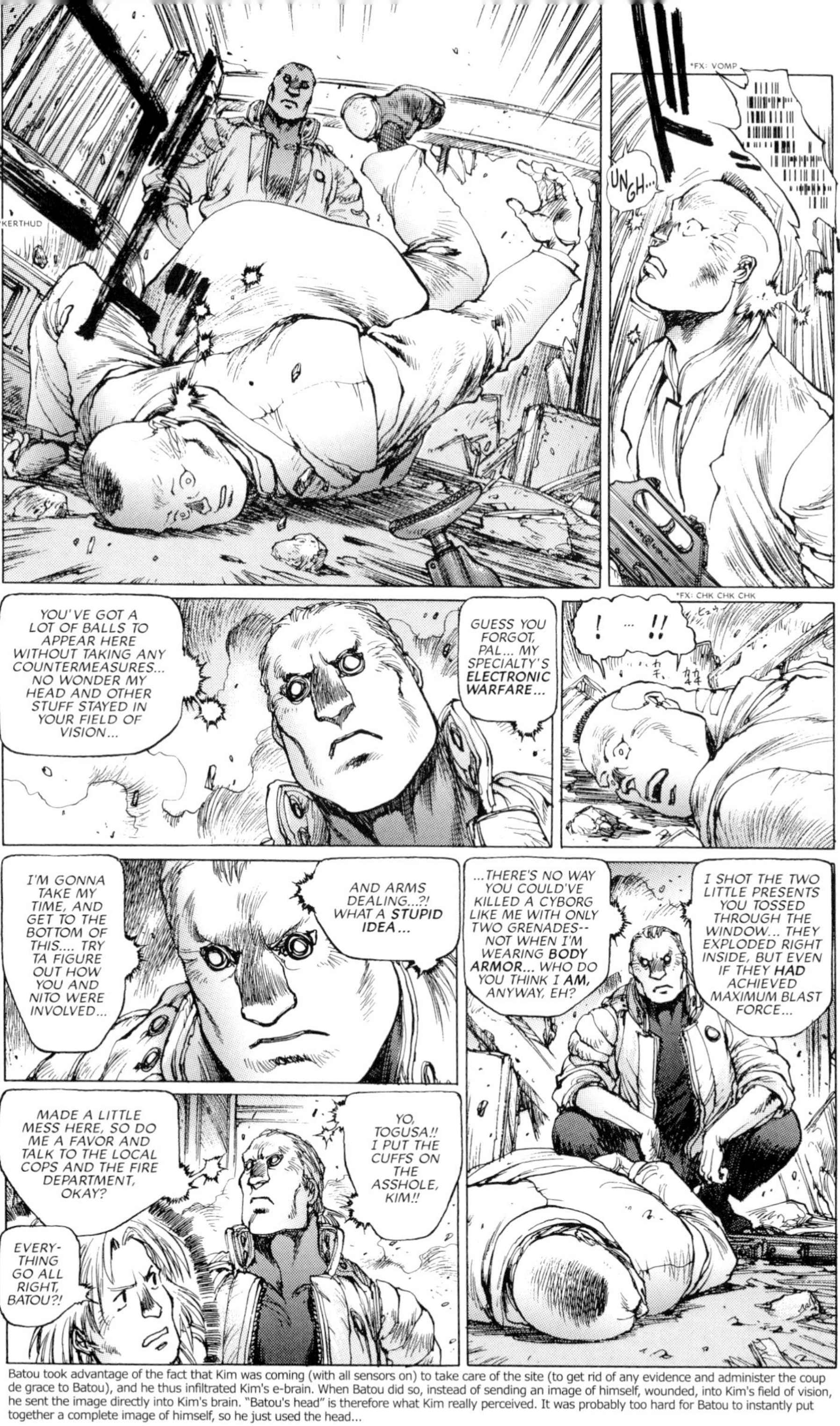
*KERTHUD
*FX: VOMP
UNGH...
*FX: CHK CHK CHK
YOU'VE GOT A LOT OF BALLS TO APPEAR HERE WITHOUT TAKING ANY COUNTERMEASURES... NO WONDER MY HEAD AND OTHER STUFF STAYED IN YOUR FIELD OF VISION...
GUESS YOU FORGOT, PAL... MY SPECIALTY'S **ELECTRONIC WARFARE...**
! ... !!
I SHOT THE TWO LITTLE PRESENTS YOU TOSSED THROUGH THE WINDOW... THEY EXPLODED RIGHT INSIDE, BUT EVEN IF THEY **HAD** ACHIEVED MAXIMUM BLAST FORCE...
...THERE'S NO WAY YOU COULD'VE KILLED A CYBORG LIKE ME WITH ONLY TWO GRENADES-- NOT WHEN I'M WEARING **BODY ARMOR...** WHO DO YOU THINK I **AM,** ANYWAY, EH?
I'M GONNA TAKE MY TIME, AND GET TO THE BOTTOM OF THIS.... TRY TA FIGURE OUT HOW YOU AND NITO WERE INVOLVED...
AND ARMS DEALING...?! WHAT A **STUPID IDEA...**
EVERY-THING GO ALL RIGHT, BATOU?!
YO, TOGUSA!! I PUT THE CUFFS ON THE ASSHOLE, KIM!!
MADE A LITTLE MESS HERE, SO DO ME A FAVOR AND TALK TO THE LOCAL COPS AND THE FIRE DEPARTMENT, OKAY?

Batou took advantage of the fact that Kim was coming (with all sensors on) to take care of the site (to get rid of any evidence and administer the coup de grace to Batou), and he thus infiltrated Kim's e-brain. When Batou did so, instead of sending an image of himself, wounded, into Kim's field of vision, he sent the image directly into Kim's brain. "Batou's head" is therefore what Kim really perceived. It was probably too hard for Batou to instantly put together a complete image of himself, so he just used the head...

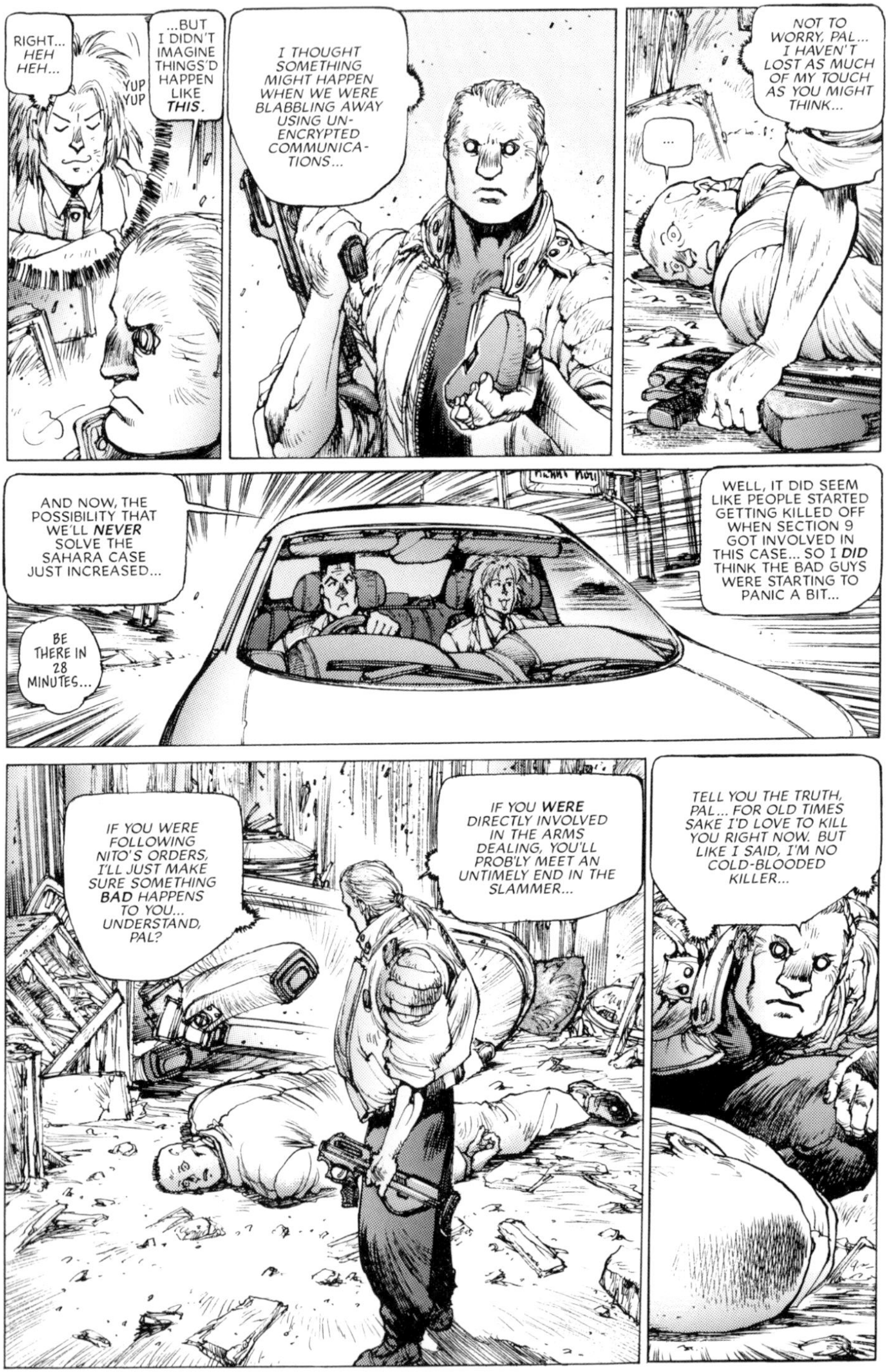
NOT TO WORRY, PAL... I HAVEN'T LOST AS MUCH OF MY TOUCH AS YOU MIGHT THINK...
...
I THOUGHT SOMETHING MIGHT HAPPEN WHEN WE WERE BABBLING AWAY USING UN-ENCRYPTED COMMUNICA-TIONS...
...BUT I DIDN'T IMAGINE THINGS'D HAPPEN LIKE *THIS*.
RIGHT... HEH HEH...
YUP YUP
WELL, IT DID SEEM LIKE PEOPLE STARTED GETTING KILLED OFF WHEN SECTION 9 GOT INVOLVED IN THIS CASE... SO I *DID* THINK THE BAD GUYS WERE STARTING TO PANIC A BIT...
AND NOW, THE POSSIBILITY THAT WE'LL *NEVER* SOLVE THE SAHARA CASE JUST INCREASED...
BE THERE IN 28 MINUTES...
TELL YOU THE TRUTH, PAL... FOR OLD TIMES SAKE I'D LOVE TO KILL YOU RIGHT NOW. BUT LIKE I SAID, I'M NO COLD-BLOODED KILLER...
IF YOU **WERE** DIRECTLY INVOLVED IN THE ARMS DEALING, YOU'LL PROB'LY MEET AN UNTIMELY END IN THE SLAMMER...
IF YOU WERE FOLLOWING NITO'S ORDERS, I'LL JUST MAKE SURE SOMETHING **BAD** HAPPENS TO YOU... UNDERSTAND, PAL?

*FX: WOPPA WOPPA WOPPA WOPPA

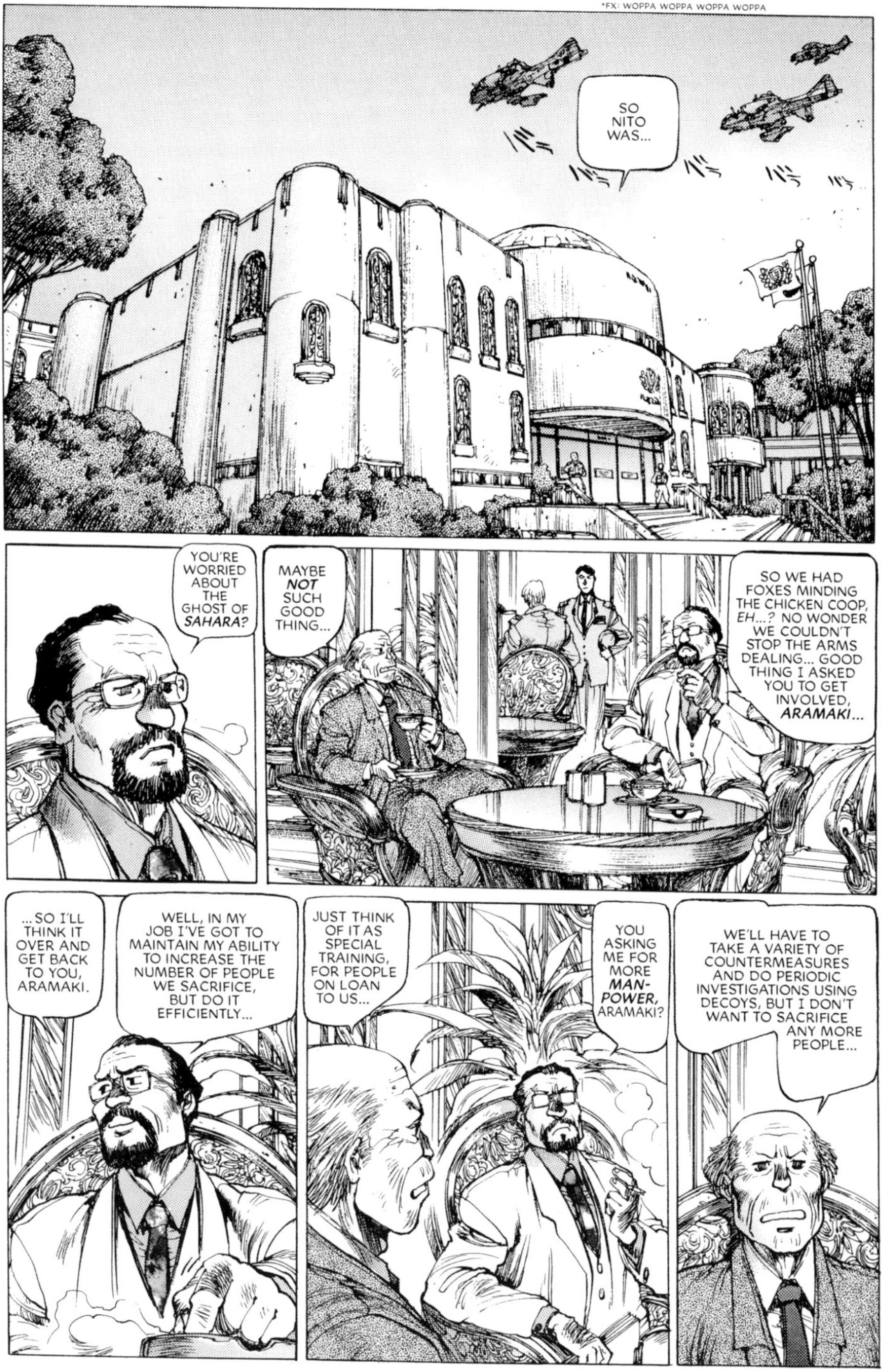
SO NITO WAS...
SO WE HAD FOXES MINDING THE CHICKEN COOP, *EH*...? NO WONDER WE COULDN'T STOP THE ARMS DEALING... GOOD THING I ASKED YOU TO GET INVOLVED, ***ARAMAKI...***
MAYBE ***NOT*** SUCH GOOD THING...
YOU'RE WORRIED ABOUT THE GHOST OF *SAHARA?*
WE'LL HAVE TO TAKE A VARIETY OF COUNTERMEASURES AND DO PERIODIC INVESTIGATIONS USING DECOYS, BUT I DON'T WANT TO SACRIFICE ANY MORE PEOPLE...
YOU ASKING ME FOR MORE ***MAN-POWER,*** ARAMAKI?
JUST THINK OF IT AS SPECIAL TRAINING, FOR PEOPLE ON LOAN TO US...
WELL, IN MY JOB I'VE GOT TO MAINTAIN MY ABILITY TO INCREASE THE NUMBER OF PEOPLE WE SACRIFICE, BUT DO IT EFFICIENTLY...
...SO I'LL THINK IT OVER AND GET BACK TO YOU, ARAMAKI.

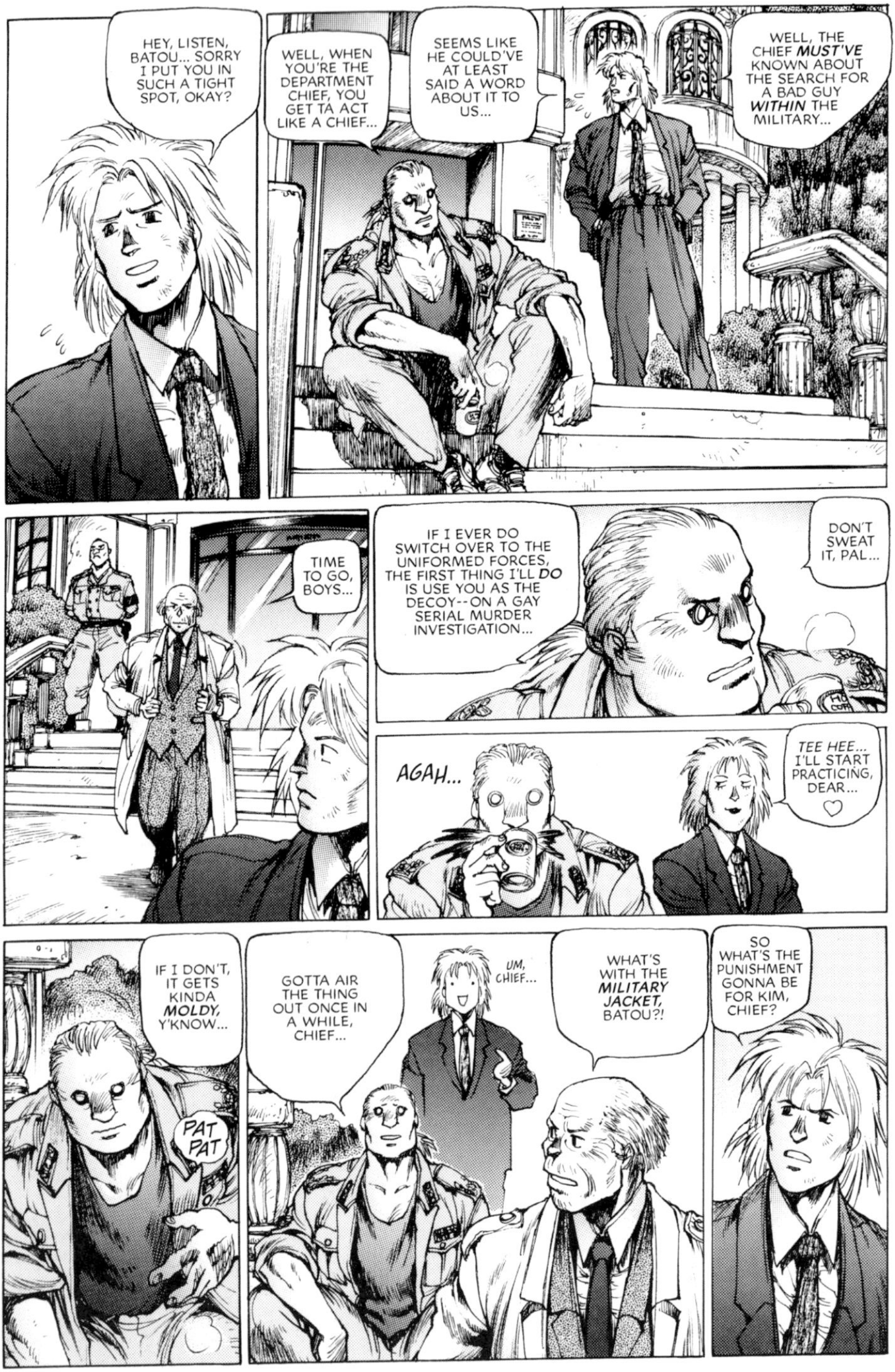
HEY, LISTEN, BATOU... SORRY I PUT YOU IN SUCH A TIGHT SPOT, OKAY?
WELL, WHEN YOU'RE THE DEPARTMENT CHIEF, YOU GET TA ACT LIKE A CHIEF...
SEEMS LIKE HE COULD'VE AT LEAST SAID A WORD ABOUT IT TO US...
WELL, THE CHIEF ***MUST'VE*** KNOWN ABOUT THE SEARCH FOR A BAD GUY ***WITHIN*** THE MILITARY...
TIME TO GO, BOYS...
IF I EVER DO SWITCH OVER TO THE UNIFORMED FORCES, THE FIRST THING I'LL ***DO*** IS USE YOU AS THE DECOY--ON A GAY SERIAL MURDER INVESTIGATION...
DON'T SWEAT IT, PAL...
AGAH...
TEE HEE... I'LL START PRACTICING, DEAR... ♡
IF I DON'T, IT GETS KINDA ***MOLDY,*** Y'KNOW...
PAT PAT
GOTTA AIR THE THING OUT ONCE IN A WHILE, CHIEF...
UM, CHIEF...
WHAT'S WITH THE ***MILITARY JACKET,*** BATOU?!
SO WHAT'S THE PUNISHMENT GONNA BE FOR KIM, CHIEF?

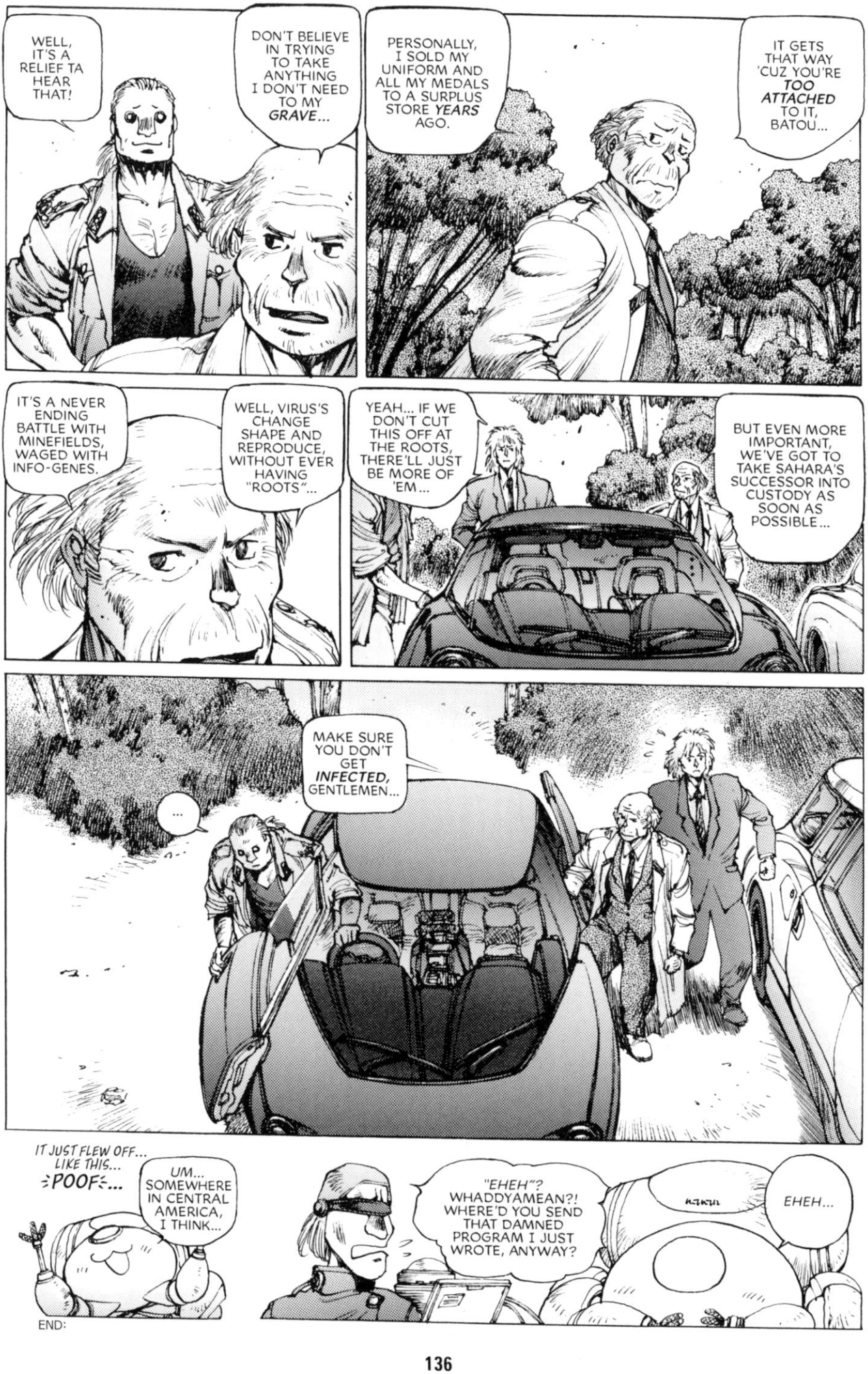
IT GETS THAT WAY 'CUZ YOU'RE *TOO ATTACHED* TO IT, BATOU...
PERSONALLY, I SOLD MY UNIFORM AND ALL MY MEDALS TO A SURPLUS STORE *YEARS* AGO.
DON'T BELIEVE IN TRYING TO TAKE ANYTHING I DON'T NEED TO MY *GRAVE*...
WELL, IT'S A RELIEF TA HEAR THAT!
BUT EVEN MORE IMPORTANT, WE'VE GOT TO TAKE SAHARA'S SUCCESSOR INTO CUSTODY AS SOON AS POSSIBLE...
YEAH... IF WE DON'T CUT THIS OFF AT THE ROOTS, THERE'LL JUST BE MORE OF 'EM...
WELL, VIRUS'S CHANGE SHAPE AND REPRODUCE, WITHOUT EVER HAVING "ROOTS"...
IT'S A NEVER ENDING BATTLE WITH MINEFIELDS, WAGED WITH INFO-GENES.
MAKE SURE YOU DON'T GET *INFECTED,* GENTLEMEN...
...
EHEH...
"EHEH"? WHADDYAMEAN?! WHERE'D YOU SEND THAT DAMNED PROGRAM I JUST WROTE, ANYWAY?
UM... SOMEWHERE IN CENTRAL AMERICA, I THINK...
IT JUST FLEW OFF... LIKE THIS... POOF...

END:

LOST PAST 07

1996

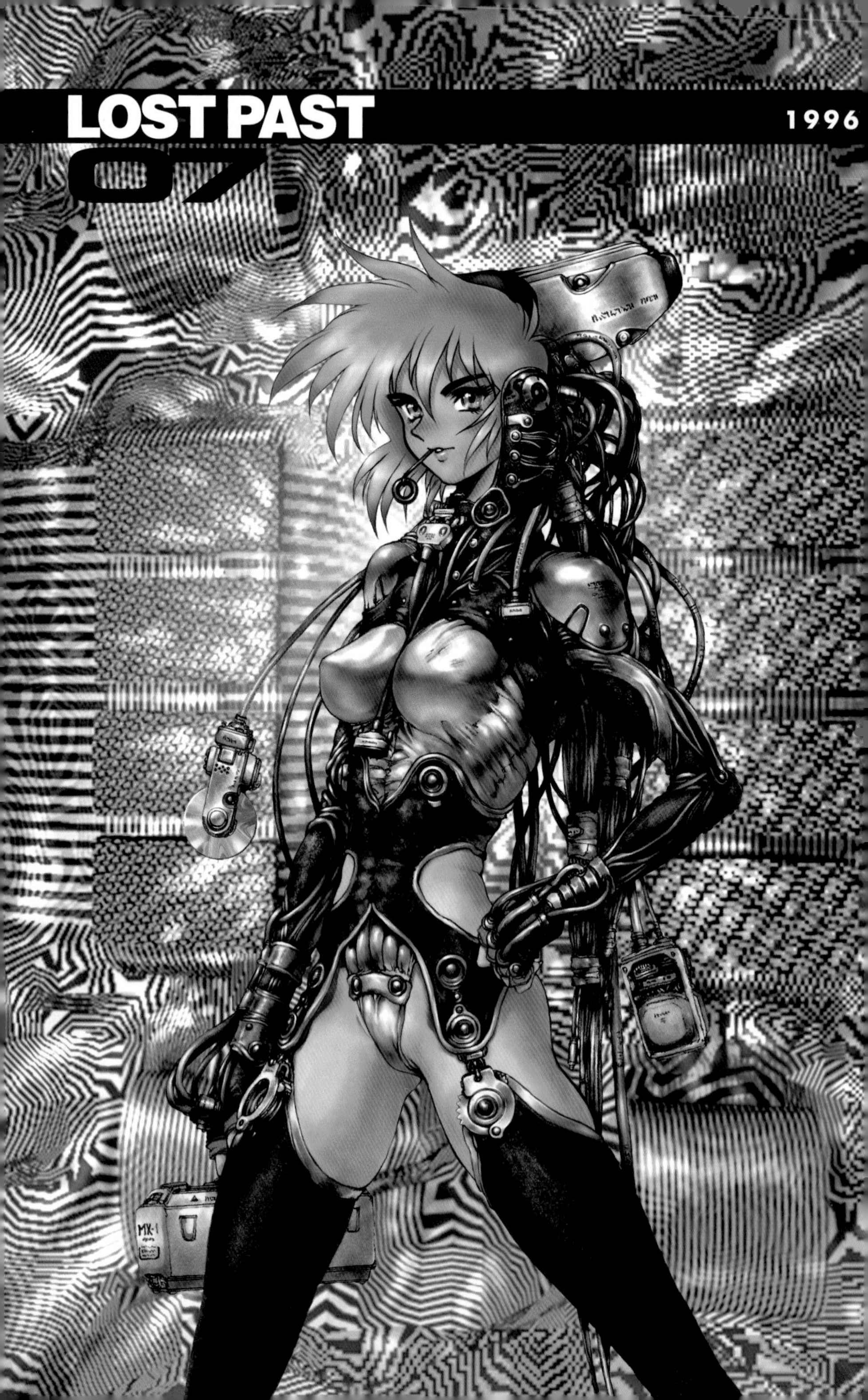

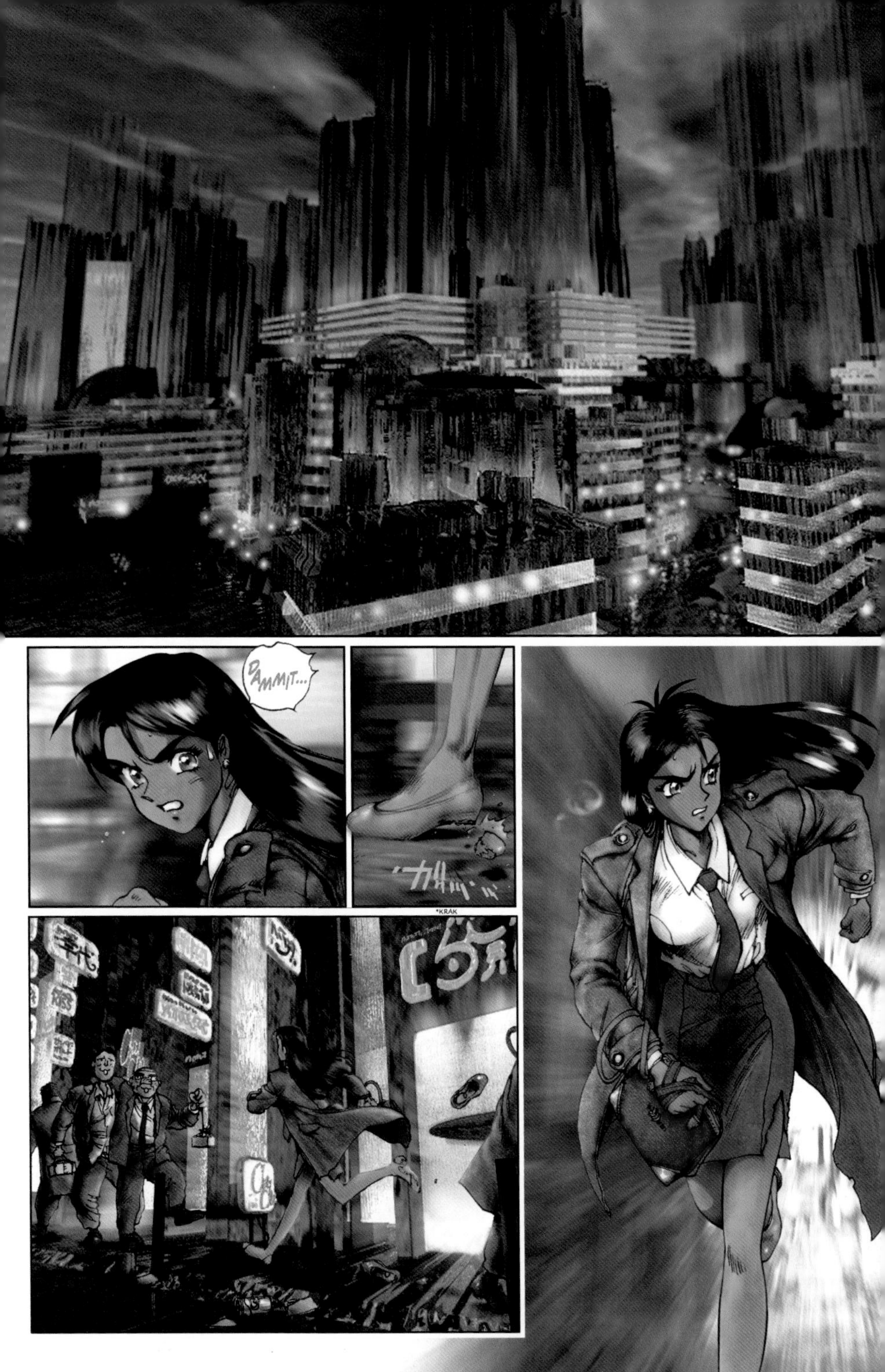
DAMMIT...
*KRAK

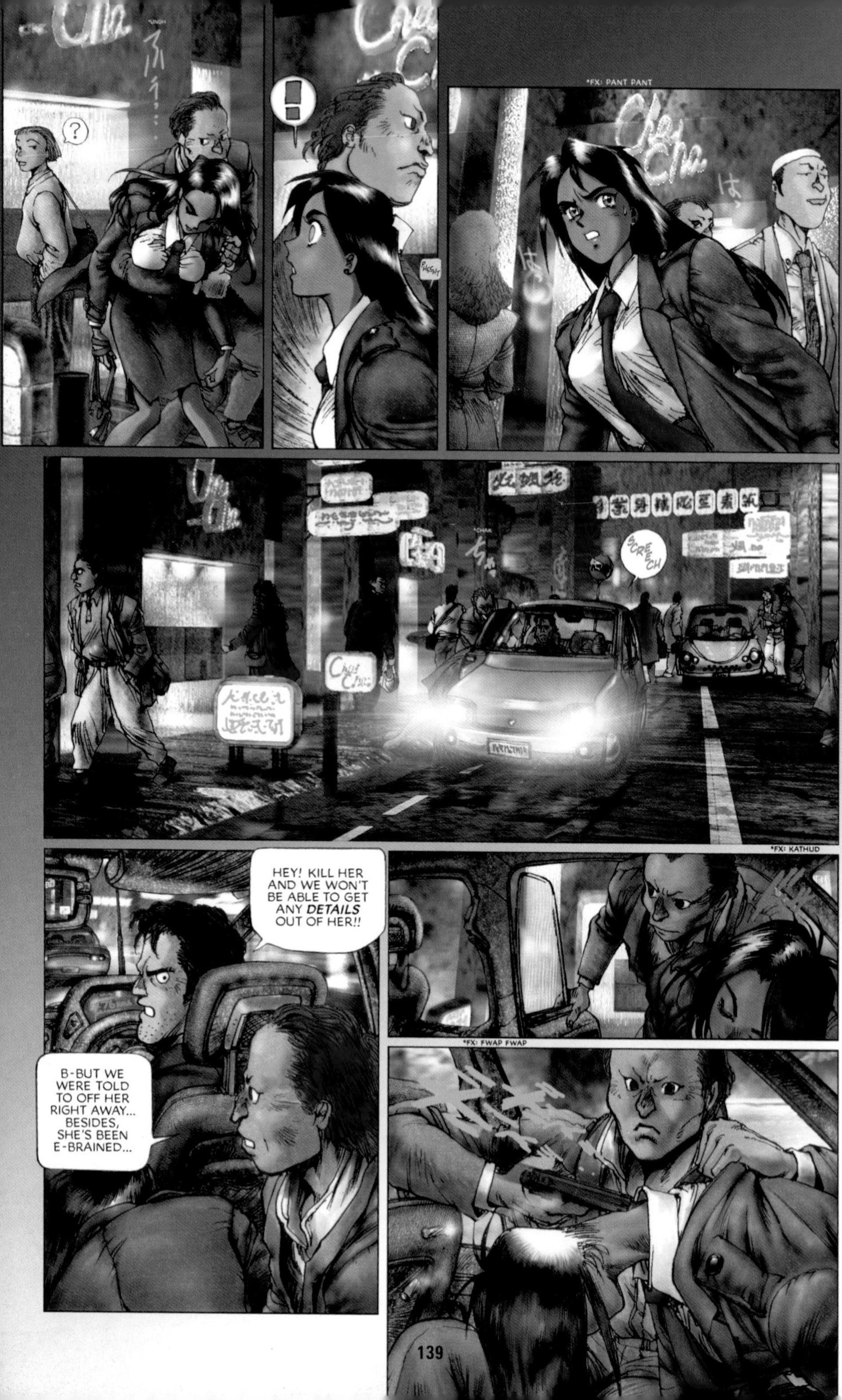
*FX: PANT PANT
*FX: KATHUD
*FX: FWAP FWAP
HEY! KILL HER AND WE WON'T BE ABLE TO GET ANY ***DETAILS*** OUT OF HER!!
B-BUT WE WERE TOLD TO OFF HER RIGHT AWAY... BESIDES, SHE'S BEEN E-BRAINED...

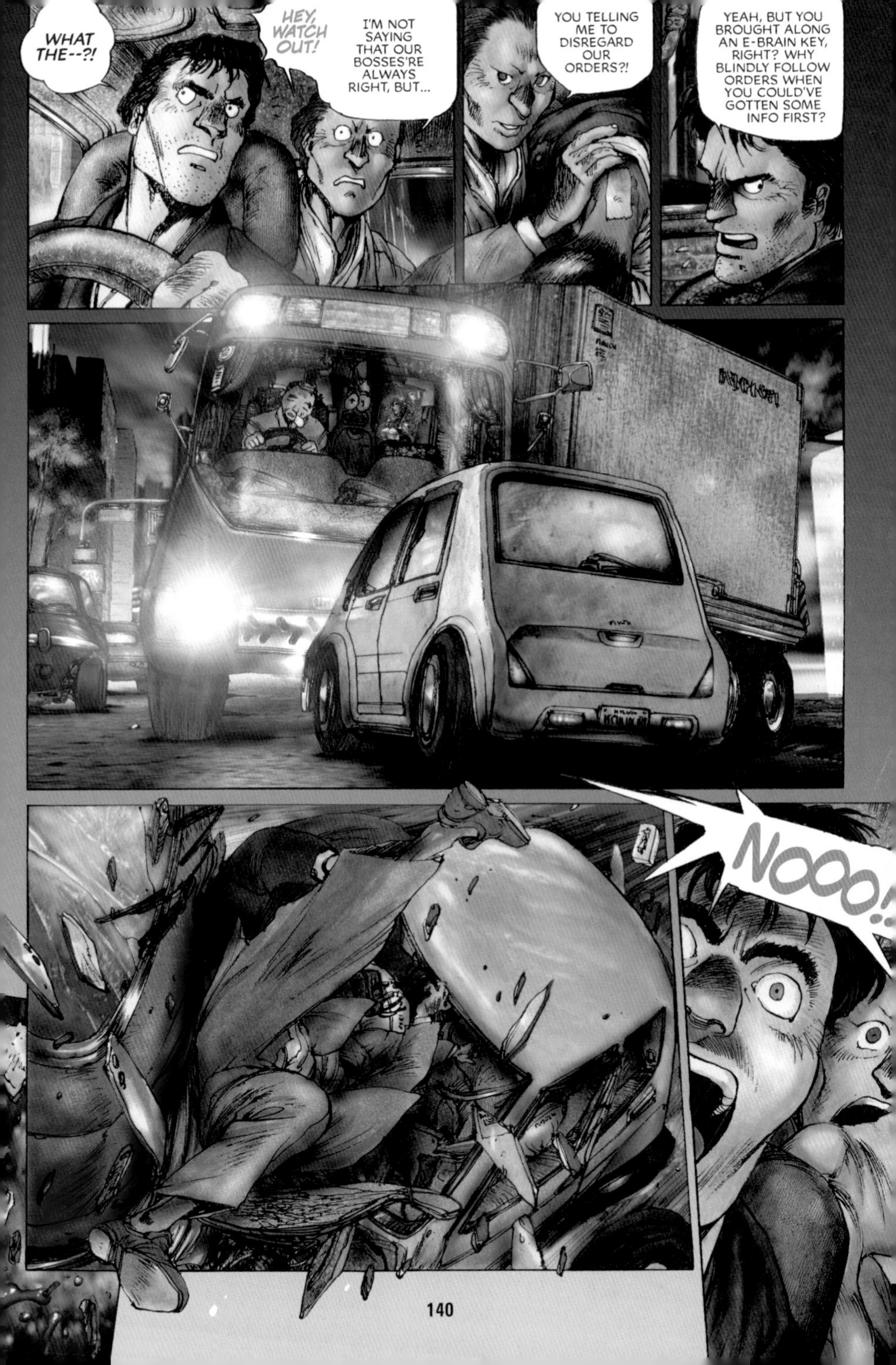
YEAH, BUT YOU BROUGHT ALONG AN E-BRAIN KEY, RIGHT? WHY BLINDLY FOLLOW ORDERS WHEN YOU COULD'VE GOTTEN SOME INFO FIRST?
YOU TELLING ME TO DISREGARD OUR ORDERS?!
I'M NOT SAYING THAT OUR BOSSES'RE ALWAYS RIGHT, BUT...
HEY, WATCH OUT!
WHAT THE--?!
NOOO!!

*truck: YAMAMURA TRANSPORT

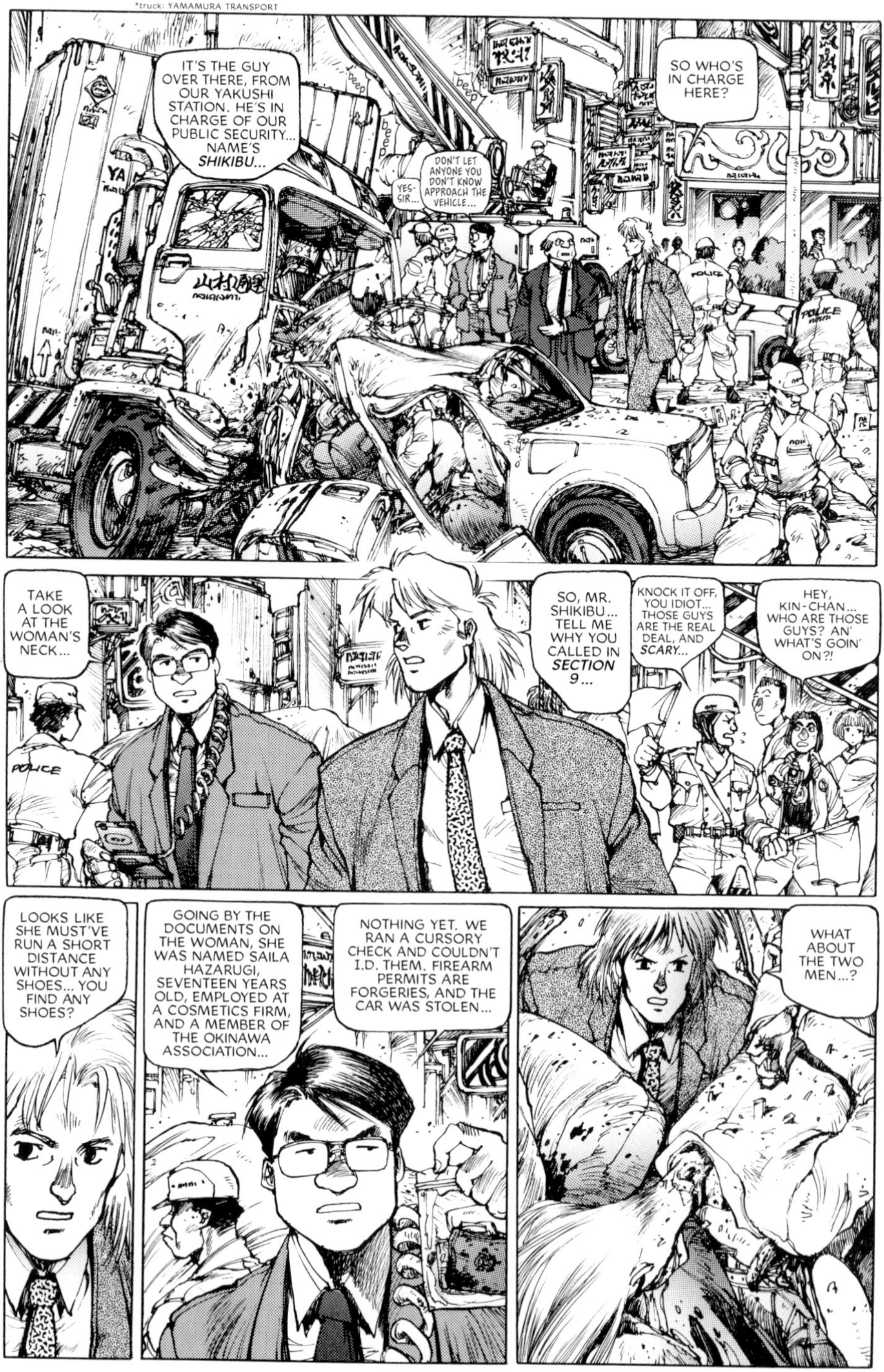

SO WHO'S IN CHARGE HERE?
beep
beep
DON'T LET ANYONE YOU DON'T KNOW APPROACH THE VEHICLE...
YES-SIR...
beep
IT'S THE GUY OVER THERE, FROM OUR YAKUSHI STATION. HE'S IN CHARGE OF OUR PUBLIC SECURITY... NAME'S *SHIKIBU*...
POLICE
POLICE
HEY, KIN-CHAN... WHO ARE THOSE GUYS? AN' WHAT'S GOIN' ON?!
KNOCK IT OFF, YOU IDIOT... THOSE GUYS ARE THE REAL DEAL, AND *SCARY*...
SO, MR. SHIKIBU... TELL ME WHY YOU CALLED IN *SECTION 9*...
TAKE A LOOK AT THE WOMAN'S NECK...
POLICE
WHAT ABOUT THE TWO MEN...?
NOTHING YET. WE RAN A CURSORY CHECK AND COULDN'T I.D. THEM. FIREARM PERMITS ARE FORGERIES, AND THE CAR WAS STOLEN...
GOING BY THE DOCUMENTS ON THE WOMAN, SHE WAS NAMED SAILA HAZARUGI, SEVENTEEN YEARS OLD, EMPLOYED AT A COSMETICS FIRM, AND A MEMBER OF THE OKINAWA ASSOCIATION...
LOOKS LIKE SHE MUST'VE RUN A SHORT DISTANCE WITHOUT ANY SHOES... YOU FIND ANY SHOES?

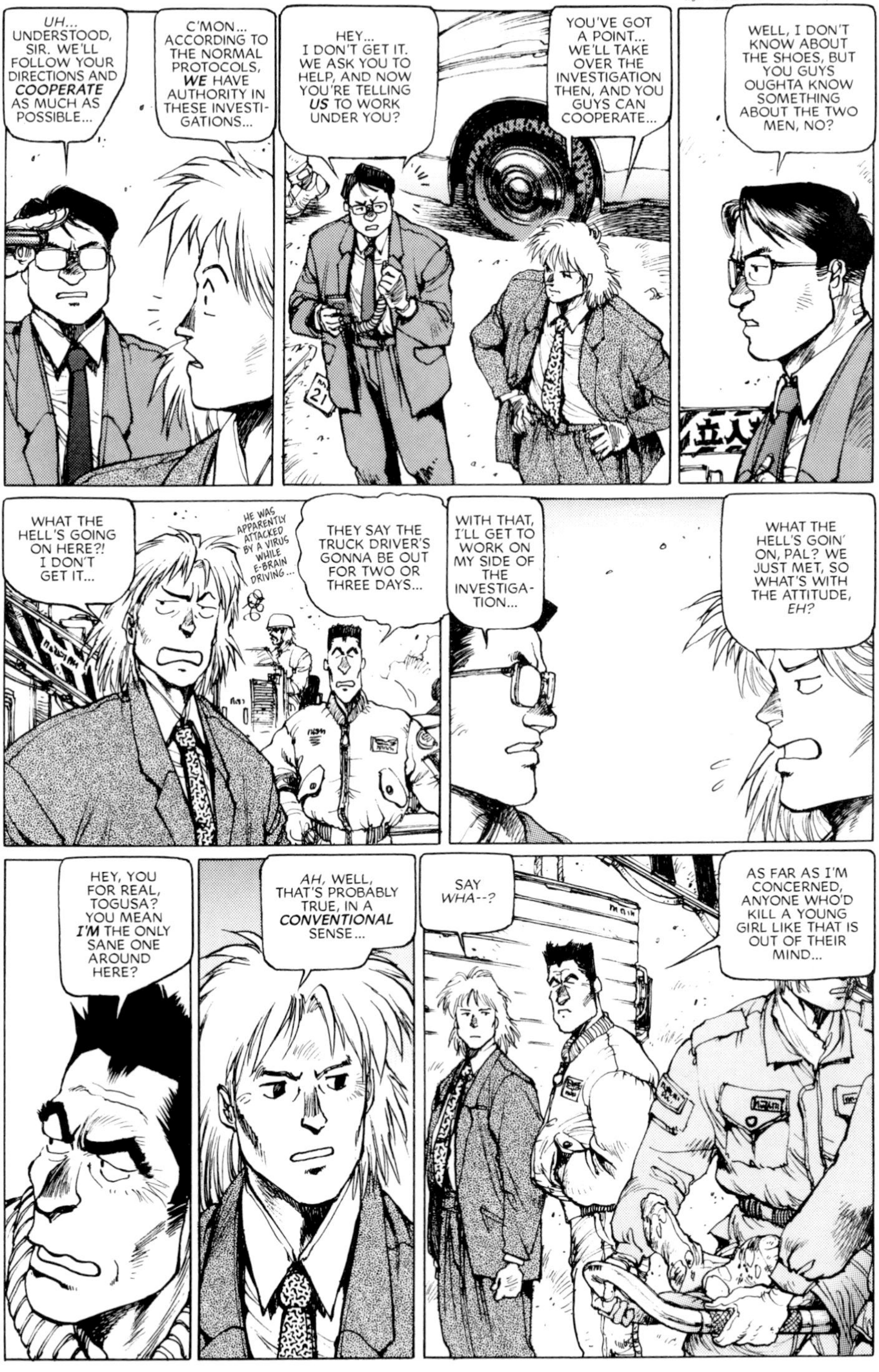
*sign: POLICE LINE – DO NOT CROSS
WELL, I DON'T KNOW ABOUT THE SHOES, BUT YOU GUYS OUGHTA KNOW SOMETHING ABOUT THE TWO MEN, NO?
YOU'VE GOT A POINT... WE'LL TAKE OVER THE INVESTIGATION THEN, AND YOU GUYS CAN COOPERATE...
HEY... I DON'T GET IT. WE ASK YOU TO HELP, AND NOW YOU'RE TELLING *US* TO WORK UNDER YOU?
C'MON... ACCORDING TO THE NORMAL PROTOCOLS, ***WE*** HAVE AUTHORITY IN THESE INVESTIGATIONS...
UH... UNDERSTOOD, SIR. WE'LL FOLLOW YOUR DIRECTIONS AND ***COOPERATE*** AS MUCH AS POSSIBLE...
WHAT THE HELL'S GOIN' ON, PAL? WE JUST MET, SO WHAT'S WITH THE ATTITUDE, *EH?*
WITH THAT, I'LL GET TO WORK ON MY SIDE OF THE INVESTIGATION...
THEY SAY THE TRUCK DRIVER'S GONNA BE OUT FOR TWO OR THREE DAYS...
HE WAS APPARENTLY ATTACKED BY A VIRUS WHILE E-BRAIN DRIVING...
WHAT THE HELL'S GOING ON HERE?! I DON'T GET IT...
AS FAR AS I'M CONCERNED, ANYONE WHO'D KILL A YOUNG GIRL LIKE THAT IS OUT OF THEIR MIND...
SAY *WHA--?*
AH, WELL, THAT'S PROBABLY TRUE, IN A ***CONVENTIONAL*** SENSE...
HEY, YOU FOR REAL, TOGUSA? YOU MEAN ***I'M*** THE ONLY SANE ONE AROUND HERE?

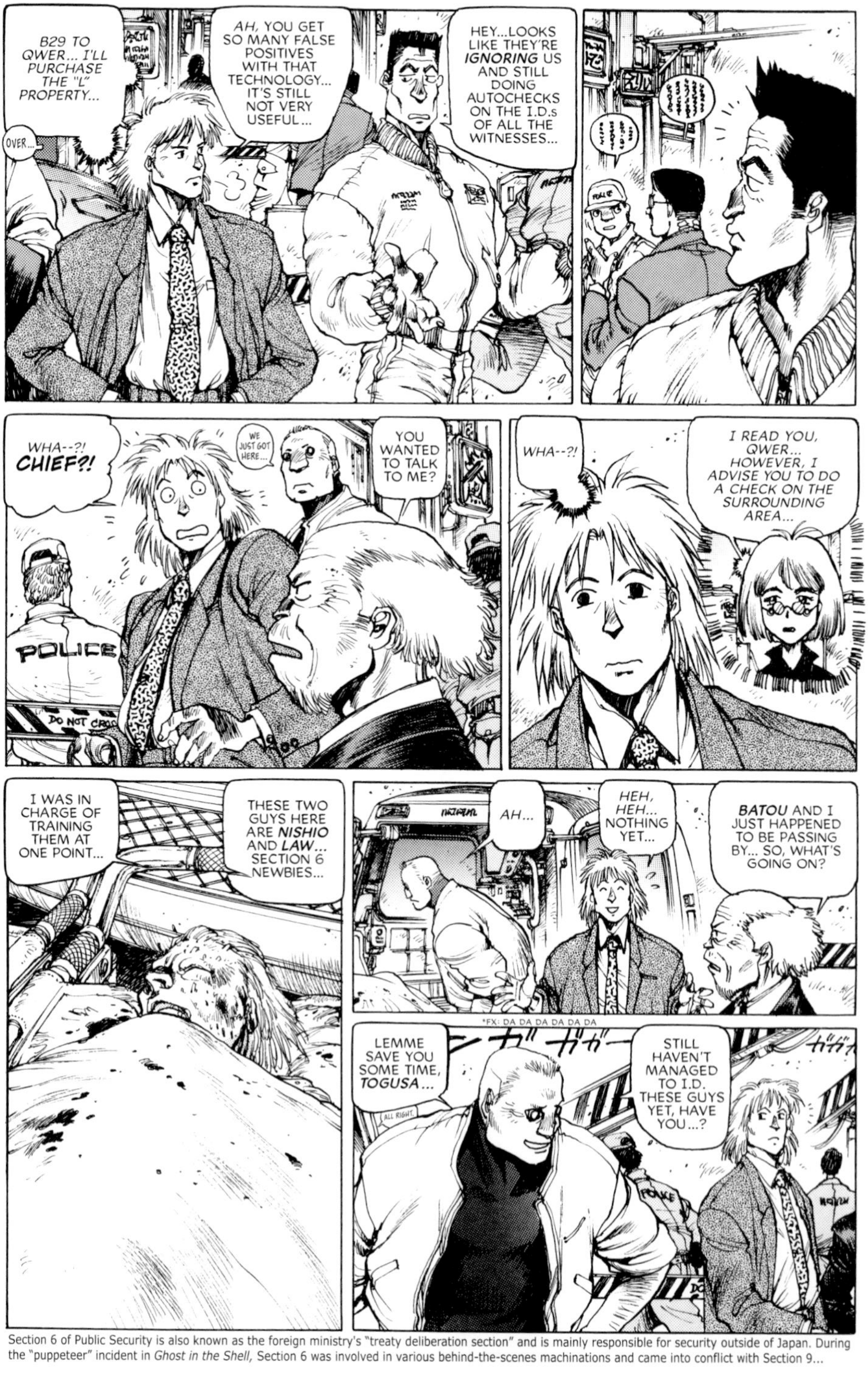
B29 TO QWER... I'LL PURCHASE THE "L" PROPERTY...
OVER...
AH, YOU GET SO MANY FALSE POSITIVES WITH THAT TECHNOLOGY... IT'S STILL NOT VERY USEFUL...
HEY...LOOKS LIKE THEY'RE ***IGNORING*** US AND STILL DOING AUTOCHECKS ON THE I.D.s OF ALL THE WITNESSES...
WHA--?! ***CHIEF?!***
WE JUST GOT HERE...
YOU WANTED TO TALK TO ME?
POLICE
DO NOT CROSS
WHA--?!
I READ YOU, QWER... HOWEVER, I ADVISE YOU TO DO A CHECK ON THE SURROUNDING AREA...
BATOU AND I JUST HAPPENED TO BE PASSING BY... SO, WHAT'S GOING ON?
HEH, HEH... NOTHING YET...
AH...
STILL HAVEN'T MANAGED TO I.D. THESE GUYS YET, HAVE YOU...?
LEMME SAVE YOU SOME TIME, ***TOGUSA***...
ALL RIGHT.
THESE TWO GUYS HERE ARE ***NISHIO*** AND ***LAW***... SECTION 6 NEWBIES...
I WAS IN CHARGE OF TRAINING THEM AT ONE POINT...
*FX: DA DA DA DA DA DA

Section 6 of Public Security is also known as the foreign ministry's "treaty deliberation section" and is mainly responsible for security outside of Japan. During the "puppeteer" incident in *Ghost in the Shell,* Section 6 was involved in various behind-the-scenes machinations and came into conflict with Section 9...

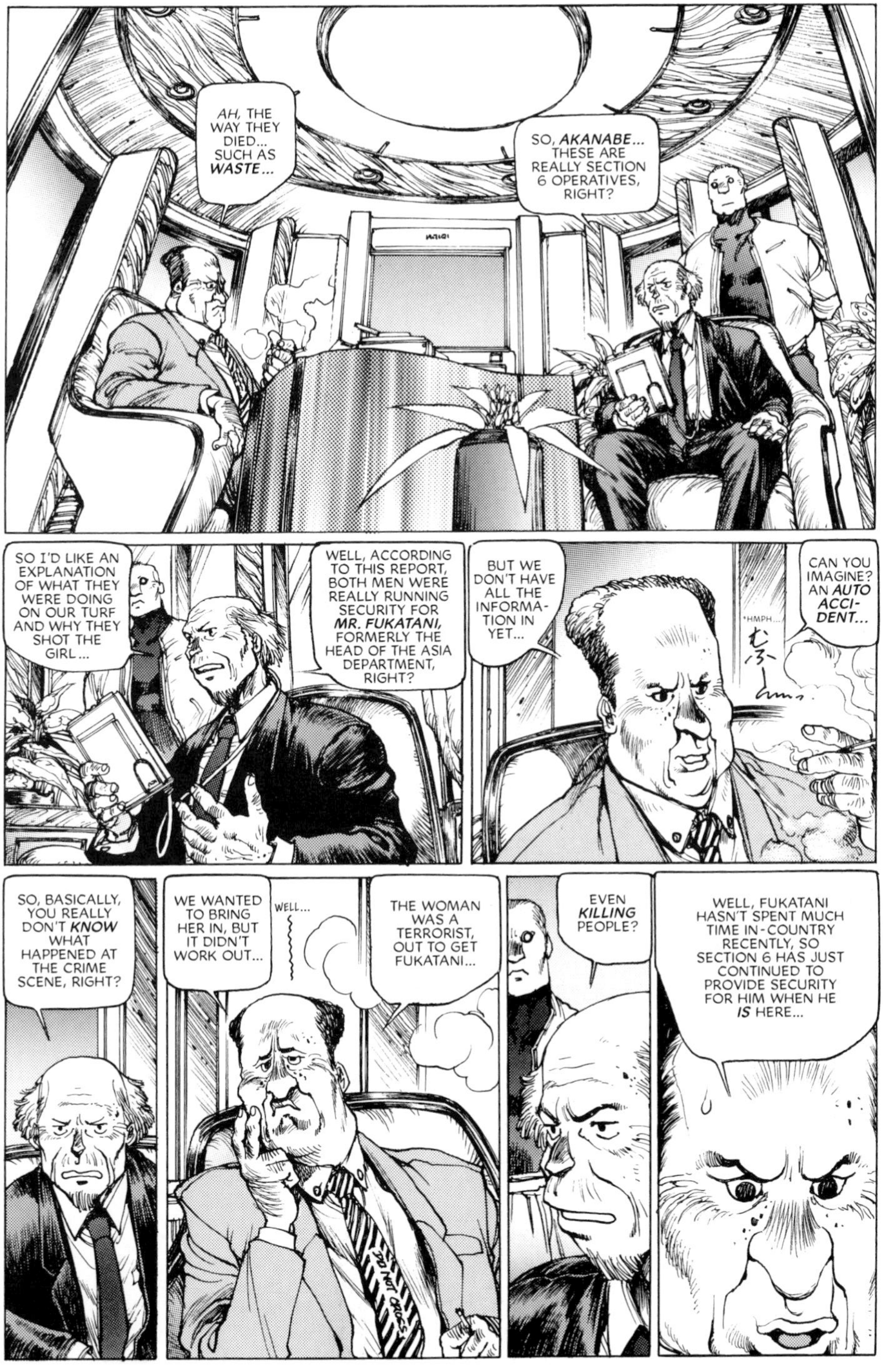
AH, THE WAY THEY DIED... SUCH AS WASTE...
SO, AKANABE... THESE ARE REALLY SECTION 6 OPERATIVES, RIGHT?
SO I'D LIKE AN EXPLANATION OF WHAT THEY WERE DOING ON OUR TURF AND WHY THEY SHOT THE GIRL...
WELL, ACCORDING TO THIS REPORT, BOTH MEN WERE REALLY RUNNING SECURITY FOR MR. FUKATANI, FORMERLY THE HEAD OF THE ASIA DEPARTMENT, RIGHT?
BUT WE DON'T HAVE ALL THE INFORMATION IN YET...
*HMPH...
CAN YOU IMAGINE? AN AUTO ACCIDENT...
SO, BASICALLY, YOU REALLY DON'T KNOW WHAT HAPPENED AT THE CRIME SCENE, RIGHT?
WE WANTED TO BRING HER IN, BUT IT DIDN'T WORK OUT...
WELL...
THE WOMAN WAS A TERRORIST, OUT TO GET FUKATANI...
EVEN KILLING PEOPLE?
WELL, FUKATANI HASN'T SPENT MUCH TIME IN-COUNTRY RECENTLY, SO SECTION 6 HAS JUST CONTINUED TO PROVIDE SECURITY FOR HIM WHEN HE IS HERE...

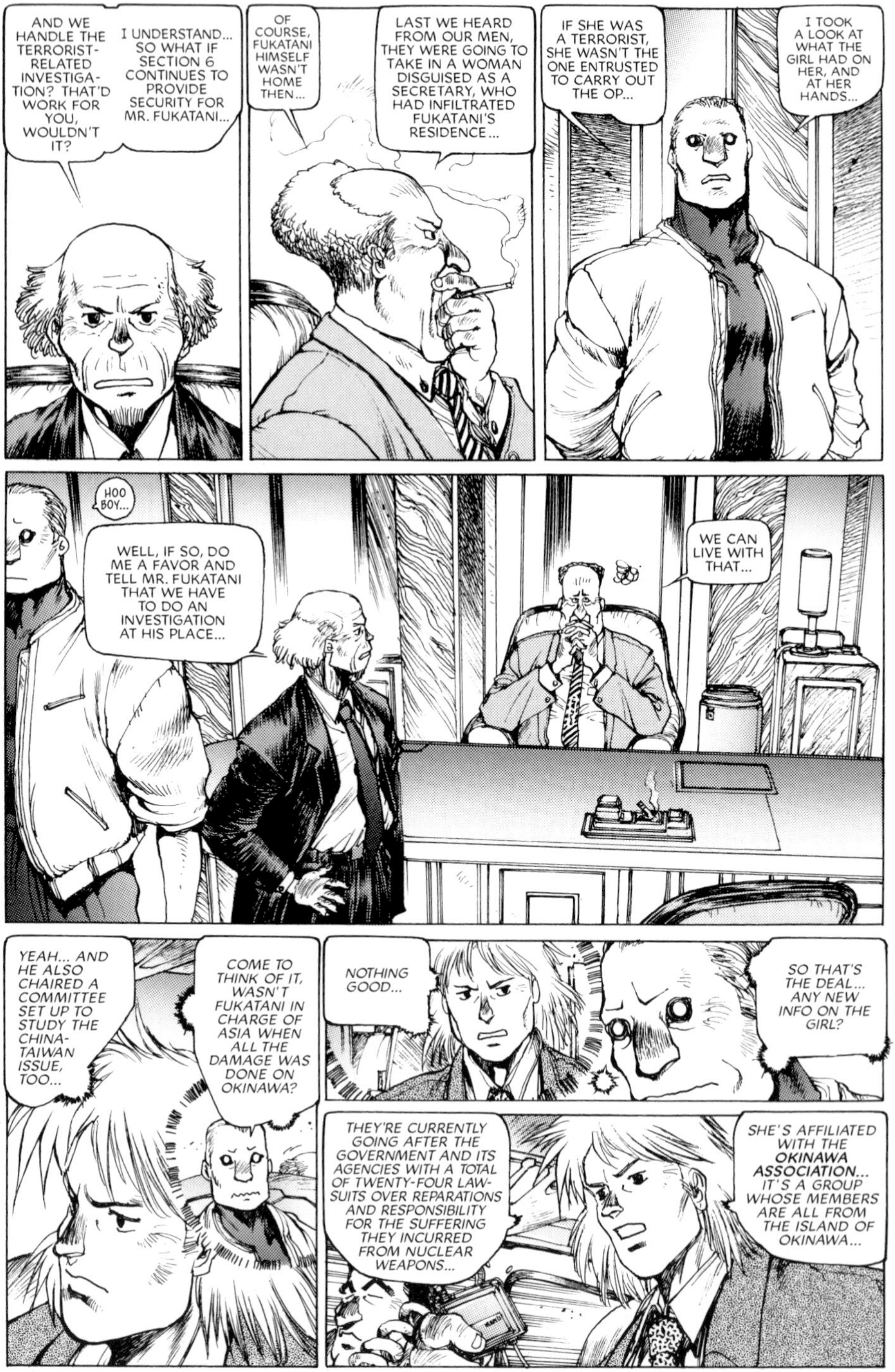
I TOOK A LOOK AT WHAT THE GIRL HAD ON HER, AND AT HER HANDS...
IF SHE WAS A TERRORIST, SHE WASN'T THE ONE ENTRUSTED TO CARRY OUT THE OP...
LAST WE HEARD FROM OUR MEN, THEY WERE GOING TO TAKE IN A WOMAN DISGUISED AS A SECRETARY, WHO HAD INFILTRATED FUKATANI'S RESIDENCE...
OF COURSE, FUKATANI HIMSELF WASN'T HOME THEN...
I UNDERSTAND... SO WHAT IF SECTION 6 CONTINUES TO PROVIDE SECURITY FOR MR. FUKATANI...
AND WE HANDLE THE TERRORIST-RELATED INVESTIGATION? THAT'D WORK FOR YOU, WOULDN'T IT?
WE CAN LIVE WITH THAT...
WELL, IF SO, DO ME A FAVOR AND TELL MR. FUKATANI THAT WE HAVE TO DO AN INVESTIGATION AT HIS PLACE...
HOO BOY...
SO THAT'S THE DEAL... ANY NEW INFO ON THE GIRL?
NOTHING GOOD...
SHE'S AFFILIATED WITH THE **OKINAWA ASSOCIATION**... IT'S A GROUP WHOSE MEMBERS ARE ALL FROM THE ISLAND OF OKINAWA...
THEY'RE CURRENTLY GOING AFTER THE GOVERNMENT AND ITS AGENCIES WITH A TOTAL OF TWENTY-FOUR LAW-SUITS OVER REPARATIONS AND RESPONSIBILITY FOR THE SUFFERING THEY INCURRED FROM NUCLEAR WEAPONS...
COME TO THINK OF IT, WASN'T FUKATANI IN CHARGE OF ASIA WHEN ALL THE DAMAGE WAS DONE ON OKINAWA?
YEAH... AND HE ALSO CHAIRED A COMMITTEE SET UP TO STUDY THE CHINA-TAIWAN ISSUE, TOO...

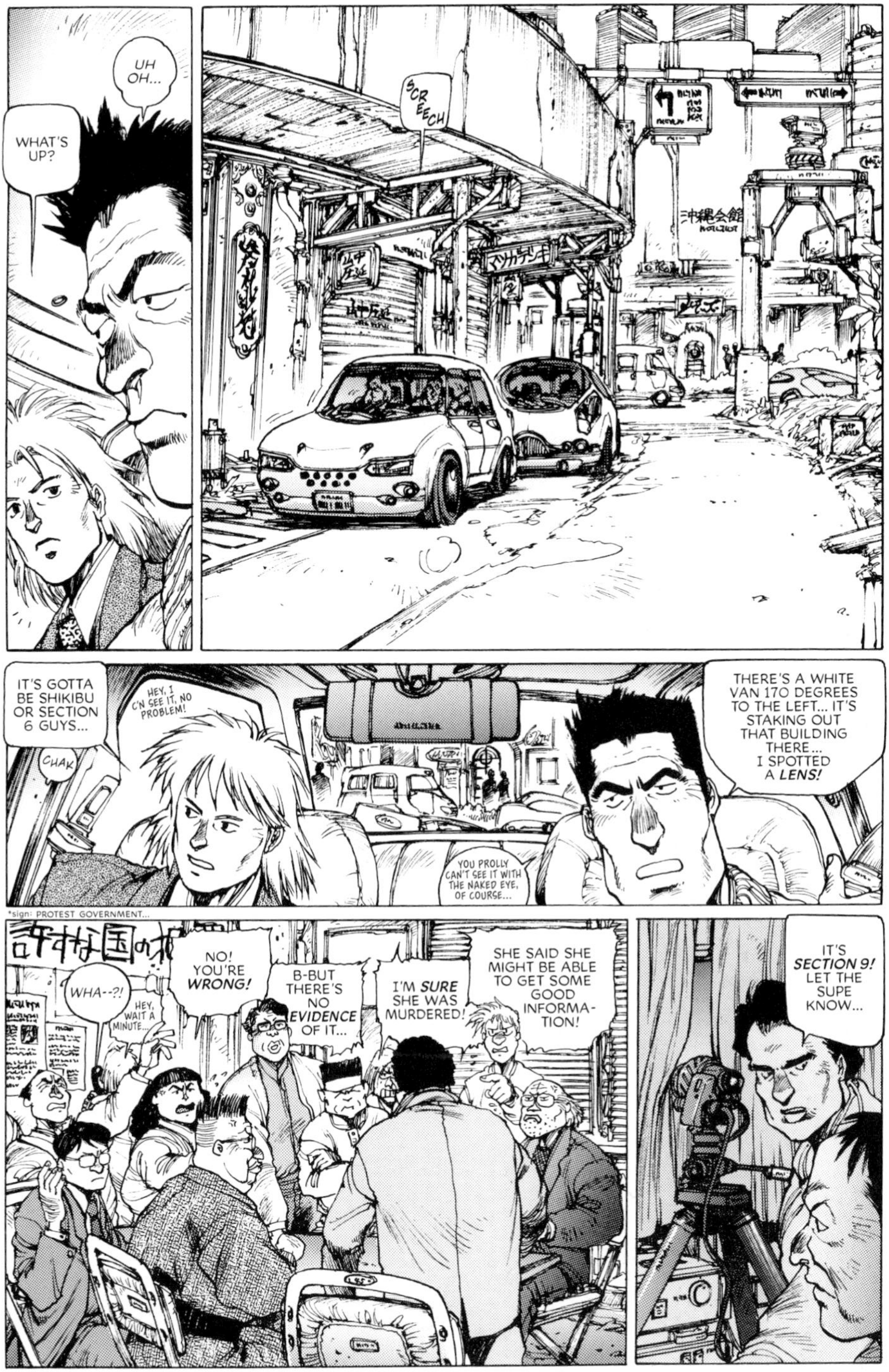
WHAT'S UP?
UH OH...
SCREECH
THERE'S A WHITE VAN 170 DEGREES TO THE LEFT... IT'S STAKING OUT THAT BUILDING THERE... I SPOTTED A **LENS!**
YOU PROLLY CAN'T SEE IT WITH THE NAKED EYE, OF COURSE...
IT'S GOTTA BE SHIKIBU OR SECTION 6 GUYS...
CHAK
HEY, I C'N SEE IT, NO PROBLEM!
許すな国の
SHE SAID SHE MIGHT BE ABLE TO GET SOME GOOD INFORMA-TION!
I'M **SURE** SHE WAS MURDERED!
B-BUT THERE'S NO **EVIDENCE** OF IT...
NO! YOU'RE **WRONG!**
WHA--?!
HEY, WAIT A MINUTE...
IT'S **SECTION 9!** LET THE SUPE KNOW...

*sign: PROTEST GOVERNMENT...

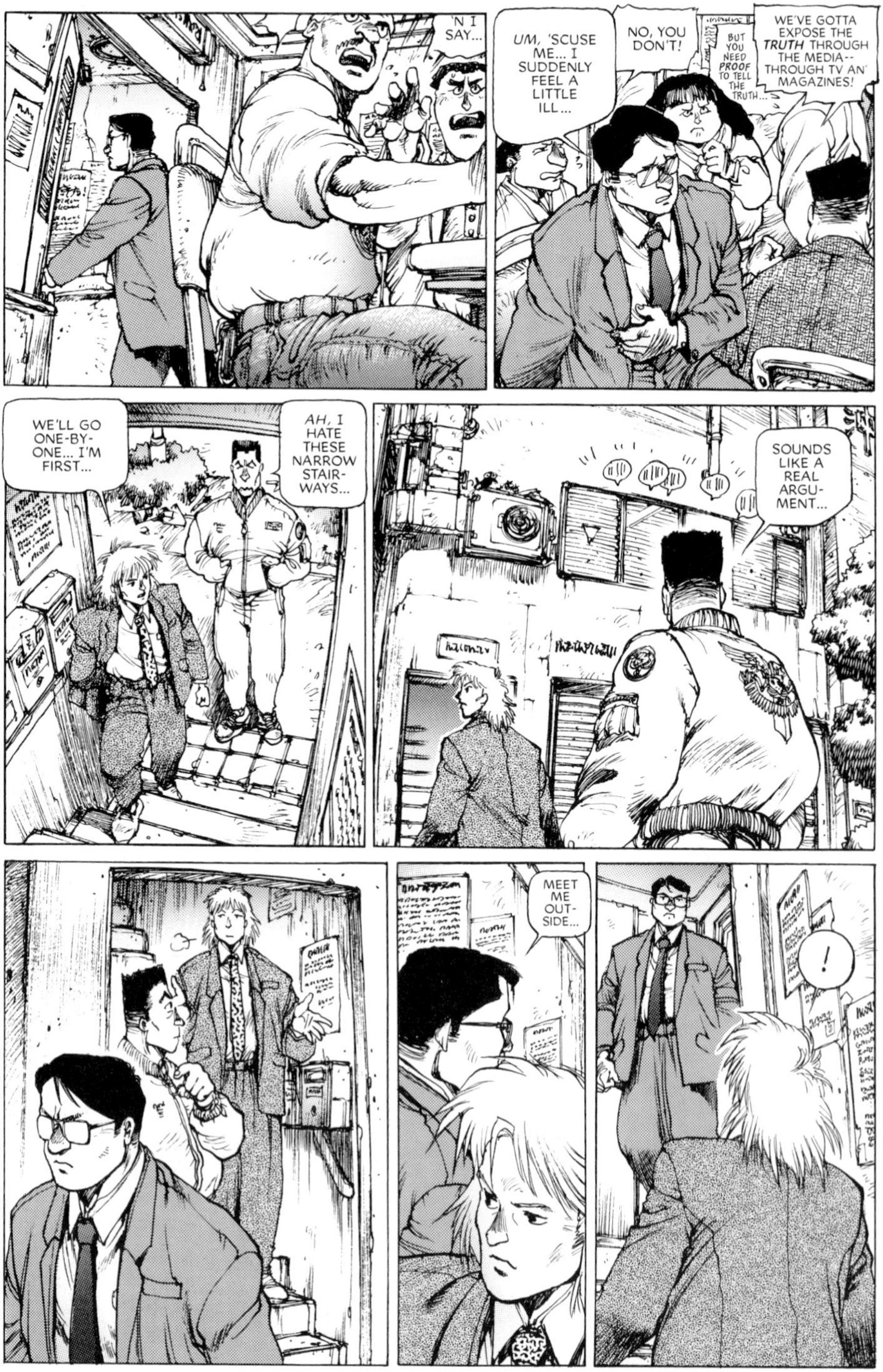
'N I SAY...
WE'VE GOTTA EXPOSE THE *TRUTH* THROUGH THE MEDIA-- THROUGH TV AN' MAGAZINES!
BUT YOU NEED *PROOF* TO TELL THE TRUTH...
NO, YOU DON'T!
UM, 'SCUSE ME... I SUDDENLY FEEL A LITTLE ILL...
WE'LL GO ONE-BY-ONE... I'M FIRST...
AH, I HATE THESE NARROW STAIR-WAYS...
SOUNDS LIKE A REAL ARGU-MENT...
MEET ME OUT-SIDE...
!

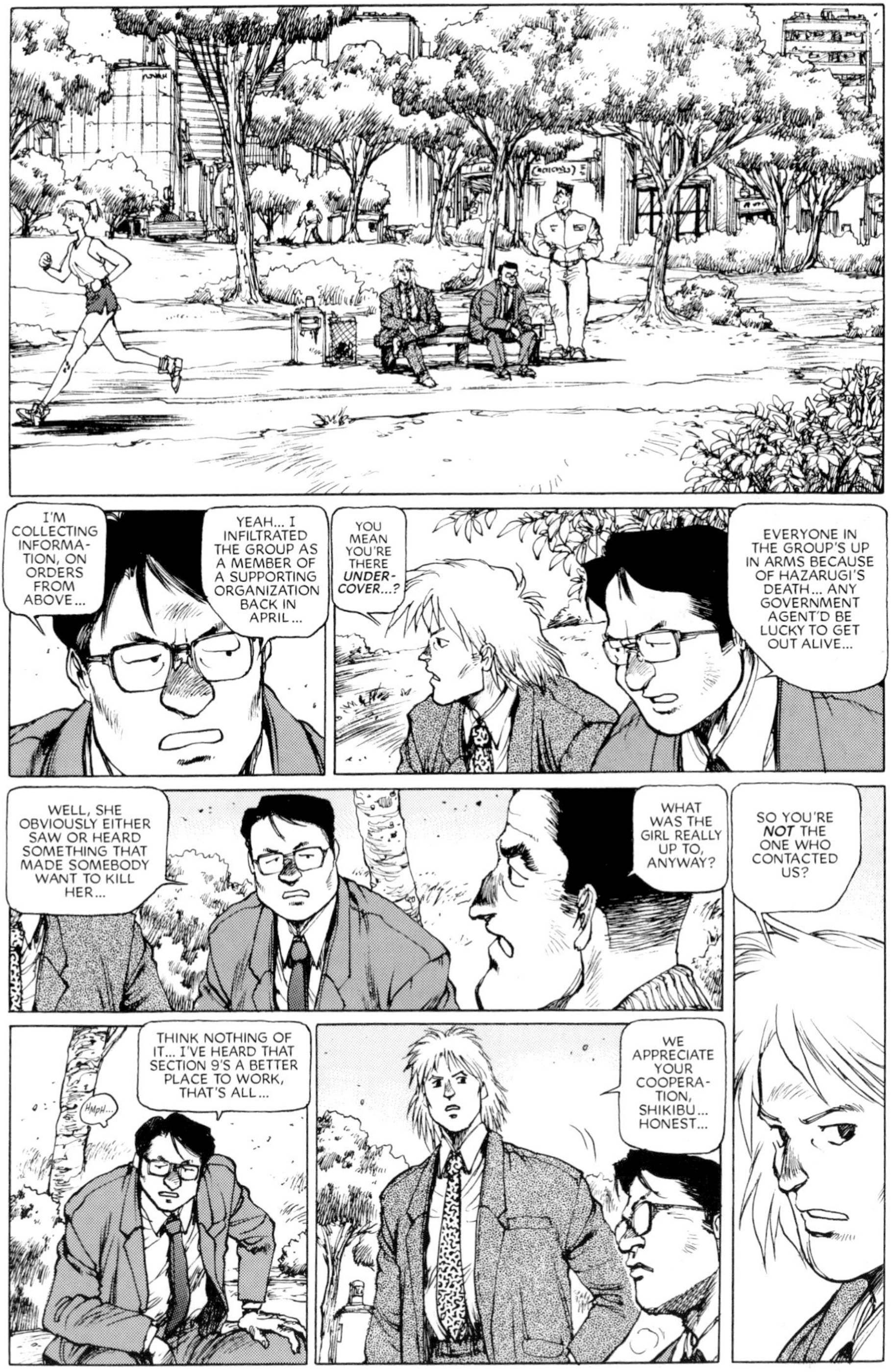
I'M COLLECTING INFORMATION, ON ORDERS FROM ABOVE...
YEAH... I INFILTRATED THE GROUP AS A MEMBER OF A SUPPORTING ORGANIZATION BACK IN APRIL...
YOU MEAN YOU'RE THERE *UNDERCOVER*...?
EVERYONE IN THE GROUP'S UP IN ARMS BECAUSE OF HAZARUGI'S DEATH... ANY GOVERNMENT AGENT'D BE LUCKY TO GET OUT ALIVE...
WHAT WAS THE GIRL REALLY UP TO, ANYWAY?
WELL, SHE OBVIOUSLY EITHER SAW OR HEARD SOMETHING THAT MADE SOMEBODY WANT TO KILL HER...
SO YOU'RE ***NOT*** THE ONE WHO CONTACTED US?
THINK NOTHING OF IT... I'VE HEARD THAT SECTION 9'S A BETTER PLACE TO WORK, THAT'S ALL...
HMPH...
WE APPRECIATE YOUR COOPERATION, SHIKIBU... HONEST...

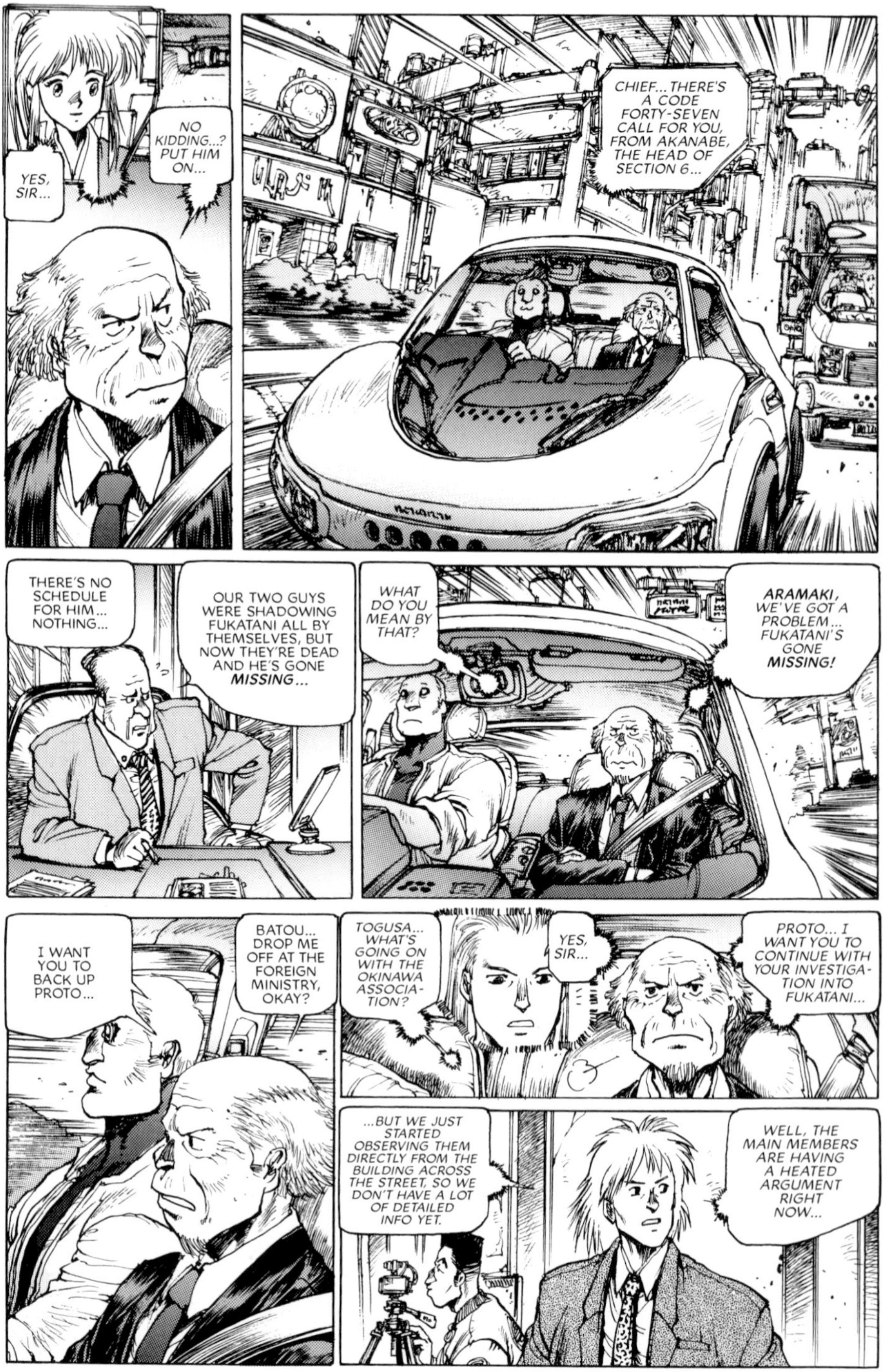
CHIEF... THERE'S A CODE FORTY-SEVEN CALL FOR YOU, FROM AKANABE, THE HEAD OF SECTION 6...
NO KIDDING...? PUT HIM ON...
YES, SIR...
ARAMAKI, WE'VE GOT A PROBLEM... FUKATANI'S GONE MISSING!
WHAT DO YOU MEAN BY THAT?
OUR TWO GUYS WERE SHADOWING FUKATANI ALL BY THEMSELVES, BUT NOW THEY'RE DEAD AND HE'S GONE MISSING...
THERE'S NO SCHEDULE FOR HIM... NOTHING...
PROTO... I WANT YOU TO CONTINUE WITH YOUR INVESTIGATION INTO FUKATANI...
YES, SIR...
TOGUSA... WHAT'S GOING ON WITH THE OKINAWA ASSOCIATION?
WELL, THE MAIN MEMBERS ARE HAVING A HEATED ARGUMENT RIGHT NOW...
...BUT WE JUST STARTED OBSERVING THEM DIRECTLY FROM THE BUILDING ACROSS THE STREET, SO WE DON'T HAVE A LOT OF DETAILED INFO YET.
BATOU... DROP ME OFF AT THE FOREIGN MINISTRY, OKAY?
I WANT YOU TO BACK UP PROTO...

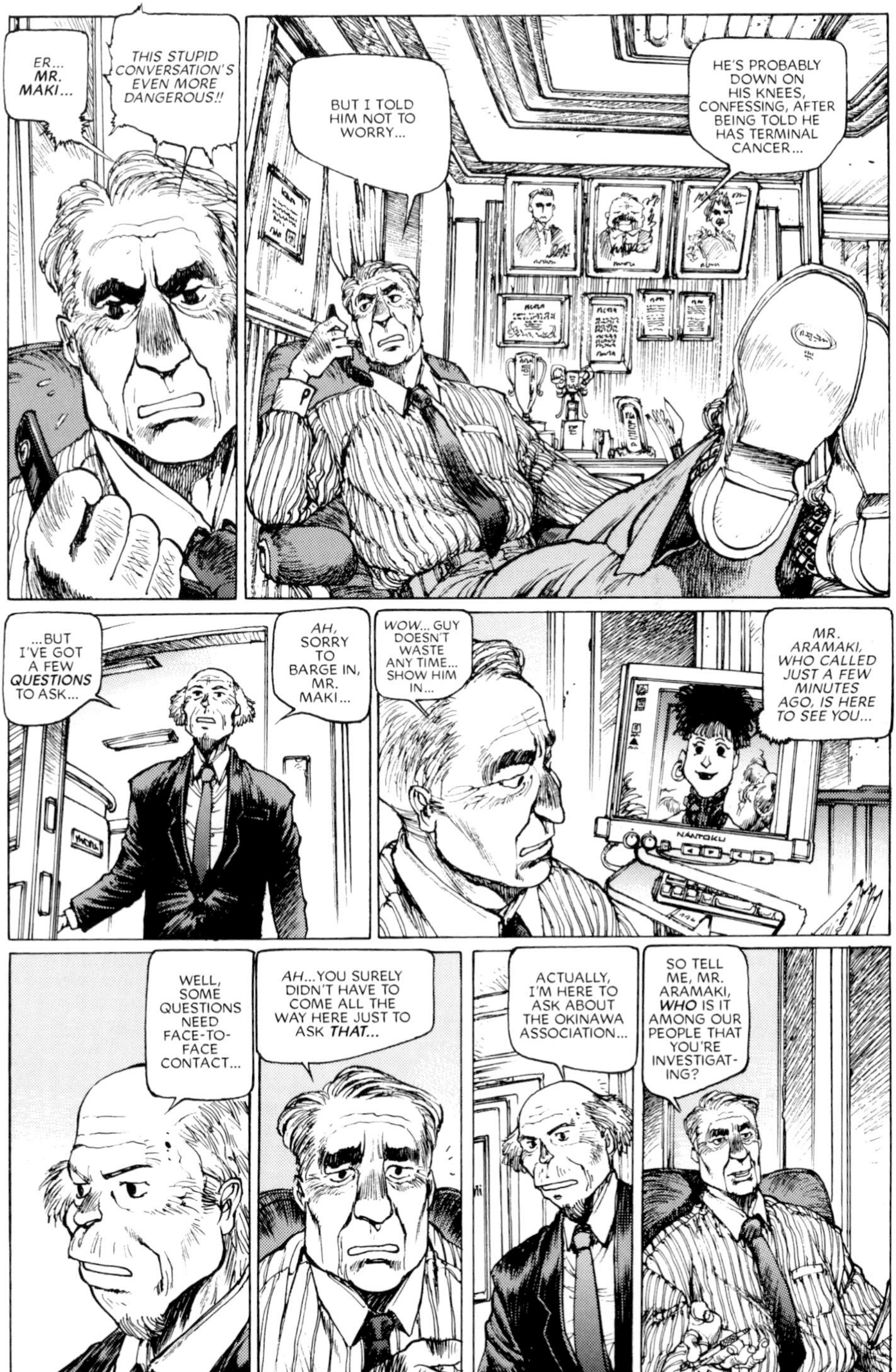
HE'S PROBABLY DOWN ON HIS KNEES, CONFESSING, AFTER BEING TOLD HE HAS TERMINAL CANCER...
BUT I TOLD HIM NOT TO WORRY...
THIS STUPID CONVERSATION'S EVEN MORE DANGEROUS!!
ER... MR. MAKI...
MR. ARAMAKI, WHO CALLED JUST A FEW MINUTES AGO, IS HERE TO SEE YOU...
WOW... GUY DOESN'T WASTE ANY TIME... SHOW HIM IN...
NANTOKU
AH, SORRY TO BARGE IN, MR. MAKI...
...BUT I'VE GOT A FEW QUESTIONS TO ASK...
SO TELL ME, MR. ARAMAKI, WHO IS IT AMONG OUR PEOPLE THAT YOU'RE INVESTIGAT-ING?
ACTUALLY, I'M HERE TO ASK ABOUT THE OKINAWA ASSOCIATION...
AH...YOU SURELY DIDN'T HAVE TO COME ALL THE WAY HERE JUST TO ASK THAT...
WELL, SOME QUESTIONS NEED FACE-TO-FACE CONTACT...

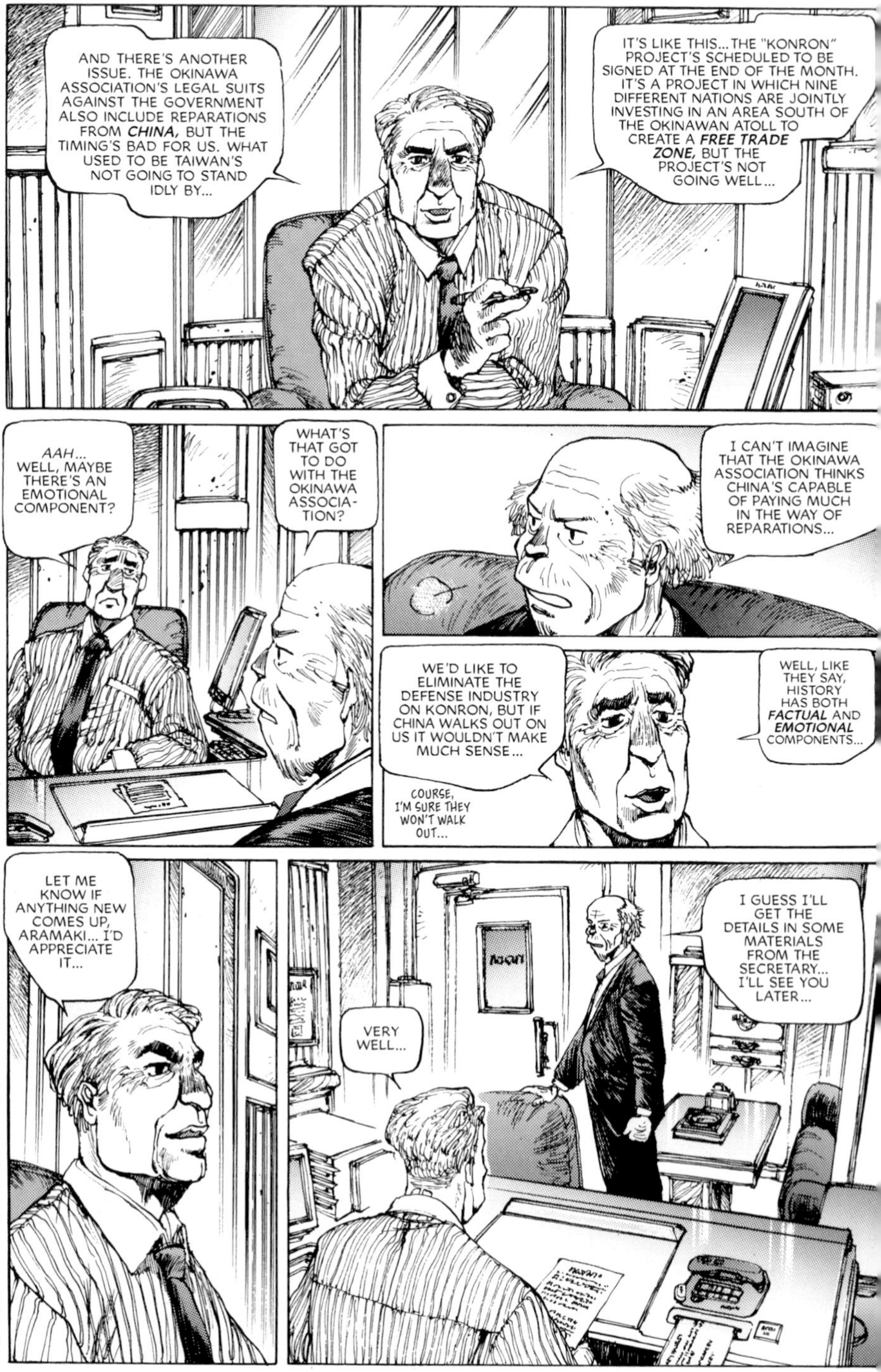
AND THERE'S ANOTHER ISSUE. THE OKINAWA ASSOCIATION'S LEGAL SUITS AGAINST THE GOVERNMENT ALSO INCLUDE REPARATIONS FROM *CHINA,* BUT THE TIMING'S BAD FOR US. WHAT USED TO BE TAIWAN'S NOT GOING TO STAND IDLY BY...
IT'S LIKE THIS... THE "KONRON" PROJECT'S SCHEDULED TO BE SIGNED AT THE END OF THE MONTH. IT'S A PROJECT IN WHICH NINE DIFFERENT NATIONS ARE JOINTLY INVESTING IN AN AREA SOUTH OF THE OKINAWAN ATOLL TO CREATE A ***FREE TRADE ZONE,*** BUT THE PROJECT'S NOT GOING WELL...
AAH... WELL, MAYBE THERE'S AN EMOTIONAL COMPONENT?
WHAT'S THAT GOT TO DO WITH THE OKINAWA ASSOCIA-TION?
I CAN'T IMAGINE THAT THE OKINAWA ASSOCIATION THINKS CHINA'S CAPABLE OF PAYING MUCH IN THE WAY OF REPARATIONS...
WE'D LIKE TO ELIMINATE THE DEFENSE INDUSTRY ON KONRON, BUT IF CHINA WALKS OUT ON US IT WOULDN'T MAKE MUCH SENSE...
COURSE, I'M SURE THEY WON'T WALK OUT...
WELL, LIKE THEY SAY, HISTORY HAS BOTH ***FACTUAL*** AND ***EMOTIONAL*** COMPONENTS...
LET ME KNOW IF ANYTHING NEW COMES UP, ARAMAKI... I'D APPRECIATE IT...
VERY WELL...
I GUESS I'LL GET THE DETAILS IN SOME MATERIALS FROM THE SECRETARY... I'LL SEE YOU LATER...

During the era in which this story is set, U.S. forces in the Far East are no longer mainly based in Japan and a unified Korea (I know this nomenclature isn't proper, but forgive me; it's the only thing I could come up with). U.S. forces are instead on a landfill area near Takeshima Island. (Ah, again forgive me. I know there are political problems with this name, but it's too difficult to go into the details, so please forgive me.) Now, I know that moving U.S. forces to a landfill area is probably impossible, but we are dealing with a manga, after all, so please humor me. I do wish something could be done about this issue, though. What probably can be done is to have U.S. forces disperse off Japan's main islands, and build up the defense capabilities of the Japanese self-defense forces. But that's a scary idea in and of itself... Ah, excuse the political diversion...

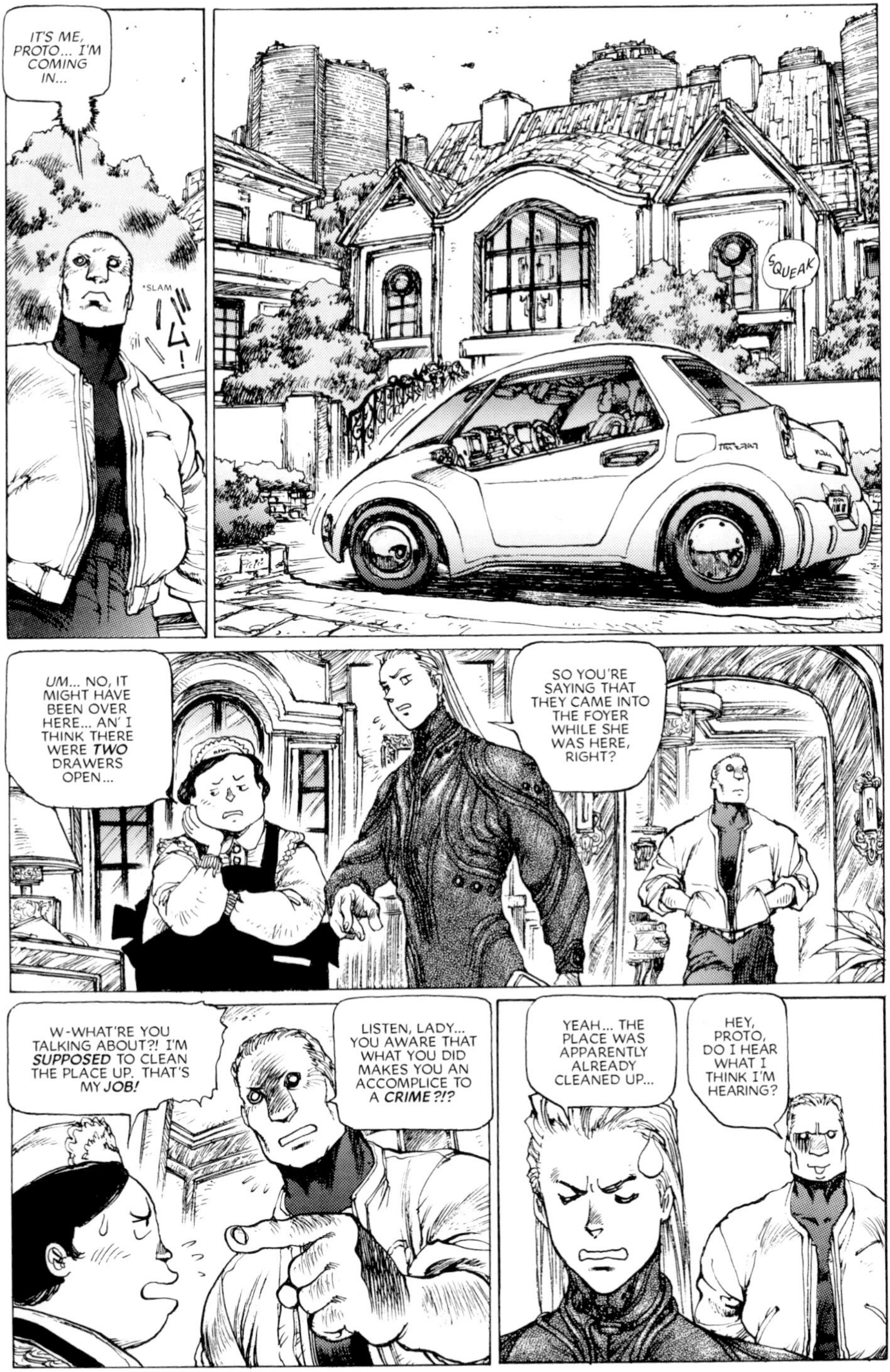
SQUEAK
*SLAM
IT'S ME, PROTO... I'M COMING IN...
SO YOU'RE SAYING THAT THEY CAME INTO THE FOYER WHILE SHE WAS HERE, RIGHT?
UM... NO, IT MIGHT HAVE BEEN OVER HERE... AN' I THINK THERE WERE ***TWO*** DRAWERS OPEN...
HEY, PROTO, DO I HEAR WHAT I THINK I'M HEARING?
YEAH... THE PLACE WAS APPARENTLY ALREADY CLEANED UP...
LISTEN, LADY... YOU AWARE THAT WHAT YOU DID MAKES YOU AN ACCOMPLICE TO A ***CRIME?!?***
W-WHAT'RE YOU TALKING ABOUT?! I'M ***SUPPOSED*** TO CLEAN THE PLACE UP. THAT'S MY ***JOB!***

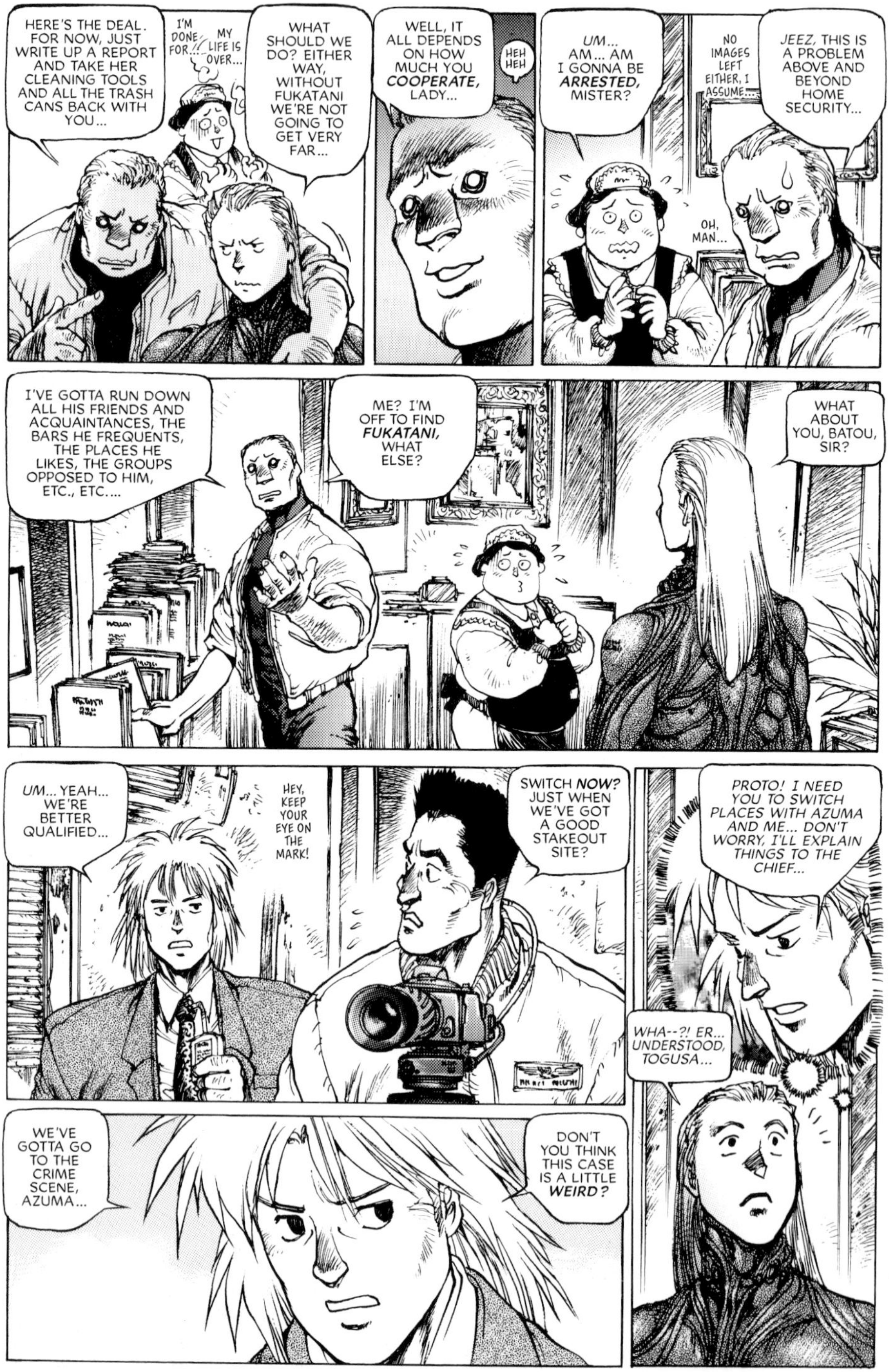
HERE'S THE DEAL. FOR NOW, JUST WRITE UP A REPORT AND TAKE HER CLEANING TOOLS AND ALL THE TRASH CANS BACK WITH YOU...
I'M DONE FOR...!
MY LIFE IS OVER...
WHAT SHOULD WE DO? EITHER WAY, WITHOUT FUKATANI WE'RE NOT GOING TO GET VERY FAR...
WELL, IT ALL DEPENDS ON HOW MUCH YOU *COOPERATE,* LADY...
HEH HEH
*UM... AM... AM I GONNA BE **ARRESTED,** MISTER?*
NO IMAGES LEFT EITHER, I ASSUME...
JEEZ, THIS IS A PROBLEM ABOVE AND BEYOND HOME SECURITY...
OH, MAN...
I'VE GOTTA RUN DOWN ALL HIS FRIENDS AND ACQUAINTANCES, THE BARS HE FREQUENTS, THE PLACES HE LIKES, THE GROUPS OPPOSED TO HIM, ETC., ETC....
ME? I'M OFF TO FIND ***FUKATANI,*** WHAT ELSE?
WHAT ABOUT YOU, BATOU, SIR?
UM... YEAH... WE'RE BETTER QUALIFIED...
HEY, KEEP YOUR EYE ON THE MARK!
SWITCH ***NOW?*** JUST WHEN WE'VE GOT A GOOD STAKEOUT SITE?
WE'VE GOTTA GO TO THE CRIME SCENE, AZUMA...
DON'T YOU THINK THIS CASE IS A LITTLE ***WEIRD?***
PROTO! I NEED YOU TO SWITCH PLACES WITH AZUMA AND ME... DON'T WORRY, I'LL EXPLAIN THINGS TO THE CHIEF...
WHA--?! ER... UNDERSTOOD, TOGUSA...

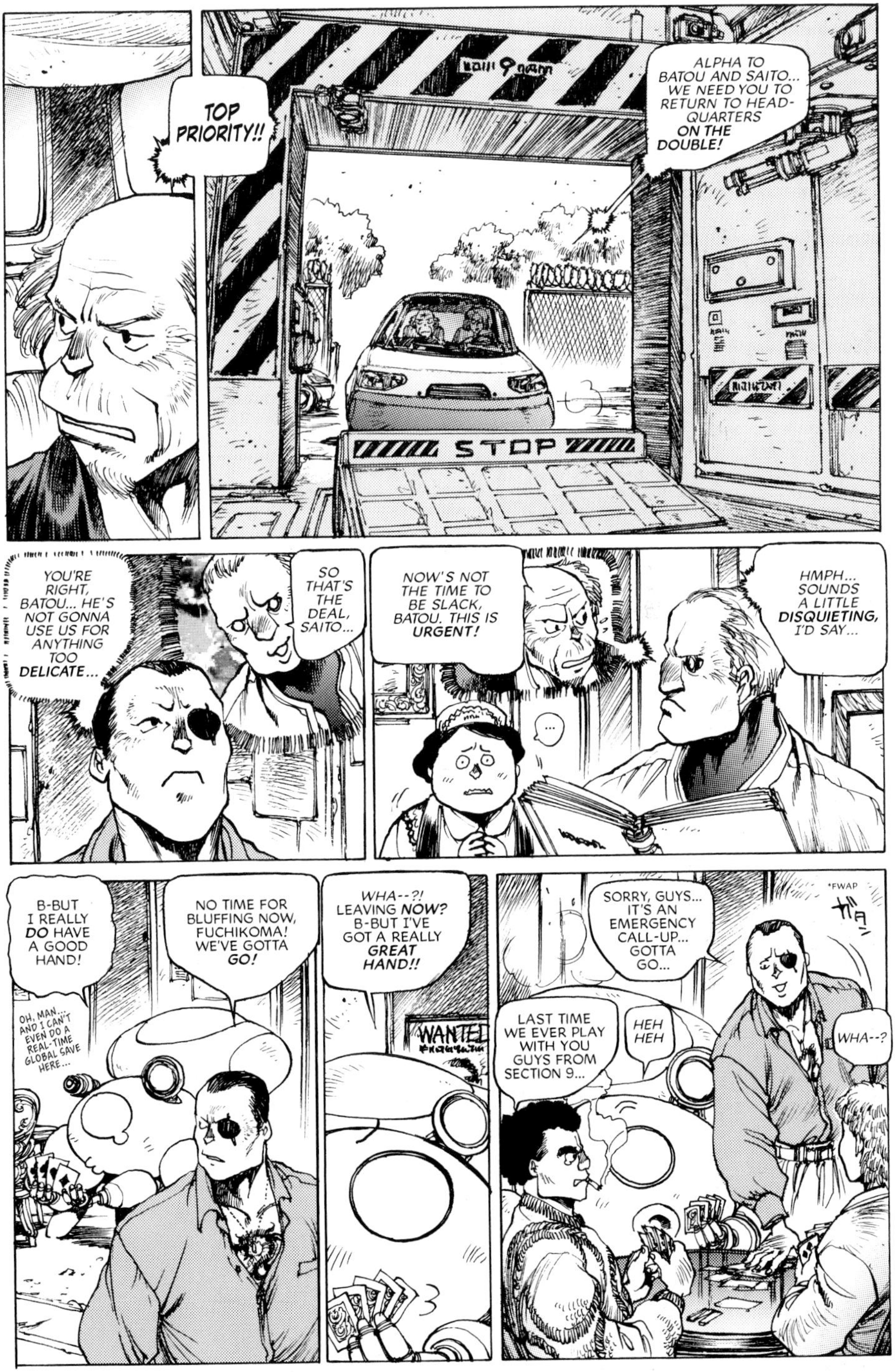
TOP PRIORITY!!
ALPHA TO BATOU AND SAITO... WE NEED YOU TO RETURN TO HEAD-QUARTERS **ON THE DOUBLE!**
STOP
YOU'RE RIGHT, BATOU... HE'S NOT GONNA USE US FOR ANYTHING TOO **DELICATE...**
SO THAT'S THE DEAL, SAITO...
NOW'S NOT THE TIME TO BE SLACK, BATOU. THIS IS **URGENT!**
HMPH... SOUNDS A LITTLE **DISQUIETING,** I'D SAY...
...
B-BUT I REALLY **DO** HAVE A GOOD HAND!
NO TIME FOR BLUFFING NOW, FUCHIKOMA! WE'VE GOTTA **GO!**
OH, MAN... AND I CAN'T EVEN DO A REAL-TIME GLOBAL SAVE HERE...
WHA--?! LEAVING **NOW?** B-BUT I'VE GOT A REALLY **GREAT HAND!!**
WANTED
SORRY, GUYS... IT'S AN EMERGENCY CALL-UP... GOTTA GO...
*FWAP
LAST TIME WE EVER PLAY WITH YOU GUYS FROM SECTION 9...
HEH HEH
WHA--?

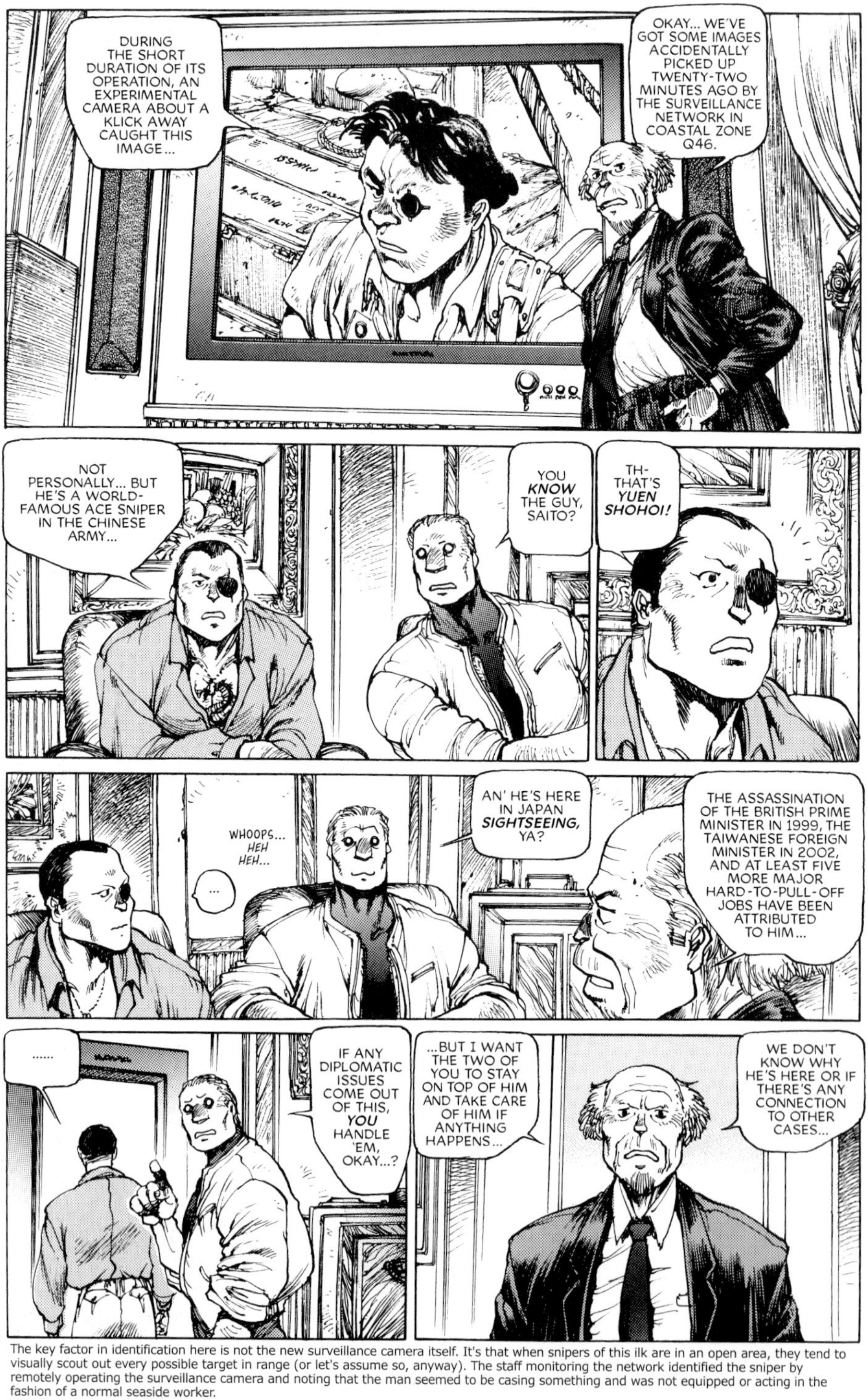
OKAY... WE'VE GOT SOME IMAGES ACCIDENTALLY PICKED UP TWENTY-TWO MINUTES AGO BY THE SURVEILLANCE NETWORK IN COASTAL ZONE Q46.
DURING THE SHORT DURATION OF ITS OPERATION, AN EXPERIMENTAL CAMERA ABOUT A KLICK AWAY CAUGHT THIS IMAGE...
TH-THAT'S *YUEN SHOHOI!*
YOU *KNOW* THE GUY, SAITO?
NOT PERSONALLY... BUT HE'S A WORLD-FAMOUS ACE SNIPER IN THE CHINESE ARMY...
THE ASSASSINATION OF THE BRITISH PRIME MINISTER IN 1999, THE TAIWANESE FOREIGN MINISTER IN 2002, AND AT LEAST FIVE MORE MAJOR HARD-TO-PULL-OFF JOBS HAVE BEEN ATTRIBUTED TO HIM...
AN' HE'S HERE IN JAPAN *SIGHTSEEING,* YA?
WHOOPS... HEH HEH...
...
WE DON'T KNOW WHY HE'S HERE OR IF THERE'S ANY CONNECTION TO OTHER CASES...
...BUT I WANT THE TWO OF YOU TO STAY ON TOP OF HIM AND TAKE CARE OF HIM IF ANYTHING HAPPENS...
IF ANY DIPLOMATIC ISSUES COME OUT OF THIS, *YOU* HANDLE 'EM, OKAY...?
......

The key factor in identification here is not the new surveillance camera itself. It's that when snipers of this ilk are in an open area, they tend to visually scout out every possible target in range (or let's assume so, anyway). The staff monitoring the network identified the sniper by remotely operating the surveillance camera and noting that the man seemed to be casing something and was not equipped or acting in the fashion of a normal seaside worker.

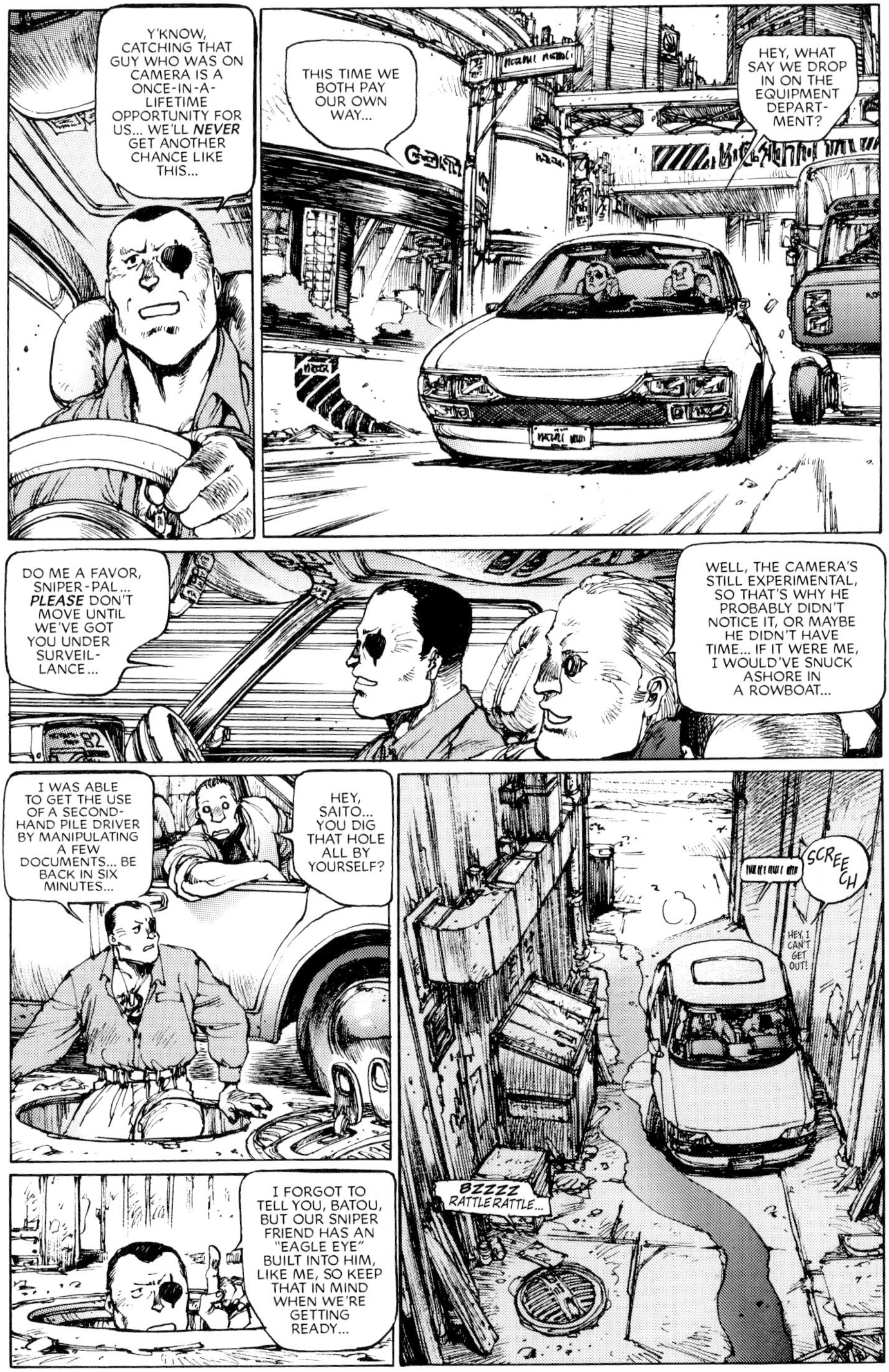
Y'KNOW, CATCHING THAT GUY WHO WAS ON CAMERA IS A ONCE-IN-A-LIFETIME OPPORTUNITY FOR US... WE'LL *NEVER* GET ANOTHER CHANCE LIKE THIS...
THIS TIME WE BOTH PAY OUR OWN WAY...
HEY, WHAT SAY WE DROP IN ON THE EQUIPMENT DEPART-MENT?
DO ME A FAVOR, SNIPER-PAL... *PLEASE* DON'T MOVE UNTIL WE'VE GOT YOU UNDER SURVEIL-LANCE...
WELL, THE CAMERA'S STILL EXPERIMENTAL, SO THAT'S WHY HE PROBABLY DIDN'T NOTICE IT, OR MAYBE HE DIDN'T HAVE TIME... IF IT WERE ME, I WOULD'VE SNUCK ASHORE IN A ROWBOAT...
HEY, SAITO... YOU DIG THAT HOLE ALL BY YOURSELF?
I WAS ABLE TO GET THE USE OF A SECOND-HAND PILE DRIVER BY MANIPULATING A FEW DOCUMENTS... BE BACK IN SIX MINUTES...
I FORGOT TO TELL YOU, BATOU, BUT OUR SNIPER FRIEND HAS AN "EAGLE EYE" BUILT INTO HIM, LIKE ME, SO KEEP THAT IN MIND WHEN WE'RE GETTING READY...
SCREECH
HEY, I CAN'T GET OUT!
BZZZZ
RATTLE RATTLE...

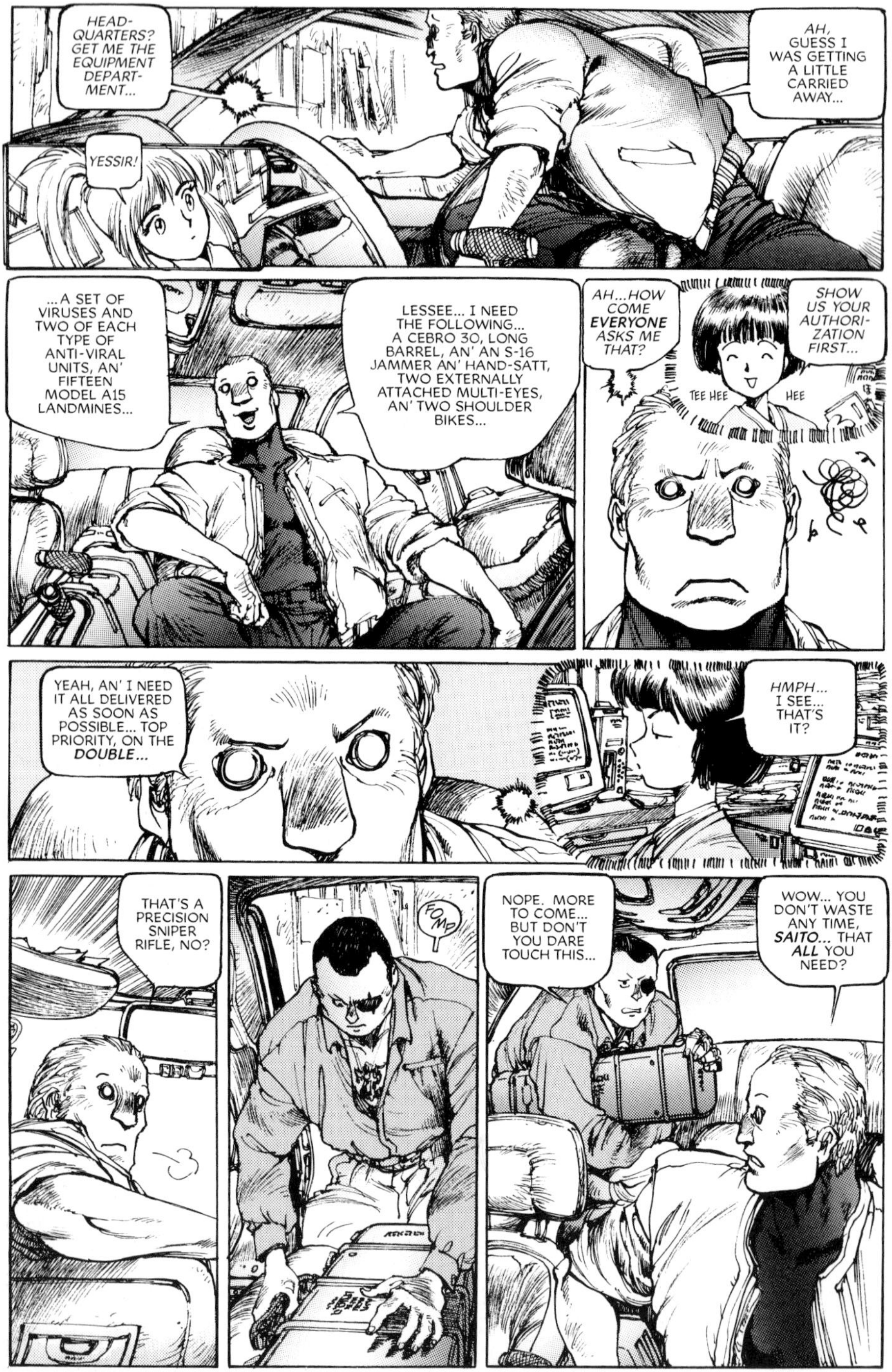
AH, GUESS I WAS GETTING A LITTLE CARRIED AWAY...
HEAD-QUARTERS? GET ME THE EQUIPMENT DEPART-MENT...
YESSIR!
LESSEE... I NEED THE FOLLOWING... A CEBRO 30, LONG BARREL, AN' AN S-16 JAMMER AN' HAND-SATT, TWO EXTERNALLY ATTACHED MULTI-EYES, AN' TWO SHOULDER BIKES...
...A SET OF VIRUSES AND TWO OF EACH TYPE OF ANTI-VIRAL UNITS, AN' FIFTEEN MODEL A15 LANDMINES...
SHOW US YOUR AUTHORI-ZATION FIRST...
TEE HEE
HEE
AH...HOW COME EVERYONE ASKS ME THAT?
HMPH... I SEE... THAT'S IT?
YEAH, AN' I NEED IT ALL DELIVERED AS SOON AS POSSIBLE... TOP PRIORITY, ON THE DOUBLE...
WOW... YOU DON'T WASTE ANY TIME, SAITO... THAT ALL YOU NEED?
NOPE. MORE TO COME... BUT DON'T YOU DARE TOUCH THIS...
FOMP
THAT'S A PRECISION SNIPER RIFLE, NO?

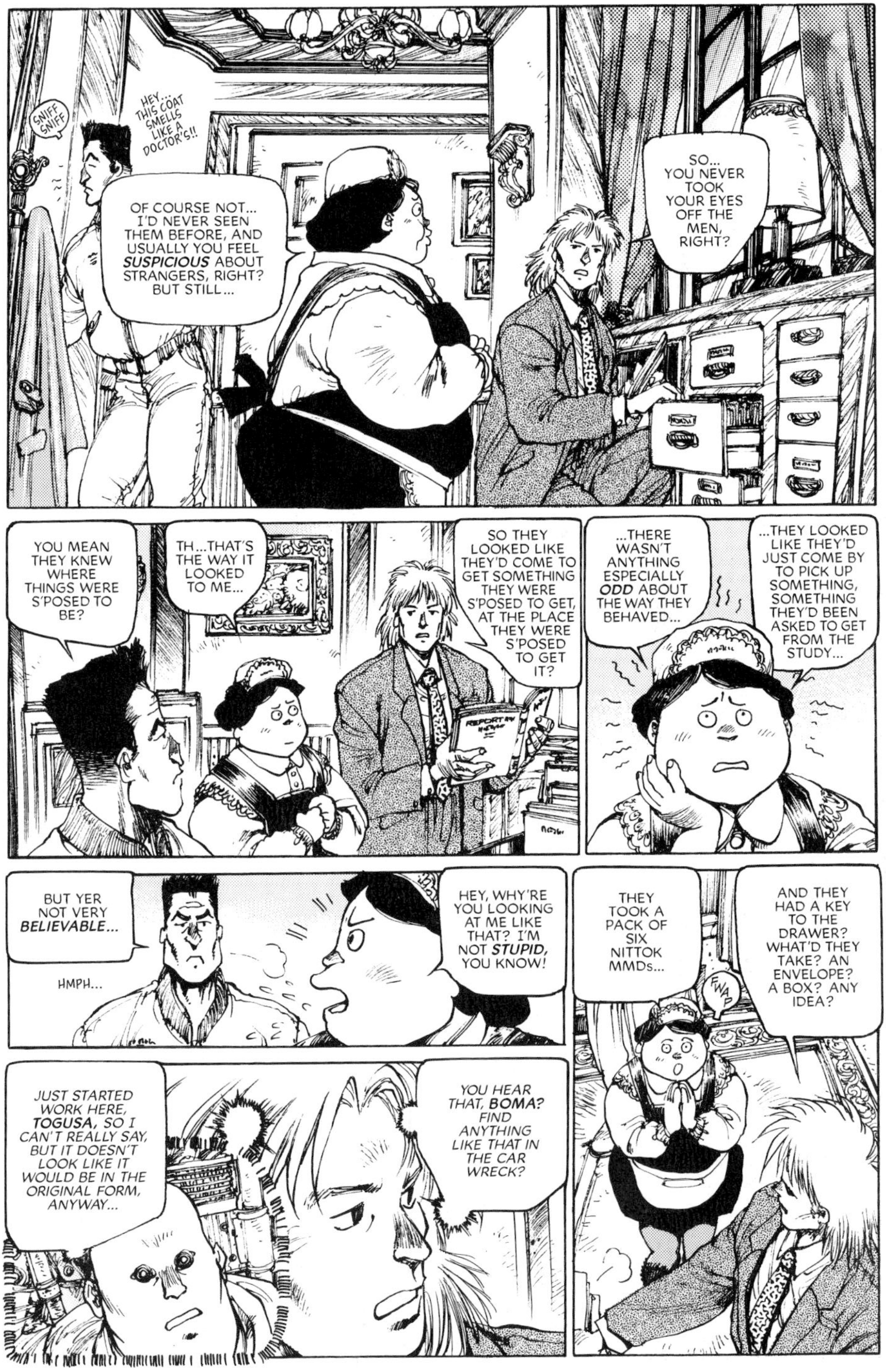
SO... YOU NEVER TOOK YOUR EYES OFF THE MEN, RIGHT?
HEY... THIS COAT SMELLS LIKE A DOCTOR'S!!
OF COURSE NOT... I'D NEVER SEEN THEM BEFORE, AND USUALLY YOU FEEL SUSPICIOUS ABOUT STRANGERS, RIGHT? BUT STILL...
SNIFF SNIFF
...THEY LOOKED LIKE THEY'D JUST COME BY TO PICK UP SOMETHING, SOMETHING THEY'D BEEN ASKED TO GET FROM THE STUDY...
...THERE WASN'T ANYTHING ESPECIALLY ODD ABOUT THE WAY THEY BEHAVED...
SO THEY LOOKED LIKE THEY'D COME TO GET SOMETHING THEY WERE S'POSED TO GET, AT THE PLACE THEY WERE S'POSED TO GET IT?
TH...THAT'S THE WAY IT LOOKED TO ME...
YOU MEAN THEY KNEW WHERE THINGS WERE S'POSED TO BE?
AND THEY HAD A KEY TO THE DRAWER? WHAT'D THEY TAKE? AN ENVELOPE? A BOX? ANY IDEA?
THEY TOOK A PACK OF SIX NITTOK MMDs...
FWAP
HEY, WHY'RE YOU LOOKING AT ME LIKE THAT? I'M NOT STUPID, YOU KNOW!
BUT YER NOT VERY BELIEVABLE...
HMPH...
YOU HEAR THAT, BOMA? FIND ANYTHING LIKE THAT IN THE CAR WRECK?
JUST STARTED WORK HERE, TOGUSA, SO I CAN'T REALLY SAY, BUT IT DOESN'T LOOK LIKE IT WOULD BE IN THE ORIGINAL FORM, ANYWAY...

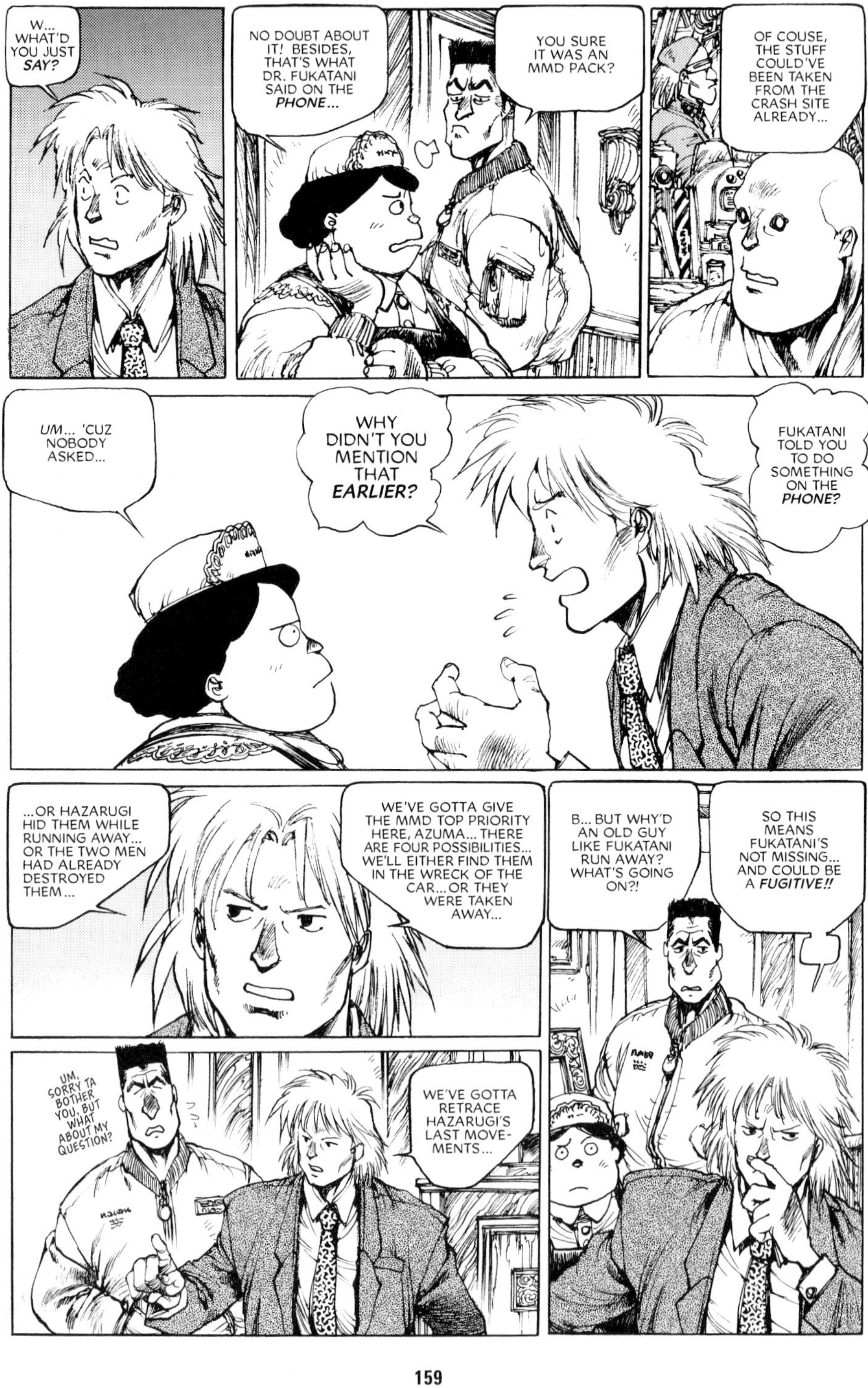
OF COUSE, THE STUFF COULD'VE BEEN TAKEN FROM THE CRASH SITE ALREADY...
YOU SURE IT WAS AN MMD PACK?
NO DOUBT ABOUT IT! BESIDES, THAT'S WHAT DR. FUKATANI SAID ON THE *PHONE*...
W... WHAT'D YOU JUST *SAY?*
FUKATANI TOLD YOU TO DO SOMETHING ON THE *PHONE?*
WHY DIDN'T YOU MENTION THAT *EARLIER?*
UM... 'CUZ NOBODY ASKED...
SO THIS MEANS FUKATANI'S NOT MISSING... AND COULD BE A *FUGITIVE!!*
B... BUT WHY'D AN OLD GUY LIKE FUKATANI RUN AWAY? WHAT'S GOING ON?!
WE'VE GOTTA GIVE THE MMD TOP PRIORITY HERE, AZUMA... THERE ARE FOUR POSSIBILITIES... WE'LL EITHER FIND THEM IN THE WRECK OF THE CAR... OR THEY WERE TAKEN AWAY...
...OR HAZARUGI HID THEM WHILE RUNNING AWAY... OR THE TWO MEN HAD ALREADY DESTROYED THEM...
WE'VE GOTTA RETRACE HAZARUGI'S LAST MOVE-MENTS...
UM, SORRY TA BOTHER YOU, BUT WHAT ABOUT MY QUESTION?

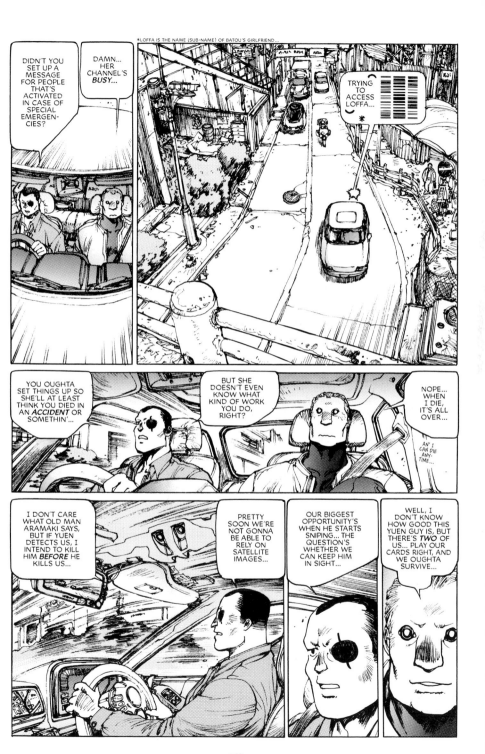

<image-description>

*LOFFA IS THE NAME (SUB-NAME) OF BATOU'S GIRLFRIEND...

DIDN'T YOU SET UP A MESSAGE FOR PEOPLE THAT'S ACTIVATED IN CASE OF SPECIAL EMERGENCIES?

DAMN... HER CHANNEL'S *BUSY*...

TRYING TO ACCESS LOFFA... ☺ ✳

YOU OUGHTA SET THINGS UP SO SHE'LL AT LEAST THINK YOU DIED IN AN *ACCIDENT* OR SOMETHIN'...

BUT SHE DOESN'T EVEN KNOW WHAT KIND OF WORK YOU DO, RIGHT?

NOPE... WHEN I DIE, IT'S ALL OVER...

AN' I CAN DIE ANY- TIME...

I DON'T CARE WHAT OLD MAN ARAMAKI SAYS, BUT IF YUEN DETECTS US, I INTEND TO KILL HIM *BEFORE* HE KILLS US...

PRETTY SOON WE'RE NOT GONNA BE ABLE TO RELY ON SATELLITE IMAGES...

OUR BIGGEST OPPORTUNITY'S WHEN HE STARTS SNIPING... THE QUESTION'S WHETHER WE CAN KEEP HIM IN SIGHT...

WELL, I DON'T KNOW HOW GOOD THIS YUEN GUY IS, BUT THERE'S *TWO* OF US... PLAY OUR CARDS RIGHT, AND WE OUGHTA SURVIVE...
</image-description>

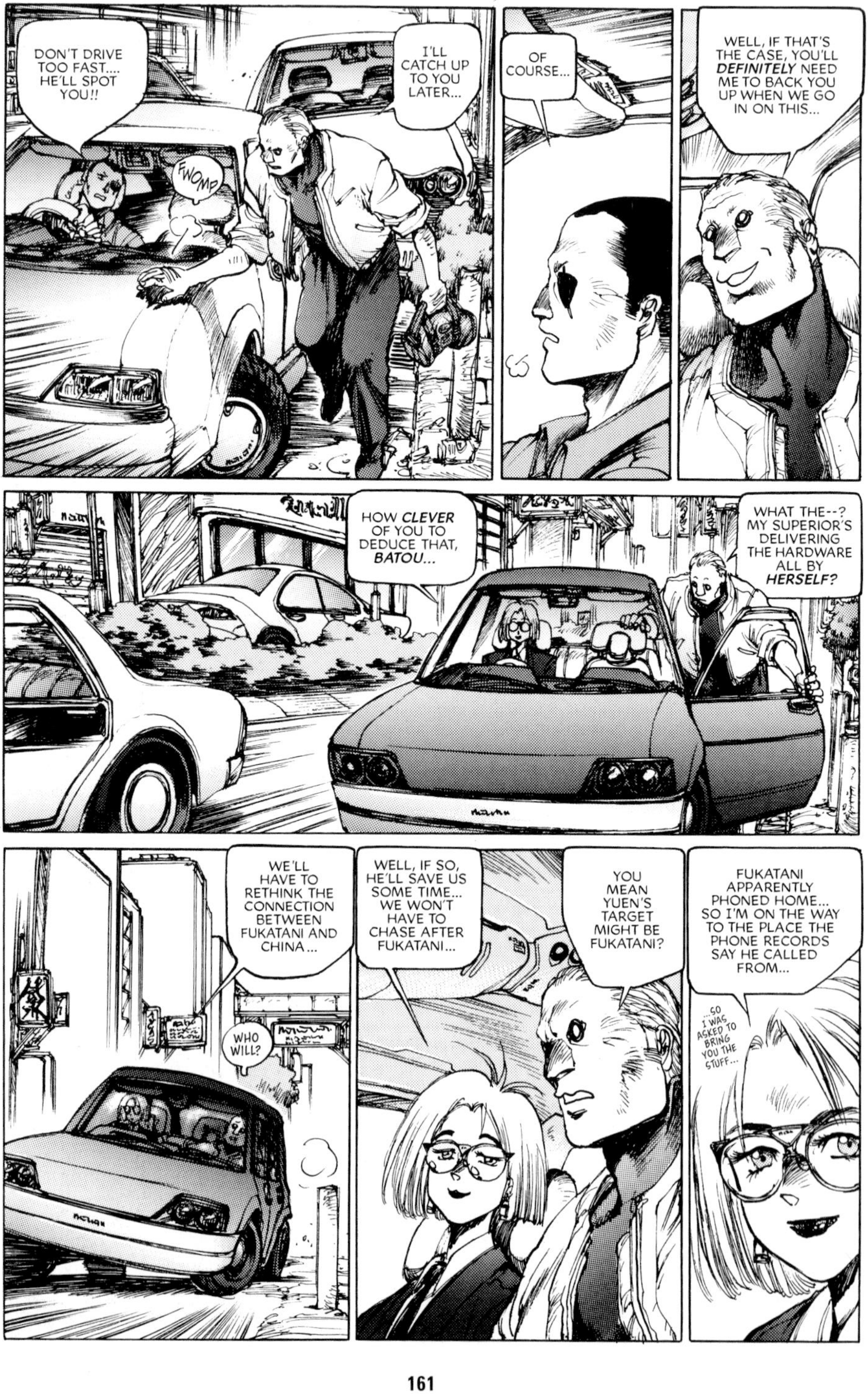
WELL, IF THAT'S THE CASE, YOU'LL *DEFINITELY* NEED ME TO BACK YOU UP WHEN WE GO IN ON THIS...
OF COURSE...
I'LL CATCH UP TO YOU LATER...
DON'T DRIVE TOO FAST.... HE'LL SPOT YOU!!
FWOMP
WHAT THE--? MY SUPERIOR'S DELIVERING THE HARDWARE ALL BY *HERSELF?*
HOW *CLEVER* OF YOU TO DEDUCE THAT, *BATOU...*
FUKATANI APPARENTLY PHONED HOME... SO I'M ON THE WAY TO THE PLACE THE PHONE RECORDS SAY HE CALLED FROM...
...SO I WAS ASKED TO BRING YOU THE STUFF...
YOU MEAN YUEN'S TARGET MIGHT BE FUKATANI?
WELL, IF SO, HE'LL SAVE US SOME TIME... WE WON'T HAVE TO CHASE AFTER FUKATANI...
WE'LL HAVE TO RETHINK THE CONNECTION BETWEEN FUKATANI AND CHINA...
WHO WILL?

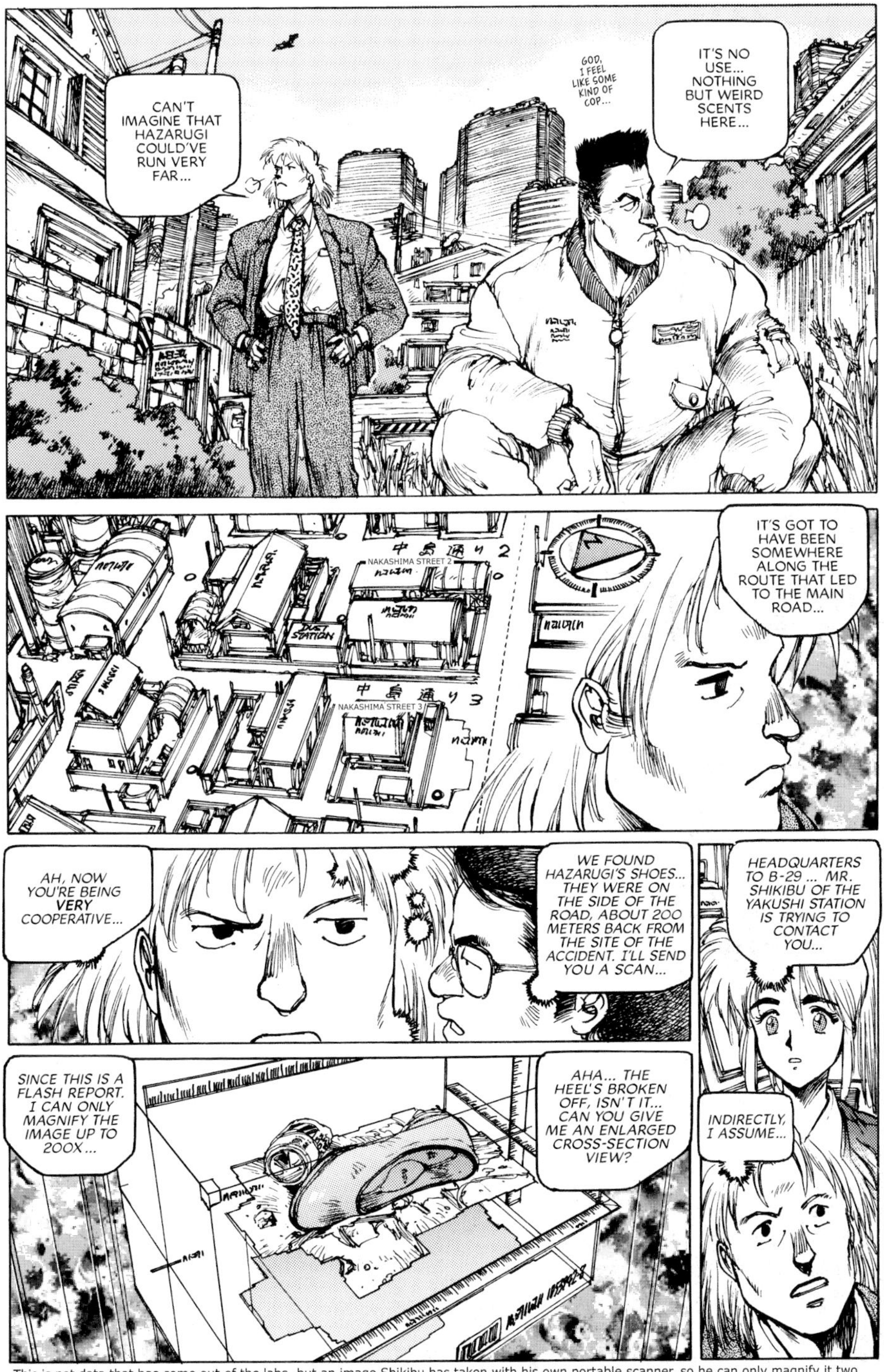
IT'S NO USE... NOTHING BUT WEIRD SCENTS HERE...
GOD, I FEEL LIKE SOME KIND OF COP...
CAN'T IMAGINE THAT HAZARUGI COULD'VE RUN VERY FAR...
IT'S GOT TO HAVE BEEN SOMEWHERE ALONG THE ROUTE THAT LED TO THE MAIN ROAD...
中島通り2
NAKASHIMA STREET 2
DUST STATION
中島通り3
NAKASHIMA STREET 3
HEADQUARTERS TO B-29 ... MR. SHIKIBU OF THE YAKUSHI STATION IS TRYING TO CONTACT YOU...
INDIRECTLY, I ASSUME...
WE FOUND HAZARUGI'S SHOES... THEY WERE ON THE SIDE OF THE ROAD, ABOUT 200 METERS BACK FROM THE SITE OF THE ACCIDENT. I'LL SEND YOU A SCAN...
AH, NOW YOU'RE BEING **VERY** COOPERATIVE...
AHA... THE HEEL'S BROKEN OFF, ISN'T IT... CAN YOU GIVE ME AN ENLARGED CROSS-SECTION VIEW?
SINCE THIS IS A FLASH REPORT, I CAN ONLY MAGNIFY THE IMAGE UP TO 200X...

This is not data that has come out of the labs, but an image Shikibu has taken with his own portable scanner, so he can only magnify it two hundred times... By this time the actual item in question is probably in a vinyl bag of some sort, being transported to the labs. Investigators greatly appreciate such preliminary data, but its use is limited because it carries little legal weight. Investigators found the shoes as soon as police sniffer dogs appeared on the scene, and luckily for them there had been no street cleaning yet that day...

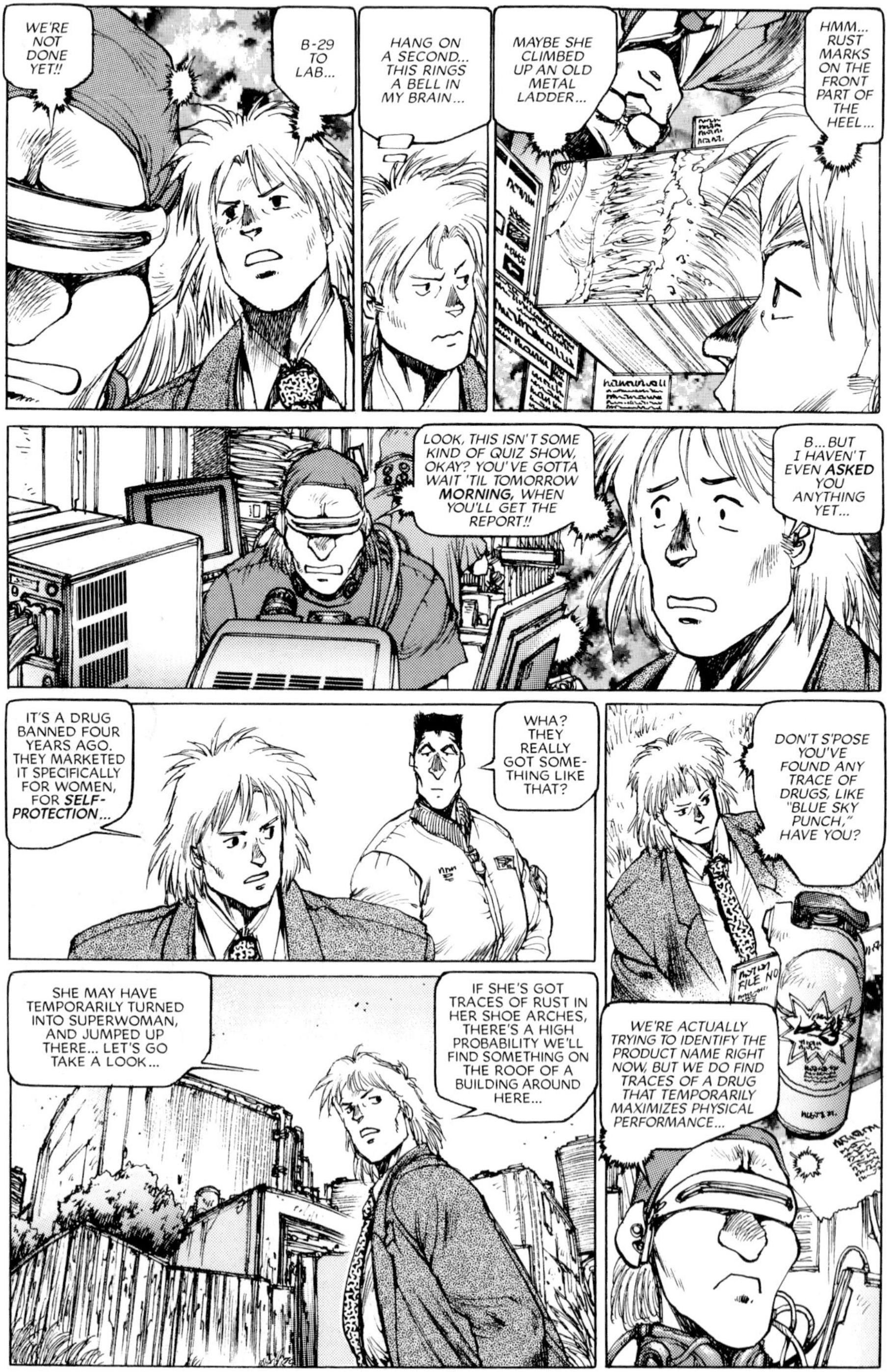
HMM... RUST MARKS ON THE FRONT PART OF THE HEEL...
MAYBE SHE CLIMBED UP AN OLD METAL LADDER...
HANG ON A SECOND... THIS RINGS A BELL IN MY BRAIN...
B-29 TO LAB...
WE'RE NOT DONE YET!!
LOOK, THIS ISN'T SOME KIND OF QUIZ SHOW, OKAY? YOU'VE GOTTA WAIT 'TIL TOMORROW MORNING, WHEN YOU'LL GET THE REPORT!!
B...BUT I HAVEN'T EVEN ASKED YOU ANYTHING YET...
DON'T S'POSE YOU'VE FOUND ANY TRACE OF DRUGS, LIKE "BLUE SKY PUNCH," HAVE YOU?
WE'RE ACTUALLY TRYING TO IDENTIFY THE PRODUCT NAME RIGHT NOW, BUT WE DO FIND TRACES OF A DRUG THAT TEMPORARILY MAXIMIZES PHYSICAL PERFORMANCE...
IT'S A DRUG BANNED FOUR YEARS AGO. THEY MARKETED IT SPECIFICALLY FOR WOMEN, FOR SELF-PROTECTION...
WHA? THEY REALLY GOT SOMETHING LIKE THAT?
IF SHE'S GOT TRACES OF RUST IN HER SHOE ARCHES, THERE'S A HIGH PROBABILITY WE'LL FIND SOMETHING ON THE ROOF OF A BUILDING AROUND HERE...
SHE MAY HAVE TEMPORARILY TURNED INTO SUPERWOMAN, AND JUMPED UP THERE... LET'S GO TAKE A LOOK...

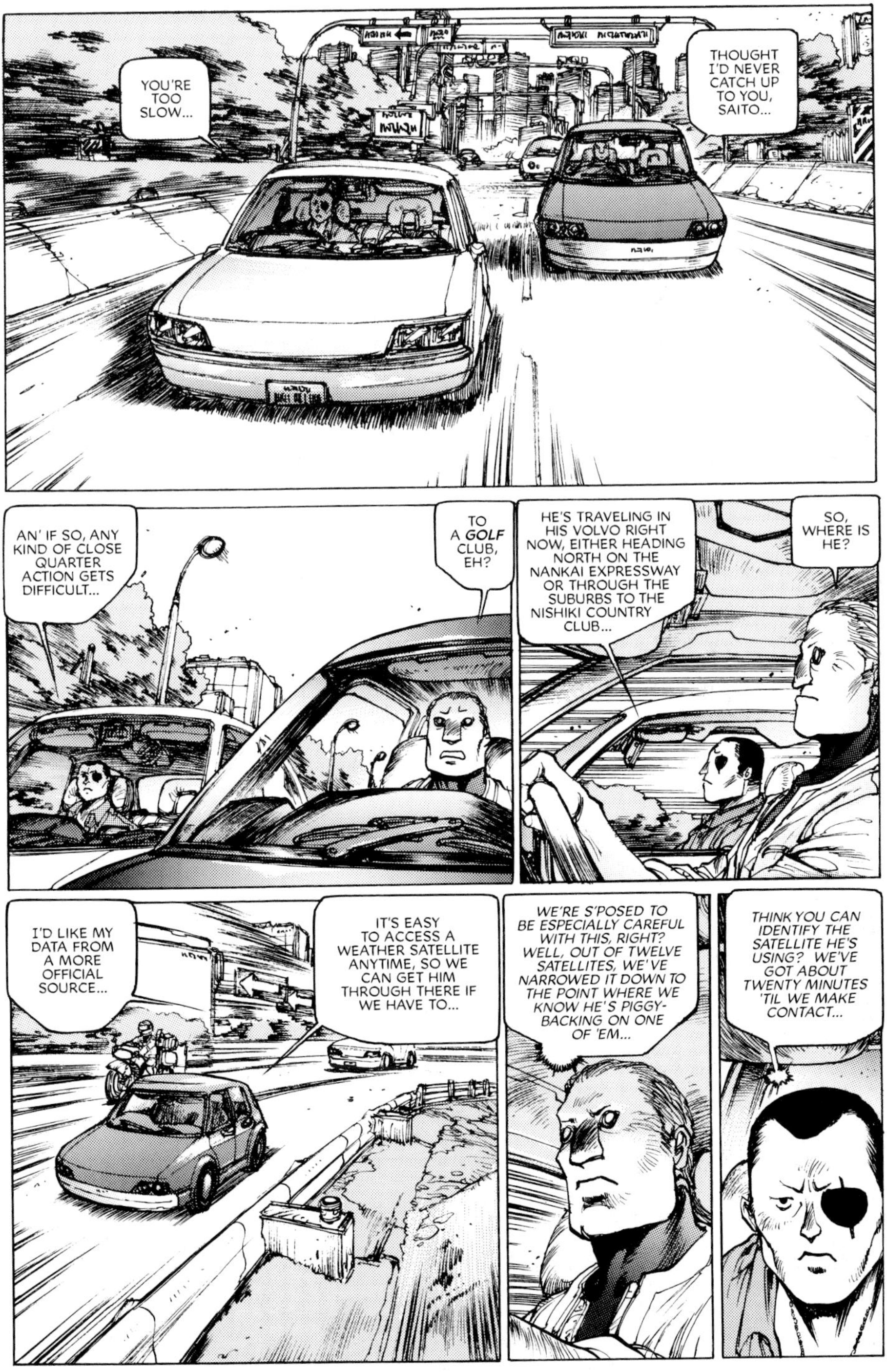
THOUGHT I'D NEVER CATCH UP TO YOU, SAITO...
YOU'RE TOO SLOW...
SO, WHERE IS HE?
HE'S TRAVELING IN HIS VOLVO RIGHT NOW, EITHER HEADING NORTH ON THE NANKAI EXPRESSWAY OR THROUGH THE SUBURBS TO THE NISHIKI COUNTRY CLUB...
TO A *GOLF* CLUB, EH?
AN' IF SO, ANY KIND OF CLOSE QUARTER ACTION GETS DIFFICULT...
THINK YOU CAN IDENTIFY THE SATELLITE HE'S USING? WE'VE GOT ABOUT TWENTY MINUTES 'TIL WE MAKE CONTACT...
WE'RE S'POSED TO BE ESPECIALLY CAREFUL WITH THIS, RIGHT? WELL, OUT OF TWELVE SATELLITES, WE'VE NARROWED IT DOWN TO THE POINT WHERE WE KNOW HE'S PIGGY-BACKING ON ONE OF 'EM...
IT'S EASY TO ACCESS A WEATHER SATELLITE ANYTIME, SO WE CAN GET HIM THROUGH THERE IF WE HAVE TO...
I'D LIKE MY DATA FROM A MORE OFFICIAL SOURCE...

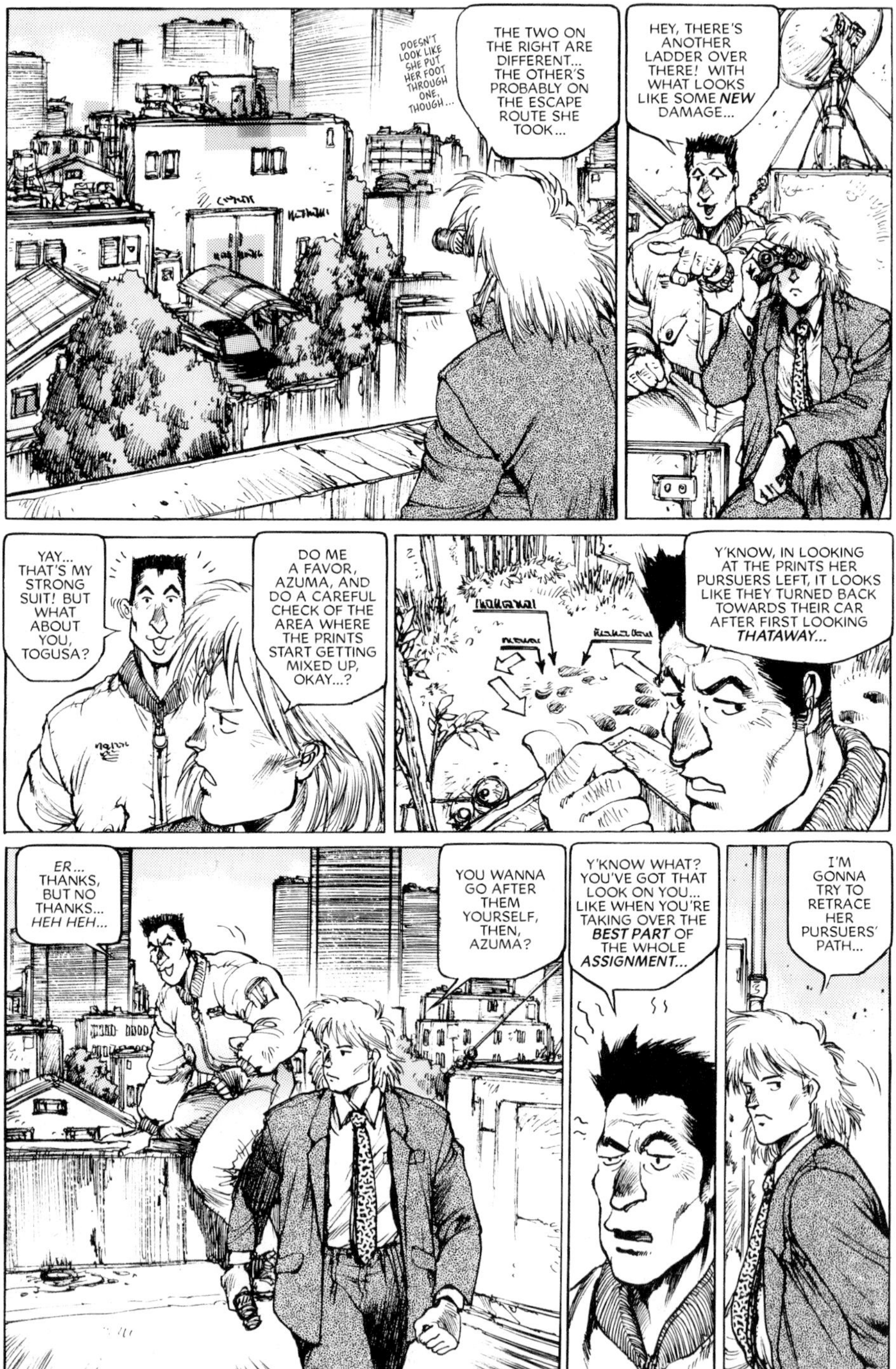

THE TWO ON THE RIGHT ARE DIFFERENT... THE OTHER'S PROBABLY ON THE ESCAPE ROUTE SHE TOOK...
DOESN'T LOOK LIKE SHE PUT HER FOOT THROUGH ONE, THOUGH...
HEY, THERE'S ANOTHER LADDER OVER THERE! WITH WHAT LOOKS LIKE SOME *NEW* DAMAGE...
DO ME A FAVOR, AZUMA, AND DO A CAREFUL CHECK OF THE AREA WHERE THE PRINTS START GETTING MIXED UP, OKAY...?
YAY... THAT'S MY STRONG SUIT! BUT WHAT ABOUT YOU, TOGUSA?
Y'KNOW, IN LOOKING AT THE PRINTS HER PURSUERS LEFT, IT LOOKS LIKE THEY TURNED BACK TOWARDS THEIR CAR AFTER FIRST LOOKING ***THATAWAY...***
YOU WANNA GO AFTER THEM YOURSELF, THEN, AZUMA?
ER... THANKS, BUT NO THANKS... *HEH HEH...*
Y'KNOW WHAT? YOU'VE GOT THAT LOOK ON YOU... LIKE WHEN YOU'RE TAKING OVER THE ***BEST PART*** OF THE WHOLE ***ASSIGNMENT...***
I'M GONNA TRY TO RETRACE HER PURSUERS' PATH...

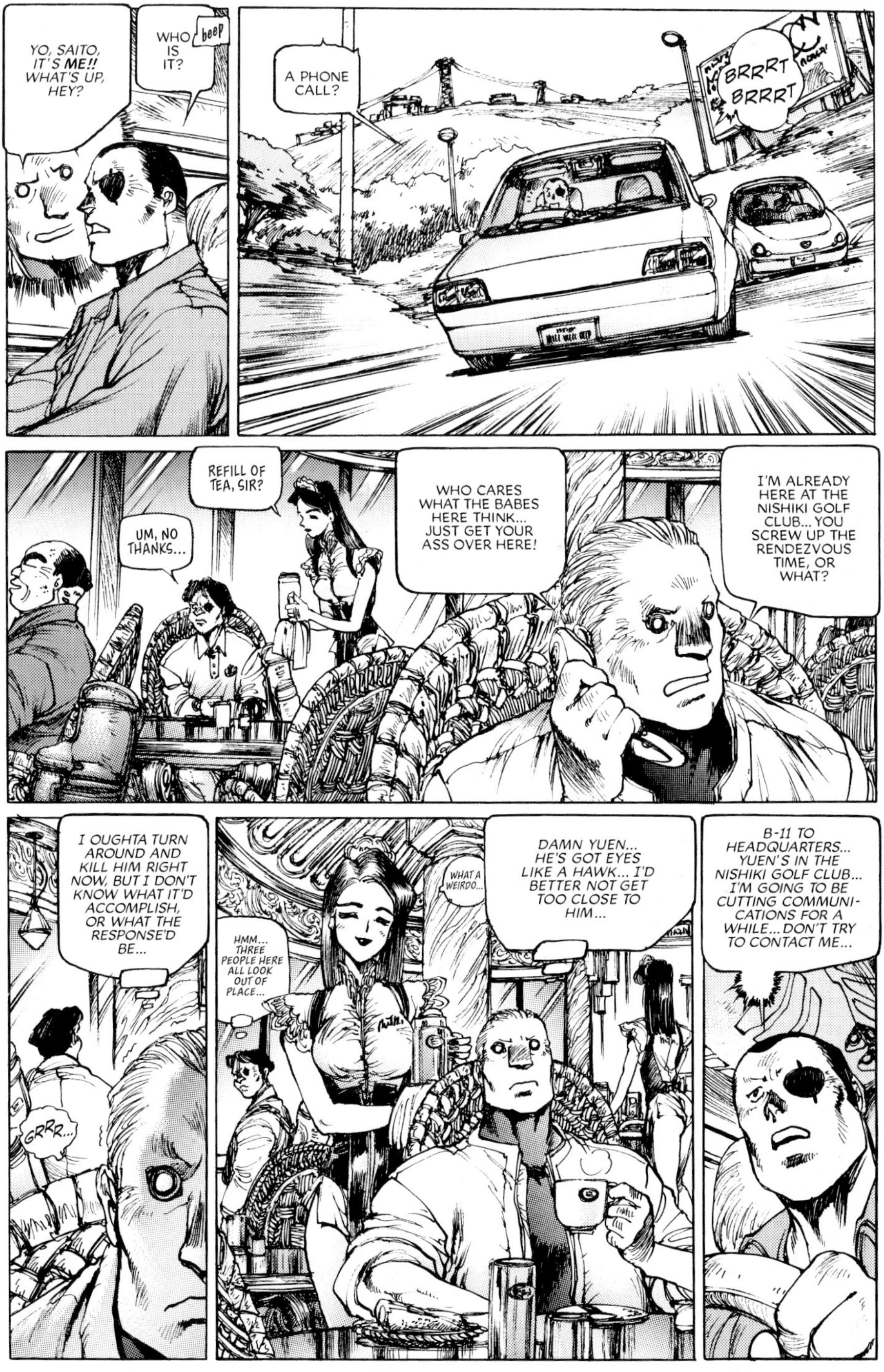

BRRRT BRRRT
A PHONE CALL?
WHO IS IT?
beep
YO, SAITO, IT'S ME!! WHAT'S UP, HEY?
I'M ALREADY HERE AT THE NISHIKI GOLF CLUB... YOU SCREW UP THE RENDEZVOUS TIME, OR WHAT?
WHO CARES WHAT THE BABES HERE THINK... JUST GET YOUR ASS OVER HERE!
REFILL OF TEA, SIR?
UM, NO THANKS...
B-11 TO HEADQUARTERS... YUEN'S IN THE NISHIKI GOLF CLUB... I'M GOING TO BE CUTTING COMMUNI-CATIONS FOR A WHILE... DON'T TRY TO CONTACT ME...
DAMN YUEN... HE'S GOT EYES LIKE A HAWK... I'D BETTER NOT GET TOO CLOSE TO HIM...
WHAT A WEIRDO...
HMM... THREE PEOPLE HERE ALL LOOK OUT OF PLACE...
I OUGHTA TURN AROUND AND KILL HIM RIGHT NOW, BUT I DON'T KNOW WHAT IT'D ACCOMPLISH, OR WHAT THE RESPONSE'D BE...
GRRR...

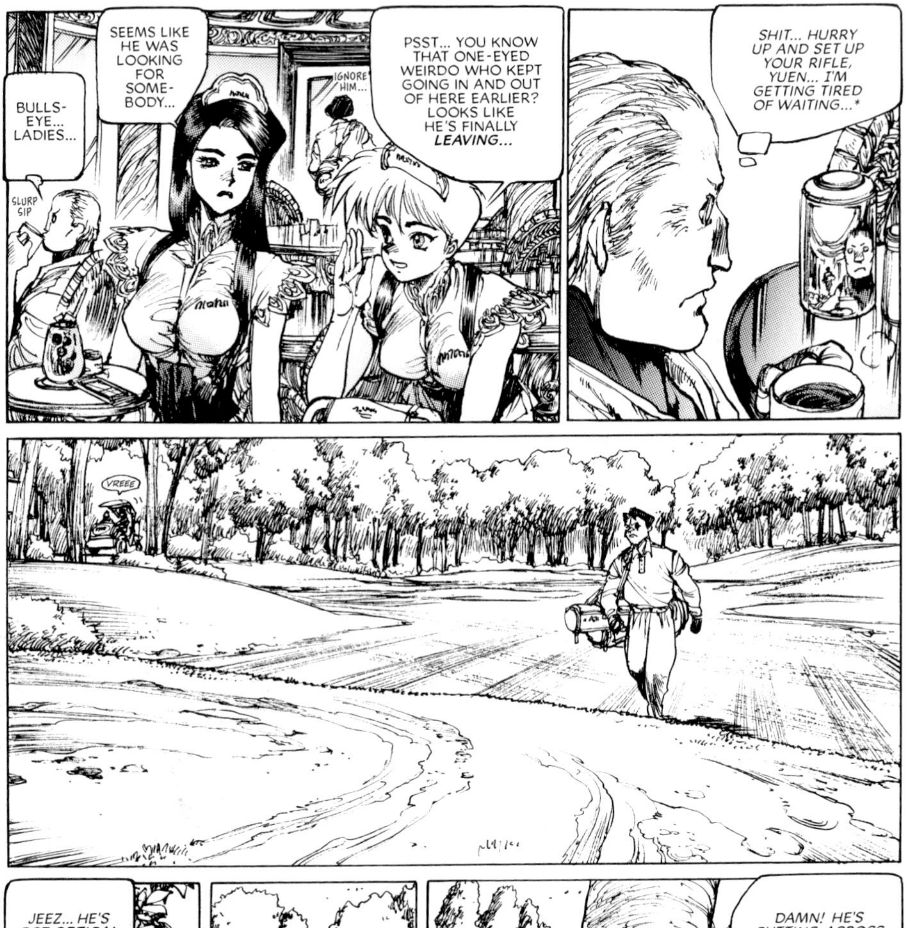
SHIT... HURRY UP AND SET UP YOUR RIFLE, YUEN... I'M GETTING TIRED OF WAITING...*
PSST... YOU KNOW THAT ONE-EYED WEIRDO WHO KEPT GOING IN AND OUT OF HERE EARLIER? LOOKS LIKE HE'S FINALLY LEAVING...
IGNORE HIM...
SEEMS LIKE HE WAS LOOKING FOR SOME-BODY...
BULLS-EYE... LADIES...
SLURP SIP
VREEE
DAMN! HE'S CUTTING ACROSS THE FAIRWAY! THE BASTARD'S BEING AWFULLY CAREFUL...**
ZIP
HUMM
JEEZ... HE'S GOT OPTICAL CAMOUFLAGE, TOO?!! UH, OH...

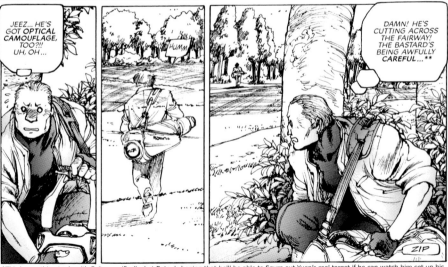

*This has nothing to do with Saito specifically, but Batou's hoping that he'll be able to figure out Yuen's real target if he can watch him set up his sniper rifle....

**Yuen looked back, right after crossing the fairway, to make sure he wasn't being tailed. That means Batou will be forced to go around the long way if he wants to continue to tail Yuen on the other side. Or at least that's what we'll assume's going on here...

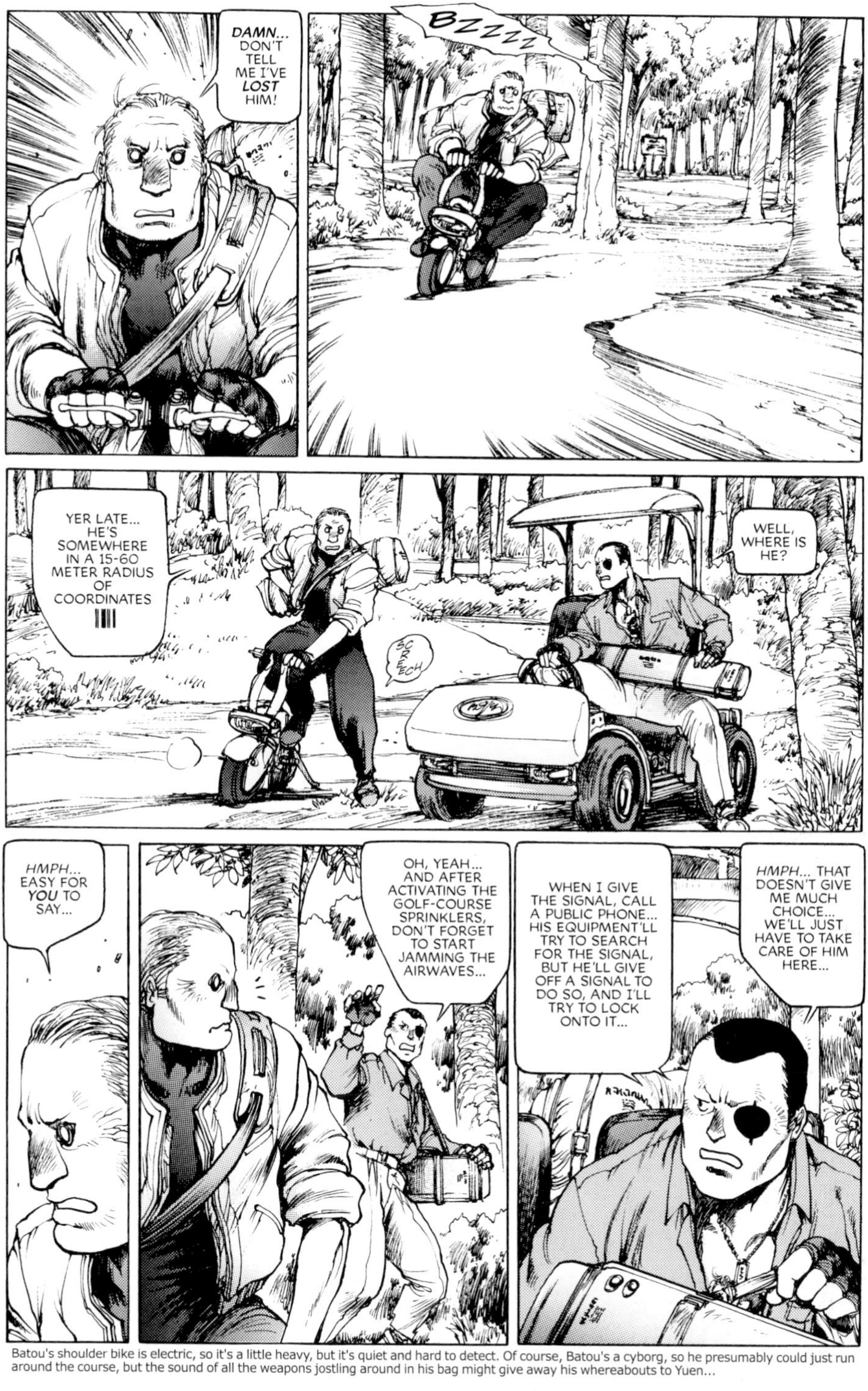
BZZZZZ
DAMN... DON'T TELL ME I'VE LOST HIM!
WELL, WHERE IS HE?
SCREECH
YER LATE... HE'S SOMEWHERE IN A 15-60 METER RADIUS OF COORDINATES
HMPH... THAT DOESN'T GIVE ME MUCH CHOICE... WE'LL JUST HAVE TO TAKE CARE OF HIM HERE...
WHEN I GIVE THE SIGNAL, CALL A PUBLIC PHONE... HIS EQUIPMENT'LL TRY TO SEARCH FOR THE SIGNAL, BUT HE'LL GIVE OFF A SIGNAL TO DO SO, AND I'LL TRY TO LOCK ONTO IT...
OH, YEAH... AND AFTER ACTIVATING THE GOLF-COURSE SPRINKLERS, DON'T FORGET TO START JAMMING THE AIRWAVES...
HMPH... EASY FOR YOU TO SAY...

Batou's shoulder bike is electric, so it's a little heavy, but it's quiet and hard to detect. Of course, Batou's a cyborg, so he presumably could just run around the course, but the sound of all the weapons jostling around in his bag might give away his whereabouts to Yuen...

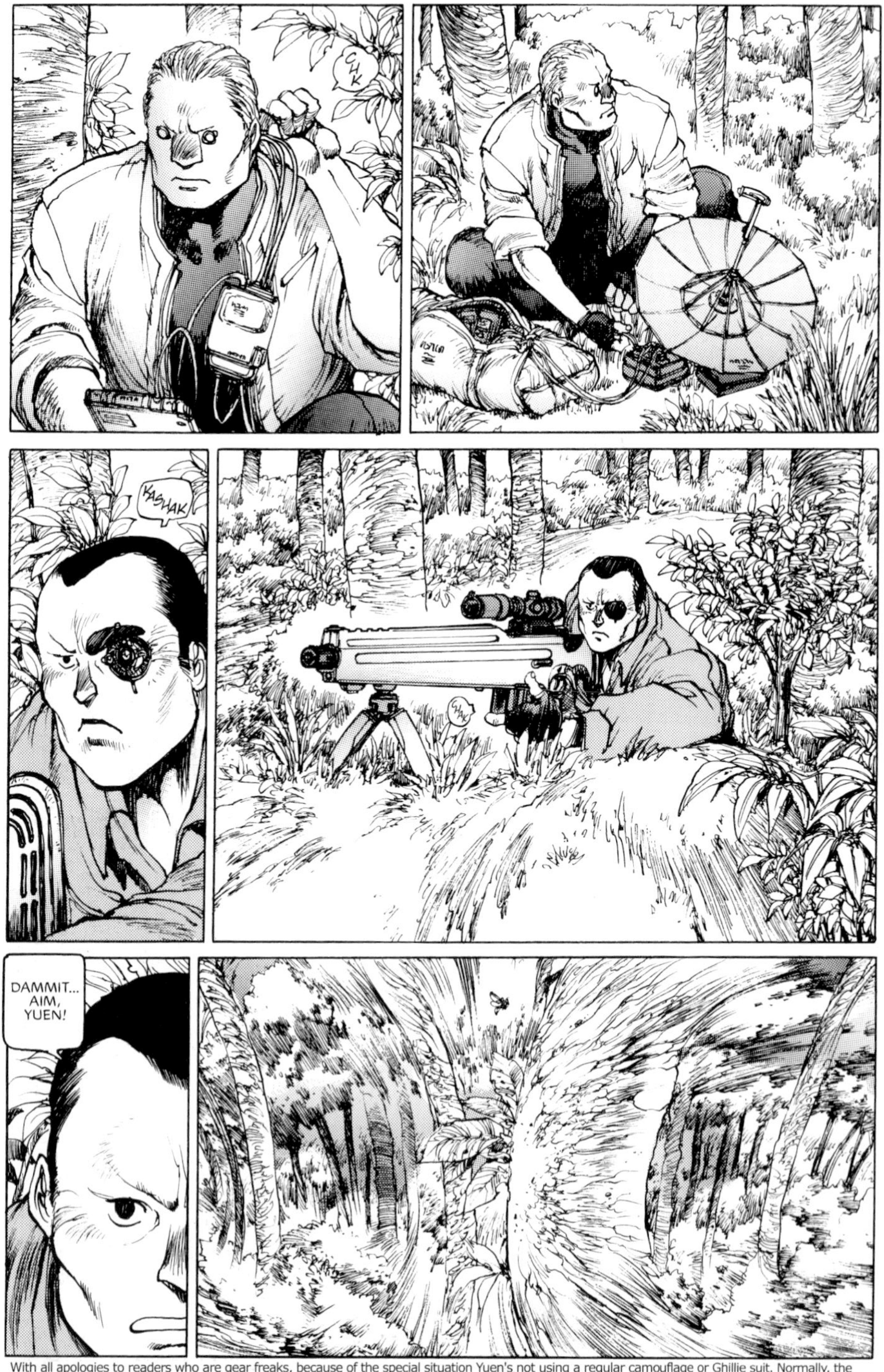
CHK
KASHAK
DAMMIT... AIM, YUEN!

With all apologies to readers who are gear freaks, because of the special situation Yuen's not using a regular camouflage or Ghillie suit. Normally, the surface of his rifle would also have some sort of optical camouflage applied, that could be changed as needed, but I've left that out, too. In the fifth panel on the page, the movement of the air would normally be converted into a specific color range and displayed as a 3-D image, but this is a monochrome manga, so I beg your forgiveness... The mid-section of the image is distorted because Saito's "eagle eye" function has enlarged it.

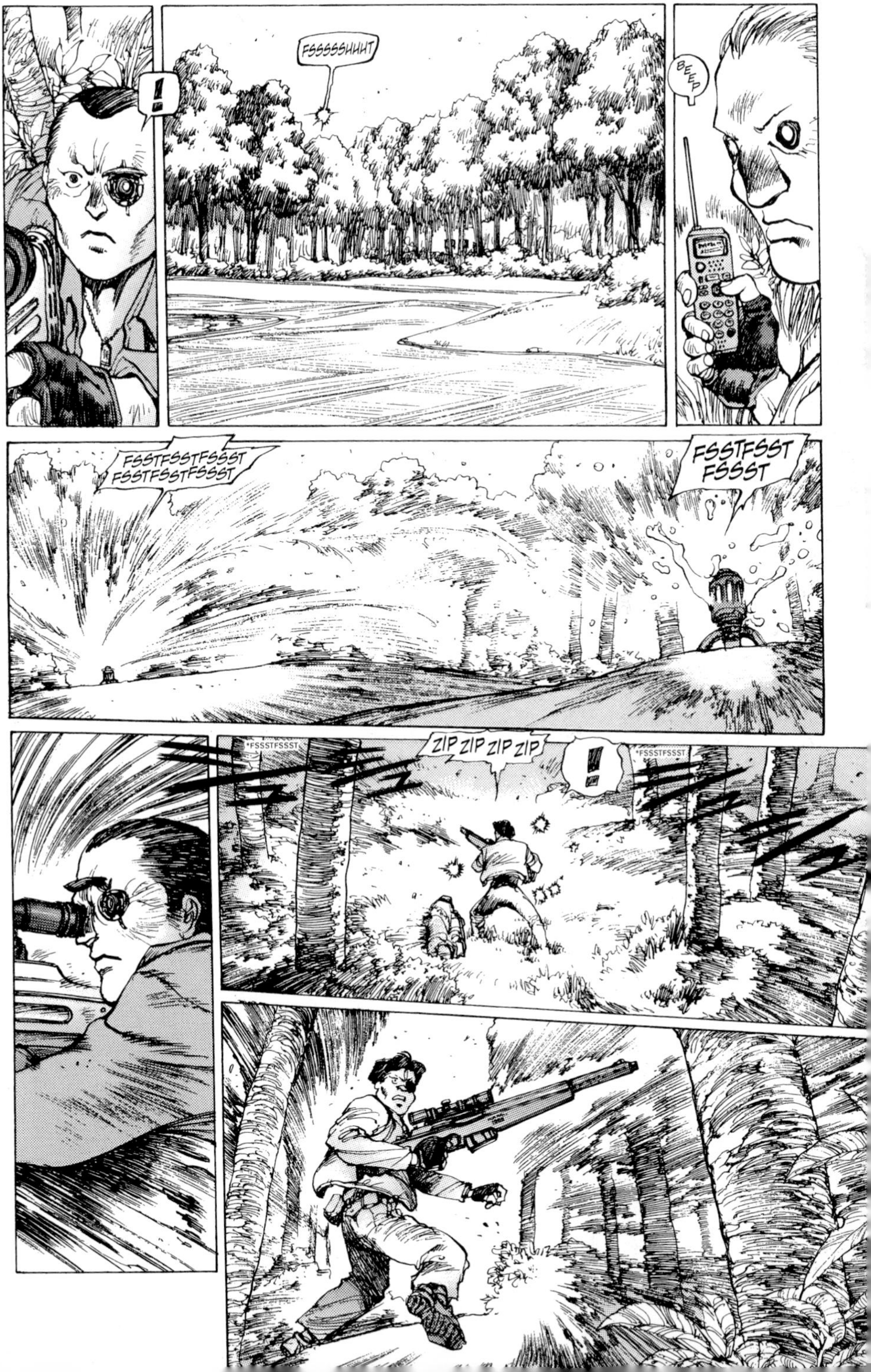
BEEP
FSSSSSHHUT
!
FSSTFSST FSSST
FSSTFSSTFSSST FSSTFSSTFSSST
*FSSSTFSSST
!!
ZIP ZIP ZIP ZIP
*FSSSTFSSST

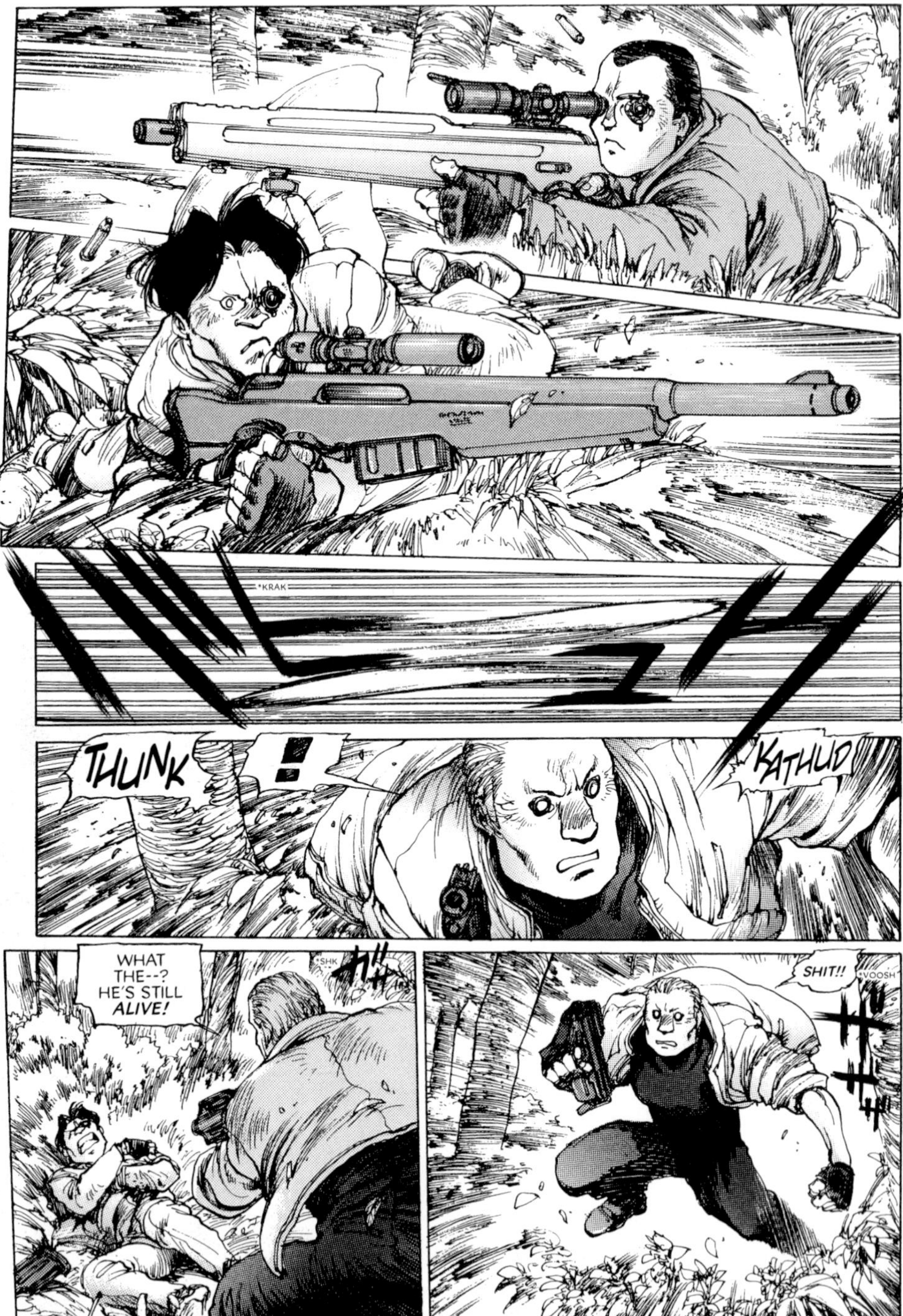

*KRAK
THUNK
!
KATHUD
WHAT THE--? HE'S STILL ALIVE!
*SHK
SHIT!!
*VOOSH

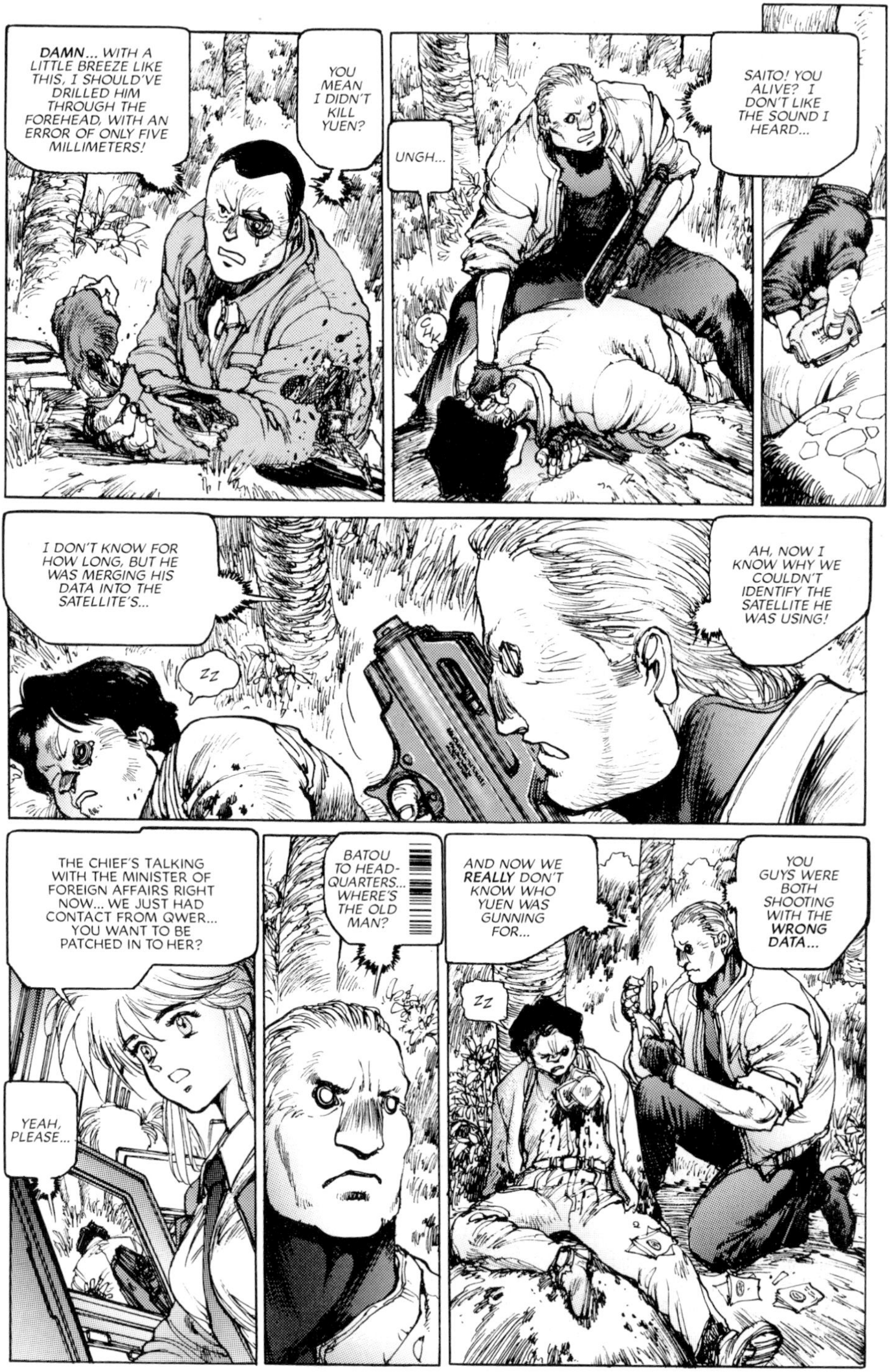
DAMN... WITH A LITTLE BREEZE LIKE THIS, I SHOULD'VE DRILLED HIM THROUGH THE FOREHEAD, WITH AN ERROR OF ONLY FIVE MILLIMETERS!
YOU MEAN I DIDN'T KILL YUEN?
UNGH...
SAITO! YOU ALIVE? I DON'T LIKE THE SOUND I HEARD...
I DON'T KNOW FOR HOW LONG, BUT HE WAS MERGING HIS DATA INTO THE SATELLITE'S...
ZZ
AH, NOW I KNOW WHY WE COULDN'T IDENTIFY THE SATELLITE HE WAS USING!
THE CHIEF'S TALKING WITH THE MINISTER OF FOREIGN AFFAIRS RIGHT NOW... WE JUST HAD CONTACT FROM QWER... YOU WANT TO BE PATCHED IN TO HER?
YEAH, PLEASE...
BATOU TO HEAD-QUARTERS... WHERE'S THE OLD MAN?
AND NOW WE REALLY DON'T KNOW WHO YUEN WAS GUNNING FOR...
ZZ
YOU GUYS WERE BOTH SHOOTING WITH THE WRONG DATA...

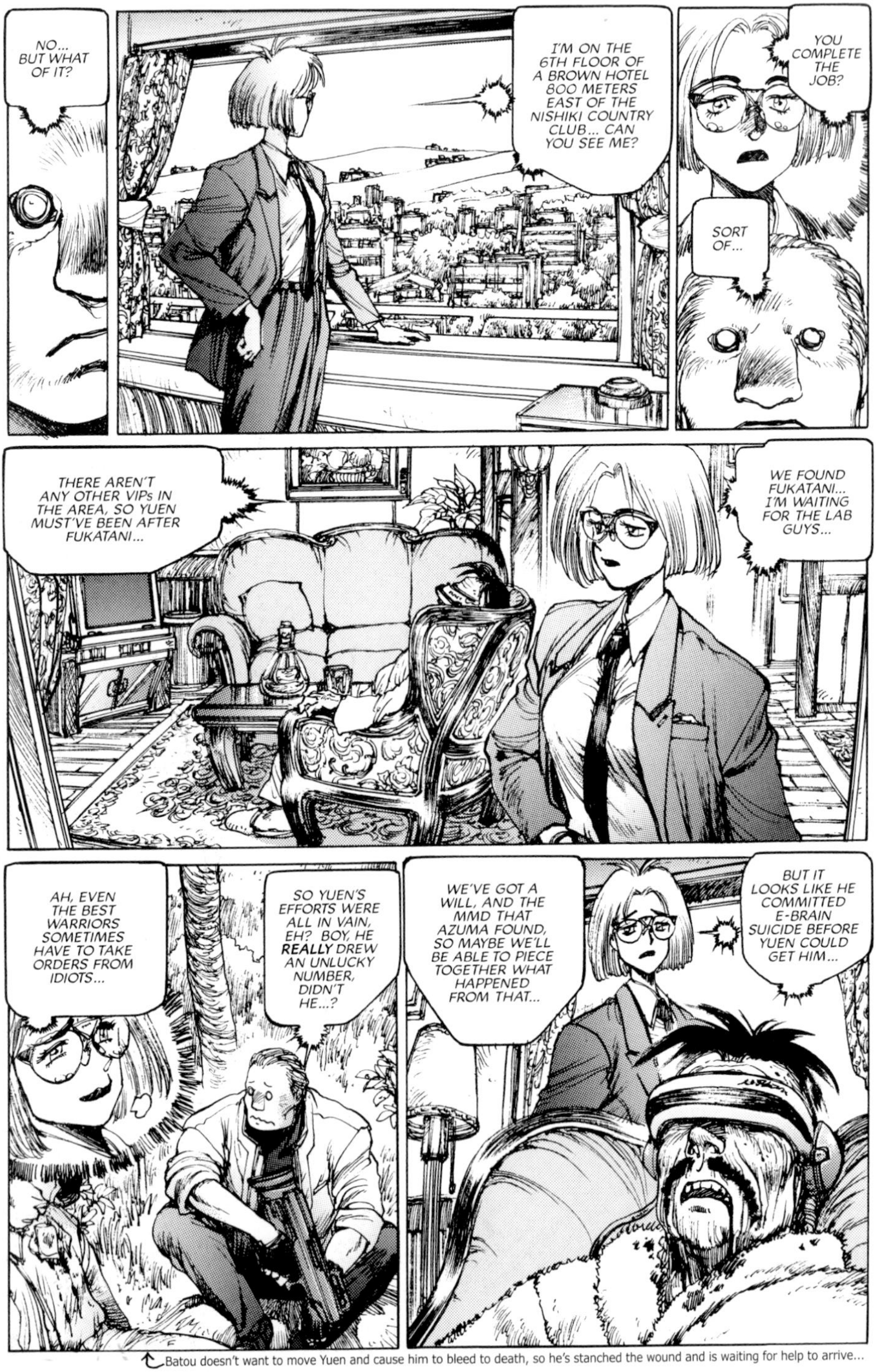
YOU COMPLETE THE JOB?
SORT OF...
I'M ON THE 6TH FLOOR OF A BROWN HOTEL 800 METERS EAST OF THE NISHIKI COUNTRY CLUB... CAN YOU SEE ME?
NO... BUT WHAT OF IT?
WE FOUND FUKATANI... I'M WAITING FOR THE LAB GUYS...
THERE AREN'T ANY OTHER VIPs IN THE AREA, SO YUEN MUST'VE BEEN AFTER FUKATANI...
BUT IT LOOKS LIKE HE COMMITTED E-BRAIN SUICIDE BEFORE YUEN COULD GET HIM...
WE'VE GOT A WILL, AND THE MMD THAT AZUMA FOUND, SO MAYBE WE'LL BE ABLE TO PIECE TOGETHER WHAT HAPPENED FROM THAT...
SO YUEN'S EFFORTS WERE ALL IN VAIN, EH? BOY, HE **REALLY** DREW AN UNLUCKY NUMBER, DIDN'T HE...?
AH, EVEN THE BEST WARRIORS SOMETIMES HAVE TO TAKE ORDERS FROM IDIOTS...

↑ Batou doesn't want to move Yuen and cause him to bleed to death, so he's stanched the wound and is waiting for help to arrive...

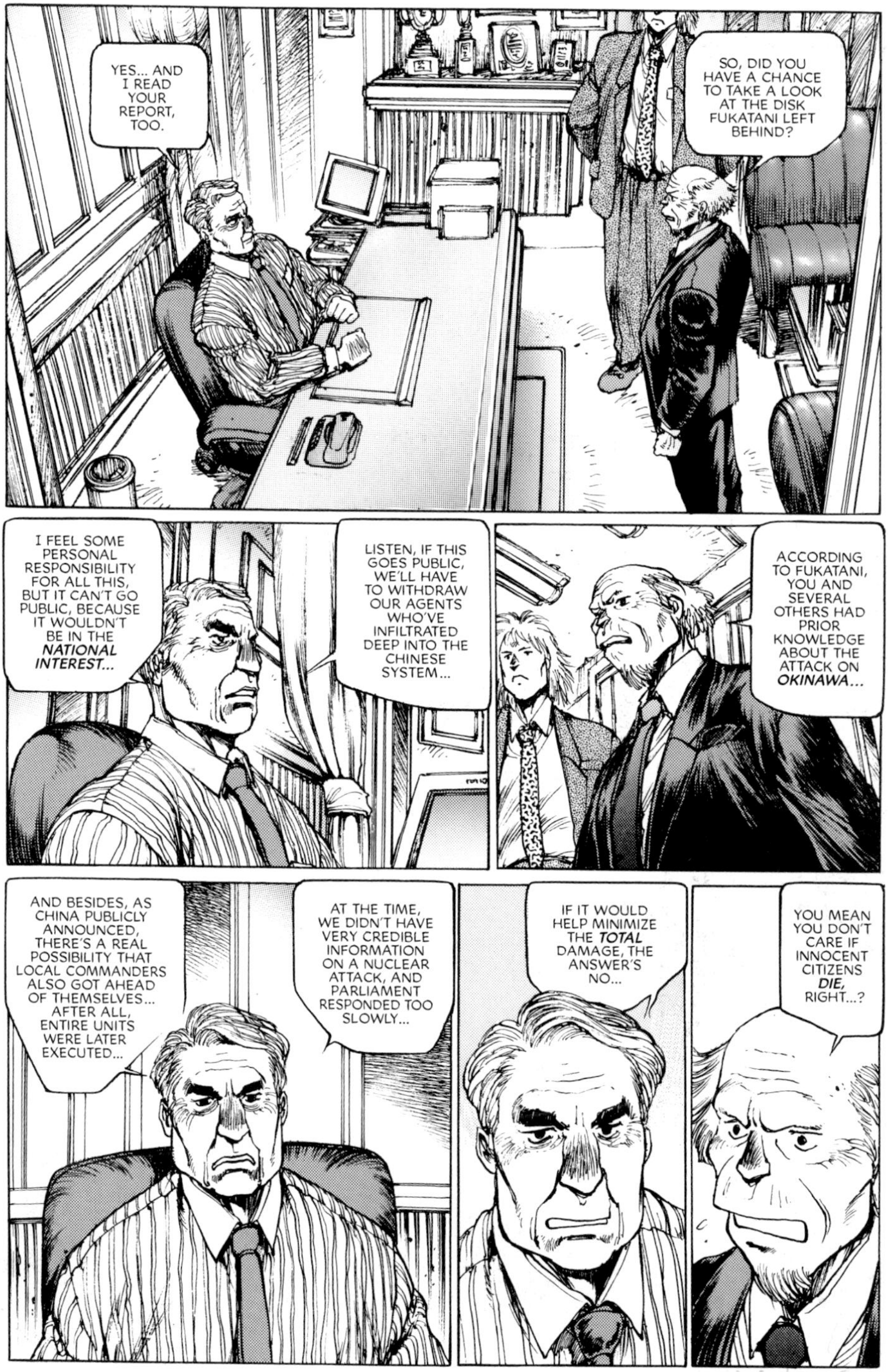
SO, DID YOU HAVE A CHANCE TO TAKE A LOOK AT THE DISK FUKATANI LEFT BEHIND?
YES... AND I READ YOUR REPORT, TOO.
ACCORDING TO FUKATANI, YOU AND SEVERAL OTHERS HAD PRIOR KNOWLEDGE ABOUT THE ATTACK ON OKINAWA...
LISTEN, IF THIS GOES PUBLIC, WE'LL HAVE TO WITHDRAW OUR AGENTS WHO'VE INFILTRATED DEEP INTO THE CHINESE SYSTEM...
I FEEL SOME PERSONAL RESPONSIBILITY FOR ALL THIS, BUT IT CAN'T GO PUBLIC, BECAUSE IT WOULDN'T BE IN THE NATIONAL INTEREST...
YOU MEAN YOU DON'T CARE IF INNOCENT CITIZENS DIE, RIGHT...?
IF IT WOULD HELP MINIMIZE THE TOTAL DAMAGE, THE ANSWER'S NO...
AT THE TIME, WE DIDN'T HAVE VERY CREDIBLE INFORMATION ON A NUCLEAR ATTACK, AND PARLIAMENT RESPONDED TOO SLOWLY...
AND BESIDES, AS CHINA PUBLICLY ANNOUNCED, THERE'S A REAL POSSIBILITY THAT LOCAL COMMANDERS ALSO GOT AHEAD OF THEMSELVES... AFTER ALL, ENTIRE UNITS WERE LATER EXECUTED...

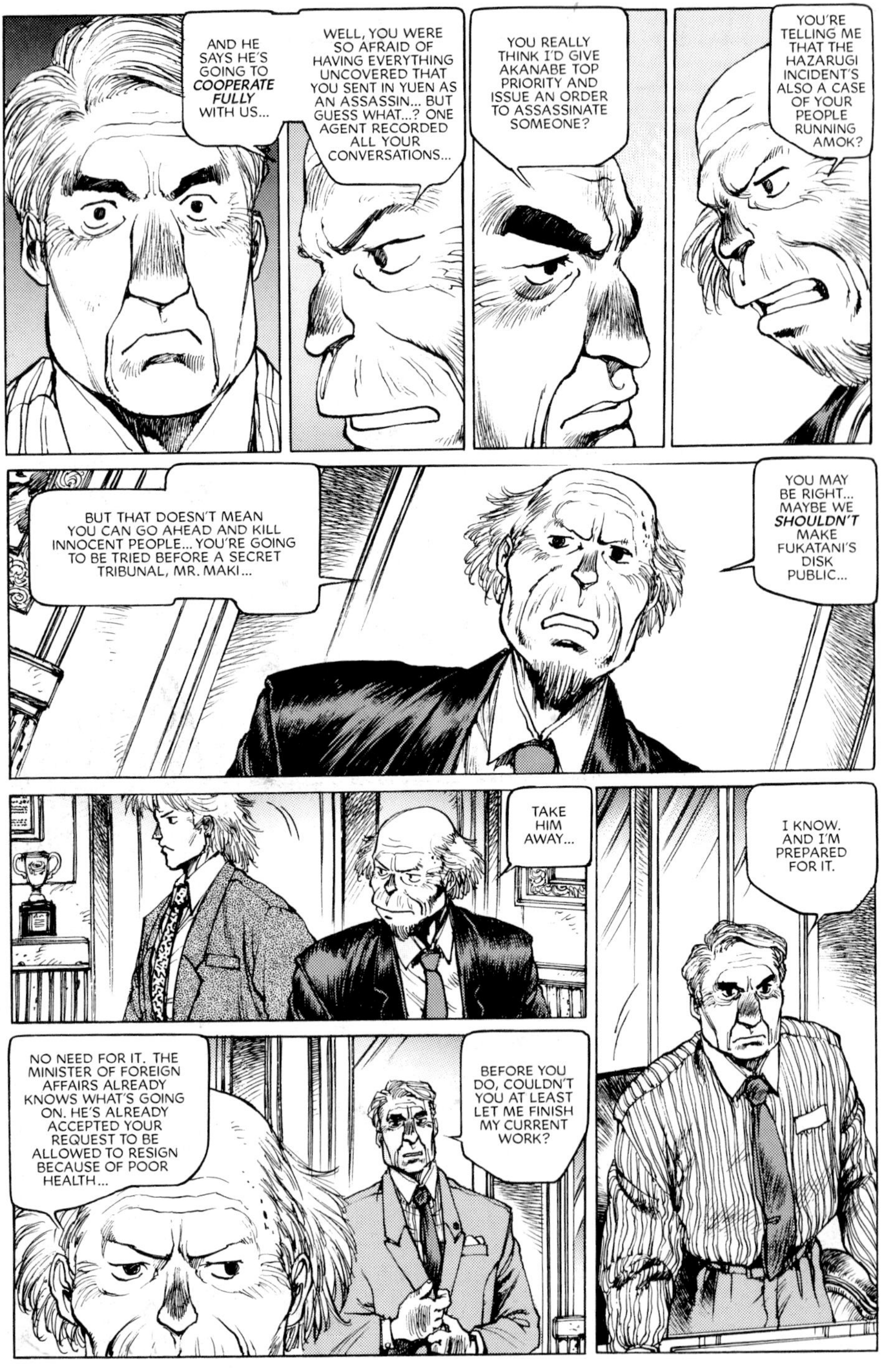
YOU'RE TELLING ME THAT THE HAZARUGI INCIDENT'S ALSO A CASE OF YOUR PEOPLE RUNNING AMOK?
YOU REALLY THINK I'D GIVE AKANABE TOP PRIORITY AND ISSUE AN ORDER TO ASSASSINATE SOMEONE?
WELL, YOU WERE SO AFRAID OF HAVING EVERYTHING UNCOVERED THAT YOU SENT IN YUEN AS AN ASSASSIN... BUT GUESS WHAT...? ONE AGENT RECORDED ALL YOUR CONVERSATIONS...
AND HE SAYS HE'S GOING TO *COOPERATE FULLY* WITH US...
YOU MAY BE RIGHT... MAYBE WE *SHOULDN'T* MAKE FUKATANI'S DISK PUBLIC...
BUT THAT DOESN'T MEAN YOU CAN GO AHEAD AND KILL INNOCENT PEOPLE... YOU'RE GOING TO BE TRIED BEFORE A SECRET TRIBUNAL, MR. MAKI...
I KNOW. AND I'M PREPARED FOR IT.
TAKE HIM AWAY...
BEFORE YOU DO, COULDN'T YOU AT LEAST LET ME FINISH MY CURRENT WORK?
NO NEED FOR IT. THE MINISTER OF FOREIGN AFFAIRS ALREADY KNOWS WHAT'S GOING ON. HE'S ALREADY ACCEPTED YOUR REQUEST TO BE ALLOWED TO RESIGN BECAUSE OF POOR HEALTH...

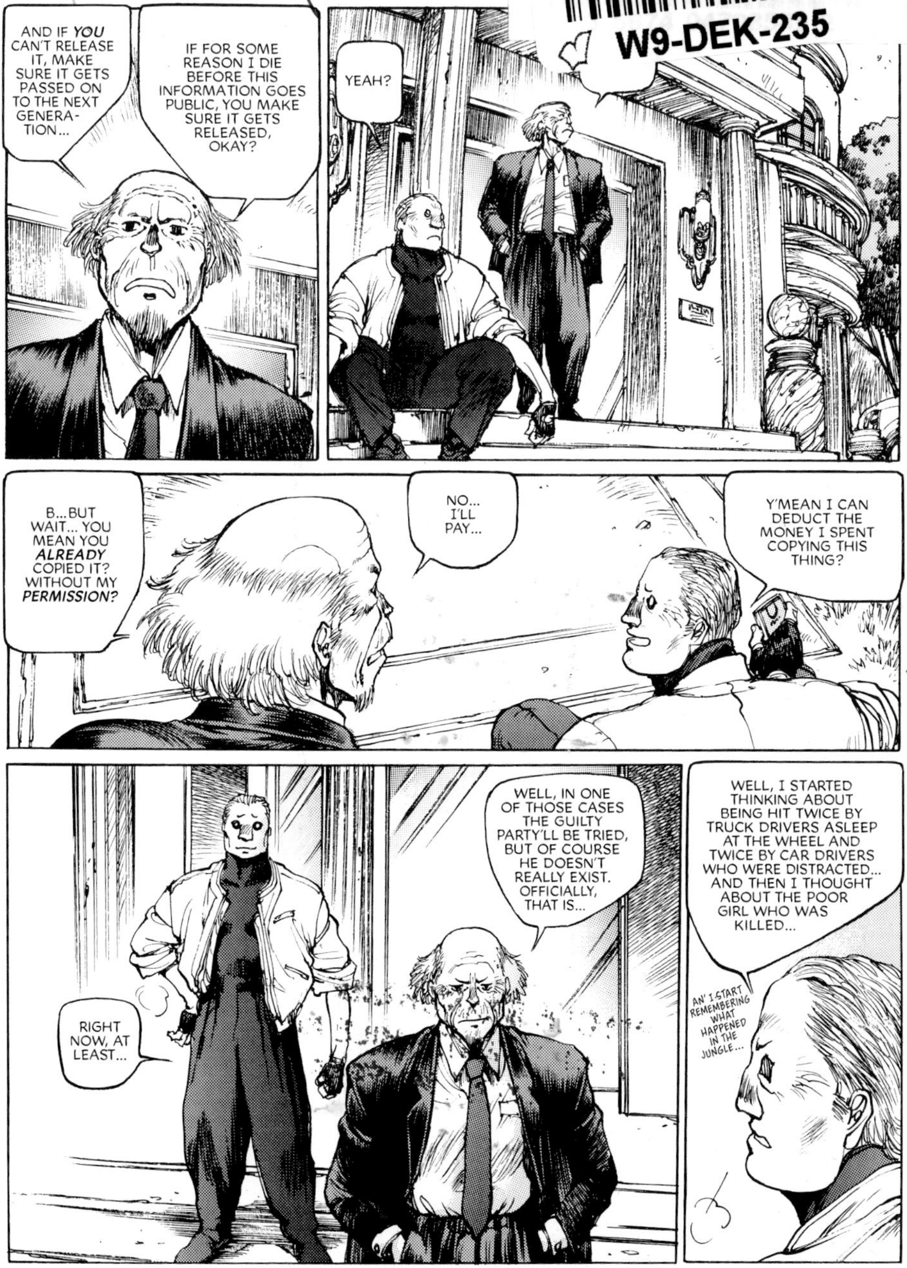
YEAH?
IF FOR SOME REASON I DIE BEFORE THIS INFORMATION GOES PUBLIC, YOU MAKE SURE IT GETS RELEASED, OKAY?
AND IF *YOU* CAN'T RELEASE IT, MAKE SURE IT GETS PASSED ON TO THE NEXT GENERA-TION...
Y'MEAN I CAN DEDUCT THE MONEY I SPENT COPYING THIS THING?
NO... I'LL PAY...
B...BUT WAIT... YOU MEAN YOU *ALREADY* COPIED IT? WITHOUT MY *PERMISSION?*
WELL, I STARTED THINKING ABOUT BEING HIT TWICE BY TRUCK DRIVERS ASLEEP AT THE WHEEL AND TWICE BY CAR DRIVERS WHO WERE DISTRACTED... AND THEN I THOUGHT ABOUT THE POOR GIRL WHO WAS KILLED...
AN' I START REMEMBERING WHAT HAPPENED IN THE JUNGLE...
WELL, IN ONE OF THOSE CASES THE GUILTY PARTY'LL BE TRIED, BUT OF COURSE HE DOESN'T REALLY EXIST. OFFICIALLY, THAT IS...
RIGHT NOW, AT LEAST...

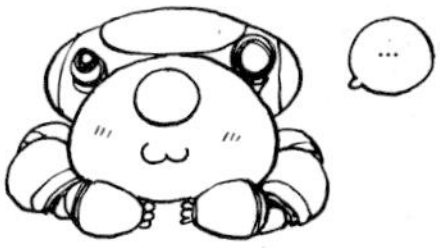
...

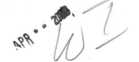